Labrador Sea
INUIT (Coastal)
Cape Mazzo
LABRADOR
Brest
Strait of Belle Isle
Brodore Bay
Newfoundland Baccalaos
MONTAGNAIS-NASKAPI
St. Marie
BEOTHUK
Trinity Bay
Cape St Mary's
Cape Race
CREE
Gulf of St. Lawrence
Gaspé
Miscou Island
Cape Breton Island
MICMAC
Prince Edward Island
Portneuf
St. Lawrence River
Massacre Island
Tadoussac
Saguenay R.
ATTIKAMEGUES
MALECITE
Canso Island
St. Maurice R.
Ile aux Coudres
St. John R.
NORUMBEGA
Medoctec
St. Croix Island
St. Croix R.
PASSAMAQUODDY
Loretteville
Québec
St. Marie
St. Francis
Chaudière R.
Penobscot R.
PENOBSCOT
Annapolis Royal
Nova Scotia Acadia
Trois -Rivières
Bécancourt
Odanak
ABENAKI
Old Town
Passama -quoddy
ALGONQUIN
Montreal
Lachine
La Prairie de la Magdelaine
Sault St. Louis
Norridgewock
Kennebec R.
Pequaket
Sable Island
Cape Sable
NIPISSING
Ottawa River
Caughnawaga
Lake Champlain
MAWOOSHEN
Pemaquid
Saco R.
HURON
Matchedash Bay
Rock
Bear
Cord
Deer
Lake Couchiching
Lake Simcoe
Etharita
Ehwae
Salmon Falls
MOHAWK
Mohawk R.
FIVE NATIONS
Lake Ontario
Nauset Harb.
TOBACCO (PETUN)
Schoharie Cr.
Genesee R.
SENECA
CAYUGA
ONONDAGA
ONEIDA
Hudson R.
NEUTRALS
Lake Erie
SUSQUEHANNOCK
ERIE
Atlantic Ocean

The Myth of the Savage

And the Beginnings of French Colonialism in the Americas

The Myth of the Savage

And the Beginnings of French Colonialism in the Americas

Olive Patricia Dickason

The University of Alberta Press

First published by
The University of Alberta Press
141 Athabasca Hall
Edmonton, Alberta, Canada T6G 2E8

Printed in Canada 5 4 3 2
ISBN 0–88864–036–6

Canadian Cataloguing in Publication Data

Dickason, Olive Patricia, 1920–
The myth of the savage

Bibliography: p.
Includes index.
ISBN 0–88864–036–6

1. France–Colonies–America. 2. French–America. 3. Indians, Treatment of–America. 4. America–History–To 1810 5. Wild men. I. Title.
E18.82.D53 970.004'97 C83–091052–2

Typesetting by The Typeworks, Vancouver, British Columbia, Canada.
Printed by Quality Color Press, Inc., Edmonton, Alberta, Canada.
∞ Printed on acid-free paper.

ALBERTA Lotteries | The Alberta Foundation for the Arts | Alberta COMMUNITY DEVELOPMENT

COMMITTED TO THE DEVELOPMENT OF CULTURE AND THE ARTS

The University of Alberta Press gratefully acknowledges the support received for its publishing program from the Canada Council Block Grant program and the Department of Canadian Heritage.

To Père Athol Murray

Notre Dame College,
Saskatchewan

Dieu a faconné l'homme & divers & semblable,
Par semblance il reduit l'espece à l'unité:
Par difference il peind en nous l'infinité,
Faisant d'un & plusieurs un sujet admirable.

–Pierre Dampmartin, *De la Connoisance et merveilles du monde et de l'homme,* (Paris: Thomas Perrier, 1585), 55v.

Contents

Preface

THE FIFTEENTH-CENTURY meeting of Amerindians and Europeans was decisive for both, but in opposite ways. For Amerindians, it meant upheavals in cultural and political landscapes; city states such as those of the Incas and Mexicas disappeared, as did a variety of hierarchical chiefdoms; only a few societies survived, incorporated more or less uneasily within new political frameworks. For Europeans, the meeting heralded an enormous impetus for forces already in action – the centralization of their nation-states and the rise of capitalism; and eventually, the opening of new intellectual horizons.

This meeting has been commonly characterized as an encounter between civilization (European) and savagery (American). But when one tries to define these terms in relation to the cultures involved, their meanings become elusive. The word "civilized" is usually applied to societies possessing a state structure and an advanced technology; the general presumption is that their members must therefore have attained a relatively high degree of refinement in their manner of living.[1] The term "savage" is applied to societies at an early stage of technology, a stage at which they are believed to be dominated by the laws of nature. Its use implies that Amerindian societies did not match the refinements of those of Europe, and that they were more cruel. Neither of these premises stands up under examination; the sophistication of a cultured Peruvian or Mexica of the fifteenth century stemmed from value systems so different from those of the French, English, or Spanish as to elude comparison; yet we know that it was highly developed. On both sides of the Atlantic, public executions of selected victims were ritually practised. So was public torture. Europeans regarded it as a necessary practice for the administration of justice, using fear to inspire respect for state authority, in the belief that it was the most effective way of controlling certain elements within their own societies. Most Amerindians who followed the practice belonged to non-state societies, and used torture, not against their own people, but against outside enemies. Their goal was to consolidate their own communities by dominating hostile alien forces. Efforts to establish that one form was civilized while the other was savage could result in some strained exposition as when, in the seventeenth century, the Jesuit Jean-Paul Mercier tried to explain the French use of torture to a Huron.[2]

This study is not about the clash of civilizations; as anthropologist A.I. Hallowell has observed, cultures do not clash – people do. However, the reactions aroused in such encounters are profoundly influenced by the cultural orientations of the individuals involved. It is with these considerations in mind that I examine some of Europe's responses to the richly varied spectrum of Amerindian societies during the sixteenth and early part of the seventeenth centuries.

At this point it is appropriate to take a brief look at the civilizations Europeans found in the New World. In respect to political organization, fifteenth-century America possessed a greater variety of societies than did Europe of the same period. In the Old World, the formation of states had reached the stage where only a few of the earlier types of societies remained in remote areas. In America the situation was reversed and the majority of societies were without states. Their characteristics were the ones Europeans attributed to the New World.

The most striking of these characteristics were that the people for the most part wore few, if any, clothes and that they did not have externalized institutions, such as written codes of law. Power was not the prerogative of a class or an individual; it existed in the society itself, and each man was his own master. Not only did these societies not vest coercive power in their chiefs, they were organized to prevent such a development from taking place.[3] The chief's influence was based on his eloquence and generosity; the result was that he was often the poorest man in the community. He could persuade, but not command, as then no one would follow him. If a rival succeeded in attracting followers, and a split occurred within the group, there was always the option of breaking away. This tendency of non-state societies toward fragmentation was largely responsible for their ineffectiveness when confronted with centralized, aggressive nation-states. In Peru and Mexico, where centralization had occurred, the process had not evolved sufficiently for the people to make a united stand against the Spanish invaders. It is well known, for example, that Hernán Cortés owed much of his success in conquering Mexico to the help of tribes that had not been fully incorporated by the Mexica into their imperial organization; and in confronting the Peruvians, the Spaniards were greatly aided by the disloyalty of the *yanaconas*, who constituted the clerk-servant-craftsman class. In the northern regions of North America, lack of unity more than any other single factor assured the destruction of native autonomy. Not even such a great leader as the Shawnee Tecumseh (1768?–1813) from Ohio, who understood the problem, was able to overcome Amerindian aversion to separating power from the corpus of society. With all of his prestige, Tecumseh could not convince either his allies or his people to take the steps that could have welded them into a united front. Yet, ironically, that very reluctance has also made possible some measure of cultural survival.

While Amerindian non-state societies could be, and often were, in continual hostility with their neighbors, rather like European nations of the period, they fought for prestige and booty rather than for territorial aggrandizement. In their manner of conducting a war, they did not make the same distinctions as did Renaissance Europeans (at least in principle) between combatants and non-combatants; on the other hand, they were not as likely to seek total destruction of the enemy. An illustration of this is the 1615 expedition in which Samuel de Champlain, founder of New France, marched as an ally of the Huron against the Five Nations. The Huron were content to lift their siege after they had taken some prisoners, despite the French leader's best efforts to encourage his new allies to destroy the village. In the Huron view, the taking of prisoners represented victory. Champlain was not impressed.

In the realm of subsistence, Amerindian goals were also different from those of Europeans. Amerindians sought to produce only enough for their needs, on the basis of mutual sharing. Surpluses were accumulated for specific social purposes such as the feasts that were part of the ritual calendar, or the official needs of the chief. In economics (if one can use that term) as well as in warfare, Amerindians and Europeans operated on different principles. Jesuit Joseph Jouvency wrote concerning Canadians (as the Amerindians of the north shore of St. Lawrence and by extension, of New France, were originally called), that there were "six hundred matters . . . in which their customs differ very widely from Europeans."[4] It took a long time before it was fully realized that those differences masked some fundamental similarities.[5]

When members of the two worlds came into contact, first impressions set the patterns by which they saw and evaluated each other. Amerindians were quick to modify initial reactions as they sought for more adequate responses; they were not immediately successful. Europeans, on the other hand, were able to establish their hegemony over the New World, making it unnecessary to alter initial assumptions; only recently have these shown signs of changing. These assumptions were not substantially modified by subsequent firsthand relationships, such as occurred when Amerindians visited Europe or when Europeans went to the New World. The fact that such views had little to do with reality did not mitigate their fundamental importance in colonization. By classifying Amerindians as savages, Europeans were able to create the ideology that helped to make it possible to launch one of the great movements in the history of western civilization: the colonization of overseas empires.[6]

The course of these events as they concerned France has governed the organization of this book. The first four chapters deal with the development of Europe's beliefs about, and attitudes toward, Amerindians. By way of contrast, the fifth chapter contains a series of ethnographic sketches of several New World societies as they are believed to have been about the time of first contact with Europeans, and some of the immediate consequences of that contact. The remaining seven chapters touch on the outcome of European beliefs and attitudes as they determined relations with Amerindians and colonization of the New World.

Because attitudes and ideas cannot be reduced to a calendar, as can events, a strict chronology has not been maintained. It is often difficult to trace origins of concepts, as most of them are far older than is usually credited. In this sense, it is profoundly true that "plus ça change, plus c'est la même chose"; even in the midst of changing social opinion, concepts can be remarkably persistent. Sometimes an idea becomes identified with a particular nation at a certain period although it may have had quite different origins, both as to time and place. *Le bon sauvage* is usually perceived in the context of eighteenth-century France, but it is clearly present in the writings of Pietro Martire d'Anghiera (1457–1526), an Italian scholar who lived at the court of Spain at the time of Columbus's voyages. It is also found in Tacitus, the Roman historian who wrote at the turn of the first century. What caught on during the eighteenth century was the phrase "le bon sauvage," which, along with the writings of Jean-Jacques Rousseau (1712–78), gave the concept a new importance. In other words, it was not the idea that was new, but its formulation. What is more, formulations of ideas into the written word sometimes bear little relation to their period of greatest influence in the realm of practical politics. The concept of *l'homme sauvage,* for example, was most influential during the sixteenth century, particularly the first part, when it was used to help justify the destruction of whole populations of Amerindians. Yet it was not until toward the middle of the century that Amerindians were fully identified as hommes sauvages—a verdict ensured by the recently accomplished conquest of the Mexica followed by that of the Inca. And it was not until the nineteenth century that this concept developed into its most extreme form, with the aid of Darwin's and Spencer's "survival of the fittest," and with the mass publication of textbooks for expanding school systems.

As I am dealing with concepts rather than events, I have chosen those sources that seemed most likely to reflect the climate of opinion in the age under consideration. This has meant a reliance on printed works, as they would have received the widest distribution. The actual influence of a given work can be extremely difficult, if not impossible, to assess at this late stage; the number of its editions and the number of the languages into which it was translated can be used as guides, as can the reputation of the publishing house. Works with less impressive publication records, however, were not ignored. On the contrary, I have tried to include as wide a sampling as time and resources would permit, on the premise that any pertinent work that was published at all would by that very fact reflect an element of contemporary opinion. If Renaissance literature is truly a window to the opinions of the age, it reveals a very wide spectrum. Theoretically, Renaissance man may have been dedicated to absolutes in religion (one God, one truth) as well as in politics (one king), not to mention in other matters; but in actual fact he had by no means realized these ideals. But one opinion, at least, became unanimous for all practical purposes–the characterization of Amerindians as savages.

While this study is primarily concerned with the French experience, non-French sources were consulted when they seemed pertinent. Although the spread of concepts across language barriers can be difficult to assess, it should be remembered that during the Age of Discovery, Latin was in international use. Navigation and discovery were cynosures of international attention, just as space travel is today. Materials dealing with these matters received wide and careful consideration: voyage accounts were quickly published in Latin as well as in an astonishing array of vernacular languages. The example of Columbus's letter, at the beginning of Chapter 1, could be extended to much of the published writing on exploration. In this connection the role of religious orders was fundamental, because of the importance of missionary work. Such orders were often international, and in any case had well-developed avenues of communication within their own ranks, with other orders, and with Rome. The great bulk of New World accounts was written by missionaries; as expressions of attempts to realize the universal church, these writings often transcended national boundaries. This means that for the epoch beginning with Columbus's 1492 voyage and ending with the permanent establishment of a New France early in the seventeenth century, I have drawn fairly extensively from Spanish sources, particularly those that were translated into French. Throughout this period, Spain was the dominant power both in Europe and in the New World. Spaniards were the first to meet Amerindians and to colonize them; their experiences set the tone and, to a large extent, the pattern of New World colonialism. While France was a principal challenger to Spain, in the Americas she followed in her rival's footsteps; only later, in the eighteenth and early nineteenth centuries, would the situation be altered and even reversed, particularly in literary fields.[7] All this is not to say that the French colonial experience was not distinct from that of Spain or England. It was; the French added their own particular dimension to Europe's basic intellectual and social baggage. This *petite difference* in turn gives a distinctive quality to the story of French overseas expansion. Nevertheless, to consider the French experience without taking cognizance of the international situation would be to present at best an incomplete picture that would be misleading, if not actually false.

This is particularly true when one is dealing with beliefs and attitudes. However, I have used French versions of the source material where circumstances permitted. Any translations from French or Spanish texts into English not otherwise credited are mine.

Because of the importance of the time frame, persons who are of consequence either in themselves or for their writings are identified with their birth and death dates at their first significant mention.

A word about names. In the interest of simplicity, I have used national forms for those from Europe, with the major exception of Christopher Columbus and his brother. For Amerindian names, it seemed easiest to stay with Europeanized forms, although there is a move toward closer approximations of original pronounciations. Thus, "Montezuma" has given way to "Moctezuma." The people whom the Spaniards knew as "Aztec" referred to themselves as "Mexica," the form used here. The names of Capuchin missionaries present a special problem. Claude (d'Abbeville) was baptized Clement Foulon; Claude is his religious name. "D'Abbeville" identifies his institutional affiliation and is not part of his name. The same applies to Yves (d'Evreux), Candide (de Nant) and Arsène (de Paris). Accordingly, I refer to them simply as Claude, Yves, and so on. Identification of New World peoples is more complicated, as European terminologies for them were seldom standardized. In general, I have used names that are recognizable today. It should be remembered that in the sixteenth century, "Brazilian" referred to the Amerindians of Brazil; "Canadian", to the natives of the north shore of the St. Lawrence; and "American" could apply to the natives of either North or South America. Such general terms were not usually employed; the common practice was to be more specific, and to use European versions of tribal names.

Acknowledgments

It is axiomatic that no one can research and write a book without considerable help from a wide variety of persons. This work is based on my doctoral dissertation done at the University of Ottawa (1977) under the supervision of Cornelius J. Jaenen, with the aid of funding provided by Canada Council. Among those to whom I owe particular debts are Margaret Carter, National Historic Sites; Gordon M. Day, National Museum of Man; Joseph Gatner, Parliamentary Library; Corrie Klugkist, The Hague; Hugh Honour, whose area of research coincided with my own while he was preparing the exhibition "The European Vision of America" for the two-hundredth anniversary of the American Declaration of Independence; Robert Mandrou, Université de Paris; and, at the University of Alberta, Nicholas Wickenden, whose criticisms of the manuscript were particularly valuable and who was most generous in sharing his knowledge of Medieval and Renaissance Europe (among many other items, he brought to my attention the poem that appears as epigraph); Alison White, whose way with English was invaluable, and Ronald Whistance-Smith, curator of maps, so proficient in tracking down ancient place names.

There are also the many archivists, librarians, and other personnel of such institutions as La Bibliothèque Nationale, Paris; the municipal libraries of Rouen, La Rochelle, and Dieppe; the departmental archives of Charente-Maritime, Seine-Inférieure, and Seine-et-Oise; La Bibliothèque de Versailles; Jesuit Archives at Chantilly; The Reading Room, British Museum; John Carter Brown Library, Brown University; The Huntingdon Library (California); and above all, Canada's Public Archives and National Library. Also very helpful were the directors of the Musée des Antiquités and the Musée des Beaux-Arts at Rouen. This book has been published with the help of a grant from the Social Science Federation of Canada, using funds provided by the Social Sciences and Humanities Research Council of Canada.

I would like to express my warmest appreciation to the Department of Computing Services of the University of Alberta, whose hard-working staff transformed my much worked-over manuscript into presentable copy; and to John L. Honsaker, programmer-analyst. And finally, a word of thanks to Jacques Monet, now president of Regis College, Toronto School of Theology, but then at the University of Ottawa, whose sympathy and support did much to make it all possible.

MER OCCEANE:
MER DESPAIGNE:
MER DE FRANCE:
Terre des bretons
TERRE NEUFVE
Canada
Grande baye
CANAD
Canada
Terre du Laborador
TIQVE:

PART I

American Discoveries and European Images

Descelliers's world map, 1550, shows the Atlantic Ocean as being divided between Spain and France. C-18165 British Library, London.

CHAPTER 1

Some First Reactions

Amerindians flee in terror from arriving Spaniards. Dati, *Isole trovate novamente*, 1493.

EARLY IN 1493, the Spanish court received unexpected news. Christopher Columbus, the Genoese captain whom the Spanish monarchs Ferdinand and Isabella had sent in search of a sea route to the Orient the previous summer, had discovered a land inhabited by "immense multitudes" of strange non-Christian people. These people were not dog-headed, as might have been expected if Columbus had reached the Far East, where such a race was reputed to live in the mountains. On the contrary, these unknowns were reported to be well formed and good-looking, an easily verifiable observation as they were largely innocent of clothing. In view of his initial belief that they were inhabitants of the Asiatic subcontinent, Columbus called them "Indians"; but in his last will and testament, he referred to them as "cannibals," by which appellation they were widely known at the time of his death in 1506. Columbus wrote in his letter announcing his discovery:

> The people... all go naked, men and women, just as their mothers bring them forth.... They have no iron or steel, nor any weapons; nor are they fit thereunto; not because they be not a well formed people and of fair stature, but that they are most wondrously timorous... they are artless and generous with what they have, to such a degree as no one would believe but him who had seen it.... And whether it be a thing of value, or of little worth, they are straightways content with whatsoever trifle of whatsoever kind be given them in return for it.... They took even pieces of broken barrelhoops, and gave whatever they had, like senseless brutes; insomuch that it seemed to me ill. I forbade it, and I gave gratuitously a thousand useful things that I carried, in order that they may conceive affection, and furthermore may be made Christians; for they are inclined to the love and service of their Highnesses and of all the Castillian nation, and they strive to combine in giving us things which they have in abundance, and of which we are in need... they are men of very subtle wit, who navigate all those seas, and who give a marvellously good account of everything.[1]

Columbus's announcement caught Spain's immediate interest, not so much because of its revelation of a new world, inhabited by a people previously unknown to Europeans, but because he reported there was every indication that it harbored immense and largely unexploited wealth.[2] This was quickly seized upon, although the full implications of Columbus's landings on Guanahari and other West Indian islands were to be a long time in being fully realized. In the short term, news of the New World had to compete with the much greater interest aroused by the opening of the Orient as well as with Europe's rediscovery of its own classical antiquity.[3] The difficult task of sorting out and assessing New World information in the light of Christian orthodoxy and of practical political ideology would be long and arduous. Conflicting reports did not help matters: initial impressions of timorous, gentle people, anxious to accommodate, were soon confused by accounts of monstrous men and bestial customs. If, in the meantime, Columbus's letter was disseminated with unheard-of speed, thanks to the new technology of the printing press, it was largely among an elite whose interest was sharpened by the prospect of economic opportunity.[4]

Columbus's letter dated 15 February–14 March 1493 was published in its original Spanish in Barcelona in April. Latin versions appeared in Rome, Antwerp, Basel, and Paris that same year. Because of the international standing of Latin at the time, these versions can be presumed to have been the most widely read. But the letter was also translated into other languages. An Italian version was published in Rome in 1493, in the form of a poem by Giuliano Dati, which also appeared twice that year in Florence, and twice again in 1495. Strasbourg saw a German translation in 1497, the same year that a second Spanish edition was issued in Valladolid. In all, twenty-two editions of Columbus's letter are known, sixteen of which appeared in the fifteenth century.[5] It is not certain how widely they were circulated; however, news of the discoveries apparently reached Poland between 1495 and 1501, and published accounts began to appear there in 1512.[6] The sole contemporary English-language report of Columbus's voyages, *Of the newe lãdes*, was published in Antwerp by Jan van Doesborch probably between 1510 and 1515, and possibly as early as 1508. Only three other accounts of Columbus's voyages are known to have been published before 1522.[7]

The publicity, spotty as it was, heralded a new fashion in literature, the voyage account, which was to reach its peak during the seventeenth and eighteenth centuries. Even romances lost out in this switch in reading tastes, a French chancellor noted.[8] In France, the new fashion can be traced to the appearance in Paris in 1497 of Sebastian Brant's *Le Nef des folz du monde*,[9] only twenty years after the publication in that city of the first book in the French language. Interestingly enough, Brant was not enthusiastic about voyages of discovery; rather, he criticized the desire to discover and describe new regions as one of the follies of mankind. When Brant's work had first appeared in German in 1494 it had been the only commentary to be published during Columbus's second voyage.[10] In France, it appears to have been the first printed reference to the New World and its inhabitants following the appearance of Columbus's letter. It was also probably the first in French.[11]

An incident in Vespucci's voyage of 1501, concerned a sailor sent ashore to charm a group of Amerindian women who had gathered on the beach. They killed and ate him within sight of his shipmates. This woodcut illustrated one of the German translations of Vespucci's letters, 1509.

Brant's criticisms did not prevent the taste for travel literature from developing. When Amerigo Vespucci (1451?–1512), the Florentine merchant who in 1505 had become chief navigator for the Casa de Contratación de las Indias in Seville, wrote letters describing his voyages, they were given far more exposure than the reports of Columbus had received.[12] Between 1502 and 1529, Vespucci's letters saw sixty editions in various cities in what is today Switzerland, Germany, France, Italy, The Netherlands, and Czechoslovakia, but none in Spain. This suggests censorship. Thirty-seven were in vernacular, of which almost half were in German, reflecting financial as well as scholarly interest in the discoveries.[13] One of the best-known editions appeared in the *Cosmographiae Introductio* of Martin Waldseemüller

(1470–1521?) and his collaborators, published at Saint-Dié in Lorraine in 1507. Besides Vespucci's "Four Voyages," the Waldseemüller edition included a map in which the New World was labelled America. The name had found ready acceptance by geographers perhaps because it was already in popular use. Its origins are uncertain; it may have been adapted by early voyagers from aboriginal place names that had been found along the coasts of Brazil, Guiana, and Venezuela. Variations included Amaracao, Maracaibo, Emeria, and Amaricocapana.[14] It could also have arisen from the tendency of Amerindians upon first seeing Europeans to regard them as superior beings. Among their words to express this were Tamaraca, Tamerka, and Maraca, the latter also appearing as a place name.[15] In any event, its usage was given an added fillip by its resemblance to Vespucci's baptismal name.

In 1515, twenty-two years after Columbus's letter had been printed in Paris in Latin, and about ten years after the appearance of Vespucci's letters in that same language, a collection of voyage accounts appeared in French. They had been translated and abridged by lawer Mathurin Du Redouer from Professor Fracanzano da Montalboddo's prototype compilation, *Paesi novamente retrovati*, first published in Italian in Vicenza in 1507.[16] Besides the accounts of Columbus and Vespucci, it included those of Pigafetta, Cadamosto, Cortés, and others. Du Redouer's adaptation, *Sensuyt le nouveau monde & navigations faictes par Emeric Vespuce Florentin: Des pays & isles nouvellement trouvez auparavant a nous inconnuz tant en l'Ethiope que Arrabie, Calichut et aultres plusieurs regions etranges*, went through five editions after its first appearance in Paris.[17]

The comparative speed with which news of the New World was diffused in Europe becomes clearer when it is realized that during the late sixteenth century, it took approximately ten days for news to travel from Paris to London.[18] Before the printing press, when dependence had been greater on word of mouth, it had not only taken longer for news to be disseminated, but its acceptance had been very slow. For example, Greenland first appeared on maps during the fifteenth century, although it had been discovered during the tenth.[19] Neither the oriental voyages of Marco Polo (1254–1323?) nor those of the Friars Minor in the late thirteenth and early fourteenth centuries had exercised the least influence on medieval cartography; until the beginning of the fourteenth century, maps were a continuation of Greco-Roman geography. It was not until the fifteenth century that the influence of Marco Polo began to be noticeable.[20] The much more rapid assimilation of the geographical information from Columbus's voyages stemmed from the presumption of the discovery of a fabled land of great riches, as cartographers clung to the classical belief in the existence somewhere in the Orient of Cryse and Argyre, islands of gold and silver.[21] Columbus's conviction that he had reached the Orient would have been reinforced by the sight of Amerindians wearing golden ornaments.[22] Intensifying the excitement was the search going on at the time in Africa for the legendary Rio Doro, river of gold.

Columbus's somewhat naive vision of New World natives in a state of primordial innocence awaiting the privilege of being exploited by the "men from heaven," as they called the Spaniards, did not endure past his second voyage. To his amazement he found that the garrison he had left behind at La Navidad had been annihilated in a dispute with those very Amerindians who the previous year had been so helpful when the *Santa Maria* had been wrecked. In the interval, the Amerindians had apparently realized that the Spaniards were all too human. What Columbus

In this engraving by Theodor de Bry, 1594, fearful Amerindians on Hispaniola offer gifts to their strange new visitors.

had taken to be artless generosity and boundless cooperation had been actually anxious maneuvers to establish good relations with these strange new beings, whatever they might be. Spaniards were later to exploit this initial reaction on the part of Amerindians by claiming descent from the sun whenever they met new peoples.[23] This was to simplify and accelerate the process of conquest, at least in the beginning.

Another unpleasant realization awaited the admiral on his second voyage: cannibal Caribs were more difficult to deal with than he had anticipated. In fact, he reported,

> These Islanders appeared to us to be more civilized than those we have hitherto seen; for although all the Indians have houses of straw, yet the houses of these people are constructed in a much superior fashion, are better stocked with provisions, and exhibit more evidence of industry, both on the part of the men and the women.[24]

A cannibal Amerindian family from *Of the newe lādes*, c. 1508–11.

"Cannibal" derives from a Carib word meaning "valiant man," an appellation which soon turned out to be apt from the European point of view. Even when captured after a brush with the Spaniards, Caribs maintained an "atrocious and diabolical regard" that inspired fear in the beholders. "I spoke with a man who told me he had eaten 300 men," Vespucci later reported, adding that fathers ate their children and husbands their wives. He had seen preserved human flesh hanging from the beams of houses "as we hang pork." He insisted on the veracity of his observations: "Of this be assured, because I have seen it. I tell you also that they wonder why we do not eat our enemies, as they say human flesh is very tasty."[25] If Columbus was horrified when he first encountered the practice, he was also pragmatic: he sent captured Caribs to Spain as slaves in order, he said, to get them to abandon their bad habits.[26]

Vespucci agreed with Columbus that Americans lived in "great multitudes,"[27] that they were generally good-looking and remarkably free from deformities. But he found that although they had "honest" faces, they destroyed them by piercing cheeks and lips, nostrils and ears. "I have seen as many as seven holes in one man's face, which holes they fill with colored stones as well as other objects. It makes them look like monsters." He calculated that the stones in one man's face weighed "sixteen ounces," adding, apparently with some relief, that the women did not indulge in this custom.[28]

There was some uncertainty as to the color of these new people, which Vespucci saw as "pulling toward red." Being naked, they were tanned by the sun. According to Columbus, however, they were "the color of the people of the Canaries, neither black nor white." Antonio Pigafetta

(1480/91–c. 1534), a gentleman from Vicenza who sailed on the three-year voyage around the globe headed by Ferdinand Magellan, reported on his return in 1522 that the natives were olive-hued.[29] Official Spanish historian Gonzalo Fernández de Oviedo y Valdés (1478–1557) agreed that the people were all about the same color, a light brown.[30] They were without any hair on their bodies except for their heads, men as well as women,[31] and what they had was always black.

Vespucci's letter, *De novo mundo*, 1505, was illustrated with this version of Amerindians.

Childbirth was observed to be easy and treated casually; Vespucci had noted that the women maintained their youthful figures even though they nursed their own babies.[32] These people practised polygyny, and Vespucci could detect no order in their sexual relations: he gained the impression that sons slept with mothers, brothers with sisters, and strangers with strangers upon chance encounters whenever they pleased.[33] When the matrilineal line of descent was recognized, it was in a way that reflected European concerns: "They take as heirs their sisters' children, to be certain of their parentage and blood line."[34]

In other aspects as well, apart from the sexual, Europeans could not at first detect order in the way of life of Amerindians, although their manner was sweet and gentle, "very like the manner of the ancients."[35] It was "wonderful that we never saw a quarrel among them."[36] Columbus had reported that they had no government. Vespucci also noted they were without churches, without faith, without markets, living according to nature.[37] Neither did they have art nor order in their combat, and after battle, they ate their prisoners of war.

More positively, Amerindians lived mainly on fish, which to the European thinking of the day provided a contrast in virtue with the evil of cannibalism.[38] But certain elements in their diet very quickly raised the suspicion that Amerindians were in association with devils, a natural consequence of the belief that one acquired the characteristics of the food one ate. To Europeans this seemed to be indicated by the fact that they ate serpents, even poisonous varieties, as well as lizards, toads, grubs, insects, and other "filth."[39] With horrified fascination, it was frequently noted that Amerindians "esteem serpents as we do capons"; in fact, they ate serpents instead of bread.[40] A milder view, such as that of Dr. Diego Alvarez Chanca, who accompanied Columbus on his second voyage, was that such a diet meant "that their degradation is greater than that of any beast in the world."[41] A question discussed during a thesis examination at the University of Montpellier in 1574 asked, "Is the flesh of poisonous animals poisonous to eat?"[42] However, Jean de Léry (1534–1611), a Huguenot minister who showed an aversion to stereotypes, tasted and found lizard so good that he talked of nothing else. The experiment was repeated by Jean Mocquet (1575–1618?), geographer

The great stores of food maintained by Amerindians impressed sixteenth-century Europeans. Jacques Le Moyne de Morgues depicts the gathering and transportation of game and agricultural produce to storehouses, where it was kept for time of need. However, the king could take whatever he pleased. Le Moyne was with the Ribault-Laudonnière expedition to the Carolinas and Florida, 1562–65. Engraving by Dietrich de Bry, 1591. C-116134 Public Archives Canada.

to the king, who found crocodile meat fairly good but somewhat tasteless, much in need of spicing.[43] The question of the connection between devils and diet faded away rather than ever being formally settled; but suspicion lingered, and certain elements of Amerindian diet never were considered "civilized." Jesuit missionaries were later to report with wonder that strawberries and raspberries were eaten with oil by Amerindians of New France, who would also "bite into a piece of solid white grease as we would bite into an apple; this is their high living."[44]

Some New World foods were readily accepted as being "merveilleusement bon"–pineapple, for instance, which to this day is known in France by the Amerindian name with which it was introduced during the sixteenth century, *ananas*. Vespucci tried a "bread" made of fish paste, and found it good.[45] Chocolate also eventually proved eminently acceptable, although sweetened rather than spiced and frothed as the Mexica preferred it. The French essayist Michel de Montaigne (1533–92) tasted cassava and found it sweet and bland. According to one report,

French explorer Jacques Cartier (1491–1557), being offered a muskrat, found it tasty.[46]

In spite of everything, the general impression was that Amerindians ate very well. Cartier explained that this was because "they took care of nothing else." Cosmographer André Thevet (1501–90), referring to the same people whom Cartier visited, reported that they ate a lot, which accords with Columbus's report that the people of the West Indies ate "luxuriously."[47] On the other hand, Amerindian moderation in food intake also impressed Europeans in an age when they considered eating to excess to be a status symbol: "The savages are very moderate in their eating, for fear of falling sick. Would to God that Christians would exercize such discretion and free us from our large and excessive banquets."[48] An Amerindian would walk all day on six biscuits, reported Melchisédech Thévenot (c.1620–92), scholar and traveller. An Englishman concurred: "It may puzzle belief to conceive how such lustie bodies should have their rise and daily supportment from so slender a fostering."[49] It was the consensus that their houses were mean, their food intake moderate in the midst of plenty, and their drink consisted of water, but still they were healthy and lusty.[50] On the rare occasions when they were sick, they cured themselves with herbs, the uses of which they knew very well. Reports that they lived as long as 150 years were generally accepted:

> Qui croiroit que sans Medecins
> Il fût possible de tant vivre?[51]

The "great stores" of food maintained by the Amerindians afforded a point of high interest to sixteenth- and seventeenth-century Europeans, in whose homelands the spectre of famine was continuously present for the peasants.[52] They were not slow to develop techniques for taking advantage of Amerindian hospitality, going from village to village and moving on before their welcome wore out.[53] Antonio de Herrera y Tordesillas (1557–1625) reported that the Spanish made themselves unwelcome by billeting their men with Amerindian families because the Spaniards "eat more in a Day than the Indians in a Month."[54] Consequently, Amerindians preferred paying tribute to having the Castilians in their houses, in spite of their lack of personal wealth and possessions.[55]

What was more, Europeans noted with considerable interest, this sufficiency in food was achieved without much effort.[56] Women, it was generally agreed, worked harder than the men, as they had to labor in the fields as well as look after their households; among nomadic hunters, they carried the burdens when on the move. Only later was it realized that the women's lot often went hand in hand with considerable power and influence.[57] Europeans rarely noted, however, that Amerindian men cleared land in preparation for planting. But toil in the European sense was noticeably absent, and individuals were not worn down with excessive labor. To Europeans, the type of sustained effort needed to be a good hunter could not be classed as work,[58] as in their society hunting was an aristocratic privilege; it was in this context, as well as that of the martial arts, that they much admired Amerindian skill in archery.[59]

Equally appreciated was New World craftsmanship; explorer Giovanni da Verrazzano, for one, noted that Amerindian arrows were worked with great beauty.[60] Although these men were without iron, they built canoes after the manner of rowing galleys, some of them large enough to hold eighty men. The speed of these craft was "a thing beyond belief."[61] Columbus, in spite of regarding Amerindians as "wild" people, felt that they were "fit for any work . . . very intelligent, and who, when they have got rid of the cruel habits to which they have become accustomed, will be better than any other kind of slave."[62]

Very early during the time of contact, Europeans attempted to show what Amerindians looked like.[63] The first illustrations appeared with original editions of Columbus's letter. A 1493 Basel edition in Latin, *Insula hyspana*, depicted a trading scene, while Italian versions that appeared in Rome and Florence the same year represented Ferdinand seated on a throne extending his hand across a body of water to some

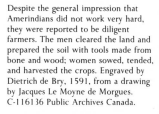

Despite the general impression that Amerindians did not work very hard, they were reported to be diligent farmers. The men cleared the land and prepared the soil with tools made from bone and wood; women sowed, tended, and harvested the crops. Engraved by Dietrich de Bry, 1591, from a drawing by Jacques Le Moyne de Morgues. C-116136 Public Archives Canada.

In this woodcut, of the earliest and most widely published representations of Amerindians, the subjects have the air of classical Romans. This illustration by Johann Froschauer was first published in a German version of Vespucci, 1505.

natives fleeing on the shore. Both versions illustrated points made by Columbus in his letter: that New World people, of an "incalculable number," were naked with long flowing hair, and they tended to run away timidly at the first sight of Spaniards. Even in the trading scene, one group was fleeing as another timorously made its offerings to the reciprocating Europeans.

The best-known early pictorialization is the so-called Augsburg woodcut by Johann Froschauer, believed to date from 1505. It illustrates a cannibal scene of the sort Léry had in mind when he criticized the tendency to represent Amerindians in the midst of hanging pieces of humans, as at a butcher's, observing that the artists had never seen what they were trying to depict.[64] The men looked not unlike Roman centurions with plumed crowns. The women also had feather headdresses, and all wore small feather capes over their shoulders. These figures set the pattern for European representation and became the stereotype for Amerindians, such as those shown in cartographical illustrations. A collection of engravings of the New World, published in 1638 under the title *L'Amerique historique*, begins with a feather-skirted couple symbolizing America, complete with a cannibal scene in the background. A less favored early method of portraying Amerindians showed the men with curling locks and full beard, as in the seventh Latin edition of Vespucci's letter, *De novo mundo* (c.1505). Another well-known example is the initial family group in the "bas-relief du Trésor" of St. Jacques church in Dieppe, believed to have been sculpted about 1530.[65] A Portuguese painting from about the same date, called "The Adoration of the Magi," has one of the wise men looking like a Tupinambá from Brazil, with feathered crown. He also wears a European shirt and breeches.[66]

The first known actual portraits of Amerindians by a European were done in 1529 by Christoph Weiditz, a German artist who saw the Mexica brought to the court of Charles V by Hernán Cortés (1485–1547).[67] Less successful in this regard was Alejo Fernández, painting a panel entitled "Virgin of the Navigators" about 1535 for the chapel of Casa de Contratación in Seville. He depicted a group of rather negroid-looking Amerindian converts in the background.[68] François Deserpz, in his work on fashions around the world published in Paris in 1567, included a pair of naked Brazilians, the woman with a large flower coquettishly placed on one thigh, and a *sauvage en pompe* in feathered cloak, as well as a hairy man and woman labelled l'homme sauvage and la femme sauvage. The latter two figures did not represent Amerindians at all, although they were frequently confused with them.[69]

Another popular subject for illustration showed Brazilians collecting dyewood for waiting ships.[70] One of the most effective of these is a bas-relief in wood dating from the middle of the sixteenth century. The figures resemble those of classical antiquity rather than of Amerindians, and display a striking vigor and vitality.[71] This period's most accurate, if rather sketchy, representations of New World life are considered to be those illustrating Hans Staden's account of his captivity among the Tupinambá.[72] A mid-sixteenth century Portugese painting entitled "Inferno" has the Devil sporting an Amerindian feather headdress.[73]

Some of the works of two artists who actually visited the New World have survived. Jacques Le Moyne de Morgues was in Florida with the Ribault-Laudonniére expedition (1556–58); and John White was in the Arctic with Martin Frobisher in 1577, and in Virginia intermittently between 1585 and 1590. Drawings by both of these artists were engraved by Theodor de Bry and his sons in de Bry's thirteen-part series published at Frankfurt am Main between 1590 and 1634 under the general title *Grands Voyages*. It is generally acknowledged that White's drawings are the only ones that catch something of the characteristic postures of Amerindians;[74] Le Moyne, while providing a wealth of detail, did not differentiate Amerindians from Europeans, except to make them bigger and more athletic-looking, rather as if they had stepped out from the Coliseum. The de Bry engravings accentuate this tendency, which is also evident in the illustrations for Thevet's *Cosmographie*.[75] In the latter case, the figures are treated in the manner of the school of Fontainebleau. Such difficulties in depicting Amerindians were not unrecognized at the time. In the words of Léry, "because their gestures and countenances are so different from ours, I confess it is difficult to represent them properly in words or even in painting. In order to see them as they are, one must visit them in their own country."[76]

The best representations of New World men are found in the genre painting of England and northern Europe. In France, such art was at the bottom of the hierarchical ladder, a position endorsed by the Royal Academy of Painting and Sculpture, founded in 1648. Consequently, despite France's reputation for accommodation with Amerindians, they appear comparatively rarely in her art during the sixteenth and seventeenth centuries.

Neither did Amerindian art influence European art. Albrecht Dürer might have exclaimed in delight at the wonders of Moctezuma's treasure, but neither he nor any other European artist appears to have been affected by these creations. An exception to this is found in certain capitals in the Palais des Princes-Evêques (c.1526) in Liège, which display Mexica influence. (Interestingly enough, the map of Tenochtitlan brought by Cortés to the Spanish court had also shown Mexica influence in its execution.) On the other hand, New World fauna were readily incorporated, and were rendered in prevailing European styles.[77]

New Ideas in Old Frameworks

As European voyages increased so did the "rage to know" about strange people and strange customs; an urge usually satisfied by collecting curiosities.[78] Ferdinand of Hapsburg owned Mexican carvings and feather work that Cortés had brought to Europe; a feather mosaic in the possession of Polish King Sigismond III Vasa may have had the same provenance.[79] Montaigne owned Tupinambá items such as a hammock, a sword club, a wrist guard, and a stamping tube. Although it is far easier to collect objects or information than it is to put them into context, at least one early collector began to put objects into series. Michele Mercati of San Miniato (1541–93), keeper of the botanic garden of Pius V and museum organizer for the Vatican, was among the first to establish that flint arrowheads were man-made.[80] Noting that they had been used by ancient Jews as well as contemporary Amerindians, he speculated that they had also been employed by early inhabitants of Italy.

Mercati's effort was unusual. Generally, during the sixteenth and seventeenth centuries, information and objects were collected fervently but with comparatively little analysis. In the material published during the sixteenth century, the only New World culture to receive much attention was that of the Tupinambá of Brazil, as it was principally in their territory that dyewood was obtained; in the seventeenth century, it was the Huron of Canada, and for a similar reason, the fur trade. Even though it was to their economic advantage to learn about these peoples, Europeans did not systematize the information they collected about the Tupinambá or the Huron until the present century.[81]

The accepted model for describing people of other lands was provided by ancient authorities such as Pliny (A.D. 23/24–79) and Herodotus (fifth century B.C.)–a model constituted largely of sweeping generalizations.[82] In spite of this, a good deal of first-rate ethnographic information was collected during the sixteenth and seventeenth centuries. Much was done by the Spaniards; but their interest was in conquest and administration rather than in learning about New World people as such. Spanish imperial considerations reinforced a penchant for secrecy; this, combined with strong doubts as to the advisability of publicizing pagan customs and beliefs, inhibited the publication of ethnographic material. Some of it did not appear until comparatively recently.[83] This was particularly true for information concerning the peoples of Mexico, Central America, and Peru.

Thus the authority of the ancients continued to maintain its grip even after they had been proved to be incompletely informed, if not completely wrong, about the nature of the world, a situation that was reinforced by the fact that some classical geographical ideas were vindicated.[84] Still, reason, to be effective, had to take into account the findings of experience–an array of strange new facts that did not accord with some cherished beliefs. Writers of the sixteenth and seven-

Flying dragon, ingeniously concocted out of a skate or ray, and known as a "Jenny Haniver." The origin of this name is unknown. Ogilby, *America*, 1671, from Albertus Montanus. National Map Collection, C-118524 Public Archives Canada.

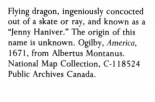

teenth centuries apparently never tired of pointing out that Aristotle had erred when he had argued against the habitability of the Torrid Zone, as had Lactantius Firmianus (c.260–c.340) and St. Augustine of Hippo (354–430) when they had maintained that it was absurd to think of man living feet above head in the Antipodes. Reason had its pitfalls–witness the logic of Lactantius's arguments against rain falling upward–so experience should not be ignored. When Cartier, in his report on his second voyage (1535–36) wrote that the ancients had theorized about the habitability of the world without testing their statements by actual experience,[85] he was repeating a point that had been made again and again since the time of Columbus. But it was easier to prove authorities wrong than it was to change patterns of thought, and the ancients were still relied upon even while their errors were reported with undisguised satisfaction.[86]

Where Europeans had been reluctant to believe in the existence of unknown races of men, they willingly (even eagerly) conceded the existence of monsters. During his first voyage to the West Indies, Columbus, while admitting that he did not actually see any monsters, accepted without question a report that on another island he did not visit, "the people are born with tails."[87] Such an easy acquiescence could well have been based on the legendary existence of people with tails–descendants from an era when men and apes mated.[88] He also repeated that on still another island the people were said to have no hair.[89] From his own observations he reported that sirens were not beautiful, as was commonly believed, but had faces like those of men.[90] While he did not consider sirens to be monsters, cannibals were traditionally classed as such,[91] and had inhabited European geographies since classical times. Columbus never did find that favorite variety supposedly inhabiting the Orient, the dog-headed man; but more than half a century later, a stranded English sailor wandering up the North American Atlantic seaboard reported that cannibals "doe most inhabite betweene Norumbega & Bariniah, they have teeth like dogs teeth, and thereby you may know them."[92] Belief in such creatures was not easily shaken; had not even St. Augustine discussed whether the descendants of Adam had produced monstrous races of men? However, the church father had been careful not to equate strangeness of appearance with non-humanity: "let no true believer have any doubt that such an individual is descended from the one man who was first created."[93] Conversely, Vadianus (1484–1551) was not convinced by reports from Africa of men who had nothing human about them except their physical form and ability to speak. He denied the existence of monstrous men: "Homines monstrosos non esse."[94] But folklore would have it otherwise;

Renaissance version of the cynocephalus, or dog-headed man, from Ulisse Aldrovandi's *Monstrorum Historia*, 1642.

a popular tale of the late Middle Ages told of Adam warning his daughters against eating certain plants that could make them conceive *semi-homo* monsters with plantlike souls.

Learned physicians of the Middle Ages and Renaissance thought that monsters were generated because of the influence of the stars, which in certain conjunctions prevented the fetus from assuming human form. Others believed that an abnormal quantity of semen was responsible, or perhaps illicit intercourse. Cornelius Gemma (1535–79), professor of medicine of Louvain, pointed to sin in general as the cause, although he indicated that the universal cataclysm and confusion of Babel also had been factors.[95]

Anecephales, also known as blemmyae, or men with heads in their chests, are shown in a New World setting by German geographer Levinus Hulsius, 1623.

The process of eliminating notions of men with one foot, faces in their chests, without mouths or anuses, or with ears so large they could use them for blankets, was to take the better part of three centuries. In fact, the immediate effect of the New World discoveries produced an efflorescence of monsters; new varieties were reported faster than the obviously unverifiable ones died out.[96] For example, years in Cuba did not prevent Governor Diego Velasquez from instructing Cortés to look for men with great flat ears and dogs' faces during his projected expedition to Mexico in 1519.[97] One seventeenth-century historian extolled the bravery of those who crossed the seas and fought monsters. Later in the same century, Pliny's pygmies were reported living in seclusion in mountainous regions of coastal New Spain; and in the Arctic, a tribe of Inuit was said to consist of persons equipped with only one leg and foot, who could truly be called half-men.[98] As late as 1724 Joseph-François Lafitau

(1681–1746) included a drawing of an *anecephale* (man with his head in his chest) among illustrations of Amerindians, despite some reservations on the subject.[99] Earlier, another had written that he did not believe there were Amerindians who lived on odors,[100] but such defiance of general belief was rare. Credulity, however, had its limits; some huge bones found in the Dauphiné in 1613 and exhibited in Paris as those of the giant Theutobochus were finally pronounced to be fraudulent, in spite of widespread belief in giants at the time.[101]

Monstrous men receded from the popular imagination as the slow intrusion of other worlds on the European consciousness revealed peoples with cultures diverse enough to satisfy the most developed taste for the bizarre. When Columbus met the Arawak and later the man-eating Carib, he found physical differences to be less than previously imagined, but differences in culture appeared to be much greater. For instance, it was one thing to detect classical affinities in New World nudity, but quite another to accept absence of clothing as a basic condition of everyday life. Spaniards had subdued naked Canary Islanders during the fifteenth century, and varying degrees of nudity had been observed in Africa. Even in Europe, nudity was acceptable under certain circumstances. Indeed, extreme tolerance existed alongside an excessive formalism,[102] in an age when sartorial ostentation was approaching its climax. The much acclaimed pageantry that marked the entry of Henry II into Rouen in 1550 included a tableau featuring fifty naked Brazilians and 150 Norman sailors playing at being Brazilians, all presumably naked (at least, that is how they are depicted in illustrations of the event).[103] The tableau was much praised without reference to the nudity. What particularly surprised Europeans about New World nudity was to see everyone, including those in authority, naked all the time.[104] Columbus, addressed by an eighty-year-old cacique "who seemed respectable enough though he wore no clothes," was surprised when he observed "sound judgment in a man who went naked."[105] Very often, their nudity was the only thing reported of Amerindians, as it was the most obvious characteristic that differentiated them from Europeans.[106]

Cannibalism made an even more profound impact than nudity. The word "cannibal" (cambialle and canibali were among the various spellings) almost immediately became the appellation by which Amerindians were known in Europe. A story that became a favorite toward the end of the sixteenth century told of some Caribs who died as a result of eating a friar; after that, men of the cloth were safe, at least on that island.[107] From the Brazilian coast about Cape Frio, came reports of men who "eate all kinde of people, Frenchmen, Portugals, and Blackamoors."[108] The ritual aspects of cannibalism were missed at first, and it was assumed that the New World men ate each other for food, hunting each other "to eat, like savage beasts."[109] Such a conclusion was perhaps to be expected. In Europe cannibalism was, not infrequently, a result of famine, as indeed it sometimes was in the Americas.[110]

In spite of a general revulsion against cannibalism, and a tendency to look for monsters, the first descriptions of New World men are moderate in tone, although a note of condescension is usually detectable. Even such defenders of Amerindians as Isabella could not resist observing, on being informed by Columbus that the trees of the New World did not have deep roots, "this land where the trees are not firmly rooted, must produce men of little truthfulness and less constance."[111] Many observers, however, seemed to agree with Pigafetta: "They are men and women disposed as we are. Although they eat the flesh of their enemies, it is because of certain customs."[112]

Visitors From Another World

As for Amerindians, they also made queries, wondering how these strangers fitted into the cosmos. Were they gods? If so, what were their intentions? When they first saw mounted Spaniards, Amerindians presumed man and horse to be one;[113] later, discerning man from mount, they continued to believe that the horse was a god, or at least immortal. To put this reaction into context, it should be pointed out that the people concerned had never before seen an animal as large as a horse; the fauna native to the areas overcome by the Spaniards did not include any animal of that size. Eventually, realizing their error, some enterprising Mexicans skinned a horse, stuffed it to appear as in life, and displayed it in a temple.[114]

Two centuries after the event, Fontenelle tried to imagine what the effect had been on the Amerindians of the first arrival of the Europeans:

> Enormous structures, which appeared to have white wings and to fly over the sea, vomiting fire from all sides, came and disgorged onto the shores men all encased in iron. They subjected their racing mounts to their will, holding thunderbolts in their hands with which they felled everything that resisted them. . . . Are they gods? Are they Children of the Sun?[115]

Amerindians, however, quickly displayed a well-developed spirit of enquiry in their attempts to decide whether or not Spaniards were indeed children of the Sun.[116] In one well-publicized instance, in Puerto Rico in 1508, they held a Spaniard under water to see if he would drown, and

In San Juan de Porto-rico, Amerindians had at first believed that Spaniards were immortal. They tested this theory by holding a Spaniard under water until he drowned, watching over him for several days to see if he were truly dead, then taking the body to their chief to inform him of their findings. The Amerindians then rose up against the Spaniards. The incident is described by Benzoni, *Historia del Mondo Nuovo*, 1565, and the engraving is by Theodor de Bry, 1596. C-116257 Public Archives Canada.

then sat by his body for three days to observe what would happen next.[117] Later, in Mexico, Amerindians, upon killing a Moor who was with the Spaniards, cut him into small pieces to make sure he was dead.[118] Once they lost their fear of horses and arquebuses, and having learned that Spaniards could fall from the blow of a stone or an arrow as well as anyone, they became much bolder in armed encounters, and the Jesuit Acosta (c.1539–1600) warned that they should not be underestimated as warriors.[119] In a more peaceful vein is the story of the aged Jamaican cacique (the same who had impressed Columbus with his authority despite his nudity) who, upon presenting Columbus with a basket of fruit, delivered an oration, concluding with the words: "If you are mortal, and believe that each one will meet the fate he deserves, you will harm no one."[120]

These reactions to the confrontation reveal the universality of human nature as well as particular characteristics of the two civilizations involved. As each sought to come to terms with what was often unwelcome new information, both Amerindians and Europeans operated on the premise that they were the only "true men." Around the world and throughout time, peoples have expressed their feeling of superiority over others by uncomplimentary appellations; for instance, Eskimo comes from an Algonkian term meaning "eaters of raw meat," which explains why present-day Arctic peoples are insisting that the term be replaced with their own name for themselves, Inuit, meaning "the people." Iroquois seems to be the French version of an Algonkian term that meant "adder" or "snake"; the Iroquois in their turn named the Sioux, which has the same meaning. Naskapi means "rude, uncivilized people"; their name for themselves is Ne-e-no-il-no, "perfect people." In Africa, the Zulus called all other tribes "animals"; whites were not people, but "those whose ears reflect sunlight."[121] Greeks rejected those who were not of their own culture as "barbarians," using a word referring to the speech of foreigners, which they thought resembled the twittering of birds. St. Augustine had been even more categoric when he said that a man was better off in the company of a dog he knew than of men whose language he did not know; he cited Pliny to the effect that a foreigner is not like a man.[122] "Each one calls barbarous that which is not of its own

Europeans giving courage to Amerindians terrified by volcanic eruptions. Ogilby, *America*, 1671, from Albertus Montanus. National Map Collection, C-118523 Public Archives Canada.

usage," Montaigne wrote with his usual perception, but with more than a little touch of irony. Montaigne was well aware of the pejorative implications of the word "barbarian," which at its kindest meant "foreigner," but with suggestions of coarseness, customs that were reprehensible if not downright wicked, and lack of manners.[123]

As Europeans and Amerindians met in the New World, this type of reaction was modified by cultural factors. Their superior technology, coupled with their belief that man was made to dominate nature, and Christians to dominate the world, did nothing to mitigate their conviction that Europeans were indeed the "true men," and that New World men were of an inferior order. Amerindians, finding themselves outclassed technologically and viewing man as a cooperative part of nature rather than as its master, wondered at first if Europeans were not more than human. Was not domination the prerogative of the gods? If one is to judge the merits of these positions on the basis of the survival of their respective cultures, the less generous response had the advantage. That the reaction of the Amerindians may have been in the nature of a self-fulfilling prophecy is suggested by the story of the bearded white-faced god they were reportedly awaiting from across the sea.[124]

In the meantime, in Europe, information about New World men accumulated haphazardly, adding much detail to Columbus's first impressions, but without seriously modifying them.

CHAPTER 2

What Manner of Men Are They?

A Latin version of Columbus's letter, published in Basel in 1493, illustrates the ambiguous reactions of Amerindians: one group flees in terror, while another offers gifts. The artist has erroneously transformed Columbus's ship into a galley, which was not designed for crossing the ocean.

THE DISCOVERY of an inhabited new world immediately raised questions for Old World theorists concerning the threefold *oikoumene* of the Christian cosmos. This concept, which conditioned European thought of the early Renaissance, divided the world into three parts, Europe, Africa, and Asia; it was symbolized by the Pope's triple crown;[1] and had hindered Ferdinand of Aragon from believing that Columbus could have found a new world. Besides, such a conclusion seemed to run counter to Holy Writ – St. Paul had written that the Gospel had been heard "unto the end of the World" (Romans 10:18).[2] Thus it had not been difficult for Europeans to ignore indications of "strange" men across the ocean. Official historian Herrera told the story of Columbus in the Azores hearing about wood of an unknown type being washed up after storms; sometimes it was artificially wrought and apparently not by iron. Another time it was the bodies of two men with broad faces "and different features from Christians"; also found were two canoes or "almidies," which did not sink and which had a removable covering.[3] But as long as it was possible to do so, such hints were ignored; Brant had reflected accepted wisdom when he had classed the urge to enquire into strange regions as one of the follies of mankind.

Once faced with irrefutable evidence of the existence of peoples previously unknown to Europe, Pope Alexander VI moved quickly. He ruled in 1493 that these people "being in peace, and, as reported, going unclothed, and not eating flesh," were human and capable of being Christianized.[4] In declaring the Amerindians to be "sufficiently disposed to embrace the Catholic faith and be trained in good morals," Alexander was stating church doctrine. St. Augustine had been firm: no matter how strange a man might appear in his person or in his customs, and no matter where he came from, there could be no doubt that he was descended from Adam.[5] The great authority of Cicero was also cited in support of this position, for he had written, "all the people of the world are men; and there is only one definition for each and every man, that he is rational."[6] Alexander may have been encouraged by the first reports of Columbus, who felt that these people "could better be freed and converted to our Holy Faith by love than by Force."[7] More than forty years later, Cartier was to make a similar observation of the Laurentian Iroquois.[8] But acknowledging Amerindians as belonging to the family of man was one thing; establishing their position in relation to Europeans was another.

What exactly had Christ meant when he had said, "other sheep I have that are not of this fold" (John 10:16)? In 1513 a presentation to Pope Leo X had claimed of Amerindians, "they are our brothers."[9] But there were others who were not so sure, and from the very first, opinion was sharply divided on the subject. As spiritual conformation was considered to be all-important, it was immediately asked why Amerindians had not been informed about the Christian God. Pope Alexander's bulls notwithstanding, there were those, even in the church, who held that the answer lay in the fact that Amerindians were brute beasts and incapable of learning the mysteries of the faith.[10] The Dominican Domingo de Betanzos was one of the most successful in propagating this view during the 1530s. Although he retracted the opinion on his deathbed in 1549, it had gained wide currency in the meantime.[11] It received general approval in an age when religious conformity was fervently supported by the people. This is reflected by André Thevet, the French Cordelier turned cosmographer, who wrote that Amerindians were "a remarkably strange and savage people, without faith, without law, without religion, without any civility whatever, living like irrational beasts, as nature has produced them, eating roots, always naked, men as well as women."[12] Columbus had reported as much, although not quite so categorically: "they do not hold any creed nor are they idolators; but they all believe that power and good are in the heavens." On his second voyage, when he was accompanied by thirteen priests, Columbus noted that each village had a house that contained "wooden images carved in relief," where Amerindians prayed and performed ceremonies. But as far as the priests could discern, Amerindians had no concept of a God in the Christian sense.

Reports that Amerindians had no religion were bad enough; worse were those that claimed they were devil-worshippers. "The principal God of Hispaniola is the Devil," wrote Francisco López de Gómara (1510–60?), who never visited Mexico but who served as Cortés' private chaplain and secretary after the conquistador had returned to Spain in 1540.[13] Peruvians, who had built great cities connected with a network of highways, each month sacrificed their most precious possessions, including their children, to their idol, washing its face as well as the doors of their temple in blood.[14] The Amerindians of the Caribbean propitiated the Devil because he was thought capable of raising hurricanes, a belief shared by Europeans.[15] Sir Francis Drake (1541?–96) in his report of his 1577–80 voyage around the world, said that the Brazilians could make it difficult for mariners by conjuring up hurricanes.[16]Amerindians, for their part, were convinced that the arrival of the Spaniards had increased the intensity of storms. Apparently the most violent hurricane in living memory struck Hispaniola in June 1494,[17] only to be followed by terrible tempests in 1508 and 1509. Whatever the Devil's association with hurricanes, Spaniards were so persuaded of Amerindian association with Satan that they sent out commissions to investigate.

Europeans early suspected Amerindians of association with devils; however, the relationship was not always a comfortable one. Jean de Léry reported from Brazil that devils could attack without warning, sometimes in the midst of a conversation between Amerindians and French. The animal at upper left represents the Europeans' impression of a three-toed sloth. The French called it "Le Haut" from the Brazilian "Amahut"; the English named it "Bear-Ape." *Histoire d'un voyage fait en la terre du Brésil*, 1580.

The charge of devil worship does not seem to have been perceived as implying a contradiction with the companion claim that Amerindians had no God and no religion. It was even conceded that they believed in immortality of the soul, and that not all the supernatural beings they believed in could be classed as devils. And had not Cicero written that there was not a people so savage that they did not have some idea of God?[18] Loys Le Roy (c.1510–77), professor of Greek at the University of Paris, used this to argue that Amerindians must have a religion.

When Amerindians showed a tendency to identify their supernatural beings and ritual practices with those of Christianity, they met with missionary resistance. However, some missionaries themselves noted some puzzling resemblances, of which the story of a flood was a favorite example. More disturbing was the presence of the symbolism of the cross among both Mayas and Mexicas; indeed, the cross was the sign of Quetzalcoatl.[19] Peruvians even seemed to believe in a trinity, and had a ceremony similar to communion.[20] Among the Mexica, there were also rituals that so closely resembled Christian forms of baptism and confession that they were regarded by the Spanish as satanic parodies, one more proof of Satan's determination to keep these people from accepting the true religion.[21] Protestant reactions were not dissimilar; majority opinion had Amerindians in league with the Devil.[22] From there it was but a short step to the opinions expressed by Spain's official historian, Oviedo, who represented Amerindians as "naturally lazy and vicious, melancholic, cowardly, and in general a lying, shiftless people. Their marriages are not a sacrament but a sacrilege. They are idolatrous, libidinous, and commit sodomy. Their chief desire is to eat, drink, and worship heathen idols and commit bestial obscenities."[23] Dominican friar Tomas Ortiz had been hardly more complimentary in 1525 when he told the Council of the Indies that Amerindians had no justice, no respect for law and truth, exercised none of the human arts and industries, and were incapable of learning. What was more, they had no beards, and carefully removed any hair that appeared.[24]

As such views became powerful in Spanish official circles, and were encouraged by the economics of colonization, the papacy once again intervened, as Alexander VI had done in 1493. The bull *Sublimis Deus Sic Dilexit*, issued by Paul III in 1537, declared that Amerindians were not to be treated as "dumb brutes created for our service" but "as truly men . . . capable of understanding the Catholic faith." Furthermore, he added,

> the said Indians and all other people who may later be discovered by Christians, are by no means to be deprived of their liberty or the possession of their property, even though they may be outside the faith of Jesus Christ . . . nor should they in any way be enslaved.[25]

This stand was to be reiterated by Pope Urban VIII in 1639, when he decreed excommunication for those who deprived Amerindians of their liberty or property.[26]

Despite papal injunctions, the debate continued: were Amerindians descended from the children of Noah, or did they represent an earlier form of humanity? Had man risen from a state of bestiality, or descended from a state of innocence?

In the basic work on worldwide customs and manners available in the sixteenth century, *Omnium gentium mores* by Johann Boem,[27] first published in Latin in 1520,[28] the cultures of Europe, Asia, and Africa are discussed in detail without mention of the New World. Indeed Boem included little recent data from any source. Instead he relied principally upon existing compilations, particularly Coccio's *Enneades*.[29] The 1542 Paris edition of Boem's work, however, was enlarged to include information from contemporary explorations, and in 1556 a Spanish version added a 190-page section on America. The work was a major influence on writers who sought to describe the world during the years 1540–75, a period known as the great age of cosmographers.

Boem saw human history in terms of a universal hierarchy, implying man's slow rise from a state of bestiality. However, because this theory had troublesome theological implications, he avoided the difficult question of the Fall of man from an original state of grace, and instead began his account with the Flood. The Flood had dispersed Noah's family, who had then lived in groups,

> without any trade with each other . . . each was equal to the other even to holding all things in common . . . each was happy with his few belongings to live in the open fields . . . with one or several women. . . . They wandered . . . no more nor less than the other animals and had no special place to take their rest, but stopped where the night caught them, in the greatest tranquility, without fear of thieves and brigands.[30]

These primitive men ate human flesh and mated with whichever women they encountered, without any concern about incest, among other vices and imperfections.[31] The descendants of Noah's sons Shem and Japhet, because they had been content with smaller holdings, had not been dispersed so widely as those of his brother, the rejected Ham.[32]

Coming down to particulars, Boem described Tartars, descendants of Japhet, as having little hair, loving hunting and fishing, and living on little. Despite their occasional predilection for roasting and eating their enemies, within their own communities they lived peacefully, never arguing with each other. The resemblance of this description to early portrayals of New World men is obvious; the principal difference was that the Tartars were depicted as deformed, something that was seldom reported of Amerindians.[33] The terms used to describe Old World "savages" were soon to become indistinguishable from those designating New World peoples.[34]

It was one thing to find resemblances between New World and Old World men, particularly if the latter belonged to classical antiquity, but it was quite another matter to establish where New World men had originated. Awkward as the fact was to deal with, it seemed that the New World had been left out of the division of the world among Noah's three sons, Shem having peopled Asia; Japhet, Europe; and Ham, Africa.[35] The debate that arose as to the origins of the Amerindians was inspired not so much by scientific curiosity, although that was a factor, as it was by a concern to defend Christian dogma and traditions.[36] The great volume of writing upon this theme gives an indication of the seriousness accorded the theological problems posed by the mere existence of people in the New World.

If Amerindians were descended from Adam, they must also be descended from Noah – but from which of his three sons?[37] The two favored candidates were Japhet and Ham, with the former enjoying a preference as he was supposed to have fathered the Tartars and the western peoples generally.[38] This was reinforced when similarities were noted in the customs of Tartars, and even more so of Scythians, with those of Amerindians. Aristotle himself had written of "certain savage tribes on the coasts of the Black Sea [Scythians] who are alleged to delight in raw

Scythian stringing a bow. From a gold bottle, fourth century B.C., now at the State Hermitage Museum, Leningrad.

meat or in human flesh, and others among whom each in turn provides a child for the common banquet."[39] All of these practices, or similar ones, were reported at various times of Amerindians. The premise of descent from the Scythians was initially expressed in print by Martire in his First Decade, reporting the voyage of Vicente Yáñez Pinzón, who had accompanied Columbus: "We consider them to be like Scythians, wanderers without fixed habitations living off the fruits of the land."[40] It was noted that Amerindians shared with Scythians the practice of scalping, and more intriguingly, a high skill in working gold. Such evidence favor ing a connection was reinforced by Acosta's well-presented argument that the people of the Americas must have migrated from northern Asia because of its proximity to North America, a theory which had been partially anticipated by Huguenot pastor Urbain Chauveton (c.1540–1614).[41] The belief was later supported by reports that Amerindians themselves had a tradition of coming from the northwest.[42] Such ideas had perhaps influenced the Jesuits of New France when they remarked that the Iroquois waged war in the manner of the Scythians and Parthians.[43]

Ham was advocated because of his cursed destiny, which had caused his descendants for the most part to fall inextricably into error.[44] Chauveton, however, took exception to this position, feeling that it slandered Amerindians. He was particularly hard on Gómara, one of its more vocal advocates.[45] Those who favored Shem as ancestor based their arguments on the existence of cannibals in the New World. They reasoned that this proved a connection with the Orient, believed to be the traditional home of man-eating peoples.[46] Since it seemed to be impossible to agree on one of the sons, the question was inevitably raised as to the possibility of Flood survivors other than Noah and his family. It was quickly denounced.[47] By the mid-seventeenth century, Isaac de La Peyrère sought to circumvent the question by reviving Paracelsus's theory of two Adams; such a view, of course, ran afoul of Christian dogma, and La Peyrère was forced to recant.[48]

A side issue to such speculations was the question of who were the first people on earth. Boem had cautiously observed that many accorded the honor to the Ethiopians, since their country, being nearest the sun, was the first to be heated.[49] Renaissance historian Polydoro Virgilio (1470?–1555) repeated Boem's arguments, but attributed the belief to the Ethiopians themselves.[50] Le Roy listed the most ancient nations as those of the Ethiopians, Indians (Asiatic), and Armenians, in that order.[51]

However, the question of primacy never engaged attention as did that of origins. Boem's version of man after the Flood, blending aspects of an animal-like existence with those of the classical Golden Age, was widely accepted; the implied contradiction was not reconciled. If anything, it intensified with the passage of time.

Boem hurried over the difficult question of primacy to theorize that, whatever his beginnings, man eventually set about improving the land. Boem speculated that the pressures for such a development arose from scarcity of food caused by growing populations, which made hunting, fishing, and gathering no longer practical. Small villages were established and slowly grew into large towns. In the words of cosmographer Sebastian Münster (1489–1552), who borrowed heavily from Boem, "Thus little by little, the people shed their barbarism and ferocity and began to live with order and 'honnesteté'."[52] During the process of acquiring civility, man had so changed the world that someone who had seen it in its original state would have taken it for another world entirely, an untouched garden resembling paradise.[53]

The discrepancies in such theorizing, not to mention those in reports

Vespucci awakens an Amerindian and gives her the name of America. Theodor Galle, after Stradanus (Jan van der Street), 1521. *L'Amérique historique*, 1638, pl. 6. Bibliothèque Mazarine, Paris.

coming in from the New World, reflected not only the unresolved views of Europeans, but also different aspects of the Amerindian personality. Cosmographer François de Belleforest (1530–83) expressed this in a verse about "ces sauvages inhumains":

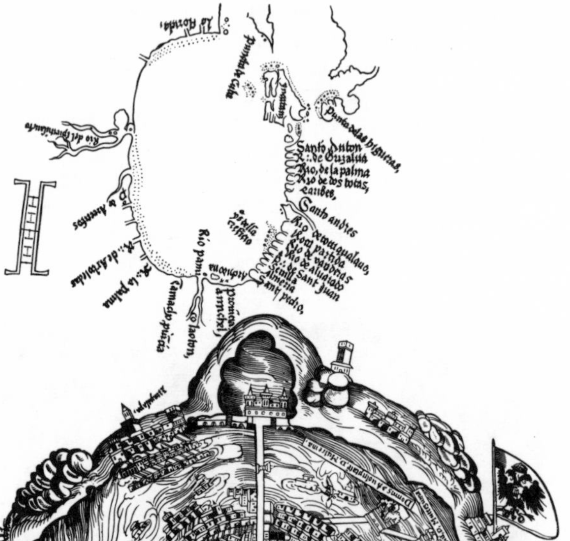

Detail of a map of the island city of Tenochtitlan sent by Hernán Cortés, and published in the first Latin edition of his second letter, *Praeclara* (Nuremberg, 1524). It shows the principal temples in the main square that had been destroyed in the conquest; they have been rediscovered near Mexico City's Zocalo, and are now being excavated. The causeways connecting Tenochtitlan with the mainland are shown, as well as the freshwater aqueduct.

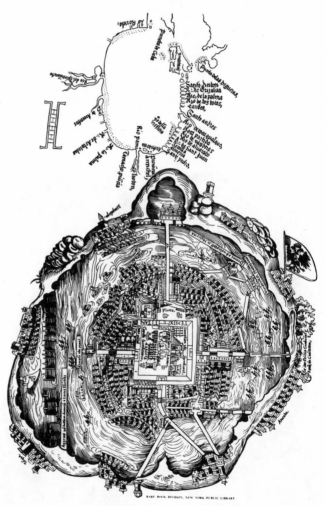

RARE BOOK DIVISION, NEW YORK PUBLIC LIBRARY

Desquels quand la façon viens lire
Avec tant d'inhumanitez,
D'horreur, de pitié, et puis d'ire,
Je poursuis ces grands cruautez.
Quelquefois de leur politique
Je loue la saincte pratique,
Avecque leurs simplicitez.[54]

For Etienne Jodelle, the contrast was not between degrees of savagery, but between savagery and civility:

Ces barbares marchent tous nuds,
Et nous nous marchons incognus,
Fardez, masquez. Ce peuple estrange
A la piété ne se range.
Nous la nostre nous mesprisons,
Pipons, vendons et deguisons.
Ces barbares pour se conduire
N'ont pas tant que nous de raison,
Mais qui ne voit que la foison
N'en sert que pour nous entrenuire?[55]

If Europeans were of two minds in their attitudes toward Amerindians, Amerindians showed no such ambivalence in their attitudes toward themselves. During the eighteenth century, a French official reported that "our Indians, while the most savage in the world, believe themselves to be the most noble of men. Next to the arts of war, they seek only to perfect themselves in the skills of hunting."[56] Another observer hinted at le bon sauvage when he wrote that "they each still believe with some justice that they are more thoughtful and more human than others."[57]

Those Amerindian cultures that came closest to the European ideal were the city-states of Mexico, Central America, and Peru. Cortés wrote that Tenochtitlan had several marketplaces, one of which was larger than the one at Salamanca. He described the central temple as being in itself as large as a town of five hundred, with a tower as high as that of the cathedral of Seville. Its citizens were not so different from Spaniards:

> Their customs in general are very similar to those of Spain, as is their orderliness and organization. One is continually struck by the surprising civility of such a barbarous people, separated from civilized nations and so far removed from knowledge of God.[58]

In other words, the sophistication of the city did not shake Cortés in his conviction that somehow this was not "civility."[59] Indeed it was not, if the evaluation of Renaissance Europe were strictly interpreted; its yardsticks were religion, political organization, and technology. Christian was superior to pagan; state to non-state; and the age of iron to the age of stone. A Christian sailing in a ship armed with artillery was not only technologically but also morally superior to a Pagan armed with bows and arrows in a canoe.[60] In the words of an anonymous sixteenth-century writer,

> although they have been formed by as many different skills and usages as we have been, their nature is still half-way between man and beast, as they have not developed and learned the arts of peace and war as have the people of the other three parts of the habitable world.[61]

The Near to Far East, in spite of deep and obvious differences, had at least one point in common with Europe: many of its societies were organized into states, well enough articulated to be able to face Europe on its own terms. In other words, Europeans could identify to some extent with Orientals.[62] In the struggle of strength that inevitably seems to follow contacts between disparate cultures, neither side was capable of completely overpowering the way of life of the other; of necessity, a modus vivendi developed. Fascination with the East was reflected in European geographical literature of the sixteenth century. Between 1580 and 1609, there appeared in France twice as many works on Turkey as on America; and in the pamphlets, the proportion is ten to one in favor of Turkey. If one were to add other parts of the Orient, the disproportion would become even greater.[63] Much has been made of this, but as far as ethnology is concerned, these statistics are misleading; in all the literature, surprisingly little was written on the people of the Orient, whereas in that on the New World, a comparatively large amount of space was devoted to its peoples.[64] As far as the East was concerned, Europe realized very quickly that it could only exploit and evangelize by taking indigenous state societies into account. In the Americas, on the other hand, cultures appeared so strange that Europe had difficulty in detecting their underlying order: at first the majority of Amerindians seemed to present a *tabula rasa* ready to be inscribed in any way that Europeans wished.

At Cumaná, a wife of a principal chief called on the Spanish governor, placed a basket of fruit before him, and sat on a bench. He was taken aback by her strange appearance: she was old, painted all over her body, and her earrings so weighted down her ears that they hung to her shoulders. She had long fingernails, her teeth were black, and she had a ring in her nose. Benzoni, *Historia del Mondo Nuova*, 1565.

If the gold and silver and pearls of the New World, not to mention its dyewood and fish, initially ensured development of contact, it was the urge to save souls, to "humanize" idolators and devil worshippers, that infused ideological life into the enterprise. This drive received tremendous impetus from the existence of attitudes, customs, and practices among New World peoples that raised fundamental questions concerning biblical accounts. For instance, how did the easy childbirth reported of New World women relate to the difficult childbirth imposed on Eve and her descendants?[65] Similarly, what about Amerindians' lack of shame in their bodies, and what about their social structures, which allowed for absence of toil and often even of hierarchy? All these ran counter to what was perceived as the biblical tradition; the concept of the universal church demanded that these strange people be brought within its fold. In the words of Emery de La Croix (c.1590–1648), eminent theorist in politics and economics, "They must be . . . shown the road to humanity and true honor, so that they live no longer like brutes. Reason and justice must prevail, and not violence which is suitable only for beasts."[66]

The drive to destroy Amerindian cultures and to rebuild them according to Christian principles began immediately. According to Oviedo,

Amerindians quickly found themselves mining placer gold for Spaniards. Here, Floridians recover gold-bearing sand by means of long tubes (right); the sand was then sieved (left). This 1591 engraving by Theodor de Bry was taken from a drawing by Jacques Le Moyne de Morgues. C-116116 Public Archives Canada.

it was because Amerindians were addicted to unspeakable abominations that God had permitted their destruction and imminent banishment from the face of the earth.[67] He supported this stand by citing Genesis 6.[68] Gómara also lauded Spaniards for removing Amerindians from their stubborn idolatry and human sacrifices. What the Spanish were teaching New World peoples was worth more than the gold, silver, and pearls they were taking. However, Gómara was honest enough to admit:

> it is certainly true that we would have done better not to have taken their goods and property from them, and to have contented ourselves with what we obtained from the mines, from the depths of their tombs and the rivers. That amounted to more than sixty millions in gold, without counting the pearls and emeralds . . . all of which represents a far greater value than what we took from them.[69]

He also regretted the Spanish practice of killing Amerindians through overwork in the mines. But these excesses on the part of the conquerors did not alter the fact that Amerindians were idolators who had to be cured of their habits, by force if necessary. Gómara's sentiments were endorsed by Richard Hakluyt (1552?–1616), the clergyman who compiled the first major collection in English of voyage accounts from around the world.[70] In Hakluyt's view, "if gentle polishing will not serve, then we shall not want hammerours and rough masons enow, I meane our old soldiours trained up in the Netherlands to square and prepare them to our Preachers hands."[71]

Remolding Amerindian cultures was a Procrustean task that was to absorb the energies of generations of officials, missionaries, and soldiers. But the primary need was to sort out contradictory impressions and to bring new facts into an Old World focus.

CHAPTER 3

To Each a Place and Rank

Cosmographer Ortelius's view of different types of man and civilizations, 1587: Africa (right), in the blazing sun, holds a flowering branch; Asia (left), in silks, holds burning incense; naked America (below), with bows and arrows, displays a human head. Crowned and sceptered Europe presides over all. Bibliothèque Nationale, Paris.

THE UNFOLDING complexities of the Americas challenged the Western World at a time when it was devoted to the Christian ideal of absolute truth. Europe reacted by reemphasizing its belief that man was part of a cosmic hierarchical order, a Great Chain of Being of collective units enclosed one within another. But a statement of faith, no matter how deeply felt, did not mean that certain questions were easily resolved: if the world represented a single order, how had it been possible for other "civilities" to develop value scales so different from those of Europe? Conversely, how could disparate civilizations possess similar cultural traits without having been in contact with each other?

The easy answer was that there must have been pre-Columbian contact. Such speculations became active when a Roman coin was reported found in Central America; Marineo Siculo, one of Ferdinand's historians, argued that this proved prior Roman presence.[1] A more solid case was provided by Corte-Real on his 1501 voyage, when he met a northern Amerindian wearing silver earrings and possessing a gilded sword. However, the earlier contact involved probably did not predate Giovanni Caboto.[2] The debate enlivened. How did "civilities" develop in the first place? Renaissance Europe's attempts to answer these questions only multiplied the contradictions. In the face of such difficulties, the simplest solution was to place New World cultures beyond the pale of "civility" and to think of Amerindians as hommes sauvages. Thus the faith of theologians and the reasoning of scholars, after some doubts and hesitations, came to reinforce a conclusion that had already been reached at the popular level.

To the Medieval and Renaissance mind, the order of the world was seen in terms of ascending importance culminating with the Heavenly Host. One view of this Great Chain of Being has been left to us by the Armenian geographer Vartan (d.1271):

> First there is the tabernacle where the divine throne is above all that exists. No created being can enter or see into this tabernacle; it is inhabited only by the Holy Trinity in inaccessible light. Next comes the home of the angels: the seraphims, cherubims, and thrones in that order, perpetually occupied in glorifying God. They are chained to Him by love, and they do not wish to be separated from Him ... As they are incorporeal, one cannot say they are in a certain place; their space is in their desire and love, and it is because they wish it that they are there ... After them come the dominations, virtues and powers, which form the middle hierarchy. Then come the principalities, the arch angels and angels who make up the last hierarchy ... The fixed and motionless heaven is their home. Then there is the Aquatic Belt placed by

> the will of the Creator who was always in movement and Who for that reason is known as the Prime Mover . . . Next comes the firmament with a great number of stars in circular motion . . . Then the zone of the seven planets . . . then the four elements that envelope earth. First the sphere of fire, which envelops the others; then air, water and finally, earth . . . which is in the midst of all the others.[3]

At the center of this world was man, for whose sake it had been created. Species were fixed, falling naturally into well-differentiated classes rather than into a qualitative continuum.[4] However, there were imperfections to be ironed out, such as the existence of wild predators: "if all countries were peopled and made subject to law and order as they should be, then there would be no animals that would attack man."[5]

Among the factors that were seen to influence this slow climb up the technological and cultural ladder were geography and climate. The appearance in 1484 of the first Latin version of Ptolemy's *Tetrabiblos* had given enormous impetus to this school of thought. Ptolemy, astronomer and geographer active in the second century A.D., had written that those who lived in the tropics were burned by the sun, had black skins, were shrunken in stature, sanguine of nature, and in habits were for the most part savage because their homes were continually oppressed by the heat; they were known as Ethiopians. Those of the north were the opposite. Being white, tall, and somewhat cold by nature, they were also savage because of low temperatures; they were called Scythians. Those who lived in between were medium in coloring and were civilized; those in the east were more masculine, vigorous, and frank, partaking of the nature of the sun; while those of the west were more feminine, softer of soul and secretive, as this region was lunar.[6] Leonardo da Vinci (1452–1519) noted a variation of this—that the men of hot countries were black because they loved the refreshing nights and hated light, while Nordics were blond for opposite reasons.[7] A Paris physician concluded that whatever is cold can be called white, and whatever is hot can be called black.[8] Ptolemy's theory was used by Le Roy without modification.[9]

The Ptolemaic explanation of the colors of mankind, which had appeared so logical in the Old World, simply did not apply to the New. Further, accounts flowing in from various parts of the New World soon made it apparent that instead of varying from white to black from the Arctic to the equator, Amerindians maintained an "astonishing similarity."[10] Columbus had noted that Amerindians at the same parallel as Ethiopians were not of the same color. Martire, in reporting this, exaggerated the difference: "The Ethiopians are black and have curly,

Amerindians of the Americas by Rossmässler. C-3649 Public Archives Canada.

woolly hair, while these nations are on the contrary white and have long, straight, blond hair."[11] Martire speculated that this puzzling discrepancy must have something to do with the disposition of the land in relation to the heavens in the American tropics. Marc Lescarbot (c.1570–1642), a lawyer who spent a year (1606–07) in Canada, varied the question: why was the hair of Amerindians black when that of French at the same latitude was not?[12] Eventually the phenomenon was explained as being due to the presence of rivers and lakes, which modified the effects of the sun so as not to turn the inhabitants black. This was a logical enough conclusion to draw from the discovery that the Torrid Zone abounded in water, contrary to the opinion of the ancients that it was arid and therefore uninhabitable. Another explanation for the uniformity of color of Amerindians was suggested by their assumed recent arrival in their lands. According to this theory, which was not explicitly formulated until the eighteenth century, since Amerindians had come only a few hundred years before the Spaniards, the climate had not had time to do its work.[13]

It was not only color that was affected by climate and geography. Jean Bodin (1530–96), the great French jurist who was renowned for his learning, saw northerners as big and strong, southerners as small and weak; men living on fertile lands as easy-going and timorous, those on sterile lands as vigilant and industrious.[14] Later, Montesquieu (1689–1755), philosopher and man of letters, was to extend such views to theorize that southern peoples' cowardice was responsible for their becoming slaves, while northerners were able to maintain their liberty.[15] Thevet, writing about the New World, took it for granted that northerners were more courageous than southerners among Amerindians.[16] Pierre Charron (1541–1603), theologian, philosopher, and close friend of Montaigne, noted that the world could be divided into

A Brazilian couple (upper) and Atahuallpa and a noble Peruvian lady (lower) in a parade of fashions from around the world. *L'Amérique historique*, 1638, pl. 3. Bibliothèque Mazarine, Paris.

north (cold), south (hot), and middle (temperate), from which he concluded that individual physical and temperamental differences were caused by internal temperatures.[17]

Ptolemy's observations about the personalities of medium-colored easterners and westerners were extended by Renaissance thinkers to include the Orient and Occident and then elaborated. Bodin reported that according to Spanish observations, the Chinese, being furthest east, were the most ingenious and cautious, while the Brazilians, being furthest west, were the most barbarous and cruel.[18] Guillaume Postel (1510–81), professor of languages and mathematics at the University of Paris, whom François I had once sent to Constantinople and Egypt in search of manuscripts, detected two heritages drawn from a common father, Noah: "the one spiritual, masculine, oriental, ascendant, heavenly, immutable; the other temporal, feminine, western, descendant, infernal, mutable." The further west one got, the closer to the infernal, until in the New World the people worshipped the Devil.[19]

Theorists encountered even greater difficulties in applying Old World cultural patterns to the New World. How could the equable climate of Brazil have produced a people with such ferocious customs?[20] "It is strange, considering the agreeableness of their country, that they are so uncivilized and rude."[21] Worse than that, the people of "Terre Australe" did not appear to have made an effort to lift themselves out of the bestial state in which all men originated.[22] Girolamo Cardano (1501–76), Italian physician and mathematician, thought he had the answer: the prevalence of savagery in the New World, he wrote, was due to the violent changes of the weather in those lands, which were caused by the great diversity between days and nights.[23] While it was generally agreed that climate affected physique and disposition and, consequently, character, others wondered whether the fertility of the land might not explain the existence of so many savage nations in America. That fertility made it possible to acquire the necessities of life with a minimum of labor, so that these people had felt no compulsion to pull themselves out of their unfortunate state.[24] Herrera thought the Old World better adapted to human life than the New, as it stretched further from east to west and so kept "more equality, with regard to the Cold of the North and the Heat of the South."[25] But how did it happen in the New World that men developed different cultures in similar climates? How could civilized Peruvians and Mexicans be living in the midst of savages?[26] Bodin concluded that social conditions could modify the effects of climate. He illustrated this with the example of the French, who, from being naturally courteous and humane, had become ferocious through civil war.[27] Bodin also theorized that different customs could be effected by the personalities of princes who imposed their preferences on their people.[28]

The beginnings of different customs were indeed hard to understand, admitted Heinrich Cornelius Agrippa von Nettesheim (1486–1535), writer, physician, and, by popular reputation, a magician. But once started, customs were handed down through generations

> according to the use of time, and agreement of manner: whereof it cometh to passe that which at one time was vice, another time is accomplished vertue; and that in which in one place is vertue, in another is vice . . . according to the opinion, or lawes of time, of place, of estate and of men.[29]

The scholar-printer Henri Estienne (1531–98) observed that not only did customs vary among different peoples, but even among the same people in different areas.[30] Complicating the issue even further, he translated Horace to the effect that to travel and to change air did not necessarily involve a change in customs. And such changes as did occur were not always for the best,

> because we have followed in the steps of our predecessors not only in industry but also in vice, for which we have greatly increased the occasion by multiplying both the extent and volume of our trade and commerce to a degree unknown to our ancestors.[31]

At the root of such ponderings lay the conviction that in the Golden Age mankind had possessed a uniform culture, and therefore the diversity now unfolding around the world could indicate only degeneration and decay, leading to eventual death. This idea was as generally accepted in the days of the Renaissance as that of progress is today.[32] Boem reflected prevailing sentiment in holding that cultural diversity implied the introduction of evil; hence cultural diffusion could only hasten the process of degeneration. Had not the Tower of Babel been "the biggest scourge that ever afflicted man?"[33] Bodin concurred that man, animals, and plants degenerate when they undergo a change of environment.[34] The abundant array of languages and cultures in the New World only served to indicate how far Amerindians had degenerated from man's pristine state before the Fall.[35] The riches of the New World had complicated the issue by arousing the greed of Europeans. This was morally disastrous for themselves and physically so for the Amerindians.[36]

But was cultural multiplicity necessarily inimical to the unity of the world? Le Roy thought not: he saw the ways of the world as forming a complex whole that could be grasped only as its interlocking relationships were understood.[37] New and previously unknown cultures presented a challenge for the spreading of Christianity; the Spanish had shown great courage in tackling vast unexplored seas and the terrors of cannibalism in order to undertake the task.[38] In his consideration of manners and morals from earliest times (in which he had included the Amerindian and his canoe[39]), Le Roy never doubted that Christian Europe represented the summit of man's development. It was destined to be the major factor in bringing together the disparate elements of the world, overriding the evils of cultural diffusion. The unity of the Christian God transcended all, its essence eternal and immutable.[40]

Similarly, Charron opposed the prevailing pessimism, arguing that Scripture applied to all people and all nations, "a universal communion and consensus."[41] But he realized that converting the world would not be easy because of the "unjust and tyrannical" control that custom exercises over judgment. Traditional European attitudes did not provide a good basis for judging men "without beards, without the use of fire, wheat or wine." Some customs were very strange indeed: for instance, to kill and eat one's aged or infirm parents as an act of devotion, a practice for which Charron found some justifications;[42] or allowing sexual freedom to single girls who when pregnant could abort at will, but who when married became chaste and faithful.[43] Even more difficult was the phenomenon of similarity. The concept of universality took an unexpected turn when certain beliefs and customs, which Europeans had believed to be exclusively theirs, were found to exist among Amerindians. The classic example of this was the story of the Deluge, wide-

In one strange custom of the Timucuans, a first-born child is offered as a sacrifice to the chief, while the mother weeps before the block on which her child will die. The executioner stands in readiness in the background. Engraved by Dietrich de Bry, 1591, after Jacques Le Moyne de Morgues. C-116123 Public Archives Canada.

spread in Amerindian mythologies.[44] Europeans were also surprised to find Amerindians using a system similar to theirs for dividing the calendar year.[45]

As for going naked, which a substantial part of humanity had now been found to do, Charron maintained that there was every indication that this was the original condition of man: "Nature did not teach us that certain parts are shameful; we did that for ourselves, through our own fault even though nature hid them and placed them far from our eyes."[46] The loss of innocence led to the adoption of clothes. Once that step was taken, it was inconceivable that man would have regressed to nakedness, ignoring considerations of health and modesty.[47]

Where Charron sought to put nudity into context as a natural stage in human development, others used it to argue that Amerindians were at best an inferior order of humanity, as obviously they had not shared in the experience of the Garden of Eden. In its extreme form, this argument was used to justify enslaving New World men.[48] In the books of costume that began to appear during the sixteenth century, dress symbolized the differences between peoples, the widest gap being between the totally naked Amerindian and the elaborately dressed European, whose clothing during the Renaissance was the heaviest in the history of the West. His dress indicated rank and authority: the more powerful the prince the more ostentatious his costume and retinue. The lavishly dressed prince epitomized civility; the naked Amerindian, the state of nature.[49] One theory even stated that it was the acceptance of clothes that had given rise to law, authority, and power, reasoning that ignored the New World's "naked governors." In the matter of clothed civility, as in other areas, wrote Thevet, God had "uniquely favored Europe over all the other parts of the world." To those taking such an attitude, reports of Europeans (usually Spanish, because of their more extensive contacts, but also French and others) "going native" and living naked with the Amerindians were truly shocking.[50]

It was thus the association of nudity with lack of social order, rather than nudity itself, that made it all but impossible for Europeans to accept Amerindian unconcern, or, as it was usually put, their lack of a sense of shame, about covering their bodies. Léry, for instance, while under no illusions that dress itself led to modesty, was astounded when he saw Amerindian woman objecting to clothing because it interfered with their bathing:

> At every spring and stream that they come to, they splash water on their heads, wash themselves and plunge into the water like dogs, on some days more than a dozen times. They say it would be too much

Satouriona and his queen display naked majesty. Engraved by Dietrich de Bry, 1591, after Jacques Le Moyne de Morgues. C-116118 Public Archives Canada.

> trouble to undress so often. How about that for a good and pertinent reason?[51]

Even whips used to force Amerindian women prisoners to wear clothes supplied by the French had only limited results: "As soon as the night fell, they took off the clothes we had given them for the pleasure of strolling naked about the island before going to bed."[52] How to explain such resistance to "civility"? Could it be, wondered one sixteenth-century writer, that nudity had something to do with the process of digestion, heating the body so that the need for clothes was not felt?[53] The struggle to clothe Amerindians was to be long and drawn-out; in 1722, Brazilians were still reported to be going naked, except on feast days when they dressed for celebrations.[54]

On this question as on others, the two themes of innocence and bestiality developed side by side, opposite aspects of the same reality. Nudity symbolized the concept of man as emerging from a state of primordial innocence.[55] This was supported by the formidable authority of the ancients, who had depicted virtue as a nude figure, unconcerned about the acquisition of riches, and often accompanied by the slogan, *nudo homine contenta est*. Such a "savage" lived in a golden age of purity of morals, of "neither mine nor thine," sharing and helping others, all of which qualities were at one time or another attributed to Amerindians.[56] The opposing theme of man arising out of bestiality was also symbolized by nudity.[57] Such an individual ate repulsive foods, had chaotic sexual habits, and worshipped the Devil, who was believed to be living on a Caribbean island.[58] These attributes of bestial man were also identified with Amerindians. As the negative and positive views of Amerindians polarized and crystallized, the one upholding their superior virtue became chiefly a literary and theoretical position, while the one downgrading them became the guide for practical politics.

The negative view was expressed in negative terms; practically every description of New World men by Renaissance Europeans was presented in terms of what they did not have: "They lived together without King or Emperor; each man is his own lord."[59] Not only was each man a law unto himself, Gómara agreed, he was also without writing, money, iron, grain, wine, and any animal larger than a dog.[60] Many New World peoples, such as the Inuit, did not cultivate the land,[61] and besides, they had no seeds to sow.[62] Being without any culture,[63] they had no alphabet, no printing,[64] no legal suits, no written books,[65] no arts or crafts.[66] It was not surprising, under the circumstances, that the New World people were also reported to be without refinements and without cares;[67] in the words of poet Pierre de Ronsard (1524–85), they "knew the names of neither virtues nor vices."[68] The negative list at times became a bit strained: Amerindians, besides being without wine, were also without bread.[69] Neither did they possess ports, firearms, or swords;[70] they were without "polite conversation,"[71] and so ignorant that they were not even aware of their deprived state.[72] Without morals, vagabonds without homes, they were without possessions, and without a country.[73]

The negative position reached its culmination with Thomas Hobbes (1588–1679):

> Hereby it is manifest, that during the time men live without a common Power to keep them all in awe, they are in that condition which is called Warre, and such a warre, as is of every man against every man. . . . In such condition, there is no place for Industry; because the fruit thereof is uncertain, and consequently no Culture of the Earth; no Navigation, nor use of the commodities that may be imported by Sea; no commodious Building, no Instruments of moving, and removing such things as require much force; no Knowledge of the face of the earth no account of Time; no Arts; no Letters; no Society; and which is worst of all, continuall feare, and danger of violent death; And the life of man, solitary, nasty, brutish and short.[74]

Although this gloomy picture was inspired by the civil wars in England (1642–49) rather than by New World societies, Hobbes assumed that it reflected man's condition in non-state societies, or, as he thought, "pre-social" man. In this he was in accord with the most advanced anthropological thinking of his day,[75] which viewed Amerindians as undomesticated and inveterately belligerent toward their own kind. This confusion apparently stemmed, at least in part, from early reports of the implacable hatred of New World men for their enemies. Overlooked were the unanimous statements that they got along "marvellously" well within their own communities.[76]

A different but still negative idea of "pre-social" man, which can be traced back directly to Columbus's reports, was best summed up by Montesquieu, a century after the appearance of *Leviathan*: "Such a man would at first only be sensible of his weakness. His timidity would be extreme, and if we need experience of that, there have actually been found "wild men" in the forests: they are afraid of, and run away from, everything."[77] However, Montesquieu was no more successful than Hobbes in selecting examples from which to argue, for the "wild men" he referred to were the insane, mentally retarded, or otherwise handicapped individuals, all too familiar on the periphery of Medieval and Renaissance society, who scrounged for themselves in the woods. Montesquieu was depicting unsocial man, just as Hobbes had depicted anti-social man, and was equating him with man in non-state societies. Neither Montesquieu nor Hobbes conceived of human society without a state, and it was the lack of state structure that caused them, along with most other early observers, to fail to see order in the majority of New World cultures. The logical conclusion of this line of thinking, as well as of the negative form of description, was another negative, the concept of New World society as essentially non-human.[78]

Sometimes, however, descriptions in negatives led to positive conclusions:

> They are in the Golden Age, neither digging ditches nor building fences to guard their possessions. They leave their gardens open, without law, without records, without judges, but following a natural justice esteeming those wicked who would injure others.[79]

Similarly, Capuchin missionary Claude (d.1632) depicted Brazilians as noble savages enjoying life, happy and lighthearted, without cares or the anxieties of earning a living, which could consume a man and reduce him to nothing.[80] Pedro Fernandes de Queiros (d.1615), petitioning the King of Spain for permission to discover the "fifth part of the world," speculated that its inhabitants would be virtuous, without need of walls or forts, or even of kings and laws.[81] A seventeenth-century Frenchman

The idealized couple. *L'Amérique historique*, 1638, pl. 1. Bibliothèque Mazarine, Paris.

in Guiana, enumerating the virtues of that country's Amerindians, did so by means of negatives: "they are neither dissolute nor dissemblers, nor liars, nor critical; neither are they vain, proud, ungrateful, thieves, mockers or hypocrites."[82] Conversely, Biard sometimes resorted to positive terms to express his negative reactions to the Micmac, whom he saw as extremely lazy and self-indulgent.[83]

Contributing to this medley of impressions was the attitude of Amerindians toward the gold and silver they possessed in abundance but did not particularly prize in an unworked state. In European eyes, this meant that they did not appreciate their "true" value.[84] Early accounts abound in references to Amerindians fishing with golden fish hooks, wearing golden breast plates or golden rings in ears and noses, not to mention pearl necklaces and bracelets. Perhaps the culmination of such stories was the tale of the conquistadors shoeing their horses with gold because there was no iron to be had.[85] Spaniards reported counting eighty houses in Cuzco that were not only roofed with gold but also lined with it.[86] A house in Collao was said to be roofed with pure gold worked to resemble straw.[87] The legend of the gilded chieftain El Dorado dates from about 1535, when Spaniards heard of the story from Amerindians.[88] The chieftain lived in a land so rich in gold that each day he covered his body with a fine film of the dust, removing it at night and letting it lie where it dropped. His investiture was marked by the jettisoning of a cargo of gold and emeralds in the middle of Lake Guatavita, situated in northeastern Bogota.[89] The legend shifted locations as the Spaniards sought the elusive cacique, in a quest that was to haunt them for many generations.

In quite another mood was the story of Amerindians commiserating with the Spanish horses for having iron bits in their mouths, and bringing gold for a substitute because they thought it would be better for the animals.[90] According to Lescarbot, Spanish women living in Peru had their shoes plated with gold and silver and garnished with pearls.[91] Not surprisingly under the circumstances, tales later circulated of Amerindians hiding more gold than they yielded to the Spaniards.[92]

Yet the need to rationalize New World peoples, to incorporate them into Europe's scale of values remained. One method for achieving this, seized upon very early, was to identify Amerindians with peoples of Europe's classical antiquity. This was evident first in the visual arts.[93] Such identification satisfied the desire for absolutes by placing Amerindians in the early stages of a universal cultural development. It opened up the possibility that in time, they would become like Europeans. "Whoever considers the Amerindians of this day, not only studies the manners of a remote present nation, but he studies, in some measure, the antiquities of all nations," wrote Edmund Burke.[94] This approach preserved the perceived unity of the world. It followed, then, that New World cultures were in their infancy, in an unevolved state. If this were so, then they must have remained unchanged while European societies were developing,[95] as their assumed youth was not sufficient in itself to explain existing disparities.

It has been realized today, of course, that American societies were no more unchanging than those of Europe.[96] As with human societies everywhere, those of America were evolving, but in a manner that had little, if any, apparent resemblance to the European model. Even now the nature of these civilizations is not fully understood, and some, such as that of the Olmec, which flourished from about 1200 to A.D./B.C., and perhaps much longer, and of the Chimú, conquered by the Inca in

Peruvian goldsmiths at work in front of a house of fine Inca stonework. Benzoni, *Historia del Mondo Nuovo*, 1565.

the late fifteenth century, remain mysterious. Others are little better known. It was not surprising, then, that Renaissance Europe, stumbling upon a New World, dazzled by the sudden appearance of great riches, controlled by a world view that relied on faith and authority, got the impression that American societies were unevolved, even static. This assumption remained throughout the sixteenth and seventeenth centuries, and, indeed, is still extant. Even such an independent thinker as Montaigne fell in with it when he wrote, "Our world has first discovered another . . . so new and so infantile that it is still being taught its ABC."[97] The fact that most New World societies were preliterate would have contributed to such a conclusion, which was further strengthened by the persistent European habit of describing the New World in negative terms, in itself an assumption of an incomplete, unfinished state. In the eyes of Estienne Pasquier (1529–1615), advocate general at the Paris *cour des comptes* and minor member of the Pléiade, America was truly a New World, even though he recognized that its physical age paralled that of Europe. What proved the point, he thought, was "the rusticity of their [Amerindians'] customs compared to the civility of ours."[98] Cannibalism and human sacrifice also illustrated this argument, as these were seen as manifestations of immature societies.[99]

Montaigne, despite his acceptance of the belief in their immaturity, came closest to perceiving that Amerindians were fully fledged human beings. They had a trait in common with Europeans, he wrote, and that was the use of reason. Interviewing sailors, merchants, and particularly "three savages who came to Rouen during the time of the late Charles IX," he found that Amerindians could and did best Europeans in debates. They were also industrious, as their cities testified. Although he was against colonization, Montaigne was more interested in using Amerindians to evaluate European society than he was in advocating Amerindian rights. Still, he denounced "false elements" in Europe that prevented the appreciation of the qualities of Amerindian life and allowed the reasoning of New World men to be disregarded because they did not wear breeches.[100] Cannibalism, he said, was not cruel in the sense that torture was. (At the time that Montaigne wrote, torture was an established part of the judicial processes throughout Europe, and burning people alive was a common method of execution.[101] In the lists of vices attributed to Amerindians, particularly in the Spanish debates that had culminated with the confrontation of the Dominican Bartolomé de Las Casas against Juan Ginés de Sepúlveda at Valladolid in 1550–51, torture had been noticeably absent.) Concluded Montaigne: better to eat your dead enemy, as do the Amerindians, than to eat a man alive, in the manner of the Europeans.

Renaissance Europe never succeeded in considering Amerindians in anything like their own terms. The general tone of Renaissance writing is overwhelmingly unfavorable toward Amerindians, in spite of efforts of individual writers to be at least impartial. Even the most sympathetic of accounts were written from the viewpoint that these nations were savage and needed to be "humanized."[102] Part of the difficulty can be attributed to the fact that much of the written European commentary about the New World, including some of the best, was the work of men who had never crossed the ocean–Montaigne and Charron being outstanding examples. Another example was Pasquier, who followed his comments on the New World with the remark, "as for myself, I pass on to you this information for the price it cost me; it is better to believe it than to go and verify it."[103] Even Jacques-Philippe Cornut (c. 1606–51) compiled his authoritative *Canadensium plantarum aliarumque nondum editarum historia* (1635) from samples brought to Paris,[104] and geographers could and did accumulate information that permitted them to draw increasingly accurate maps, often without sallying forth themselves.

The replete cannibal. *L'Amérique historique*, 1638, pl. 29. Bibliothèque Mazarine, Paris.

The French raise the Christian cross, the symbol of "humanization," establishing their colony at Maragnan, while Tupinambá are depicted as looking on in adoration. Engraving by L. Gaultier in Claude's *Maragnan*, 1614.

But the major difficulty lay in the disturbing revelation of a new world that had not only developed outside the Christian ethos, but in some cases in contradiction to it. Some Amerindian practices, such as human sacrifice, violated European taboos, yet instead of fearful consequences, as was to be expected, they seemed to result in the reverse: New World peoples were reported to be happy, healthy, and long-lived, attributes Europeans had believed to have been possessed only by patriarchs of the Old Testament.[105] Europeans reacted to such revelations according to their interpretation of Christianity. It was no coincidence that the most impassioned debates as to the nature of Amerindians arose in intensely orthodox Spain. Similarly, in France, with its long tradition of intellectual curiosity, the concept of le bon sauvage received its fullest expression during the eighteenth century.[106] This concept was not without antecedents: during the thirteenth century, the poetic image of the "noble heathen," represented by such men as Saladin, had influenced Europe to begin substituting missionary projects for the military expeditions of the Crusades.[107] Intensified missionary activity in Asia was to pave the way for similar campaigns in the New World.

Thus Europeans arrived at the consensus that Amerindians were in a state of pre-civilization, or perhaps in its early, "immature" stages. The best that could be posited for them was that they were capable of becoming fully men; according to Christian doctrine, they were perfectible. Hence, the French used the verb *humaniser* when referring to teaching and evangelizing Amerindians. There was never any doubt as to the meaning of humaniser: it signified the transformation of savages into Europeans.[108] If the idea of savagery made it possible for Europe to bypass the complexity and integrity of New World societies,[109] it also greatly eased the task of bringing about the acceptance and assimilation of new facts that did not accord with cherished beliefs.

CHAPTER 4

L'Homme Sauvage

Theodor de Bry's version of a devil being worshipped by Amerindians, as described by Benzoni, *Historia del Mondo Nuovo,* 1565. C-104182 Public Archives Canada.

EUROPE'S DISCOVERY of the Amerindian is usually represented as affording her the first large-scale encounter with man living in a state of nature. According to this view, that discovery was largely responsible for the development of the European idea of l'homme sauvage, the savage who could be either noble or debased, but who in any event was not civilized. Such achievements as the city-states of Mexico, Central America, or Peru were either overlooked or else were dismissed as being, at best, barbarous. An examination of the concept of savagery reveals that its origin is both more complex and far older than such a view would indicate. In fact, it involved the well-known Renaissance folkloric figure of the Wild Man; early Christian perceptions of monkeys, apes, and baboons; and the classical Greek and Roman tradition of the noble savage.[2]

Columbus's encounter with the Arawaks and Caribs did not introduce Europeans to a previously unknown kind of man; what it did was to add a new dimension to an already existing idea, that of l'homme sauvage, by revealing multitudes of people in the New World who appeared, to Europeans, to fit the concept, at least to some degree. Alternatively, Renaissance Europe applied the term "barbarian" to these new peoples, often as a synonym for "savage" but sometimes to indicate an ameliorated form of savagery. Eventually, the sheer weight of numbers of those they had so readily labelled "savage" caused Europeans to give new attention to their concept of l'homme sauvage, and consequently to the whole question of man in relation to his society. The idea of savagery had been around for a long time, but what exactly did it mean? How did it differ from civility?

A modern French definition of the word "sauvage," that of Larousse, says that among other things it means not cultivated, tamed, or domesticated; that which frightens easily. Applied to man, it denotes a person who lives away from society, beyond the pale of its laws, without fixed abode; by analogy, one who is rude and fierce.[3] Larousse introduces such definitions with the statement that in ancient French the adjective "salvage" or "sauvage" simply signified the forest habitat, and was a synonym for the Latin *sylvaticus*. The time boundaries implied by the word "ancient" are not specified; but it can be assumed that the sixteenth and seventeenth centuries are included. A survey of French writing during that period, however, does not support the thesis that at that epoch sauvage meant simply living in the woods. In that intensely religious age, the medieval habit of viewing man in moral terms was still far too deeply implanted for such a neutral use to have been anything but desultory, and highly individual. While shades of emphasis could and did vary from writer to writer, the general implication was always clear:

La femme (above) et l'homme sauvage (right), as conceived by François Deserpz in *Recueil de la diversité des habits*, 1567. Bibliothèque Nationale, Paris.

to be savage meant to be living according to nature, in a manner "closer to that of wild animals than to that of man."[4] The beast far outweighed the innocent.

Sainte-Palaye said the word sauvage was used in this sense well before the Age of Discovery. He compiled his *Dictionnaire historique* during the eighteenth century; in it he traced the meanings of words from their origins to the time of Louis XIV. He listed eight meanings for sauvage, of which the first was "not tamed" and the last, "extraordinary." In between are such definitions as solitary, uncivilized, ferocious, demented, and foreign.[5] Richelet, whose dictionary was published in 1680, said the word applied to fierce persons who were the enemies of society and agreeable conversation.[6] Furetière's *Dictionnaire universel* (1691) defined a savage as a man without regular habitation, without religion, law, or civility. Nearly all of America, he said, had been found peopled with savages, most of whom were cannibals. He added, "the Savages go naked and are shaggy, covered with hair."[7]

The immediate reaction of Europeans had been to refer to New World men as cannibals; even Columbus had come to comply with that designation. He did not call them savages, except in the case of armed encounters.[8] Neither did Vespucci, although he found some of them brutish and animal-like in their appearance, bad of faith and utterly savage in their manner of living.[9] In general, however, Spaniards and Portuguese immediately adopted the term *indios*, although the Portuguese sometimes referred to nomadic hunters as *selvagens*, people whom the Spaniards usually called *indios bravos*. The French initially referred to New World men as *hommes, gens, habitants, indigènes*, or most likely, *cannibales*. The Germans, interested but not so directly involved, opted for *indianer*.

It is nonetheless evident from early voyage accounts that the French, as well as Europeans in general, had quickly equated New World men with savagery. This is indicated, for example, by Cartier's comment, reporting on Amerindians he met on his first voyage in 1534: "This people may well be called savage, for they are the sorriest folk there can be in the world, and the whole lot of them had not anything above the value of five sous, their canoes and fishing nets excepted."[10] Cartier did not explain what he meant by savage beyond the lack of material possessions and a consequent style of living, which he did not consider acceptable. This equation of New World men with savagery is also evident in those early illustrations that attempted to depict *la frayeur subite* (sudden fear), which Amerindians initially experienced at the approach of Europeans.[11] One of the definitions of sauvage considered above was "that which frightens easily." However, the term sauvage does not appear frequently in print until the middle of the sixteenth century: by the third quarter, it was in general use in French and English; in Spanish and in Portuguese, the term indios became hardly less pejorative. During the seventeenth century, French and English writers were calling all the inhabitants of the New World savages, whether they were descended from the court poets of the city-states of Central and South America, or were nomadic hunters following caribou in the austere north.

In his benign aspect, the savage was represented during these two centuries as living in the "infancy of nature" or, more ideally, in a Golden Age, that concept from classical antiquity that had never ceased to haunt Europeans' minds. "They are, in effect, happy with so little";[12] or, in the words of Vespucci, "they live content with what nature gives them."[13] In his adverse aspect, the savage was "a statue of flesh and blood, an artificial man who could only be moved by the use of force."[14] He was without heart for his natural responsibilities, had no eye for the beauties of nature, did not even have names for painting and sculpture; he could not appreciate music or fine perfume, and ate his food raw, bloody, and alive. Solitary and alone in the midst of others, he was indifferent to suffering and cruelty, as he was without natural affections.[15]

Such representations, while graphic, were not considered satisfactory explanations of savagery, even at the time. How was it to be defined? First of all, it was far removed from reason. In the words of d'Avity, "One must consider barbarous those whose manners and customs are far removed from true reason."[16] The belief of the day held that this was a natural consequence of a lack of knowledge of God, the knowledge considered to be a prerequisite for mental activity, according to St. Augustine. That it had long been held to be applicable to Amerindians is indicated by the commission Cartier received for his third Canadian voyage from François I, which refers to the people of Canada as living without knowledge of God and without use of reason.[17] La Croix wrote, "I rank with beasts those savage peoples who do not use reason."[18] Oviedo's view of the mindless savage was equally unflattering: "The bones of their heads are so hard, so strong and thick, that the principal care of Christians, when they are fighting with them, is not to hit them on the head for fear of breaking their swords."[19] According to such opinions, the contemporary savage was a retrograde figure; the first man, living off acorns and chestnuts, was more polite and polished than he.[20] This position, however, was not so clear to Antoine de Montchrestien (c.1575–1621), dramatist and economist, who found that Amerindians were

> subtle enough mentally, but ignorant of our arts, whether of peace or of war. They do not believe that land belongs to individuals, any more than does the light of the sun. They only labour and cultivate enough

> to provide for their sustenance.... They are totally given to liberty, and are not very industrious. They value bravery above all.... In short, if it were possible to remove from them their faults, replacing them with our virtues without our vices, they would be worthy men.[21]

In other words, it was not so much lack of reason or even retrogression that made them savages, but rather that they were not like Europeans.

To d'Avity, the non-use of reason was the most important of five "degrees of brutality."[22] By using the term "degrees" he imparted a hierarchy to brutishness, a concept congenial to the Renaissance ethos. The second level of savagery he found in the manner of procuring food – hunting and gathering, living like beasts off the land, rather than practising agriculture. There was also the nature of the food to consider. The Amerindian diet contained elements that in the eyes of Europeans could at best be considered "savage." Herrera said of the people of Cuba that they ate "many filthy things, as large Spiders, Worms breeding in rotten Wood and other nasty Places, and Fish half raw, for as soon as taken, before boiling, they pull'd out their eyes, and eat them, which things any Spaniard would loath."[23]

This concern with the diet of the Amerindian was the logical consequence of the widespread belief that we are what we eat.[24] The implication of this, for the Renaissance mind, was that "savage food necessarily produces a savage nature and temperament."[25] Amerindians made

Virginians eating off the ground, a practice considered "very savage" by Europeans. Theodor de Bry, 1590, after John White.

similar observations concerning Europeans. A shaman accused Hennepin of eating serpents and poison, adding that such folk as he also ate thunderbolts.[26] Amerindians also shared the European belief that one develops the characteristics of the food one eats. A hunter, for instance, who ate of a slow-moving animal risked losing his speed;[27] and as is generally accepted in the case of cannibalism, eating the heart of a brave enemy was motivated by the desire to acquire his courage. Lack of regular meal hours was also cited by Europeans to prove Amerindian savagery. Even worse, Amerindians took their food from the ground, without napkin or any other cloth, eating out of earthen pots or calabashes.[28] According to one unsympathetic Recollet missionary, they often ate "crouched like dogs," and generally behaved like animals.[29]

Nudity was d'Avity's third degree of "brutishness," indicating "a complete absence of a sense of morality when persons do not cover even their shameful parts."[30] In fact, held d'Avity, it was a sense of shame that distinguished men from animals. His fourth level concerned types of habitation: the most barbarous people lived in caves and trees, although nomads living in tents were not much better. Lack of government was fifth: "They are entirely barbarous who live without any laws and without chiefs in times of peace, only accepting them during wars." On this point, however, d'Avity conceded that some New World peoples, such as those of "Tlascalla & Chilolla" and New Spain, had what qualified by European standards as government. Peruvians even had a form of civility, although they did not have the arch; but their ingenuity in building bridges up to 300 feet long over very deep gorges had to be admired.[31] Others were not so prepared as d'Avity to grant that the Peruvian government could be classed as civilized. Acosta, for one, found it to be tyrannical, and therefore barbarous, because it treated the people as beasts and the rulers as gods.[32]

Other attempts at defining brutishness included lack of writing[33] and the "elusive" or even "defective" structure of languages that impeded the communication of Christian doctrine.[34] Without the letters "f,l,r," how could Amerindians have "foy, loy et roy"?[35] This linguistic characteristic, first reported of Brazilians, was found to apply to Canadians as well.[36] A favorite word for describing their languages was *baragouin*, gibberish.

These efforts at definition were based on the assumption that if savagery were a condition, it must have certain characteristics that would make it recognizable as such. From this point of view, d'Avity's list is as interesting for what it leaves out as for what it contains. Contemporaries would have been struck by the fact that the cosmographer did not include lack of order in sexual matters, although this had been widely reported of New World peoples. This indicates some independence of

An attack on a Seneca village depicted in picture writing. The cabin with the two trees emerging from it at "F" is the emblem of the Seneca; the six symbols on either side each represent a dozen individuals who were taken by surprise, as indicated by the sleeping figure. At "G," eleven of them were killed, as indicated by the war club and the heads, and five dozen taken away as prisoners, lower right. Lahontan, *Voyages dans l'Amerique septentrionale*, 1705. C-00247 Public Archives Canada.

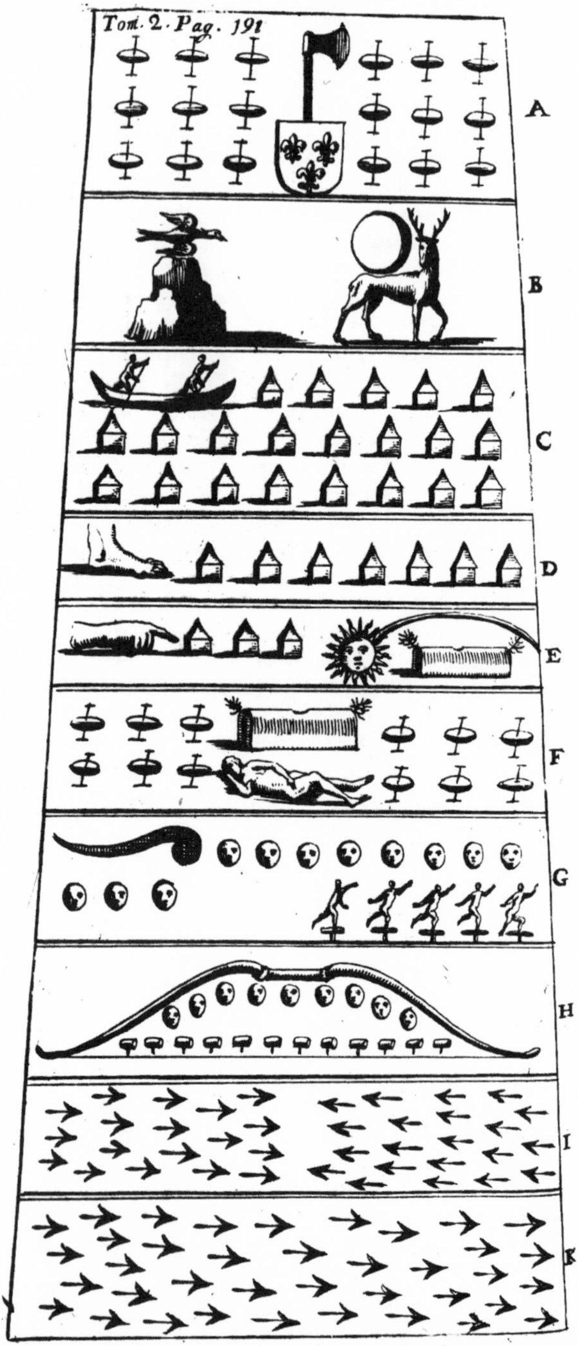

judgment on his part, for although it was being realized that these reports were exaggerated, to say the least, they were still generally believed.[37] Neither did d'Avity include cannibalism as such, but rather as a manifestation of the lack of reason. Cannibals, he wrote, must be considered as enemies of humankind, or else as maniacs who must be first rendered capable of reason and humanity, and then instructed in virtue and the Christian faith.[38]

D'Avity also omitted dirtiness, which came to be used by latter-day writers as one of the characteristics of savagery, Amerindian or otherwise. But during the sixteenth and seventeenth centuries, Europeans were struck by the frequency with which Amerindians bathed. It was told of Moctezuma ("the chief who shoots to heaven when he is angry") that he bathed every day, "were it ever so cold."[39] Léry considered it worth reporting that the Tupinambá of Brazil washed their mouths and hands before eating.[40] European standards were not as high. Erasmus (1466?–1536), in his tract entitled *De civilitate morum puerilium* (1530), said that it was necessary to wash hands before sitting down at the dining table. Among European upper classes, this was done by extending the hands so that a page could sprinkle them with perfumed water.[41] There is no indication, in Erasmus or elsewhere, however, that such refinements were suggested for the masses. Generally speaking, Europeans were of the opinion that bathing could be followed by colic, fevers, headaches, and vertigo, and that therefore the best course of action was to consult a physician before indulging in what was regarded as a pleasure rather than a health measure. In any event, it should be done only in summer and not in winter.[42] As European standards of cleanliness developed, so did criticisms of those Amerindians who were found not to wash their hands before meals, nor the meat nor even the pot before cooking.[43] However, one could wonder upon what standards such comments were based, and whether the authors were comparing a certain group of Amerindians with a comparable group of Europeans, if such inquiry would have been feasible or even possible.

An even more striking omission from d'Avity's list is that of cruelty, particularly as historians of the nineteenth and twentieth centuries have been at great pains to "prove" the savagery of Amerindians because of their war practices. Apart from their cannibalistic aspects, these practices were not considered in the days of d'Avity to be more cruel than those of Europe. Quite the contrary, in fact, as far as torture was concerned. Sixteenth-century accounts are dominated by reports of Spanish torture of Amerindians, especially during the early part of the century, when decimation of the New World peoples was at its height. The description "very cruel," which Renaissance Europeans so often applied to New World men, was a label habitually tagged onto unfamiliar people as well as onto enemies in war, and did not usually point to specific practices.[44] However, in the case of Amerindians, it often referred specifically to their cannibalism.[45]

Cardano did not consider cruelty a particular characteristic of savages, as he noted that such people were often very gentle. Observing that they could be more humane than many Greeks and Italians,[46] he went on to say that they were neither immoral nor lacking in intelligence. Their savagery lay, rather, in a psychological instability: "Before a matter is understood they begin to rage and after they have become excited it is very difficult to quiet them."[47] This lack of emotional control made them liberty-loving and seditious; it also left them vulnerable to being imposed upon.

Wild Man of the Woods[48]

When he wrote his description, Cardano thought he was depicting men of the New World, among other "savages." In fact, both his description and the definitions were strongly influenced by one of the most familiar of the folk figures of this period, the Wild Man of the Woods. In much of the sixteenth-and seventeenth-century writing on savagery, the influence of this figure is evident. Found in folklore throughout Europe, but particularly in the northern and central regions, he was known by such names as Wildemann in Flanders and Germany; Wild Man, *wodewose*, or *woodhouse* in England, Ireland, and Scotland; and l'homme sauvage in France. He was also known as Pilosus, Orcus, Schrat, and Ogre; or perhaps as *homo sylvestris* or *homine agreste*. All of these terms were more or less synonymous with savage, satyr, or faun. Wodewose derived from the Old English *wode* or *wod*, meaning furious or in a state of insanity. Like Odin or Wodin, the great God of the northern nations who presided over war and feasted on the slain, wode expressed the rage of battle. It also had implications of unrestrained sensuality and of the demonic. A glimpse of forerunners of wodewoses or wild men is provided by Pausanias, who during the second century told of satyrs attacking a woman from a Greek ship and treating her "in such a way as we will not venture to describe."[49]

The Wild Man appeared in a theatrical play in Padua as early as 1208, and was first pictorialized during the mid-thirteenth century in grotesques decorating manuscript margins.[50] His period of popularity began during the latter part of the fourteenth century, reaching its peak during the Renaissance; after the seventeenth century he went into a de-

Fifteenth-century stone carving of a hairy man. Musée des Antiquités, Rouen.

cline. His origins can be traced back to classical antiquity or even to Babylon and Uruk, as well as to the ancient Hebrews. In Roman mythology, he was descended from the Titan Saturn whose reign was described as a Golden Age of innocence and purity, although Saturn himself was a monster who ate all but three of his own children: Jupiter (air), Neptune (water), and Pluto (earth, underworld). Orcus, also descended from Saturn, carried the dead to the underworld. Saturn has certain similarities to the Greek Cronos, the son of Gaea and Ouranos (Earth and Heaven), two aspects of the same identity before they were separated by their son. Although associated with the Golden Age, Saturn symbolized life-devouring hunger and insatiable desire. Incapable of allowing his people to evolve, he was emasculated by his sons and returned to the heavens.[51] The Wild Man's physical resemblance to the satyr Silenus has frequently been noted,[52] and he has also been identified with Hercules. For the Hebrews, the Wild Man was represented as a spiritual rather than as a physical condition: he was a rebel against the Lord, insane, accursed, and destructive.[53]

Such traditions merged, more or less under the influence of Christianity, to produce the Renaissance wodewose or l'homme sauvage. He was a minor figure representing the negation of the Christian ideal, a folk version of Antichrist. In the days of courtly love he was the embodiment of brute sensuality as opposed to the chivalrous love of the knight. He was usually depicted as covered all over with hair, except for knees, elbows, and face; and he had a full beard. His hairiness symbolized the enormous strength on which he depended as he stood alone against all, even his own kind. This strength was suggested also by his habit of carrying a knotty club or an uprooted tree. Unable to speak, he shunned man and was devoid of knowledge of God, an indication that he did not have the use of reason or that he did not possess it.[54] He was intimately acquainted with nature's secrets, which he sometimes shared with peasants; at times he would tend their cattle or would heal a wounded knight with herbs. But his closest associates were bears and devils; unable to control his passions, he assaulted lone women in the woods.[55]

In Edmund Spenser's vivid imagery, this being was outsized, "all overgrowne with haire . . . With huge great teeth," he "fed on fleshly gore, The signe whereof yet stain'd his bloudy lips afore." This unprepossessing figure lived on the "spoile of women," whom he raped and then ate. He had already caught and eaten seven by the time he appeared in *The Faerie Queene*.[56]

A gentler version of the Wild Man in the same work, Satyrane (his father was a satyr) rescued ladies instead of preying on them. Whether the hairy man was presented as fierce or gentle, his portrayals were remarkably uniform, reflecting his lack of personal development, and consequently, of individuality.

This solitary homme sauvage, "black and hairy, like a chained bear," owed his origin to more than the mythologies of classical Greece, Rome, and the Middle East. He also contained elements from early reports of anthropoid apes, usually described in the Renaissance as speechless human beings, homines sylvestres. According to Pliny,

> the Choromandae are a savage and wild people; distinct voice and speech have they none, but in steed thereof, they keepe an horrible gnashing and hideous noise: rough they are and hairie all over their bodies, eies they have red like the houlets and toothed they be like dogs.[57]

There is now no doubt that Pliny was actually describing a troupe of large monkeys or gibbons. The Medieval and Renaissance tendency was to transform these animals into quasi-human beings by exaggerating their human aspects. The Spanish, for instance, were reported to regard baboons as a race of people who refused to speak so that they would not be forced to live in subjection.[58] Similarly, the great apes and orangutans were said to be descended from people who had grown weary of work and the restraints of village life, and so had retreated to the forests and an animal-like existence. They were supposed to have been the products of miscegenation between women and animals.[59] Albertus Magnus saw apes as being intermediate between man and beast, *similtudines hominis*, an early version of the missing link.[60] Men could even turn into apes: "of the Poets, it is fained that there were two bretheren most wicked fellowes, that were turned into Apes."[61] Prester John's list of wild creatures, dated 1164, included homines agrestes,[62] which Cardano said resembled Wild Men.[63] As late as the mid-eighteenth century, an Englishman published an illustration of a "man in the wood," complete with his gnarled stick, and labelled him "The Satier, Savage, Wild-Man, Pigmy, Orang-outang, Chimp-anzee, etc."[64]

From such hesitations and confusions, it had not been a long step to the idea of dual creation, of the Devil acting in competition with God but being capable only of producing a distorted version of the original being that had been divinely created. This concept was firmly established in Christian folklore: horse and ass, lion and cat, sun and moon, day and night.[65] An ape, as imperfected man, symbolized carnal desire; the apple-eating ape was seen in very much the same perspective as the sexually unrestrained Wild Man. The ape was also believed to remember injuries and to harbor hatreds for a long time.[66] Thus, men who were of a vengeful disposition or who nursed the desire for revenge were acting in the manner of apes rather than as fully fledged human beings. In describing Amerindians (with more or less truth) as people who never forgot an injury, who were so vengeful that they even ate the lice that tormented them, and who had no order in their sexual relations, Renaissance writers were putting them into a context popularly associated with apes and Wild Men.

The positioning of l'homme sauvage between man and animal meant that he could act in concert with beasts as an intermediary between human beings and the underworld. In Renaissance Flanders he was included with the wild animals who guarded the fountain of life in the forest, represented as a giant covered all over with hair, with eyebrows meeting over his nose, and armed with a large, uprooted sapling. He had the power of granting or refusing entry into heaven.[67] Near the forest was the *Nobiskrug*, where passports to the other world were obtained; its insignia was a hairy giant. In this capacity as intermediary the Wild Man was known as Orcus.[68] In Rouen during the sixteenth century, this figure was frequently placed above doors of houses, and appeared as a fireplace guardian[69] against the underworld. He is found on the North Portal of Rouen Cathedral, and guards the principal entrance to San Gregorio in Valladolid in Spain, as well as that of Casa de Montejo in Yucatán, built in 1549. In his demonic aspect he appears on tombs, particularly in northern and central Europe, where he is usually being trampled underfoot by the commemorated figure.

Seventeenth-century interpretation of a cercopithecus, showing the blending of human and apelike characteristics, from Ulisse Aldrovandi's *Monstrorum Historia*, 1642.

An extremely ancient version of the Wild Man, Enkidu, was the embodiment of natural innocence. Seduced by a harlot, and consequently rejected by his former companions the wild animals, he had no recourse except to go to the city and become civilized. He bewailed his fate at his death.[70] Among French names for l'homme sauvage or similar beings are found "Ankou" and "Annequin," the latter approaching Hellekin or Harlequin.[71]

In Renaissance France the prankish side of l'homme sauvage prevailed, and he became identified with the Germanic comic devil, Hellekin, leader of the Wild Horde. Hellekin was particularly strongly entrenched in the north; his marriage to the mythical Luque La Maudite in Rouen during the thirteenth century is said to have resulted in a spree that caused considerable damage to the city.[72] When animal skins and feathers were not available for the costuming of Hellekin in pageants, rags were substituted, and eventually became stylized into the diamond design associated with his theatrical descendant, Harlequin.[73]

Although the first record of a theatrical play featuring a wild man dates back to 1208 in Padua, it was in pageants and spectacles where he was most in evidence, particularly those of Carnival and Twelfth Night. Here his disguise was regarded as a licence for rampaging violence.[74] At one point he even took part in tournaments, challenging knights. One of the best-known incidents involving a wild man masquerade occurred on 28 January 1392 at an event that later became known as the "Bal des Ardents," Ball of the Burning Men, at the court of Charles VI ("the Mad") of France, when several revellers dressed as Wild Men burned to death.[75] Sometimes the carnival Wild Man, girdled and crowned with feathers, pretended to feed only on raw meat, which was handed to him on the end of a stick.[76] In Quercy the first Sunday of Lent was formerly called "lou dimenge dei Salvagi," Sunday of Savages, which the youth celebrated "by imitating Satyrs."[77] In the pageant celebrating the entry of Charles V into Bruges, Wild Men were shown as the city's earliest inhabitants.[78] At other times they prefigured Amerindians, as in the entry of the "Damoiseulx de Valenciennes" into Lille in 1438, when masqueraders were dressed as Wild Men, some of them in animal skins, others in feathers.[79] In 1564, Charles IX was welcomed into Troyes by a troupe of savages and satyrs mounted on goats, donkeys, and a horse masquerading as a unicorn.[80] Jesuit Paul Le Jeune (1591–1664), seeing his first Amerindians with painted faces at Tadoussac in 1632, remarked, "I saw those masks which run about in France at Lent."[81]

Le Jeune could not have foreseen that the tradition of carnival masquerades would cross the Atlantic with the settlers. Jacques-René de Brisay de Denonville, governor-general of New France in 1685–89, noted that such practices had reached the point where his predecessor, Joseph-Antoine Le Febvre de La Barre, had had to suppress them. However, he had not entirely succeeded:

> A way of dressing up like savages, stark naked, not only on carnival days, but on all days of feasting and debauchery, has been treated as a nice action and a joke. These manners tend only to maintain the young people in the spirit of living like savages and to communicate with them to be eternally profligate like them.[82]

Dramatization of *Valentine and Orson*, in which Valentine the prince captures his brother Orson, the wild man. Woodcut by Pieter Bruegel the Elder, 1566.

Armorial bearings of the Worshipful Company of Distillers of the City of London, with a Russian and an Amerindian as supporting figures, 1639.

Early seventeenth-century representation of the armorial bearings of Newfoundland, 1637. Nova Scotia is the only other Canadian province with an Amerindian supporting figure in its coat of arms. Misc. Grants 4, f.7, College of Arms, London.

From pageantry the Wild Man retired into heraldry, where he is still seen today as a supporting figure at times difficult to distinguish from Silenus. Such a position, in heraldic terms, indicates subjection. More than two hundred European families have the subjected Wild Man in their crests,[83] and he is on the coat of arms of Charles V on a building in Tlaxcala.[84] In a pose similar to his heraldic stance he also occasionally appeared on the title pages of books.[85]

There was also a Wild Woman, but she never attained the importance of the Wild Man. This may have been partially because the church tolerated the latter, albeit reluctantly, whereas the rituals of the Wild

Woman called for offerings. She was far more closely connected with the old religions, which the church was still engaged in stamping out. In Spain, for example, dancing in the disguise of Orca could draw a year's penitence.[86]

The frequent reports throughout this period of hairy men in far-off places indicate that the Wild Man was thought actually to exist. Pliny, for example, had told of such creatures in India.[87] The Borgia Map, drawn in the fifteenth century before Columbus's voyage, is illustrated with hairy Amazons.[88] Occasionally, hairy men appear in Renaissance voyage accounts, such as those of Pigafetta.[89]

Most Europeans who sailed to the New World must have been aware of the Wild Man, who was as familiar a figure to them as Santa Claus is today; indeed, in their facial representation, they were not unlike, both being bearded and having gentle expressions. From the very first, Europeans compared Amerindians with Wild Men. Columbus referred to West Indians as "wild" but suitable for slavery; an observer, describing the New World men brought to Lisbon by Corte-Real in 1501 (who have been variously identified as Inuit, Naskapi, Beothuk, or Micmac), said they had most gentle countenances but most bestial habits and manners, "like wild men."[90] The seven Amerindians brought to Rouen in 1509 were described as homines sylvestres.[91] Shakespeare's Caliban, whose name is considered by some to be an anagram of "cannibal," is more Wild Man than Amerindian, although he is regarded as representing a New World native.[92] He was in fact a depiction of the Wild Man in which the demonic aspects prevailed. This fusion of concepts can be seen in a map illustration in a Ptolemy geography of 1522, in which Terra Nova is decorated with a cannibal scene.[93] As already noted, cannibals were stock items in pre-Columbian geographies, and were usually located in the Orient. The Ptolemy cannibals have feather skirts, similar to those of the 1505 Augsburg woodcut. The figures are smooth-skinned, but have the heads and "gentle countenances" of Wild Men. Thus Ptolemy's scene could reflect simply the belief that the new-foundland was part of Asia; far more likely, however, it also indicated that the people of the New World were believed to be like Wild Men:

> the Savages of America, cruel men of no reason, whom our fishermen are obliged to hunt as if they were beasts because, besides showing ferocious traits, their bodies are covered with hair and armed with nails remarkably long and hooked.[94]

That the Wild Man had become confused in the popular mind with Amerindians is evident from not only such obviously misinformed reports, but from the repeated efforts missionaries and colonial officials

Bearded Amerindian men and woman dining on humans. Ptolemy, *Opus geographiae*, 1522. Bibliothèque Nationale, Paris.

made to discredit the notion that New World men were hairy.[95] Such efforts were unavailing. The first published denial appears to be that of Thevet in *Les Singularitez de la France Antarctique* (1557). In the chapter entitled "Against the opinion of those who believe that Savages are hairy," Thevet asserted that those who insisted that Amerindians were hairy had obviously never seen them, for the truth was the opposite; they took great care to remove all body hair.[96] Later he theorized that the custom of the northern Amerindians of wearing furs had given rise to the erroneous belief.[97] Léry felt strongly enough about the matter to deny it repeatedly. "I reserve the right to refute the error of those who would have us believe that the savages are hairy," he first wrote. Later, he was even more specific: "In spite of what some believe and others would like to make us believe, that they are covered with hair, the fact is that they are no hairier than we are."[98] He speculated that the belief had arisen from the custom of the Tupinambá of glueing themselves all over with down or little feathers, which gave them a furred appearance,

> so much so that in that state they appeared to be covered with down like newly hatched birds. Thus if Europeans, just arrived and without knowledge of these people, first see them when they are adorned in this fashion, they will spread the rumour that the savages are furred.... It is a falsehood that is too easily believed.[99]

This line of reasoning was also repeated by Lescarbot after his year in Canada.[100]

The Recollet missionary Gabriel Sagard (fl.1614–36), who visited Huronia in 1623–24, noted that "our savages are not as hairy as some might think." Referring to a well-known incident when the Admiral Hanno had brought what were believed to be two hairy women's skins from Gorgades Islands and had placed them in the Temple of Juno, Sagard continued, "hence the belief that all savages are hairy, although this is not so, and one very seldom finds that they are."[101] "Artists make a big mistake when they represent them as hairy," wrote Jean de Laon, Sieur d'Aigremont, who had taken part in the colonizing attempt in Guiana in 1652.[102] "There is no occasion to think of them as half beasts, shaggy, black and hideous," complained Father Francisco Gioseppe Bressani (1612–72): "They are without a beard... [and are] more healthy than we."[103] A generation later the same point was still being made: "The Hurons are neither furred nor misshapen as artists capriciously represent them, and except for their long hair and olive skins, most of them are as well made as the people of Europe."[104] Army officer Lahontan (1666–c.1716) tersely corroborated this: "Those who represent Savages as hairy as bears have never seen them"; but added to the confusion by referring to Amerindians on another occasion as "real satyrs and fauns, true inhabitants of the woods," who were inured "to jumping from rock to rock, being pierced by brambles and underbrush as they race through thorns and thickets as if in open country."[105] Such descriptions only confirmed eighteenth-century Europeans' impression that Amerindians were hairy, as satyrs and fauns were thus depicted.

Missionaries were the most assiduous in their efforts to disabuse the European public of its image of hairy Amerindians: Recollet Chrestien Le Clercq (c.1641–1700) was particularly stern:

> There is one error which is only too common, and of which it is desirable to disabuse the public. It is necessary to admit that some persons in our Europe are persuaded too easily that the peoples of North America... preserve of the nature of man nothing but the name of wild man, and that they have none of those finer qualities of body and of spirit which distinguish the human species from the beasts of the fields. And they even believe these people to be all hairy, like the bears, and more inhuman than the tigers and the leopards... as a matter of fact our Gaspesians have less hair than the French.[106]

According to Dominican Jean-Baptiste Du Tertre (1610–87), "at the simple word *Sauvage* most people envision cruel and inhuman barbarians, without reason, misshapen, as huge as giants, hairy as bears ... whereas in reality our Savages are savage only in name.... For the rest, they are neither hairy nor malformed."[107]

Tupinambá partially covered with down, giving them a furred appearance, perform a ceremony with sacred *tamerakas*, rattles which are painted red and decorated with feathers. Theodor de Bry, 1592, after a description by Staden. C-116033 Public Archives Canada.

Two centuries after Thevet had denied that Amerindians were furred, an officer in the French and Indian War wrote, "The Savages of Canada are very different from the idea commonly held of them in France. Far from being hairy, as is believed, they are much less covered with hair than we are."[108] As long as the Wild Man existed in folk imagination, he influenced the European conception of the Amerindian.

From Wild Man to Le Bon Sauvage

The blending of European folklore with New World accounts produced a mythology of its own. An illustration of this is a theatrical success of eighteenth-century Paris, *Arlequin Sauvage*, first presented at Théâtre des Italiens, 17 June 1721. The play, by Louis-François de Lisle de La Drévetière (1682–1756), concerns Arlequin, whose name suggests the Wild Man, but who in this instance is an Amerindian brought to Europe. Like the Wild Man, Arlequin is unformed in his personality; he proceeds to run afoul of the law, both written (in an encounter with a merchant, when he mistakes proferred goods for a gift) and unwritten (his amatory adventures with Violette). Arlequin's simple truthfulness eventually prevails over social considerations and he wins Violette. This tale of the triumph of le bon sauvage reflects the later transmutation of the Wild Man into a "paragon of virtue lost in unfolding civilization."[109] The purging of l'homme sauvage of his bestial and demonic aspects resulted in his apotheosis into le bon sauvage, a destiny he shared with the Amerindian during the eighteenth century. This provided a folkloric counterpart of Christianizing the New World peoples, "formerly savage but now evangelized."[110]

The idea of "the noble savage" is, of course, as ancient as that of the Wild Man, as it is another aspect of the same general concept. Bernheimer theorizes that its development indicated the uneasiness of Europeans with their own civilization, particularly its organized violence. Another type of mythic transformation can be discerned in *The Faerie Queene*. During the woodland episodes, Hellenore deserts her husband to go and live with bagpipe-playing satyrs; Amoret is snatched by a Wild Man; and finally, Serena is captured by Salvages who "live of stealth and spoile," depriving poor men of the fruits of their labor. These Salvages are preparing to make a cannibalistic sacrifice of Serena when she is rescued by Sir Calepine. In this presentation of evolutionary development, the animal satyrs are dominated by their sensuality and are given to dancing and festivities; the Wild Man combines sensuality and brute cannibalism; and the Salvages, although inclined to eat Serena on the spot, are persuaded by their priest to sacrifice her to their God instead; she would still have been eaten, but as part of a sacred ritual. And so bestial sensuality is transformed into a blood sacrifice to the Gods.

Until Amerindians became eligible for the honor, Europeans had cast several different Old World peoples in the role of the noble savage. At the time of the Age of Discovery, the Scythians were the favorites. According to Boas and Lovejoy, "From the fourth century B.C., the Scythians were to the ancients what the American Indians were to the primitivists of the sixteenth to the eighteenth centuries in modern Europe."[111] Christian Europe, remolding the ideal of the Golden Age into the vision of the Garden of Eden, had developed two traditions concerning the Scythians. One presented them as admirable, the other as detestable,[112] but in either case they were regarded as savage. With the emergence of Amerindians within the European range of vision, it was comparatively simple to fit them into existing perspectives, particularly as there seemed to be resemblances between the two "savage" peoples from the Old World and the New.

The inaccuracy of the view that Amerindians lived "as unreasoning beasts in a state of nature"[113] was soon recognized by those associated with them. As Claude observed, "In truth, I expected to find fierce beasts, men totally rustic, rude and savage (as we call them), but I found that to be far from reality. Instead, I have never encountered any people with such perfection of their natural senses, whether exterior or interior, and I have never heard of a nation which excels them in this."[114] Du Tertre and others agreed that Amerindians were savage in name only, and in the *Jesuit Relations* there are several assertions that the procedures of Amerindians were not those of brute beasts.[115] But instead of convincing Europeans that Amerindians were not savage, such statements were regarded as a defence of le bon sauvage. The Jesuits, for instance, were sometimes accused of being more interested in proving that "savages" possessed a viable civility than they were in evangelizing them. Europeans, by transforming the Amerindian into an idealized and thus essentially unreal image, deprived him of his position as a fellow human, both as an individual and as a social being. Even such minor honors as being a credible hero in a first-rate drama was denied to him.[116] At the same time, a use was soon found for le bon sauvage: he became a basic ingredient for various utopias.[117]

Wild man and woman with emblazoned shield. Martin Schongauer, 1480–90. The Metropolitan Museum of Art, New York.

The classification of New World men as savage was reinforced by the speed with which even the most sophisticated American cultures were overwhelmed. The argument was that the Mexica and Inca empires could not have been very well civilized, or they would not have fallen so quickly: "How do you think it was possible for a hundred or so men to conquer so huge a country in such a short time? For so few to discomfit an army of innumerable barbarians on the field of battle?"[118] One of the ironies of the situation was that the Inca and Mexica both shared with Europeans the belief that their forebears had once lived as beasts,[119] and the Inca looked down upon the people of the Amazon as being savages. But that did not imply that any Amerindian was prepared to consider himself as savage at the time of Europe's invasion of the Americas.

According to a seventeenth-century account, some were said to have retorted that as far as they were concerned, it was the French who were the savages, "because we [the French] do not live in their manner; they have their knowledge and we have ours, as if there were two ways of knowing reality."[120] But the argument that counted in the end was that of force; might was equated with civilization. There could be sympathy for the defeated, but still they had been proven to be of an inferior order.

Another irony underlying Europe's confusion of the Wild Man with the Amerindian was in the latter's horror of hairiness. Both Columbus and Vespucci were struck by this, as was anyone who had anything to do with Amerindians during the sixteenth and seventeenth centuries. To cite Vespucci, "they do not allow any hair to grow on their eyebrows nor their eyelids nor anywhere on the body (with the exception of the head), for this reason—because they deem it coarse and animal-like."[121] Jesuits in the Canadian missions observed that their charges were repelled by the hairiness of Europeans, and sometimes openly mocked them on the subject. But the crowning irony was that the Amerindians had a mythological hairy man of their own, who was also a forest figure. This personage, sometimes female, preyed on young children rather than on women, and lived in the forests of the east as well as those of the west. Among its better-known manifestations today is the Sasquatch of the Northwest Coast, who is as familiar to Canadians as Bigfoot is to Americans of the Pacific Coast.[122]

So the processes of identifying Amerindians with savages operated on the level of ideology as well as on that of popular mythology. To Europeans, reports that Amerindians lived "by eating roots, both men and women totally naked"[123] implied not that they were living without rules at all, although that was how it was usually stated, but according to the rules of the non-human world around them. Such an image is much less securely held today, as no human society has ever been found that conforms to the conditions of animal life.[124] For instance, every human society ever studied has been found to have rules against incest; notions of what constitutes incest vary from culture to culture, but the idea of degrees of relationship within which marriage is prohibited is universal. This concept has not been found to be operating in the animal world although patterns of behavior may affect availability of mates.[125] The Stone Age men of America and Australia, of Melanesia and Polynesia, may have lived in close cooperation with the world of nature around them, but this does not necessarily imply an identification between nature's rules and those of human society.

On the contrary, it could well be that the hunting and gathering way of life, which prevailed during most of the Stone Age, provided the occasion for the development of the intellectual and social qualities that permitted the rise of agriculture, and eventually, today's technological explosion.[126] The powers of observation and evaluation, the social cooperation and sharing that made the Stone Age hunter successful are just as essential for the space-age scientist.

The line of demarcation between nature and human cultures, and when, if ever, one passes over into the other is not known.[127] It is being realized more clearly all the time that even the most technologically complex of human societies ignore nature at their peril. But in sixteenth- and seventeenth-century Europe, the world of nature was seen as having been created for man's benefit. It was the task of man, created in God's image, to reduce nature to human concepts of order. From that perspective, the man who cooperated with nature and who was thought to live within its framework was regarded as living according to nature in the manner of "brute beasts."

Youthful wild man, fifteenth century.

Supported by such an ideology, Europe's belief in the hairy man was extremely persistent in folklore despite mounting evidence against his existence. It was easier to prove orthodoxy wrong about the habitability of the Antipodes than it was to dispel popular mythology. The first was a case of intellectual argument in which some glee was found in discomfiting authority; but the second was a type of belief that existed independently of scientific knowledge. The same phenomenon was illustrated by belief in the unicorn, the mythological animal that the Wild Man was able to overcome by sheer physical force, a feat which a pure young lady could match by love. Throughout the Age of Discovery, the unicorn was reported from various parts of the world, including Canada and Florida.[128] Thevet, in denying the existence of the unicorn, as well as that of dragons, sirens, and griffons, displayed some courage. Upon seeing a rhinoceros brought to Madrid in the sixteenth century, Mendoza observed, "no one wants to say it is a unicorn, but I am persuaded of it."[129] But he was not successful in slaying the mythical beast; after all, Pope Clement VII presented François I with a unicorn horn three feet long on the occasion of the wedding of the latter's son, Henri d'Orléans, to Catherine de Medici in 1533. The gift, considered to be beyond price, was also useful, as it was believed to sweat if placed near poison. As the Jesuits said of the Huron, beliefs, no matter how apparently ridiculous, are hard to eradicate.[130]

More importantly, however, Europe's belief in the savagery of Amerindians had profound consequences in the realm of practical politics in the New World. Equally important was the interplay of European attitudes with those of Amerindians, who far from being unformed savages in the "infancy of nature," were the products of cultures that had evolved over many centuries.

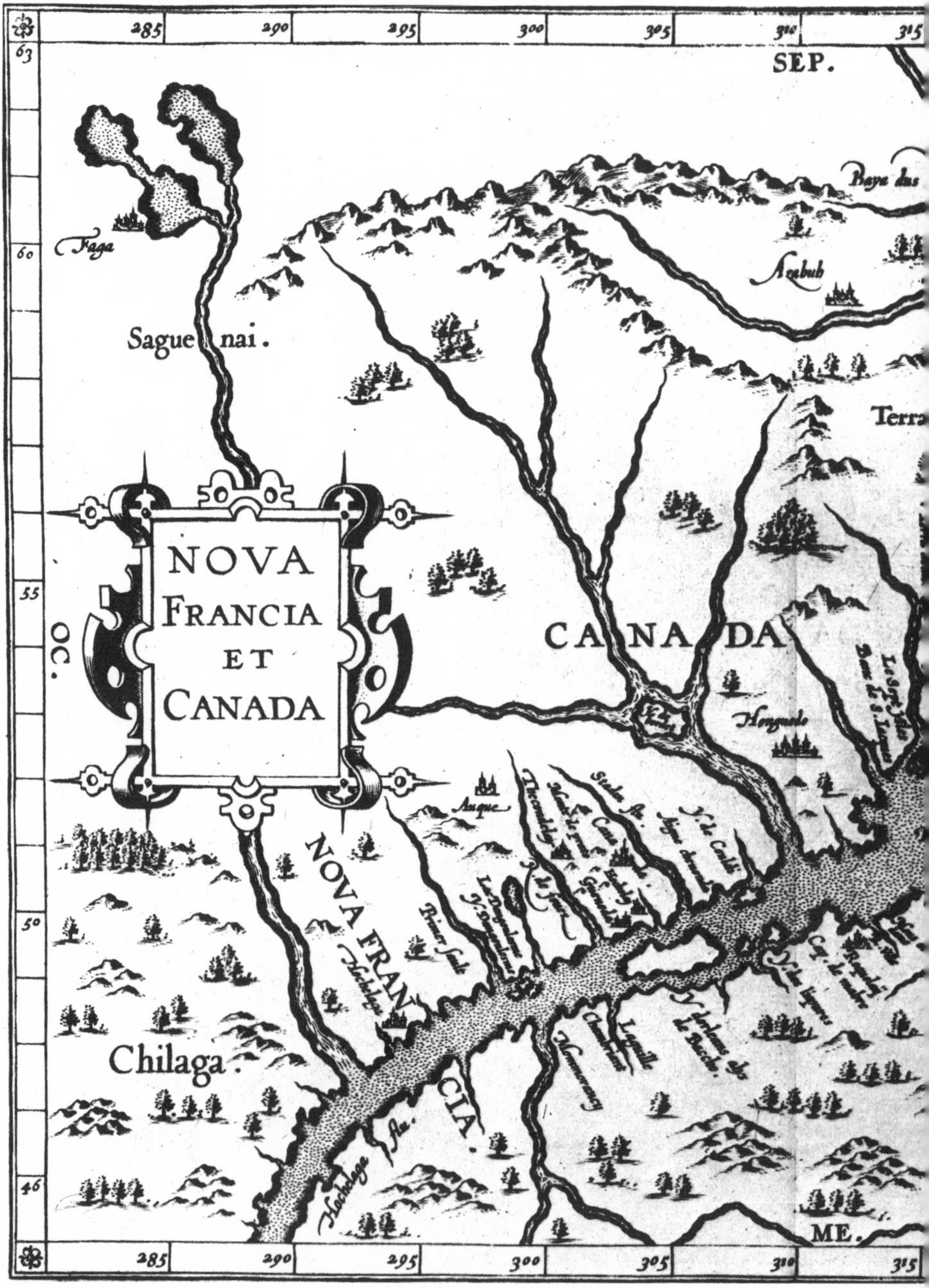
NOVA FRANCIA ET CANADA
Saguenai.
CANADA
NOVA FRANCIA
Chilaga.
SEP.
OC.
ME.
Terra
Hochelaga flu.
Hochelaga
Faga
Azabuh
Hongnedo
Auque

PART II

Early Contacts of Amerindians and Frenchmen

Wytfliet's map of Canada, 1611, showing towns along the Gulf and river of St. Lawrence. From right to left: Brest, S. Nicolas, S. Laurens, Honguedo, Canada, Hochelay, Guenoda, Thecondelay, Auque, and Hochelaga. Stadacona is not included. Bibliothèque Nationale, Paris.

CHAPTER 5

Amerindians of New France

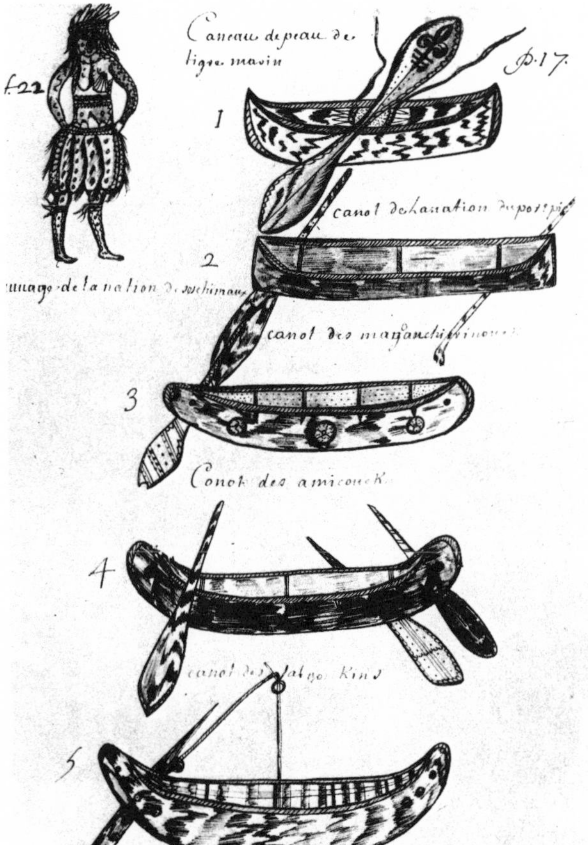

Five different styles of northeastern watercraft, from top to bottom: sealskin craft with covered deck and double-bladed paddle, more like a kayak than a canoe; and four birchbark canoes of the Montagnais, Têtes-de-Boule, Amikoues (Ottawa), and Algonquin. Bécard de Granville, *Les Raretés des Indes.* C-33287 Public Archives Canada.

RENAISSANCE EUROPEANS used savagery to explain everything about New World men, whether referring to their manner of living or personal characteristics. For instance, was not the capacity of Amerindians to orient themselves in the wilderness considered an innate instinct, the same as that possessed by animals? Experiments have not confirmed this notion; orientation by human beings has been found to rely heavily on observation, memory, and experience.[1] The capacity to find one's way in the wilderness depends upon intelligence and knowledge of the country; in a strange region, deprived of landmarks and with an overcast sky, an Amerindian could lose his way.[2] The difference between Amerindians and Europeans in this regard was cultural conditioning, because of which the former maintained constant directional orientation in contrast to the latter, who did not. But to Europeans of the sixteenth and seventeenth centuries, the Amerindian "sense of direction" appeared suspiciously animal-like. In a similar vein, it was reported of Brazilians and mountain Peruvians that they could distinguish between French and Spanish by smelling their hands.[3] And who else but savages would consider the wilderness as home?[4]

Who were the people of the north, generally characterized during the sixteenth century as "idolators, brutal, without any civility?"[5] Thevet found that their customs were not much different from those of "other barbarian peoples" in the New World.[6] The underlying similarities of Amerindians and their way of life throughout the Americas, frequently noted during this period, has been confirmed by modern ethnography. For example, all of these societies divided labor along sex lines, and individual households maintained a high degree of self-sufficiency, whether in the city-states of Central America or on the Labrador coast. A sense of community responsibility ensured that fellow tribesmen were not left without food or shelter. This is far from saying, however, that the cultures of all the New World peoples were uniform; indeed, the variety of their societies was exceeded only by that of their languages, of which about two thousand were spoken. Nowhere else in the world has such diversity been found.[7]

Amerindians living on the Atlantic Coast from Cape Breton as far south as Cape Fear belonged to the Algonkian linguistic group, apart from the Inuit and perhaps the Beothuk (who may have been distant relatives of the Algonkians, although this is not universally conceded).[8] Others of the same group inhabited the Great Lakes region. Iroquoians appeared seasonally on the coast for fishing; they lived for most of the year along the St. Lawrence in semi-sedentary towns such as Stadacona and Hochelaga. There were also the Five Nations of the Finger Lakes and Hudson River region, and the Huron, Tionontati (Pétun), Neutral,

A seventeenth-century impression of Amerindians fishing. Bécard de Granville, *Les Raretés des Indes*. C-16945 Public Archives Canada.

and Erie of the Great Lakes. The Iroquoians were, in effect, surrounded by Algonkians. The country south of the "great river" was much more thickly populated than the region to the north.[9]

The Iroquoians, as well as some of the Algonkians (such as the Abenaki, Algonquin, and Ottawa), practised farming with varying degrees of intensity. Rarely were they entirely dependent upon it, as they were at the northern limits of agriculture practicable with Stone Age technology. The Stadaconans, for instance, relied more upon the river for subsistence than did the people of Hochelaga. The Micmac had a tradition of once being agriculturalists, but at the time of contact were hunters and fishermen, confining their farming to the cultivation of tobacco.[10] The Abenaki, who during the early part of the seventeenth century were living in semi-sedentary agricultural towns, in some cases reverted under the pressures of contact to a greater dependence on hunting and fishing. However, as the resource management of hunters-gatherers becomes better understood, the line of demarcation between the two ways of life is not nearly so clear as once thought.[11] The Algonkians and Inuit of the Far North, as well as the Beothuk, were nomadic hunters and fishermen. All of these people lived within the framework of well-developed societies of varying complexities that provided for their needs, both as individuals and as social beings.

Life patterns were, of course, at least partly conditioned by the means of subsistence. For the hunters and gatherers, seventeenth-century observers unanimously reported fish as a principal means of subsistence, although moose – "very large stags like horses"[12] – bear, beaver, and caribou were important game and in the spring and fall, geese and ducks. Fishing was a low-prestige occupation, as Amerindians considered that anyone could do it, although the French were often to find themselves dependent upon the bounty of Amerindian fishermen when they themselves had no "luck."[13]

But hunting demanded skill, and the power that could be mustered by one's supernatural partners. These guardians spirits were acquired by the hunter in his puberty dream-vision.[14] Bezoars (a concretion found in the fourth stomach of ruminants) provided them with a popular hunting charm;[15] in Europe, the wearing of these stones was considered to be a safeguard against the plague.[16] New World hunters had resort to scapulamancy (reading marks on shoulder bones) and scrying (crystal-gazing) to predict success in hunting, techniques which were also familiar to Europeans. North of the St. Lawrence, where survival was more difficult, the specter of starvation was expressed in the fear of *wihtiko*, the person who developed an appetite for human flesh and turned into the most fearsome of beings.[17] In those regions, hunters had status; in areas where agriculture was practised, warriors had prestige.

Northern agriculture was based on the triple-crop complex, known to the Iroquois as the three sisters.[18] Europeans noted that Amerindians understood the culture of their crops, and selected the proper soils "with rare discrimination."[19] Enough food was grown to be used in trade and to allow for the development of symbiotic relationships. The Huron, for instance, provided the Algonquin with farm produce in exchange for products of the hunt. The Tionontati of Lakes Erie and Ontario were called Pétun by the French because they specialized in growing tobacco. The general practice at the time of contact was to abandon fields after a period of time, and to cultivate new ones that had been cleared and prepared in the meantime, a process that could involve moving the whole village.[20] The reason usually given for this practice, that the soil was exhausted after that period, is only a partial explanation. Depletion of firewood and of game were other important factors.[21] In any event, the cyclical pattern of agriculture, along with the winter hunt and fishing, meant a semi-sedentary mode of existence for northeastern farming peoples.[22] Such a cyclical life pattern, whatever its degree of nomadism, called for considerable organization. It required government, even in the absence of a state structure. Le Jeune saw this organization among the Montagnais, explaining that they maintained peace and order in their daily lives because the women "know what they are to do, and the men also; and one never meddles with the work of the other."[23]

Body-painting and tattooing were shared by all the people of the northeastern woodlands and the Great Lakes.[24] Early writers referred to tattooing under the general term *matachias*, which also included such items as hair and porcupine quill embroidery and, later, beadwork. These writers were struck with the variety and intricacy of designs with which the people of the New World adorned themselves; its resemblance to heraldry led one observer to conclude "that Heraldry was ingrafted naturally into the sense of the human Race."[25] The importance of this preoccupation was indicated by the time and thought devoted to it, as well as by the conservatism of the designs.[26] Not only did patterns express individual taste, they also served as personal identification, clan affiliation, as a record of achievements and consequently of status; they were the mark of adulthood. Bressani, who had thought deeply on Amerindian culture, observed:

> The reasons they have for painting themselves,—especially for a temporary purpose,—are certainly not barbarous. This Painting serves them in winter as a mask against the cold and ice; in war, it prevents their countenances from betraying them by revealing inward fear, makes them more terrible to the enemy, and conceals extremes of youth or age, which might inspire strength and courage in the adversary. It serves as adornment at the public feasts and assemblies. They also paint the prisoners destined to the flames, as victims consecrated to the God of war, and adorn them as the ancients adorned theirs. They do the same also to their dead, for the same reasons for which we adorn ours.[27]

Body painting endured throughout the period of New France, although the active campaign of the missionaries against it had its effect, especially among converts. The clergy thought the practice was inspired by the Devil; body painting represented a refusal by man to be a reflection

Noble Ottawa Indian, late eighteenth century. The bodypainting designs were personalized and kept for life. C-70664 Public Archives Canada.

of the divine image.[28] Such a stand, of course, was based upon a particular view of what the divine image was.

Both agriculturalists and hunters used snowshoes and toboggans drawn by a head strap and, in the regions where birch was available, birchbark canoes. The Five Nations, south of the birch tree area, used elm bark for their canoes, which made craft with a load capacity two or three times greater than was possible with the use of birchbark, but which were much slower. Skin clothing was used particularly toward the north, where hunting peoples such as the Montagnais, Naskapi, and Cree retained aspects of earlier ice-age cultures.[29]

Sweat houses were popular throughout the northeastern woodlands, as in North America generally, for ritual purposes as well as a health measure. Agricultural Iroquoians and Algonkians shared the use of the ball-headed club, effigy pipes, and longhouses; they pallisaded their villages, stored food in pits, and ate dog flesh as a delicacy in ceremonial feasts (a practice also found among the Chinese). Among the customs they shared was the use of wampum in diplomacy and to compensate for murder; another was the adoption or torture of prisoners and burning at the stake.[30] Politically, they sometimes formed confederacies, of which the most successful was the Five Nations.

Iroquoians and agricultural Algonkians had kinship systems based upon clans (in contrast to far northern Algonkians, who did not possess them),[31] which, despite variations from group to group, had denominations corresponding to water (turtle, beaver, eel), earth (wolf, deer, bear), and air (hawk, eagle, crow). Bird denominations could also pertain to water, such as heron, duck, coot, and so on.[32] Members claimed descent from a common ancestor; it was a fictive kinship, rather than one of blood. Descent was matrilineal among Iroquoians, and either patrilineal or matrilineal among Algonkians. However, community organization tended to derive not so much from clans as from moieties (from *moitié*, half), which often differed in structure and function from tribe to tribe. Among the Five Nations they were composed of clans and were exogamous; among the Fox (Algonkians of the Great Lakes), they were agamous and without reference to their clans. This dual arrangement could manifest itself in regulating any number of social events, such as marriage, trade, festivals, and ceremonies, or sports competitions, when these were not prerogatives of clans.[33] While duality itself was a constant, the institutions through which it was expressed among the peoples of the northeast as elsewhere were not only varied in their structure but ranged from permanent to highly unstable. This permeated even kinship systems, where resemblances, divergences, and transformations were such as to lead Levi-Strauss to observe:

> In societies with unilinear and exogamous clans, the system of clan names is nearly always mid-way between order and disorder. This appears to be the only explanation for the combined action of the two forces: one, of demographic origin, pushing toward disorganization; the other, of intellectual inspiration, pressing toward a reorganization as similar as possible to the previous state.[34]

Counterbalancing such institutional tensions was reciprocity, that aspect of duality which was of fundamental importance to "tribal" societies throughout the world, and the basis of the most ancient known legal system.[35] Basic to this reciprocity was exchange, which had the character of gift-giving as much as of trade in the European sense.[36] Besides being economic, these exchanges had magical, social, religious, political, judicial, and moral aspects. In other words, they represented "a total social fact."[37] Contact between Iroquoians or Algonkians and Europeans almost immediately developed into trade relationships, which for Europeans were essentially economic, but which for Amerindians represented, among other things, military alliances as well. Such differences in attitude were to contribute later to misunderstandings.

The egalitarianism marking northeastern Amerindian social organization, which early missionaries tended to regard as indicating lack of order and subordination, was reflected in spiritual relationships. Just as each individual was autonomous in dealing with the material world, so it was up to each person to establish his own contacts with the non-material world. Peoples of the northeastern woodlands practised shamanism, bear ceremonialism, and shaking-tent rituals; at least some of them, including Micmac and Naskapi, held the sun in special regard.[38] The office of the shaman was not hereditary, as it called for special personal qualities, and could be attained only after a long apprenticeship. Feats recognized as shamanistic included control of the weather, predictions, interpretations of dreams, finding lost objects, and curing. Of these, dream interpretation and healing the sick were the most important.

These Amerindians also shared myths and culture heroes: the giant Gluskap of the Micmac, Malecite, and Abenaki; the dwarf Tcïkpai of the Montagnais-Naskapi; and Nanabozho, the trickster-transformer of the Algonquin, among others. The myths that attached to such personalities, as well as to Aataentsic of the Iroquoians, the mother of mankind, had to do with the nature of the world, of how men came to be part of it, and of how they became civilized. In other words, they provided a point from which to grasp the universe as a whole, and to fit the particular tribe into the universal pattern. Geography tended to be interpreted in terms of totems and myths. The Micmac, Malecite, and Abenaki saw evidences of their hero-civilizer Gluskap in the countryside–an elongated rock was Gluskap's canoe; a vein of white rock, the entrails of a moose he had killed. A mountain was his upturned cooking kettle.[39] The desire to relate to the whole world was seen also in the roles provided for the dead in ceremonies, although there was no ancestor worship as such.[40]

A closer look at a selected few of the peoples along the northern Atlantic coast, the St. Lawrence, and some of its hinterlands at the time of first successful settlement by the French, reveals a rich kaleidoscope of vigorous cultures. These societies had been affected by Europeans well before colonization, with highly variable results. Already discernible were patterns of alliances and antagonisms, which would develop during the colonial period. The St. Lawrence Iroquois are not included here, as they had disappeared as entities by the time of French settlement. It is known, however, that they had shared the general lifestyle of the Huron, with whom they may have assimilated.

Beothuk

First descriptions of the Beothuk of Newfoundland almost unanimously represented them as "inhuman and wild." Cartier was more precise:

> They wear their hair tied on the top of their heads like a handful of twisted hay, with a nail or something of the sort passed through the middle, and into it they weave a few birds' feathers. They clothe themselves with the furs of animals, both men as well as women.[41]

Jean Fonteneau *dit* Alfonce (1483?–1557?), a Portuguese who became France's best navigator in his day, wrote of the Beothuk: "The people are big and tend toward being dark. . . . They have no more God than beasts, and are bad people . . . they call themselves Tabios. They live off fish, meat and the fruit of trees."[42] The learned Pierre Crignon (c.1464–1540), who won prizes for his poetry at Rouen and who had accompanied the Parmentier brothers on at least one of their voyages, agreed: "Between Cape Race and Cape Breton live a cruel and rude people with whom we can neither deal or converse."[43]

In spite of such attitudes, there are no indications that initial contacts were overtly hostile. During the early part of the sixteenth century, Basques left their fishing gear and boats in the whaling ports winter after winter, without loss or damage.[44] But by the end of the century this had

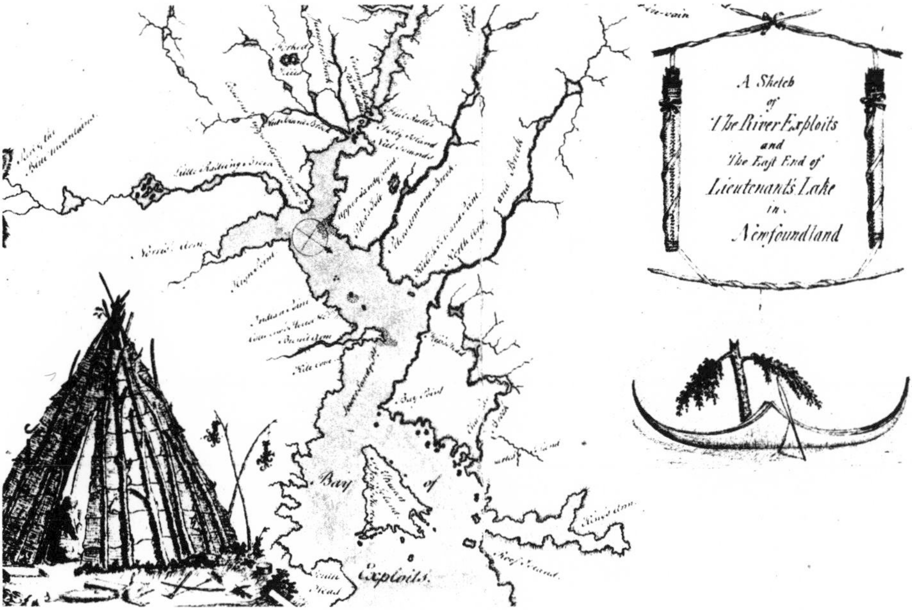

Beothuk lodge and canoe are represented on this map of Newfoundland. National Map Collection, C-17988 Public Archives Canada.

changed to the point where fishermen were arming their *pataches* to guard themselves against raids. The feud, which the Beothuk shared with the Labrador Inuit, was attributed to the action of a Malouin sailor (or surgeon) who had killed the wife of an Inuit chief in a particularly brutal way.[45] The English also found their fishing operations hampered in certain areas "because the Savages of that country doe there inhabite; many of them secretly every yeare come into Trinity Bay and Harbor, in the nightime, purposely to steale Sailes, Lines, Hatchets, Hookes, Knives, and such like."[46]

At first contact Beothuk apparently occupied most of Newfoundland, alternating between fishing on the coast and hunting caribou in the interior, depending upon the seasonal availability of species.[47] They had corn, which indicates a trading relationship to the south, as they themselves did not practice agriculture. They quickly retreated into the interior as the fishermen established themselves along the coast. By 1583 Edward Hayes, reporting on Sir Humphrey Gilbert's expedition, wrote that "in the South parts we found no inhabitants, which by all likelihood have abandoned these coasts, the same being frequented much by Christians; but in the North are savages, altogether harmless."[48] Sir Richard

Whitbourne (c.1579–1626), one of the best known of the "fishing admirals" of the Grand Banks, noted in 1620 that the natives were few in number.[49] Lahontan was under the impression the island's only natives were the occasional Inuit passing through.[50] One estimate places the Beothuk population at five hundred in 1600.[51]

The Beothuk have been called the original "Red Indians" because of their practice of painting themselves, their clothing, and their belongings with red ocher.[52] But Brazilians and West Indians could, with equal justification, be granted the distinction, as they also colored themselves red. In their case they used dyewood as well as *roucou*, from achote seeds. Roucou, like red ocher, was an insect repellant.[53]

In spite of Whitbourne's opinion that a mission would have been helpful in bringing the Beothuk into line with European civility, none was established among them by either the French or the English. In fact, quite the opposite sentiment prevailed: according to one authority, the French placed a bounty on their heads,[54] and the English hunted them at every opportunity. The last known representative of the Beothuk, a woman, died in 1829.[55] It has been speculated that their disappearance was at least partly owing to their loss of access to the coast and its food resources.[56] As far as the Europeans had been concerned, the Beothuk had not the right to defend their lands from outside intrusion.

Micmac (*Souriquois, Tarrantines, Toudamans, Gaspesians, Acadians*)

In contrast to the Beothuk, the Micmac accommodated themselves comparatively well to Europeans; if population levels are an indication, they managed the best of all the coastal peoples. Although they were among the earliest of northern Amerindians to come into contact with Europeans, if not actually the first, they were able to maintain themselves in their ancestral lands as middlemen in trade and later as guerrillas during colonial rivalries. According to the testimony of Membertou in 1610, the Micmac had formerly been "as thickly planted as the hairs upon his head," but after the arrival of the French, the "bad habits" they developed in respect to food and drink had greatly reduced their numbers.[57] Hoffman estimated that a pre-contact population of six thousand is not out of the question.[58] Some support for a large pre-contact population was given by Rouen trader Etienne Bellenger, who told of one village, probably near Cape Sable, of eighty multi-family houses.[59] By 1612, Father Biard estimated their numbers at less than two thousand, a figure which he revised four years later to between 3,000 and 3,500.[60] A century and a half later the number was almost the same.

The Micmac lived on the Gaspé Peninsula, in present New Brunswick east of the drainage basin of the St. John River, throughout Nova Scotia, including Cape Breton Island, as well as on Prince Edward Island, lands they called Megumaage. They were the Toudamans mentioned by Cartier, probably Thevet's Tontaniens[61] and the Tarantines of the English colonists.[62] To the early French the Micmac were Souriquois. Their language shares certain characteristics with Cree, the most widespread of the Algonkian group, as well as with Arapaho of the Central Plains.

The sites of approximately forty-six Micmac summer villages are known.[63] Their bark wigwams and lodges were so well fitted that it never rained within, and they were decorated with paintings of animals.[64] Archeology has confirmed that the Micmac once used pottery, as Lescarbot reported;[65] recent findings have revealed an early cultural

"The Lord's Prayer" from a Micmac catechism published by Redemptorist missionary Christian Kauder in Vienna, 1866. The hieroglyphs had been adapted from existing Micmac symbols and devices by Pierre Maillard during his years as missionary in Nova Scotia from 1735 until his death in 1762.

Micmac encampment, post-contact. The women have adopted the pointed headgear of European fishermen. Anonymous painting, nineteenth-century. National Gallery of Canada, Ottawa.

complex that suggests connections with Ohio. That the pattern of cyclical activity was altered all along the coast at about the time of contact is indicated by archeological evidence. In Maine, from about 200 to 1100 A.D., campsites were occupied during late winter and early spring; but by 1500, occupancy had shifted to late spring and summer. European trade may have been a factor in the change; also, there is the possibility of climatic shifts.[66]

The sea offered more easily accessible food than did the land, providing the Micmac with ninety percent of their diet.[67] They were therefore skilled seamen,[68] who quickly adapted themselves to European craft such as shallops. Bartholomew Gosnold (d.1607) encountered Amerindians in a Basque shallop in 1602.[69] When Lescarbot made landfall at Canso, he was met with two shallops, one of which was manned by Amerindians with a "stagge" (moose) painted on the sail.[70] French and Basque whalers described the Micmac as "willing enough to enter into the service of Europeans for a few goods or a little pay, and to do all kinds of work, such as cleaning and butchering whales."[71]

In their socio-political structure they were unique in maintaining an agricultural way of life in a non-agricultural environment.[72] Megumaage was divided into seven districts, of which Oonamagik (Cape Breton Island) was the principal.[73] Their regional chiefs, functioning with the aid of councils of elders, recognized "grand chiefs," whose heredity was calculated through the male line. Membertou, one of the earliest and most useful of French allies in the region, was one of these grand chiefs.[74] The power of such a leader was circumscribed, being based on kinship affiliations and, above all, on personal qualities, such as being a great shaman or orator; it did not include the power of coercion. This was characteristic of leadership among all the people in the northeast, even

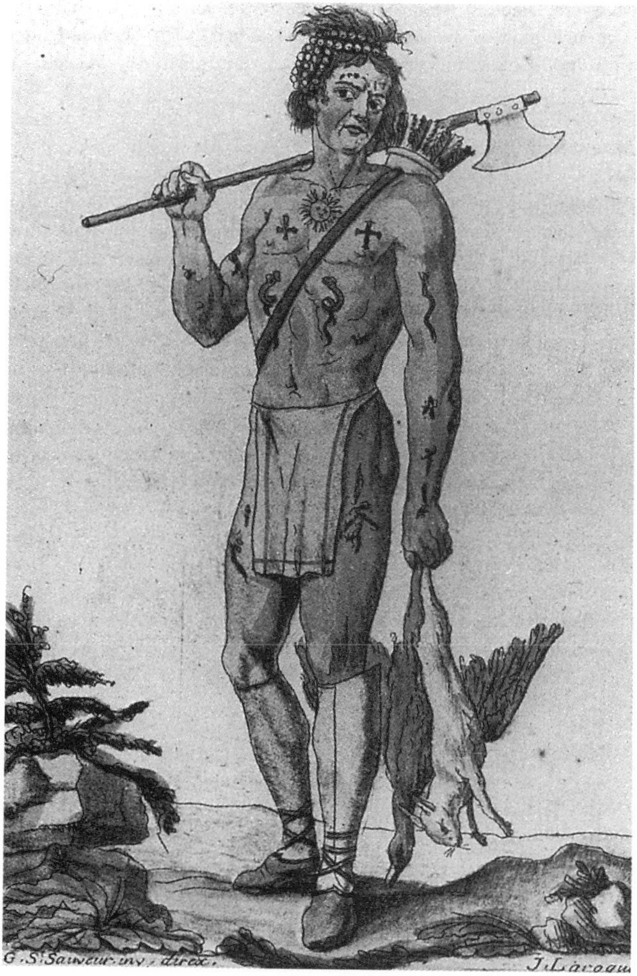

Acadian Amerindian or Micmac marked with the cross symbols that so intrigued and puzzled early missionaries. Engraving by J. Laroque, after Jacques Grasset St. Sauveur. C-21112 Public Archives Canada.

those with a more structured society, such as the Huron-Iroquois. One of the Micmac symbols, the cross, caused considerable astonishment among early missionaries,[75] who took this to mean that the Micmac had had previous contact with Christians.[76]

Cartier found the Micmac at war with the Stadaconans, and was shown scalps taken by the latter.[77] Similar clashes led to the naming of Massacre Island.[78] Lescarbot described Micmac hostilities with the Armouchiquois to the south as being perpetual.[79] The Micmac feuded with the Beothuk, and shared a common culture with the Malecite.

Malecite (*Etchemin, Eteminquois*)

Although there were some similarities in the ways of the Micmac and the Malecite, their languages were different, except for some loan words; *mel'asit* is Micmac for "corrupted speech" or "broken talk." In the words of Abbé Pierre Maillard (c.1710–62), writing in 1758: "The Mickmakis and Mariquets, who, though different in language, have the same customs and manners . . . are of the same way of thinking and acting."[80] The Malecite were also linked with the Abenaki to the south:

> The Maricheets . . . chiefly settled at St. John's . . . are often confounded with the Abenaquis, so as to pass for one nation with them, though there is certainly some distinction. They used, till lately, to be in a constant state of hostility with the Mickmakis.[81]

The "Etchemin" referred to by Champlain in 1604 on the St. Croix River probably included the Passamaquoddy, also closely related to the Malecite, and speaking a variety of the same language. The Malecite were reported to have occupied the region from Port Royal to the Kennebec

Eastern Algonkian tribal designations: Passamaquoddy, two canoeists following a fish (upper left); Malecite, two persons poling a canoe after a muskrat (upper right); Micmac, two canoeists following a deer (lower left); Penobscot, two canoeists, one with a paddle and the other with a pole, following an otter (lower right).

River at the time of contact.[82] Biard in 1612 estimated that the "Etheminqui" numbered less than a thousand, then in 1616 calculated that the "Eteminquois" numbered 2,500; he wrote that they were in association with the French through the cod fisheries and the fur trade.[83] The Etchemin seem to have been heavily affected by the epidemic of about 1617, which wrought havoc among the coastal peoples.[84]

The Micmac had another uncomplimentary appellation for the Malecite, "muskrat people." This referred to the fact that the animal was included in the Malecite diet; the Micmac would not eat it. Malecite economy was based on exploitation of inland resources such as freshwater fish and caribou;[85] the Passamaquoddy hunted sea mammals.[86] Malecite and Micmac had a common enemy in the Mohawk, and later, the English. Along with the Abenaki and the Etheminqui, they also shared a common ally, the French. But this shared alliance did not ensure accord among the Amerindians. The French quarrelled among themselves, fanning ancient animosities among their allies. Charles de Menou d'Aulnay (c.1604–50) and Charles de Saint-Etienne de La Tour (c.1593–1666), both governors of Acadia, fought what amounted to a civil war from 1635 to 1650 over their conflicting jurisdictions. In general, the Malecite and Micmac supported La Tour, and the Penobscot supported d'Aulnay. In spite of this, neither the Malecite, Micmac, nor Abenaki wavered from their attachment to the French throughout the period of New France.

Abenaki (*Eastern: Canibas, Penobscot, Arosagunticook, Norridgewock, Pigwacket, Pentagouet; Western: Sokoki, Penacook, Cowasuck, Missiquoi, Loup*)

As can be inferred from the above listing, it has not been precisely determined which of the agricultural tribes of New Brunswick and Maine, westward to Lake Champlain, were included during the sixteenth and seventeenth centuries under the label Abenaki or Wabanaki, "those living at the sunrise"; but it is known that their language had two forms, the eastern and western. Geography ensured that the eastern would be the first of the Abenaki to meet Europeans; theirs was the land reported by Purchas in "The Description of the Country of Mawooshen" in 1602. It was also known as Norumbega. According to Purchas, it counted fourteen thousand souls living in semi-permanent villages under Bashabes, the ranking eastern Abenaki chief; today the population is estimated more conservatively to have been about ten thousand.[87] Following the devastation of the 1617 epidemic, speakers of eastern Abenaki coalesced around the Kennebec and Penobscot drainages.[88] Early in the eighteenth century, four eastern Abenaki mission villages were listed as being in Acadia, two of which (Narantsouak or Norencouan, and Panouamké) were said to be entirely Abenaki, whereas the other two (Pasamoquady or Pesmonquady, and Medockeck or Medoctet) were said to be part Malecite.[89] The western Abenaki, from the lower Saco River to Lake Champlain, were included by the French, along with other tribes, under their general rubric, Loup.[90]

The large population known to the early French as the Armouchiquois, bitter enemies of the Micmac, were eastern Abenaki, and may have included other groups as well.[91] A seventeenth-century cosmographer said the land of the Armouchiquois extended from the Kennebec to Malebarre.[92] The French shared the Micmac antipathy for their southern neighbors, if one is to judge by the highly unflattering accounts. Pierre-Victor-Palma Cayet (1525–1610) scholar and chronicler, described the Armouchiquois as being deformed, with small heads and short bodies, whose knees, when they squatted on their heels, passed their heads by more than half a foot.[93] Elsewhere are reports that the Armouchiquois were "devious and treacherous, always scheming under the guise of friendliness; they must be handled by means of fear and severity." They were also suspected of cannibalism.[94] This hardly constituted a friendly beginning; however, fighting did not erupt, as it had already done with the Beothuk. The first meeting with the western Abenaki, in 1642, was more auspicious: it occurred when Algonquin

From Champlain's engraved map, 1612, an Almouchiquois (Abenaki) couple (left), and a couple identified as Montagnais (right). National Map Collection, C-38194 Public Archives Canada.

allies of the French brought a Sokoki prisoner to Trois- Rivières under the impression he was an Iroquois. When the error was discovered, the French released the prisoner, thereby winning the Sokoki's friendship.[95]

As hostilities mounted with their traditional enemies the Iroquois, and developed with English colonists, eastern and later western Abenaki found themselves siding with the French and in alliance with their former enemies, the Micmac. An English ploy forcing Mog, an eastern Abenaki leader from the Kennebec region, to sign a treaty in 1676 did not succeed in imposing acquiescence to colonial land encroachments. It was the Abenaki who, with the French, laid waste New England's norththern frontier, until the English destruction of Norridgewock in 1724 and defeat of Pequaket in 1725. Abenaki also took part in the French expeditions against the Iroquois: those of La Barre in 1684, Denonville in 1686,[96] and Frontenac in 1693. Along with the Micmac, they were the allies of Joseph-François Hertel de La Fresnière against Salmon Falls, Maine, in 1690; and of Pierre Le Moyne d'Iberville, Simon-Pierre Denys de Bonaventure and of Jean-Vincent d'Abbadie de Saint-Castin in the taking of Pemaquid in 1696. This involvement in colonial disputes was disastrous for the Abenaki, who were reduced to a fraction of their pre-contact population and eventually lost their former homelands.[97] During the second half of the seventeenth century they had begun to drift up to Canada; by 1670 there were Sokoki settled in Montreal and Trois-Rivières, and before the end of the century other groups were on the Chaudière River, at Saint-Francis (now Odanak) and on the south shore of the St. Lawrence at Bécancour.

Montagnais-Naskapi

Where the Abenaki relocated as a consequence of the European invasion, the Montagnais and Naskapi, Cree-speaking Algonkian hunting peoples, according to their own traditions had been pushed into their sub-Arctic lands by the Iroquois before the Europeans had arrived. On the north shore of the St. Lawrence, from the Atlantic seaboard to the St. Maurice River and extending north to James Bay and the Arctic Ocean, these closely related people shared a culture based on the taiga economy. The Naskapi in Labrador exploited maritime resources as well as caribou; the Montagnais, living in heavily forested inland regions, depended on moose in winter and freshwater fish during the summer. The Naskapi covered their lodges with caribou skin, and wore tailored clothes similar to those of the Inuit; the Montagnais used birchbark for their lodges, and were more casual about the tailoring of their garments.[98] Both, but particularly the Naskapi, adorned their garments with geometrical patterns, the "double-curve motif" painted or stamped predominantly in red. This was the "leather lace" described by Biard. Both Montagnais and Naskapi women carried their babies in moss bags, rather than in the *tikinagen* or wooden carrying boards of the forest peoples to the west and south. They shared with the Micmac and other Algonkians the custom of a bridegroom serving his bride's family for a year before being allowed to establish his own domicile.

It was of the Montagnais that Le Jeune penned his well-known description, after living with them in their remote forests:

> It seems as if innocence, banished from the majority of the Empires & Kingdoms of the World, had withdrawn into these great forests where these people dwell. Their nature has something, I know not what, of the goodness of the Terrestrial Paradise before sin had entered it. Their practices manifest none of the luxury, the ambition, the avarice, or the pleasures that corrupt our cities.[99]

A late seventeenth-century "Mountain Amerindian" from near Hudson Bay. C-10897 Public Archives Canada.

D'Avity reflected this when he wrote of the closely related Attikamègue of the St. Maurice River (a people who disappeared as a separate entity during the seventeenth century, but who may be partly the ancestors of today's Têtes-de-Boule of the upper Saint-Maurice River), "who, although the least instructed of nations, give the most solid evidence of a goodness that is truly Christian and have a stronger disposition and inclination than others toward the Faith."[100]

The Naskapi fought the Inuit; the Montagnais were enemies of the Iroquois. When Champlain first met the Montagnais at Tadoussac, they were celebrating a victory with the Algonquin and Etchemin; it was as their ally that he fired the famous shot that knocked down three Iroquois chiefs.

Both the Montagnais and Naskapi seem to have traded and thus allied themselves with Europeans from the earliest days of contact. It may have been these people who smoke-signalled to Cartier in the Straits of Belle-Isle to come and trade. He reported that they had no fear of boarding the French ship.[101] It appears to have been trade that initially attracted the Montagnais-Naskapi to the St. Lawrence.[102] That the Montagnais prospered from the early fur trade is indicated by d'Avity's comment as to the great quantity of presents that characterized the installation of a chief named Etouat.[103] Etouat benefited from being a Christian and a particular friend of the French; the ceremony of his installation reflected French influence.[104]

In spite of their initially favorable position from which to exploit the fur trade, and their remoteness, the Montagnais and the Naskapi suffered population declines following contact with Europeans. Their number at time of contact has been estimated at five thousand, although anthropologist Diamond Jenness thought this to be conservative. Today, the Montagnais and Naskapi together number fewer than four thousand.[105] The French, by establishing themselves at Quebec in 1608, bypassed the Montagnais. As their position in the fur trade declined, the latter tended to retreat once more into their northern fastness.

Algonquin and Related Peoples

Between the Montagnais in the east and the Ojibway in the west, the Algonquin were allies of both the Montagnais and the Huron against the Iroquois. A group of several related peoples (Weskarini or La Petite Nation, Onontchataronon), they had a symbiotic relationship with the Huron, providing them with meat and skins in exchange for agricultural produce, and often wintering with them. At the beginning of the seventeenth century, they came to Quebec with the Huron to trade, and appear to have considered themselves as middlemen between the Huron and the French. Certainly they tried to prevent the French from going to Huronia, just as at an earlier period the Stadaconans had tried to prevent Cartier from sailing up the St. Lawrence. The Algonquin's lively sense of their rights in this new trade is indicated by their practice of charging a toll on Huron canoes laden with furs passing Allumette Island in the Ottawa River. Although the Huron complained about this,[106] they themselves collected tribute on goods passing through Huronia.[107] This was in line with the general Amerindian practice of charging tolls for passage through another's territory for trade. Besides trading with the French, the Algonquin also sought an arrangement with the Dutch, but were foiled by the intervening Mohawk. Like the Micmac, Malecite, and Abenaki, they remained faithful allies to the French during the colonial wars.[108]

The Algonquin shared cultural characteristics with their close relatives the Ottawa (Odawa), Ojibway (Chippewa) and such affiliates as the Mississauga and westernmost Saulteaux, as well as with the Cree to the north and west. Like the Iroquoians, the Algonquin built longhouses; and one of their branches, the Nipissing, celebrated a Feast of the Dead similar to that of the Huron. The Algonquin as well as the Ottawa practised some agriculture, but relied heavily on hunting. However, these peoples, unlike some of their neighbors, did not torture war prisoners. After the dispersal of the Hurons, the Ottawa (who had earlier been lo-

Algonquin hunter, from Bressani's map, 1657. He is wearing a minimum of clothing, although it is winter and he is on snowshoes. National Map Collection, C-19028 Public Archives Canada.

cated on Manitoulin Island and adjacent areas, and had then expanded), successfully brought down some fur brigades to Montreal, but were unable to maintain the position of middleman.[109] Later, toward the end of the seventeenth century, the Ojibway group entered into a period of expansion, apparently for reasons similar to those that had spurred the Iroquois about sixty years earlier. The Mississauga expelled the Iroquoians from southern Ontario, and the Saulteaux began moving out onto the western plains.[110]

Huron (*Ouendat or Wendat*)

The people written about most during the contact period, along with the Tupinambá of Brazil, were the Huron, and for a similar reason: their trading alliance with the French. The name Huron is of French origin, referring to the bristly coiffures of the warriors.[111] Their name for themselves was Wendat, "Islanders," referring to the earth, which, in their cosmology, was an island on the back of a turtle. The Wyandot of Oklahoma are descendants of the remnants of the Huron and Tionontati, the Tobacco people. The Huron confederacy consisted of four principal Iroquoian tribes: the Attignawantan, referred to by the French as the Bear; the Attigneenongnahac, the Cord; the Arendahronon, the Rock; and Tahontaerat, the Deer. The confederacy may have counted a fifth tribe; more certainly, it included some smaller communities, one at least of which spoke an Algonkian language.[112] The Bear was the largest, followed by the Cord; these two were also the seniors, having lived in the region two hundred years or so at the time of the appearance of the French.[113] The most recent arrivals were the Deer, who joined the league in 1610. There has been speculation that the Rock and the Deer were descendants of the Laurentian Iroquois who had been living along the St. Lawrence at the time of Cartier's visits. By the time of Champlain, early in the seventeenth century, they had disappeared from the river. The first Huron who came to Quebec in 1609 to meet the French were of the Rock tribe, and it was with them that Champlain wintered in 1615–16. But it was the Bear who became the most receptive to Christianity.[114]

Geographically, Huronia was concentrated in an area that measured only thirty-five miles east to west and twenty miles north to south[115] between Lakes Simcoe and Couchiching on the east and Matchedash Bay on the west. At the time of the arrival of the Jesuits, it could be traversed in three or four days.[116] It was a country "full of fine hills, open fields, very beautiful broad meadows bearing much excellent hay."[117] Champlain estimated its population at thirty thousand, a figure later to be repeated by the Jesuits,[118] although Sagard set the figure at between thirty thousand and forty thousand.[119] These people lived close together in villages that were reported as numbering either eighteen, twenty, or twenty-five,[120] and shared common hunting territory. Such a way of life is strikingly different from the settlement pattern of the Five Nations, among whom the villages of each tribe were separated by hunting territory.[121] This resulted in greater uniformity of language and culture among the Huron than was the case among the Five Nations. Archeological evidence suggests that the Huron of about 1550 had a settlement pattern that resembled that of the Iroquois a hundred years later,[122] but that sometime late in the sixteenth century there was a movement northward in which the settlements were reorganized and former occupied areas became joint hunting territories. The new location, besides having soil suitable for Huron agriculture and providing a plentiful supply of fish, and initially of firewood, was strategically located at the head of a main water route for northern trade.

It has been speculated that trade, rather than fear of the Iroquois, prompted the move; it could also have been due to population pressure. The fur trade with Europeans had been developing throughout the sixteenth century along the Atlantic coast and up the St. Lawrence, and had resulted in European goods reaching Huronia well before the arrival of Champlain. This could have caused the agricultural Huron, already in a close trading relationship with the hunting Algonquin, to relocate and to consolidate their settlements in order to exploit the new development.[123] However, archeology has revealed that the Huron population expanded greatly during the 1300s,[124] an event which may have been at least as important in the relocation as was trade. By the time the Jesuits appeared, beaver had already been exterminated in Huronia.[125] Prior to their arrival, not only the Huron in the north but also the Iroquois, Susquehannock, Powhatan and Cherokee to the south had become active in the fur trade.[126] The Huron's principal trading activities were with Algonkian tribes, such as Nipissing, Ottawa, and Algonquin of the Ottawa Valley.

The presence of Ontario Iroquoian pottery in Algonkian sites in northern Ontario gives archeological evidence of prehistoric trade. The Jesuits referred to Huronia as "the granary of most of the Algonquins."[127] The elaborate trading conventions of the Huron, closely interwoven into their complex social network, reflect the fundamental importance, as well as the antiquity, of this aspect of reciprocity. Trading missions were occasions for feasts, speeches, and formal gift exchanges, rituals which could take several days before actual trading began. There was a recognized scale of values; for example, haggling over price was disapproved of.[128] The first to exploit a certain trade route had exclusive rights to it; these were hereditary. Others could receive permission to use a route in exchange for gifts. Accordingly, the Arendahronon, the Rock people, being the first to meet the French, controlled the rights to trade with them. Because of the volume of this new trade, however, they shared these rights with the other nations of the confederacy, while continuing to regard themselves as the special allies of the French.[129] Outside of the confederacy, they acknowledged that the Algonquin possessed particular rights as allies of the French, also because of their prior contact.[130] Exchange of children was an important feature of the trading relationship. Such an exchange provided hostages, and was also a gesture of good will that forged blood ties between the participants, as the children sometimes remained to grow up and marry within the adoptive tribes.

Still another indication of the importance of trade to the Huron concerned the compensation required in the case of murder. If a Huron killed a member of a friendly trading group, a higher compensation was paid than in the case of one Huron killed by another. It is interesting to note in passing that if the victim was a woman, reparations were higher than for a man. The arguments for this were that it was women who produced children, and that they had no defence. Gifts that were not acceptable had to be replaced with those that were. The largest payment of which there is a record was that of a hundred gifts made to the Jesuits in 1648 for the killing of a *donné*.[131]

Ironically, trade would be instrumental in the downfall of the Huron Confederacy in 1649, as the Five Nations acquired guns faster from the Dutch and English than the French would allow along the St. Lawrence. During the very early days of the colony, it was forbidden to trade guns to Amerindians on pain of a fine of two thousand livres.[132] That such measures were not entirely effective is witnessed by the charge of English colonists that the Tarranteens (Tarrantines, Micmac) were armed with guns secured in trade with the French.[133] Nevertheless, they appear to have been effective enough, at least during the first half of the sixteenth century, to handicap French allies in the face of the better armed enemy. Jesuit Barthelemy Vimont was vehement on that point as he reported the increasing boldness of Iroquois attacks in 1642–43. Ruefully noting that the French "have always been afraid to arm the Savages too much," he added: "Would to God the Hollanders had done the same."[134] The first Huron known to obtain a French gun was Charles Tsondatsaa in 1641, who received it as a baptismal gift. Even then, only those who became Christians acquired guns,[135] a policy which the French maintained with their allies until the pressures of trading and colonial rivalries dictated otherwise.

As closely as can be estimated today, the Huron tribes were divided among eight exogamous clans. The Jesuits did not report on such structures, although the "eight captains from the eight nations that constitute the Huron country," may be an oblique reference to such an institution.[136] As a consequence, what little is known has been inferred largely from a study of the Wyandot (the Huron of Lorette, near Quebec City, have assimilated with the whites to the extent of having lost their traditional social structures). Clans were scattered throughout the villages; each grouping of any size had its own chiefs, who managed internal clan affairs as well as representing the group on tribal and confederacy levels. Clan offices were hereditary within the group, through the holder's sister's son. Among the Huron, as among the Iroquois, the clans were responsible for settling blood feuds.

The Huron resembled the Iroquois in having two kinds of chiefs: those for civil affairs, who had seats in the main tribal and confederacy councils, and those for war. The former inherited their offices through their clan lineage, although not in any particular order, so that personal merit had a great deal to do with it; the name of the holder of a particular office stayed the same through the generations, providing institutional continuity. War chiefs were elected on the basis of valor and personal qualities, although lineage may have been a factor. Neither type had coercive powers; the chiefs did not have police forces at their disposal.

Huron warrior, from Champlain, 1632.

Influence was exercised through ability to gain the support of public opinion.[137] Civil chiefs had the most prestige. However, age was much respected; an individual who was not a chief but who became recognized as an outstanding individual could gain considerable influence as an Old Man.

No amount of prestige, nor high rank, gave a chief the right to interfere in the affairs of a clan that was not his own. Indeed, even within his own clan, his influence was restricted to his particular group within his village. Council meetings at all levels were held with considerable formality, with gifts and wampum playing a vital role.

One means available to chiefs for exercising social control was provided by fear of witchcraft and treason. Both these crimes were considered so heinous that in theory the guilty ones could be killed with impunity by anyone on the spot.[138] In practice, however, the sanction of a chief or a council was relied upon in order to establish beyond doubt that the accused was generally recognized as being guilty; if there was any doubt, such a killing could conceivably trigger a feud. The most effective form of social control, however, was community approval; children were taught that unacceptable behavior could bring dishonor upon their names.

In contrast to a witch or sorcerer, a shaman (medicine man) was much respected and was called *arendiwane*, "his supernatural power is great." He was also called *oki*, the term for those who performed extraordinary feats, as well as for certain spirits or charms. One of their most

Seventeenth-century Huron village as envisaged in nineteenth-century Italy. Giulio Ferrario, *America*, 1820. C-1994 Public Archives Canada.

important functions was the interpretation of dreams, to which the Huron looked for guidance in their daily lives; so much so that the Jesuits wrote that dreams were the "God of the country."[139] A frustrated Jérôme Lalemant reported a Huron—"a slave of Satan"—as saying: "I am quite ready to embrace the Faith and to become a Christian, whatever dread I may have of it, provided my Dreams command me to do so."[140]

Burial customs formed the most distinctive aspect of Huron culture. At the time of the arrival of the French, the Feast of the Dead was the most important of all their festivals, being held whenever a village moved. Its central feature was burial in an ossuary; the largest of these that have been found contained the bones of about one thousand individuals. Bodies were disinterred from cemeteries where they had been placed immediately after death, and the bones were cleaned and washed and wrapped in new finery such as beaver skins. Only the bodies of those recently dead were exempted. Following about ten days of ceremonies, these bones were reburied along with offerings in pits lined with beaver robes. Sometimes those from allied nations were included. This mingling has been described as the most important of all rituals for uniting the Huron tribes among themselves as well as with their allies.[141]

Neighboring Iroquoians

Immediately to the west and south lived the Tionontati, the Tobacco People (Pétun to the French), a confederacy of two nations who spoke Attignawantan. Their customs were similar to those of the Huron, with whom they traded and shared a new-found friendship with their former enemies—the Algonquin, some of whom lived amongst them.[142] The Tionontati were also allied and traded with the Ottawa to the north and west, and the Iroquoian Neutral to the south. Before contact, the Tobacco People may have numbered eight thousand; but in 1639, toward the end of the epidemics of 1634–40, the Jesuits reported that they had been reduced to nine villages. The largest of these, Ehwae (Saint-Pierre et Saint-Paul), numbering forty-five or fifty cabins, was burned in 1640 by an unidentified enemy who may have been of the Five Nations or perhaps the Algonkian-speaking Assistaeronon.[143] The Tobacco People, so-called because they specialized in growing the herb, were prevented from direct access to French trade by the Huron, jealous of their middleman position. That situation also prevented the Jesuits from establishing a mission among them. Later, perhaps because of the dislocations caused by the epidemics and tribal warfare, the missionaries were able to establish themselves at Etharita (which they called Saint-Jean), a village of perhaps six hundred families on the Tionontati's southern frontier, which was destroyed in its turn by the Five Nations in 1649.[144]

Further south but still north of Lake Erie and west of Lake Ontario were the people known to the Huron as Attiwandaron ("people who speak a slightly different language"), and to the French as the Neutral because they managed to stay on peaceful terms with both the Huron and the Five Nations. (Attiwandaron was also the name by which the Neutral knew the Huron.) Although not as populous as the Huron, they also formed a confederation, inhabiting about forty villages more widely dispersed and smaller than those of their northern neighbors. The French speculated that the Neutral had once formed one people with the Huron and Five Nations and had divided "not long ago"; in any event, their population has been estimated at twelve thousand in 1640, following the epidemics.[145] The Neutral, while managing to keep the peace to the north and east, were less successful toward the west, and fought bitterly with an Algonkian people of Michigan, the Assistaeronon, "Fire Nation" (perhaps the Mascouten). The Assistaeronon were reported to be more numerous than the Neutral, Huron, and Five Nations combined. Among the battles of which there is a record, one occurred in 1642, when the Neutral assembled an army of two thousand to attack a palisaded village of the Fire Nation, taking several hundred captive; they were reported to burn women prisoners as well as men.[146]

Although the Neutral resembled the Huron in both language and customs, they differed on certain points, such as burial customs.[147] They kept their dead in their houses for long periods of time, only taking them to cemeteries when decomposition was advanced. Later the bones were brought back to the houses until the Feast of the Dead. Like their close relatives the Tionontati, the Neutral grew large quantities of good tobacco, which they used in trade. When Recollet Joseph de La Roche Daillon visited the Neutral in 1626 and sought to establish a trading relationship with them, he attracted the instant opposition of the Huron, who would not countenance such an infringement upon their rights.[148]

Upon their dispersal in 1649, many Huron settled among the Neutral. This was a reversal of what happened a few years earlier, in 1638, when the easternmost of the Neutral associate tribes, the Wenro, neighbors of the Seneca, had fled to Huronia and had been accepted into the Huron Confederacy. This suggests that the relationship of the Neutral with the Five Nations may not have been as secure as their European name implies.

Other Iroquoians in the general area included the Nation of the Cat (Erie, Rhiierrhonon, perhaps Black Minqua), and the Andastes or Susquehannock (Connestoga or White Minqua), allies of the Huron, although separated from them by the Five Nations. At the beginning of the seventeenth century, the Huron had the Five Nations encircled by means of their alliances. The Erie, south of Lake Erie, had little contact with Europeans. The French knew of them as "La Nation du Chat"

Eighteenth-century Iroquois warrior, as engraved by J. Laroque, after Jacques Grasset St. Sauveur. C-3165 Public Archives Canada.

because of the number of raccoons (*chats sauvages*) in their lands, whose pelts the Erie used to make blankets adorned with the tails.[149] The Susquehannock lived scattered along the north branch of the Susquehannock River, almost 400 miles away. The Five Nations, after dispersing the Huron and Tionontati in 1649, defeated the Neutral in 1651, the Erie in a series of attacks between 1654 and 1656; and the Susquehannock, who in the meantime had also become embroiled with English colonists, in 1675. Another Iroquoian group, of which very little is known, the Scahentarronon, appears to have been defeated by the Five Nations in 1652. In any event, the Five Nations had smashed the encircling ring of Huron allies in an extraordinary series of victories. Of the major Iroquoian tribes in the Great Lakes-St. Lawrence system during the days of first contact with Europeans, only those of the Five Nations remained intact by the end of the seventeenth century.

A major consequence of this series of victories over farming people at the hub of Amerindian trade networks was radically altered trading patterns. Northern hunters, no longer able to obtain agricultural supplies from the Huron, began to trade directly with the French. New markets resulted in expansion of land clearing for cultivation as habitant farmers moved into the niche once occupied by the Huron.[150]

Five Nations

The League of the Five Nations comprised, from west to east, the Seneca, Cayuga, Onondaga, Oneida, and Mohawk, spread out from the Genesee River on the west through the Finger Lake region to Schoharie Creek on the east. (By the eighteenth century, this range had expanded to the Ohio Valley in the west, and the lower reaches of Lake Champlain in the east.) Its total population in 1600 has been estimated at 16,000.[151] The largest tribe was the Seneca, "The Great Hill People" (about 7,000, according to Lloyd). They were the "keepers of the west door" of the League. The smallest was the Oneida, "People of the Stone" (1,000); next were the Mohawk, "People of the Flint" (about 3,000). They were the "keepers of the east door." Politically, the important members were Seneca, Mohawk, and Onondaga. The last-named, numbering about 3,000, were called the "People of the Mountain" or "keepers of the council fire." Occupying a position that was central, not only geographically but also in inter-league relations, they served as lawmakers, arbitrators, and archivists ("keepers of the archival wampum"). The French, however, classified them as the most warlike,[152] although the Seneca played the major role in the defeat of the Huron in 1649, and later of the other western tribes;[153] and the Mohawk spread such terror among the Montagnais, Micmac, and easterners generally. The Mohawk ("Maqua" in early accounts) derived at least some of their influence from their early direct contact with the Dutch and subsequently the English. The Cayuga, "People at the Landing" (2,000), who specialized in rituals, played a lesser role as did the Oneida; in fact, the Cayuga were said to be offshoots of the Onondaga, as the Oneida were of the Mohawk. At no time did the Five Nations count more than 2,500 warriors, and these were never fielded all at once.[154]

The League is generally believed to have taken form sometime during the last half of the sixteenth century, under the leadership of Deganawidah (a Huron by birth but a Mohawk by adoption), and that of his lieutenant, Hiawatha. However, Iroquois legends support an earlier date—one as early as the mid-fifteenth century.[155] Population increases, warfare, and trade may have been factors in encouraging such a development as confederation. Archeology has confirmed the presence among the Seneca as early as 1500, of European trade goods that may have come up from the south.[156] By the end of the sixteenth century, steel had already largely replaced stone for Seneca axe blades, and arrowheads were often cut from brass.[157] In any event, the League was formed with a central council of forty-nine permanent sachemships, unequally divided among the five tribes. Technically, there were fifty, as Hiawatha's position continued to be listed but not filled.[158] As with the Huron, these offices were hereditary within the clans, although the actual person who succeeded to a vacant post was named by the clan mother acting on the advice of fellow members. In spite of unequal representation, each nation had only one vote. Regular meetings were held at the central fire at Onondaga, where the archival wampum was kept. The Onondaga sachem was permanent moderator. His was a position of great prestige but of closely circumscribed powers. The council's powers were related to external affairs, such as war, peace, and trade, and its decisions had to be unanimous. Each of the five nations was autonomous in its internal affairs. Two hereditary war chieftainships were held by the Seneca. Otherwise, war leaders rose on individual merit; the conduct of hostilities was a matter for personal initiative. The Iroquois, like the Huron, did not resolve the contradictions between the ideal of individual dignity and responsibility with the practical necessities of cooperation and authority needed to effect united action. Although their political organization was relatively complex, it was still based on the principles of non-state societies, which were fundamentally opposed to centralization of power. In practice this meant that the Iroquois were far from achieving unity of action, as the French discovered when their peace

A council of the Five Nations meets with a delegation; speeches are made with the aid of wampum "belts," one of which is shown enlarged at bottom. An eighteenth-century French interpretation, from Lafitau, *Moeurs des sauvages amériquains*, 1724.

treaty with the Mohawk in 1666 did not automatically mean peace with the other members of the Five Nations.

The Iroquois, like the Huron, were simultaneously members of their particular nation, a political unit, and of a clan, a social unit. There seem to have been nine clans, which not only cut across national lines but were not evenly divided among the five members.[159] Thus the Mohawk and Oneida each had only three clans, whereas the Seneca, Cayuga, and Onondaga each had at least eight. A nation divided its clans into exogamous moieties, a division that was reflected in social activities. In games, the moieties were lined up against each other. At ceremonial occasions such as the Strawberry Festival or Green Corn Festival, the two halves faced each other, and the speakers addressed the opposite side.[160] Functionaries at burial ceremonies were always selected from the moiety opposite to that of the deceased. This was true also for the various medicine societies such as the "False Faces," "Little Water," or "Real Life."[161] Similarly, in the dream-guessing ritual, the guesser belonged to the moiety opposite the dreamer. This dual division was also present in both national and League councils.

Much has been written about the importance of women in Iroquois life. On the family level, a man owned his tools, weapons, and wearing apparel; a woman owned household utensils, the house itself, and the land. Marriages were arranged by the mothers of the principals. On ceremonial occasions, each clan was represented by three male and three female officials. It was the women who elected new sachems to fill vacancies. Their choice had to be confirmed by the sachems of the moiety involved, and ratified by the other side. If a sachem proved to be unsatisfactory, the women of his clan could impeach him. The impeachment, if ratified by the confederate council, could result in his deposition. Though women were not members of the council, they sometimes made speeches before it as well as during ceremonies.[162]

Of all the peoples here considered, the Five Nations were initially highly successful in maintaining their league and tribal integrity in the face of European pressures. Contributing to this was their advantagous geographical position, enabling them to capitalize both on the fur trade and its concomittant alliances. They continued to do so for nearly three centuries, until the invasion of their territories during the American War of Independence.

Geography also came to the aid of the far northern peoples, such as the Montagnais, Naskapi, and Cree. For them, however, the factors were isolation and climate: the areas they occupied did not at first attract European settlement. Of the peoples in more immediately accessible and desirable areas, the Micmac and Malecite enjoyed considerable early success in maintaining their cultural identity, despite the fact they were among the first to meet Europeans. They did this at first by becoming partners with the French in the fisheries and fur trade, a partnership which became a military alliance in the colonial wars. This lasted until the defeat of France in North America in 1760. Of all the peoples of New France, the Beothuk were the least successful in maintaining themselves. Whatever their ultimate fate, all of these peoples at the time of contact led structured lives within organized societies, based upon cyclical patterns. The fact that such organization was often not centralized or that its institutions were not always stable did not mean that it was any the less operative. Amerindians possessed a comparatively simple technology that contrasted strongly with the complexity and richness of their spiritual and ritual lives. Some Europeans came to appreciate the contrast as they became more knowledgeable about Amerindians and realized that these peoples had found workable answers to the problems of living within a context that was fundamentally different from their own. But these were not the realizations to which the French and other Europeans would give precedence when it came to establishing empires.

CHAPTER 6

The Old World Embraces the New

Ferdinand's gesture of dominion over the New World appears to frighten his new Amerindian subjects. Dati, *La lettera*, 1493.

Europe moved very early to integrate the Americas into what it considered to be an acceptable Christian social order. According to the advanced political thinking of the sixteenth century, such an order meant centralization, whether of a state or of an empire, based on an absolute monarchy.[1] It was not a governmental theory that enjoyed unqualified support; Spain, for one, stood firmly for constitutional limits to royal power and insisted on the legal rights of free peoples. Just emerged from a contest with the Moors, and leading Europe both in jurisprudence and in the practice of law, Spain had an administrative apparatus well enough developed to take advantage of Columbus's discoveries by launching immediately into the conquest and colonization of the New World. Hers was a position that France was not to attain until the end of the century.

As a political theory, absolutism placed the monarch at the center of the state just as man was believed to be at the center of the natural order of the earth and God at the center of the universe. These interlocking parts of the Great Chain of Being,[2] in which rank and order were accorded overriding importance, were believed to be stable and static. Cultures could evolve, but only until the perfect, Christian form had been reached. The squabbles about precedence that characterized the history of New France were logical results of this social philosophy. Such quarrels were perhaps even more venomous in Europe than they were in her colonies. The rise of centralized states led to the development of international law, a movement accelerated by the need to establish a theoretical and legal basis for European power in the New World. As questions about the rights of discovery and procedures for claiming new territories were debated, France jockeyed to establish her transatlantic presence. Her problems were not just political: they involved such practical matters as the selection of colonists, ocean crossings, and adaptations to strange and often unforeseen conditions.

Cross found in Brazil by Staden and his companions in 1549. They could not read the inscription, and so could not determine who had erected it.

As Spain moved to exploit its sudden access to dazzling sources of wealth, France was by no means oblivious to the visions of imperial glory that were so soon to become reality:

> The French above all were spurred by a desire to do likewise in areas that had not been reached by them [Spaniards], for they did not esteem themselves less than they, neither in navigation, in feats of arms nor in any other calling. They persuaded themselves that they had not discovered all, and that the world was large enough to reveal even stranger things than those already known.[3]

Those were the words of Henri Lancelot-Voisin, Sieur de La Popelinière (1541–1608), a Huguenot and one of France's leading historians of the sixteenth century. With disarming frankness, he added that in France there was a certain jealousy occasioned by Spain and Portugal's success. In French circles it was widely believed that Columbus had originally sought Gallic support for his voyage of discovery but had been turned down. Gaspard de Saulx, Seigneur de Tavannes (1509–93), later Marshal of France, noted bitterly in his diary in 1536: "This conquest of the New World, proposed to the French and turned down by them, is witness to the lack of dedication of our counsellors, who would prefer to lose kingdoms for their master [the King] rather than see their enemies have the opportunity to conquer them."[4] By the time of Montesquieu, nearly 200 years later, the French were still bewailing the blindness of their court for having repulsed Columbus's proposal to cross the western sea.[5] Bartholomew Columbus had been at the French court in 1490, apparently looking for support for his brother's project; he was still there when the news of the discovery of the New World arrived.[6]

La Popelinière felt that national pride demanded that his country should continue where Columbus left off. He was sure there were "many singular and prodigious miracles of nature still to be found, particularly toward the south." As for the awkward question of the papal division, the Huguenot historian held that it was certain that Amerindians, if they had been consulted, would never have agreed to such a gift to Spain and Portugal; besides, the papal donation had not included "les Terres Australes" (southern lands).[7] Such a position, of course, took advantage of the vague wording of the original demarcation, as well as of the confirming Treaty of Tordesillas in 1494.

Pope Alexander VI's bulls of 1493, which had been issued in response to Spanish pressure to demarcate Spanish and Portuguese zones of influence in the new regions, had not been well received in France. The pope, a Borgia, was Spanish by birth and needed support from Spain for his policy of family aggrandizement in Italy.[8] Spain was disturbed at Portuguese claims of sovereignty in the New World by right of the Treaty of Alcáçovas, which the two countries had signed on 4 September 1479, before Columbus's discoveries had radically altered the importance of the new regions. Ferdinand's move to get Rome's sanction for Spanish claims in the New World, in return for Spain's promise to evangelize, smacked more of imperial opportunism than of acknowledged papal supremacy. In the realm of practical politics, however, it powerfully reinforced the New World claims of Spain and Portugal. In fact, Spain officially based her New World claims on the 1493 bulls, particularly the second *Inter Caetera*, even as she carefully included her "other just and legitimate titles." Portugal, having won the right to Brazil in the Treaty of Tordesillas with Spain, was careful to secure her posi-

The cacique Guarionex challenges the Spaniards at Vega Real, Hispaniola. Some of his people are pulling down and attacking the Spanish cross. Herrera, *Historia General*, 1601.

tion by obtaining papal confirmation from Julius II in the bull *Ea Quae*, issued in 1506. Ironically, papal power did not extend directly into the New World.

Although there was much criticism of the papal action, particularly in regard to its temporal aspects, no one seriously challenged its basic assumption of the right of Christians to dominate non-Christians. The legality of the bulls was based on the doctrine of universal papal dominion in temporal as well as spiritual matters. While it long antedated him, Henry of Susa, cardinal of Ostia (d.1271), came to be particularly associated with this doctrine, which was known as the Ostiensian (or Hostiensian) doctrine.[9] Henry had maintained that when Christ had become King of the earth, heathens had lost their right to political jurisdiction and to worldly possessions. He held that Jesus had transferred his temporal and spiritual dominion to Peter and hence to the popes. In practical terms, this meant that a people without a knowledge of the true God could retain its lands only with the approval of the church. The pope had the right to appoint a Christian ruler to bring such people within the fold of the faith; however, the power of such a prince was carefully circumscribed.[10] An early version of this doctrine had guided the popes in granting heathen lands to Christians during the Crusades. In 1156 Adrian IV had accorded Ireland to Henry II of England "as an inheritance," on condition that he should convince the Irish church to accept the authority of Rome, and bring order to Ireland's government.[11] The Canaries had also been the subject of a papal grant. In 1454 Pope Nicholas V had given Portugal the right to possess non-Christian lands on the West Coast of Africa, and two years later Calixtus III granted to the Grand Prior of the Order of Christ, of which Prince Henry was the administrator, spiritual control of all Portuguese dominions then and thereafter existing. A corollary and even a justification for this was later detected in the fact that a Catholic power had discovered the New World. This was cited as positive proof that Roman Catholicism was the true faith: God had thus indicated the religion he wanted taught to these strange peoples.[12]

Such reasoning made the papal demarcation even more galling to the national pride of many Frenchmen. By what right was France, a Catholic power, excluded from the New World?[13] In the words of Alfonce, "They made the said divisions without consulting Your Royal Majesty, nor any

Champlain, during his explorations of the Atlantic seaboard, 1605, encountered hostility from natives in Massachusetts. Champlain had noted that the site was suitable for settlement, and had erected a cross as depicted in his illustration of the incident (*Works*, I). C-97387 Public Archives Canada.

of Your predecessors. It was an ill-advised and bad partition, as You had as much and as great a right as they."[14] Such indignation was compounded by the immensity of the gift to the Spanish and Portuguese, once it was realized that the new lands were continents and not just islands. "I cannot believe," complained Thevet, "that the Pope has granted this huge territory from one pole to another, as it is enough for 50 Christian kings."[15] An anonymous pamphleteer proclaimed that it would be to the benefit of the barbarians themselves for France to venture forth and civilize them. Inspired by the French example, they would practically civilize themselves: "We are in an age when all that is great, all that is beautiful, all that is useful for the state is being accomplished."[16] Montchrestien was just as vehement: "If any nation has the right to take over, it is the French, who are particularly qualified because of the glory of their letters and arms, their arts and fine manners, and their true Christianity, despite the claims of others."[17] Even missionaries joined the chorus. Le Jeune, recently arrived as Superior of the Jesuits in Quebec in 1632, wondered if the French alone of all nations of the earth were to be deprived of expanding in the New World.[18] François I was thus on solid nationalist grounds when he asked to see Adam's will in order to verify the pope's right to dispose of non-Christian lands. Pressuring Clement VII for a re-interpretation of the bulls to mean that Spain and Portugal's claims extended only to territories already discovered, not to unknown lands, he formally inaugurated Franco-Spanish rivalry in the New World by sending Verrazzano to explore the North American Atlantic coast in 1524.

François I, for all his annoyance with the pope, agreed with him on one fundamental point: whatever claim to sovereignty non-Christian Amerindians might have, it was secondary to the duty of Christian Europeans to evangelize them. François's dream of an empire could have hardly allowed for any other position. But there were dissenting voices, even in his own realm. One of the most influential was that of a Scottish Dominican theologian at the Sorbonne, John Major or Mair (1469–1550). Major denied the pope's temporal dominion of the world on the grounds that Jesus had declared that His kingdom was not of this world. Therefore such dominion lay not in faith, but in natural law, which gave the infidel as much right to his land as the Christian had to his. However, Christians had not only the right but the duty to preach the Gospel; if Amerindians resisted, then Christians had the right to resort to the use of arms. In such a case the pope could authorize the seizure of political power and the levying of tribute. As for the Amerindians,

> Those people live like animals . . . it is evident that some men are by nature free, and others servile. In the natural order of things the quali-

> ties of some men are such that, in their own interests, it is right and just that they should serve, while others, living freely, exercise their natural authority and command.[19]

More subtle and perhaps more humane was the stand taken by another Dominican, Francisco de Vitoria (1480-1552), professor of moral theology at the University of Salamanca, considered by many to have been the founder of international law. In a series of lectures delivered in 1532 under the overall title "De Indis et De Jure Belli Relectiones," he outlined his position on the bulls of demarcation, Spanish imperial claims, and the rights of Amerindians. He agreed with Major that the validity of the bulls was restricted by the fact that "the Pope has no civil or temporal dominion over the earth," nor did he have temporal power over Amerindians or other pagans.[20] Even if the pope had possessed such power, he could not transfer it.[21] Neither could the Spanish emperor legally claim to be the lord of the earth. Even if he were granted such a position, that would still not entitle him "to seize the territories of the aborigines, nor to erect new rulers, nor to dethrone the old ones and capture their possessions."[22] The aborigines, he found, "undoubtedly had true dominion in both public and private matters, just like Christians, and that neither their princes nor private persons could be despoiled of their property on the ground of them not being true owners."[23] However, having granted Amerindians their theoretical rights, Vitoria proceeded to qualify this position. He supported the doctrine of the Christian right to preach the gospel and to resort to force if the infidels refused to listen,[24] and even claimed an exclusive right for Spain in this regard as one of the rights of discovery.[25] Discovery also gave the Spanish the exclusive rights to trade,[26] which could be supported by the use of arms, if necessary.[27] Further, Spaniards had the right and duty to intervene in Amerindian states to rescue people from such tyrannies as human sacrifices and cannibalistic rituals.[28] In other words, the propagation of Christianity could legitimately lead to the subjection of Amerindians to Christian princes on civil, as well as religious, grounds so long as this was done for the benefit of Amerindians rather than of Spaniards.[29] To these arguments Vitoria added, although with considerable reservation, that Amerindians could be considered unfit to administer a lawful state:

> they have no proper laws nor magistrates, and are not even capable of controlling their family affairs; they are without any literature or arts, not only the liberal arts, but the mechanical arts also; they have no careful agriculture and no artisans; and they lack many other conveniences, yea necessaries, of human life.[30]

This was reinforced, Vitoria thought, by the fact that Amerindians were by nature slaves "so they may be in part governed as slaves are"; also, "their food is not more pleasant and hardly better than that of beasts."

In spite of such ambivalences, Vitoria's lectures are often cited as the first clear statement of aboriginal rights.[31] But it was his arguments in favor of intervention that influenced his contemporaries, perhaps because they reflected the consensus of his time. In this regard, it would be difficult to overestimate the effect of Vitoria's reasoning, which, in spite of his personal humanity, provided an instrument for the rationalization of the Spanish wars of conquest and colonization that directly, or more often indirectly, resulted in the deaths of an estimated 13 to 14 millions.[32] In fairness to the Spaniards, it should be emphasized that a large proportion of these deaths were owing to European-introduced diseases to which the Amerindians had no immunity. Also, oddly enough, the spectacular multiplication of Spanish-introduced cattle contributed to an Amerindian demographic decline in some areas, as pre-Columbian agricultural lands were transformed into pasture.[33] By the middle of the sixteenth century, Spain was no longer debating its moral right to assume control of Amerindian lands, but was consolidating and extending its New World empire.

Territorial Rights of Discovery

Widely claimed by Spaniards as by others were the so-called territorial rights of discovery. As Vitoria pointed out, such claims could apply only to unoccupied lands.[34] Even those who advocated such rights, however, did not contend that visual apprehension or primacy of exploration was in itself enough; some symbolic act was also considered to be necessary for a claim to be justified.[35] Thomas Gage (1603?–56), a Dominican of English origin in the service of Spain, wrote that if the Spanish were to be accorded title to New World lands because they sailed by, then Amerindians should be accorded similar privileges if they coasted by Spain: "It is certain that the true legal and proprietary rights of these lands belong to the original inhabitants. . . . It is also certain that they can legitimately transfer those rights."[36] Purchas also supported aboriginal rights: "It was barbarous Latine to turn fides into feodum . . . to dispossesse Barbarians of their Inheritance, and by their want of Faith to increase our fees of Inheritance . . . Christ came not to destroy the Law but to fulfill it."[37]

Crosses or monuments bearing royal arms were erected by the Portuguese and French: in the case of the French, by Ribault in Florida; Cartier in the Gaspé and later on the St. Lawrence; Poutrincourt and De Monts along the Atlantic coast; and Champlain in the interior.

The Timucuan leader Athore greets Laudonnière and shows him a column with the arms of France that had been erected by Laudonnière's colleague, Ribault. The French had brought ready-made columns with a view to establishing their claims in the New World. Athore's people had reacted by considering the column an idol, had wreathed it with garlands, brought offerings, and were reported to have worshipped it. The gestures of the worshippers are European, however, rather than Amerindian. Dietrich de Bry, 1591, after Jacques Le Moyne de Morgues. C-116149 Public Archives Canada.

Daniel de La Touche de La Ravardière and François de Razilly in Brazil elicited the aid of the natives to erect crosses in two different locations. They then held a procession in which the arms of France were borne.[38] The fact that Amerindians might have been unaware of the significance of the act, or perhaps had been misled, as in the case of Cartier on the Gaspé, did not obviate the consequent French claim to those territories, at least in the eyes of France. Such a deception was to be practised by other European powers as well.

Spaniards also read the *requerimiento* to the uncomprehending natives. This was a legal document, which called upon the Amerindians to abjure their false beliefs and accept Christianity or else suffer the consequences.[39] The Dutch and then the English favored agreements, which usually took the form of nominal "purchases," in which the goods given in exchange bore no relation to the value of the land received, even in the terms of the day. These agreements were ambiguous in the sense that Europeans used them as a device for peaceful occupation of the land rather than as a tool of international diplomacy, because the latter would have implicitly recognized the sovereignty of the Amerindians.[40] Partly to avoid this ambiguity in regard to acts of possession, the French never resorted to purchase.[41] Instead they turned the Amerindian practice of usufruct to their own advantage by inverting the Ostiensian doctrine with the argument that they received the use of New World lands in return for teaching Amerindians their new religion. This was perfectly acceptable to the latter, as they regarded such agreements very much as they did alliances, as arrangements to be cyclically renewed, with appropriate gifts. The French were careful to honor this convention, and so the point did not become an issue.[42] There was no great debate in sixteenth-century France on the question of aboriginal territorial rights, although the Huguenot literary figure Urbain Chauveton insisted on the theoretical right of each man to live in liberty and be free from the danger of assault from his neighbor.[43]

This insistence had long been voiced by the papacy, beginning officially in the third decade of the sixteenth century with Paul III.[44] The fact that Urban VIII found it necessary in 1639 to repeat the official Catholic position that Amerindians were not to be deprived of their liberty or the possession of their property indicates the prevalence of abuses in this regard, which the pope could do little to control as he had no direct jurisdiction in the New World. Urban's bull was, in fact, in-

The burning of cacique Hatuey, who, with his people, had fled to Cuba from Hispaniola to escape the Spaniards. A Cordelier tries in vain to convert the cacique, who said he did not want to go to paradise because of the danger of meeting Spaniards there. An engraving by Theodor de Bry, 1591, for the Latin translation of *Brevissima Relación de las Destruyción de las Indias* by Bartolomé de Las Casas. *L'Amérique historique*, 1638, pl. 64. Bibliothèque Mazarine, Paris.

Natives of Hispaniola killing their children and committing suicide rather than be forced to work for the Spaniards. Benzoni, *Historia del Mondo Nuovo*, 1565.

spired by the situation in Brazil and Paraguay, where slave raiding had reached such a point that the Jesuits were having trouble protecting their mission Amerindians from depredations.[45] Indeed, the more firmly European powers became established in the New World, the less was their inclination to recognize aboriginal rights. As lawyer Lescarbot put it, "there is here no question of applying the law and policy of Nations, by which it would not be permissible to claim the territory of another. This being so, we must possess it and preserve its natural inhabitants."[46]

Amerindians, in the meantime, had no doubts as to their own sovereignty. One group, upon being informed of the papal donation, was reported to have laughed and to have replied that the pope was being very liberal with what was not his, and that the Spanish king must be poor because he was asking for the lands of others.[47] First told by a Spaniard, the lawyer, geographer, and navigator Enciso (fl.1450-95), with some amusement but also with some awareness of Amerindian rights, this tale was repeated by the French, less from concern for Amerindians than from anti-Spanish sentiment. For the Amerindians, clear-sighted as they might have been about what was happening to them, they could do little more than complain. In the words reported of some Nicaraguans: "What manner of being are the Christians? No sooner do they enter our houses than they ask for corn, honey, cotton, a cloak, women to bear their children; they want us to give them gold and silver. Christians do not want to work: they are liars, mockers, gamblers, perverts, and blasphemers."[48] The problem was essentially one of power. Amerindians possessed neither the political hegemony nor the technology to defend their rights. Those who were not organized into city-states were further handicapped by their social philosophy, which called for the sharing of land and its resources. This had led them at first to welcome Europeans.[49]

As these debates over Amerindian sovereignty and rights to property were going on, wealth from the New World was helping to transform the 1500s into Europe's Golden Century. Between 1500 and 1650, 181 tons of gold and 16,000 tons of silver reached Europe officially from America.[50] This movement reached massive proportions beginning with the 1530s, and culminated during the first decade of the 1600s.[51] According to Acosta, "It is incredible to see how much merchandise they take and bring back in the fleets. It is almost beyond belief that we from Europe have destroyed so much."[52] Amerindians reacted to Europeans' search for wealth by considering themselves privileged in this regard. They were puzzled, however, by the claim of Christians that their God was rich and all-powerful: "They ask why, then, did He not give riches and necessities to Christians, so they would not have to run

On a Sunday morning, the people of Amaracapanna in the province of Cumaná rose up against the Spaniards, killing all who were there. They burned houses, churches, and monasteries, sparing neither domestic animals nor even Amerindians in the service of the Spaniards. Dietrich de Bry, 1596, after a description by Benzoni. C-116250 Public Archives Canada.

such dangers by coming to America to take from those they call unbelievers"?[53] From Peru alone in 1533, Spain received "100 millions in gold and twice that amount in silver, the ransom of Atahuallpa amounting to 1,326,000 besants of gold."[54] A later writer set the ransom figure at 27,000,000 in gold, without specifying the units, although he said the total amount was more than existed in all of Spain at that time.[55] Whether this treasure trove entered Europe officially through Spanish ports or unofficially through those of France or elsewhere, the result was an unprecedented increase in Europe's supply of precious metals. Spanish coins struck with gold and silver from the New World became the legal tender of the West.[56]

In spite of its enormous contribution, America was not the only source of wealth for Spain. In *Réponse à Malestroit* (1568), Bodin pointed to the riches flowing in from the Orient and Africa as well as from the New World. In 1554, the Spanish crown's American revenue represented only eleven percent of its total;[57] in other words, America was not the sole factor in the situation, although its bullion may well have provided a principal stimulus for European capital formation.[58] On the other hand, its role in opening up new commercial opportunities may have been more important, as this created a climate of success.[59]

The sixteenth century saw prices spiralling, a phenomenon which recent studies indicate may have been accelerated but not started by the influx of bullion from the New World.[60] But that was not how it

Amerindians pouring gold into the mouths of Spaniards to satisfy the visitors' greed. Benzoni, *Historia del Mondo Nuovo*, 1565.

appeared to some contemporary observers, particularly outside of Spain; de Saulx, for one, wrote in his journal in 1536 that prices had kept pace with the new supply of gold and silver by "doubling as often as ten times."[61] Bodin later made a somewhat similar observation: "Gold and silver have arrived in such abundance from the New World that everything is ten times more expensive than before."[62] The conquistadors themselves reported that as they accumulated loot, prices "grew dear." In Europe, such effects spread rapidly and extensively, whereas the influx of wealth was both slower and more restricted. France, although her income increased four and a half times during the sixteenth century, by 1587 was faced with the necessity of raising taxes, and considered she might begin by doubling those of Paris.[63] Meanwhile, she had for some time been resorting to more spectacular means for redressing her position. Robert de Berquen (fl.1615–61) hinted at this when he observed that the Spanish were fortunate to have rich enemies, in contrast to the "brave and generous" French nobles who fought the poor Germans. He added, "there is more honor in conquering brave [rich] people than miserable ones."[64]

Piracy and Diplomacy

In her pique at having been bypassed, and confronted with the alliance of papal authority and overwhelming Spanish might in the New World, France resorted to harassment. This policy enjoyed considerable success as French privateers became the scourge of the Spanish Main. The French were not alone in use of violence as an arm of diplomacy. The

English and the Dutch contributed some spectacular personalities and episodes to this extraordinary development in international relations. This period was marked by colorful incidents, such as Jean Florin's capture of the richer of the two ships whose cargo included Moctezuma's treasures sent over by Cortés from Mexico in 1523. The Mexican ruler's treasure had been selected by Cortés for the Spanish emperor not only for its intrinsic value but also with the eye of a connoisseur; its value was placed by Martire at 150,000 ducats.[65] But François I was enamored with the arts of Italy, for which he was establishing a showcase at Fontainebleau; he had no place to house the arts of the New World. Besides, he was perennially short of money in his expensive pursuit of his country's aggrandizement. And so Moctezuma's golden treasure was melted with the rest of the loot into bullion. The total loss to Spain has been estimated at 800,000 ducats,[66] which does not take into account the loss to the art world.

Privateering and outright piracy led to an escalating series of armed encounters that by the middle of the century had developed into open warfare between the fishing fleets of the Grand Banks.[67] A Spanish

Conquistadors using two Amerindian dugout canoes to transport their horses. It would be difficult to overestimate the value of horses to the Spaniards in their New World conquests, particularly in Central and South America where there were no native animals of that size. José Amador de los Rios, 1851–55, after Oviedo.

attempt to destroy the French fishing fleet very nearly succeeded in 1554–55.[68] As Europe relied heavily upon Newfoundland cod for food, the situation called for regulation. It was complicated by economic difficulties felt throughout Europe, but particularly in Spain, which had been hit by a series of crises: the influx of New World gold and silver was contributing to conditions that Old World economies were not equipped to handle.

Thus, for a variety of reasons, Henry II of France and Philip II of Spain were forced to the negotiating table in 1559. In spite of the fact that the French had managed to isolate Spain in the New World by means of a treaty of neutrality with Portugal signed at Lyon on 14 July 1536, they were again unsuccessful in obtaining Spanish recognition of their right to go to the New World.[69] But the treaty that was hammered out, that of Cateau-Cambrésis, restored peace for a time. The Spanish and French

Cartouche of an eighteenth-century map of the British and French dominions in North America. The prayerful attitudes of the Amerindians indicate they have been Christianized, and have adopted European mannerisms. John Mitchell, 1755. National Map Collection, C-98062 Public Archives Canada.

monarchs apparently came to a verbal agreement during the negotiations, to the effect that never again would violence in the New World be considered a cause of war in the Old; also, that European treaties would not be automatically applicable in the Americas.[70] The monarchs, in trying to ensure peace in the Old World by divorcing it from the New, in effect left the latter in a perpetual state of war. This situation endured for almost two centuries.

France had to wait until 1598 for even a partial recognition by Spain of her New World claims, a reluctant move that had received its initial impetus from the defeat of the Spanish Armada in 1588. In the Treaty of Vervins, Philip II and Henry IV agreed upon a *ligne d'amitié* (line of friendship) drawn north of the Canaries, which removed the threat of Spanish molestation from France's activities in the north. This was the first of several such lines that progressively restricted the areas of activity for piracy.

The settlement of Vervins was especially important to the French Atlantic port cities with large numbers of Huguenots. These enterprising people, besides being deeply involved in imperial and commercial rivalries, had risked being persecuted for heresy whenever they had ventured into the New World.[71] The mercantile cities in Normandy and Brittany were the principal agents for French transatlantic initiative, and so Huguenot stakes were high.

Although the western monarch fought between themselves over the wealth of the New World, they were united in their belief that their divine mandates to convert the heathen included the right to make grants of New World territory to their own subjects. As they saw it, they also had the right to claim vast stretches of territory that in the European sense were not occupied at all, but were "ranged" rather than settled by their nomadic inhabitants.[72] According to the Renaissance view, God had intended land to be farmed; and so the divine mandate was extended to include the right to take over such territories in order to realize God's will. The theory was eventually given its classic formulation by Emerich de Vattel (1714–67) in *Le Droit des gens* (1758). Bolstered by such reasoning, western monarchs quickly began to make huge grants of New World lands, which were then used by the grantees to establish "legal" claims for colonization. When boundaries overlapped or grants conflicted, as inevitably happened, the ensuing disputes and hostilities were always between the rival claimants and never took into consideration the Amerindians whose territory was being disputed. When two New England Amerindians, Bombazeen and Esumuit, insisted that their lands were inalienable, the English regarded this as "insolent" and observed that "nobody doubts but that the French missionaries prompt 'em to."[73] That incident indicates not only growing restiveness of Amerindians at European infringements on their lands, but also French exploitation of that reaction as a weapon against the English.

It was very early realized that land grants were not effective unless they were reinforced with permanent settlement. France's quasi-permanent fishing establishments along the Atlantic Coast were not considered satisfactory for securing her claims, any more than were seasonal trading posts such as the one at Tadoussac. Neither the fishing nor the fur-trading interests were concerned with settlement; on the contrary, it was much simpler and more profitable to come to the New World for the appropriate season and to return home as soon as possible. This was particularly true for the fur trade, for which settlement was inimical. But political considerations caused François I to insist that forts, houses, and churches be built, the visible and permanent signs of France in America. In the words of Le Jeune, writing from Canada in 1635, "if this country is peopled by the French, it will be firmly attached to the Crown, and the Foreigners will come no more to trouble it."[74]

CHAPTER 7

Ephemeral Settlements and Unknown Hazards

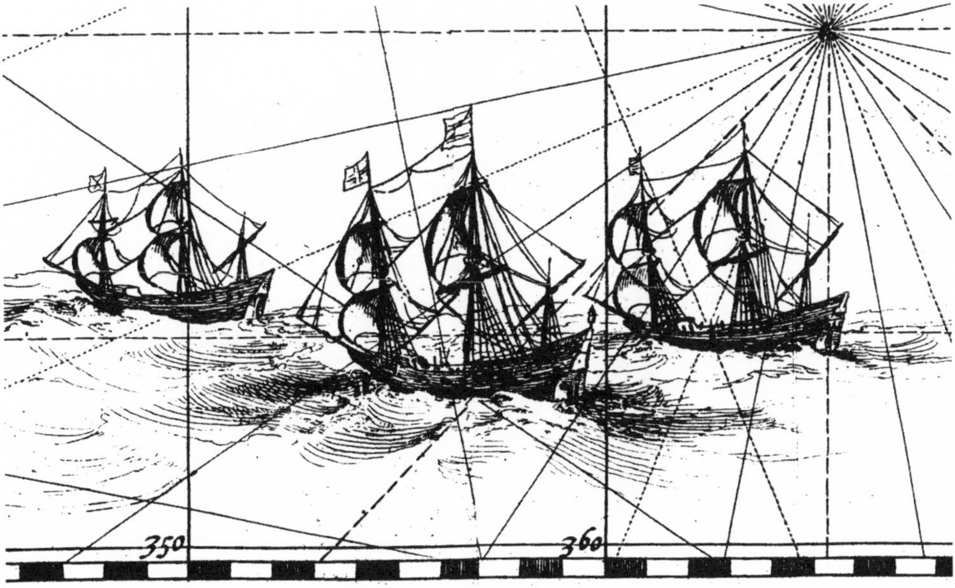

Ships, from *Tabula Nautica* [Hessel Gerritsz], 1612.

TRADING AND FISHING expeditions could be mounted with comparative ease, but actually living in the New World presented more complex problems. This was particularly true for the north, the region that first suggested itself for French settlement because of French commercial activities in the area, as well as because northern rigors had not encouraged the colonial attentions of either the Spanish or the Portugese, who in any event were fully occupied elsewhere. According to the theory of the day, the St. Lawrence Valley, being at the same latitude as La Rochelle, should have had the same climate. But the logic of that reasoning was not borne out by the facts. Something must be responsible, and so the forests were blamed.[1] The theory was that the forests held the cold; once the land was cleared and brought under cultivation, the climate would then become like that of France.[2] This concept of the forest as enemy prevailed throughout the period of the French presence in America, and extended long afterward. The wilderness, far from being regarded as either beautiful or desirable, was habitually described with the aid of such adjectives as "affreux," "hideux," "rude," and "desert." Incidentally, Europeans did not find an "untouched wilderness" as the cliché would have it; the forest had long been occupied and modified by various Amerindian peoples. The degree of modification, however, did vary with the location and intensity of settlement. The clearings left behind by early agriculturalists were a boon to such settlements as Quebec and Montreal, in providing the colonists with a base from which to attack the forest.

In contrast to such hostility to the forest, good agricultural potentialities were seen for the land itself. Thevet described it as "very temporate and fertile, like those of Gascony, suitable to produce all sorts of grains."[3] Even fur traders saw benefits: "As for the countryside, never have I seen anything so beautiful, so good and so fertile," observed one of them by the name of Bertrand.[4] Such sentiments were repeated by Champlain as well as Nicolas Denys and others.[5] The health and vigor of the Amerindians were also thought to be due at least partly to the climate, which was persistently described as "healthful." Once the French were established and flourishing along the St. Lawrence, their good health in turn was ascribed to the same cause.[6]

But hazards were also perceived. For one thing, the climate had been cited as a factor in the beardlessness of Amerindians.[7] More seriously, what effect would it have on the color of colonists after a few years? What about their children? According to the beliefs of the day, the *olivâtre* tone of the aborigines was due to the climate.[8] While olivâtre was not as extreme as black, which denoted moral depravity,[9] it was still a long way from white, which was considered the most pleasing color to

God.[10] Would European settlers eventually turn the color of Amerindians? Palma Cayet had written that the whiter the man, the darker he would become after living a few years in Barbarie.[11] He illustrated this with the example of Dom Christophe, eldest son of King Dom Antoine, who after three years in Morocco had become so dark that his old friends did not recognize him upon his return. Cayet did not suggest that the tan would disappear with time. Ronsard alluded to this problem in "Les Isles fortunées":

> De ne vouloir en France revenir
> Jusques à tant qu'on voie devenir
> Le More blanc, & le François encore
> Se basanant prendre le teint d'un More.[12]

There seems to have been comparatively little speculation as to why Amerindians and Negroes brought to Europe did not turn white.[13] As white was believed to be superior to black or any of the shades in between, Amerindians or Negroes transplanted to Europe could hardly be expected to lighten. The attitude implied was a corollary to the belief that transplanted cultures tended to deteriorate. From this was to develop the later conviction that a Frenchman or Spaniard or Englishman or indeed any European born and raised in Europe was superior to one born and raised in the colonies.

So firmly attached were Europeans to the theory that skin color was the result of climate that they had difficulty in accepting what they saw in the New World. The climate for vast areas of these lands was very similar to that of Europe. Why were not the inhabitants white? Perhaps their nakedness had something to do with it. Vespucci wrote, "I believe that if they went clothed they would be as white as we."[14] This was also the impression of Cartier, who expressed himself in similar words.[15] From the north, there were persistent reports of white Amerindians.[16] More subtle minds tried to find evidence that the further north, the lighter were Amerindians.[17] When that turned out not to be the case, they theorized that perhaps the cold, because of its intensity, could turn complexions brown as did the heat of the sun further south.[18]

Another way of indicating that Amerindians were not really colored was to refer to them as "quelque peu basané" (somewhat tanned). The term "basané" had strong connotations of rusticity and lack of sophistication, and so in effect equated Amerindians with the European peasantry. A similar identification was frequently made in regard to intelligence. Such attitudes probably account at least partly for the persistence of reports that Amerindians were born white and turned olivâtre

Amerindians were sometimes shown looking more like Africans. Ogilby, *America*, 1671, from Albertus Montanus. National Map Collection, C-118522 Public Archives Canada.

through exposure to the sun and the use of oils and paints. D'Avity, for example, noted that Amerindians were olive-hued or bronze, because "they rub themselves with oil against flies, and besides they sleep on the ground, and are exposed to heat and wind."[19] On another occasion he referred to their color being the same as that of Orientals.[20] Jesuit Julien Perrault wrote from Cape Breton Island in 1634–35: "Their skin is naturally white, for the little children show it thus; but the heat of the Sun, and the rubbing with Seal oil and Moose fat make them very swarthy, the more so as they grow older."[21] This belief in the whiteness of Amerindians at birth was shared by such diverse figures as Marie de l'Incarnation[22] and Claude, who persuaded an Amerindian father not to oil his baby, so that it would be left to its natural whiteness.[23] The worthy Capuchin did not report on the results of his experiment, but later another missionary noted rather testily, "the falsity of this proposition is proved by the fact that the savage children we have living with us have never been painted, nevertheless they are as bronzed as the others."[24] Other voices of dissent included those of Lahontan and the Jesuit Bernabé Cobo; the latter wrote in 1653 that color was part of the nature of man and was not caused by climate.[25] Such comments supported the opinion that color could not be changed by the application of paints and oils. But myths were hard to kill. And so reports as to the essential whiteness of Amerindians continued, reinforced by the observation that

Europeans who lived in the New World did not change color, not even after several generations. Therefore, if climate was not the cause of Amerindians' color, then it must lie in their customs and practices.[26]

In other respects also, Amerindians were viewed as being similar to Europeans. According to Antoine Du Perier, they resembled the French in height and facial features more than any other foreigners he had seen.[27] John Guy, governor of the first English colony in Newfoundland (1610–14), said of the natives of the island that their hair was brown and yellow as well as black, an observation which apparently supports the theory that Vikings became assimilated with the Inuit after the dissolution of the Greenland settlements during the fifteenth century. Or else it could be that men from the fishing fleets occasionally defected to the aborigines.[28]

The idea of the basic whiteness of Amerindians was to give impetus to the seventeenth-century French drive to evangelize and to intermarry with them. Whereas in New France this goal seemed to hold some prospect of realization,[29] in other parts of the New World it did not appear so promising. The Capuchin Yves reported from Brazil in 1613–14 that the Tupinambá had suggested such an alliance with the French. Yves's

The bronze skin color of Amerindians was attributed to their use of paints and oils. C-30039 Public Archives Canada.

words on this subject were almost exactly those of Champlain, but his conclusion was quite different: "we will not see such things."[30] While the policy of creating one race was doomed to failure in New France as elsewhere–Amerindians and French were still distinct entities at the end of the French regime in 1760–still there was enough intermixing for a writer in a South Carolina newspaper in 1742 to refer to the French as "swarthy brethren" of Amerindians.[31] Shortly afterward, in 1753, Abbé Maillard noted that intermixing had already proceeded so far that in his opinion in fifty years it would be impossible to distinguish Amerindian from French in Acadia.[32]

If the policy of creating one race had worked better, the French might have avoided the difficulties of recruiting colonists. The question of whom to send over to settle in the New World was not a simple one for France. As a land power fast developing to the point where she would be able to challenge successfully the predominance of Spain in Europe, she felt that she needed her population at home. Although long since demographically recovered, she still remembered the effects of the Black Death, which had wrought such devastation in Europe through the Middle Ages, particularly in 1348–50 when close to half the people had been carried off. The threat of further loss due to pestilence, famine, and war always lurked close. It was generally believed that one way of measuring a nation's wealth was by the size of its population, and that sending large bodies of people out to the colonies could only result in depopulation at home. This was cited as a reason for Spain's waning power during the second half of the seventeenth century.[33]

But to challenge Spain overseas, France needed more permanent colonists than was provided by her merchants and traders on the one hand and her privateers, flibustiers, and buccaneers on the other. Her first reaction was to turn to those elements of her population that were not far removed from pirates, those who had run afoul of the law. La Popelinière became the spokesman for this policy, basing his arguments on the belief that the negative aspects of cultural diffusion on emigrating Europeans could be neutralized, at least to some extent, by sending unruly elements out to the colonies. According to this line of reasoning, Spain had been particularly fortunate in finding new worlds to conquer just at the time when she had driven out the Moors; the men who had performed this feat were not inclined to settle down to sedentary tasks after such exciting adventures, and could well have caused trouble at home if they had not found new diversions across the Atlantic.[34] The idea had earlier been discussed by Bodin, who had used ancient Rome as an example of the successful use of colonization to siphon off undesirables.[35] Neither Bodin nor La Popelinière seemed to have been aware of the consequences of such a policy in Peru, where conquistadors had split into factions and had come close to revolting against Charles V. Michel de l'Hospital (1505–73), who was later to become Chancellor of France, had drily observed that the colonial governors were more concerned with fighting each other than with serving the emperor. On top of everything else, their tyrannies were ruining the Amerindians.[36] Cosmographer Thévenot observed that very often the ministers of the king were the persecutors of the Amerindians as they profited "from that which they took from the Indians." Such officials, he said, found it more convenient to pass the Amerindians off as rebels and criminals than to pay attention to their complaints.[37]

Beaver hunting in Canada, as illustrated in *Il Gazzettiere Americano*, 1763.

Apparently oblivious to such considerations, La Popelinière theorized that perhaps France could resolve its civil wars of the last half of the sixteenth century by undertaking a great colonial enterprise.[38] He seemed to believe that the scope of such an enterprise would attract unruly nobility as well as rogues from among the masses. In spite of such considerations, to be named leader of a colonizing expedition was considered to be an honor, and competition for such posts was keen. A powerful inducement, of course, was the prospect of wealth, particularly for the leaders and the "better sort." Even for the rank and file there was the possibility of improving one's lot. That this actually happened was illustrated by Lorenzo, one of St. Teresa of Avila's seven brothers who made the crossing. He returned as Don Lorenzo, wealthy enough to become a man of property in Avila.[39] Success stories were frequent enough to prevail over those who doubted the wisdom of such ventures. They also won over those, such as Montaigne, who were opposed to colonization in principle. The most resistance was found among the lower echelons of society.[40] This could be a reflection of a basic conservatism, of an unwillingness to risk unknown dangers when the known ones were difficult enough to deal with. Be that as it may, early French colonizing ventures found rank and file the hardest to recruit, particularly for a northern country such as Canada. The Cartier-Roberval expedition filled its complement by conscripting vagabonds and convicts.

Flotte du Canada

During much of the sixteenth century, French ships going to the New World were referred to collectively as the *flotte du Canada.* A look at shipboard life throws a sidelight on the European culture of the period, as well as providing a contrast to that of Amerindians. Subsistence set the pattern for both.

By early in the century, rations on French ships were more or less standardized. For a four-month voyage, these were calculated at the rate of one and a half pounds of biscuit per man per day (the biscuit of Dieppe being considered the best as it was white and made of fine flour. It was thought so nourishing that some crews were given only three pounds for four days per man.)[41] "Lard," which was salt pork, was calculated at forty pounds per man; cod, at fifty fish per man; as many "boisseaux" of peas as there were men, and cider at the rate of a "pot" per head per day. Water as a drink was avoided as much as possible, as it was believed that combined with the shipboard diet of salted foods it could cause a bloody flux. Other recommended provisions included olive oil, butter, mustard, vinegar, wine, and *eau-de-vie* (brandy).[42] A well-provisioned ship was expected to provide its crew salt pork for dinner and supper three or four times a week, and cod or herring on the other days at the rate of two cod for eight men or two herrings per man. Generally wine was served once a week, on Sunday. On longer voyages, eau-de-vie was recommended to be served once or twice a day, but particularly in the morning.[43] Colonists were advised to provision themselves for the voyage with the strongest eau-de-vie and the best wine from the Canaries, taking care that it be stored in well-stoppered bottles made of tin. These bottles were to be kept in a case, under lock and key, and the liquor used with the greatest of care in times of illness and other necessities.[44] Such advice relects not only the distrust that sometimes existed between passengers, but also between passengers and crew. Indeed, colonists sailing with Villegaignon in the mid-sixteenth century were pillaged by the crew.[45]

For women who were making the voyage, it was recommended that each be supplied with twenty bottles of wine, four pots of the strongest vinegar, a bottle of "cinnamon water," and, among other items, perfumes to distract from the pervading odor of tar.[46]

Sailors' table manners were not distinguished for their niceties. According to Diéreville, "each man puts his hands into the dish without having washed them, although there was no lack of water, saying as he did so, that they were Man's most natural forks." Diéreville then burst into poetry:

> Quelle malpropreté de Linge & de Vaiselle
> Jamais on n'écouroit les plats
> Qu'on entouroit d'un torchon gras,
> Pour en empécher la culbutte;
> Le plaisir que j'avois, c'etoit de voir dix bras,
> Ne pouvoir sur la table en garantir la chûte,
> Et porter sous la dent ce qu'ils prenoient à bas.[47]

It will be remembered that the manner of eating of Amerindians was listed by some authors as indicating their barbarity.[48]

The death rate on these voyages was high. On a good trip, only a fifth of those on board died. Though poor living conditions and bad diet were largely responsible for this, self-indulgence was also cited as a cause: "It is certain that each year more than fifty persons die on these voyages because of their excessive use of the brandy they brought for their refreshment." Antoine Le Febvre de La Barre, who was later to become an ill-fated governor-general of New France (1682–85), but who in 1664 had planted France's successful colony in Guiana, added that three or four sessions of debauchery with eau-de-vie were enough to put a person into the grave. That, of course, raises questions as to the quality of the liquor. Later he seemed to forget his strictures against eau-de-vie when he prescribed that it should be provided, along with wine, only for "gentlemen" and not for "persons."[49]

As for the perils of the sea, they lost nothing in the retelling.[50] Sometimes there was not much to choose between the perils of nature and those of man. Diéreville told about sailors on his ship deciding to flog a boy in order to get a favorable wind, a customary remedy for such a situation. In this case, the lad selected had stolen from one of the seamen, so he was flogged more severely than would otherwise have been the case. The boy's part in the ritual was to scream, "Northeast, good wind for the Ship!" This the unfortunate boy did. Diéreville reported that the desired wind sprang up, although he did not believe it was due to the flogging.[51]

By early in the seventeenth century, colonists were being advised that they should also provide beforehand for at least their first few months in the new land; the better prepared they were, the fewer the inconveniences they would suffer.[52] Yves urged that they bring gifts and trade goods as well. Although he was speaking specifically of Brazil, this advice would have applied also to North America. The gifts were for gaining good will; and the trade goods for purchasing slaves and useful items.[53] In his list of merchandise that Amerindians would find acceptable, he included swords and guns, which he qualified by saying that the swords be old and the arquebuses "of little cost."[54] Gifts were strongly recom-

French settlers arriving in Canada, 1541. The figure at right indicating the way is believed to represent Cartier. Detail sketch from the Vallard world map, 1547. National Map Collection, C-61596 Public Archives Canada.

Some of the most common of European first impressions of the New World are illustrated in this engraving in Theodor de Bry, ed., *America*, part 13 (1634), after Jacques Le Moyne de Morgues. These include: Amerindians as skilled canoeists and hunters in lands teeming with game; signal bonfires lit by Amerindians along the coast, often the first sight that greeted Europeans; and Amerindians' bounteous crops, which were encouraged by the use of fish as fertilizer. The result of all this abundance was plenty of leisure, symbolized by the couple in the center foreground.

mended to put Amerindians in good humor and to encourage their hospitality.

Among the items that colonists should bring over for their own use, said Yves, was clothing suitable for the country in which they would be settling. Besides a quantity of laundry soap, they would need plenty of shoes as there would be none available in the new land except for what had been brought over from France. That fact would be reflected in the price, twelve times higher than back home. Also needed were linens, a good mattress and, for those who wished to live cleanly in the French manner, a tin vessel for personal necessities, particularly in times of sickness.[55] Colonists would do well to take along their own supply of sugar and good spices, well placed in a white iron box to avoid ants, reported to have an "incredible" taste for sweets. Above all, colonists should bring along as much of their accustomed food as they possibly could to provide a cushion against too sudden an introduction to a strange diet. The most frequently heard complaint of Frenchmen in the New World was the lack of bread and wine and "ordinary" foods that made life pleasant in Europe.[56] One official did not think that a year was too long to plan for in this regard. He added that colonists should be careful to bring necessities, not luxuries, and should be prepared to establish themselves in modest dwellings at first, as expenses were high, and it would not pay to be overly ambitious at the beginning.[57]

Most important of all, colonists should be mentally and spiritually prepared before embarking. Whatever happened, they should maintain a good face, never quarrelling with the sailors "because you will gain nothing from it." Colonists should be particularly careful on disembarking, as the sailors were likely to take whatever they could lay their hands on if it were not watched.[58]

That was also the advice of La Barre, who wrote that the prime requisite for colonists was health, particularly where the stomach was concerned. Almost equally important was the willingness to work: peasants, people accustomed to labor and to eating country food, were well-suited to the task.[59] Settlers should have been briefed upon embarkation so as not to have come over with false expectations. In this La Barre was benefiting from lessons learned from previous colonization attempts, particularly those of Villegaignon and Ribault-Laudonnière. He was also reflecting the comments of Samuel de Champlain (c.1570–1635), who had finally succeeded in establishing France permanently in the New World with the founding of Quebec in 1608. Champlain had pointed to insufficient preparation as the main obstacle to colonization—or, as he put it, lack of "judgement and reason." After criticizing Ribault and Laudonnière for not sufficiently provisioning their expeditions, he remarked that this was due to the unrealistic expectation that these new lands were so rich they would produce without cultivation. Besides, added Champlain, "such voyages are undertaken improperly without practice or experience." Before attempting to settle a distant land, certain individuals should live there at least a year "to learn the quality of the country." Unfortunately, such precautions were almost never taken.[60]

One point that had been established very early was that the quality of the colonists had much to do with the success or failure of a venture. Those early notions of ensuring peace at home by shipping dissidents overseas had not worked, because, instead of setting about the hard tasks of planting settlements, such dissidents only became embroiled in quarrels and fights and killed each other off. Even worse, they occupied themselves with stealing what they needed for subsistence from Amerindian gardens and vegetable plots, and then added insult to injury by trading defective merchandise. Some had become rich by such means, but colonization as a whole had suffered. La Barre wrote with feeling when he said that young people who had passed their lives in libertinage in the cities were nothing but pests in the colonies.[61]

Thus was tempered La Popelinière's optimistic vision of creating a New France overseas with those who did not meet the mother country's requirements at home. But even that historian had had his doubts when he had noted the "insatiable desire to enrich themselves" with which Europeans sallied forth to the New World. He admitted sadly that many had hazarded their lives, their goods, their honor, and their consciences for no other purpose than to disturb the peace of the aborigines who asked nothing more than to be allowed to live out their days on the bounty of nature. However, he philosophized, in behaving thus Europeans were only following the most ancient of all laws, by which the strong took from the weak. Even the gods follow this law of nature, not to mention the beasts.[62] The trouble with that line of argument was that it put Europeans into the role of behaving like "brutes"–in other words, like savages.

Politically, the opening up of the New World had provided absolute monarchs with a splendid opportunity for aggrandizement. An overseas empire had become a means by which they could enlarge their power and prestige in Europe. However, while the establishment of such empires undoubtedly contributed to the achievement of such goals, they also created new situations that strained the very ideologies upon which the monarchies were based. The universality of the hierarchically ordered society, which in Medieval and Renaissance Europe had seemed to be beyond question, did not appear so certain in the New World. The Atlantic crossing and unfamiliar New World conditions caused a shift in the attitudes that Europeans brought with them. This was manifested as a change in expectations: soon it became a maxim that every Spaniard who crossed the ocean became a caballero, or every Frenchman a seigneur, no matter how humble his condition had been originally. But the process did not work in reverse. Amerindians who came to Europe usually just became homesick and wanted to return home as quickly as they could, if they lived long enough. Europeans were more successful in overriding aboriginal rights than they were in including New World man within a Christian social framework, either as a visitor in the Old World or as a citizen within the new Europes being established in the Americas.

Seasonal Settlements

In the meantime, as a result of the activities of the fishing fleets, European settlements had spontaneously sprung up along the Atlantic coast from a very early date. These settlements were not permanent, largely disappearing during off-seasons, but some were substantial enough to be listed as "towns" by early cosmographers. Barent Langenes, for instance, listed Ste-Marie, Cobo, Mazzo, and Brest as the principal towns of "Terra de Labrador."[63] Of these towns, the largest seems to have been Brest, sometimes referred to as a "metropole."[64] Even after the establishment of a permanent colony, Brest was listed as the principal town of Canada, as distinguished from New France, whose principal city was Quebec.[65] In 1705, the French merchant Augustin le Gardeur de Courtemanche, setting himself up Phélypeaux Bay (known today as Bradore Bay,) found traces of houses, roofs, stoves for melting oil from seals (and probably whales as well), and "other similar things."[66] According to the Amerindians, this had been a Spanish establishment that had been dispersed by the Inuit.[67] The probability of at least a summer settlement there known by the French name of Brest is attested to by seventeenth-century maps. The name was sometimes accompanied by an illustration suggesting a town, probably inspired by reports that the French had a fort there and a population of one thousand.[68]

Even more elusive than the existence or identity of such a town is the tradition that a Baron de Leri had attempted a settlement on Sable Island in 1518. The documentary evidence for this stems from Lescarbot.[69] According to Flemish scholar and geographer Johannes de Laet (d.1649), the French had been attracted by the advantages of the spot, but it turned out to be too sandy for agriculture and further, had an insufficient water supply. For these reasons they abandoned it, leaving behind their pigs and cattle.[70] Another version has it that de Leri was forced to land his livestock on Sable Island because he had run out of water and food at sea.[71] It could also be that the presence of livestock on the island was owing to the frequent shipwrecks that had occurred there, and had no particular connection at all with colonization on the island. Both Champlain and Sir Humphrey Gilbert referred to the livestock as being of Portuguese origin, and Champlain implied that it had been there since before 1553. Later, Champlain said that the animals were from the wreck of a Spanish ship on the way to colonize Cape Breton.[72] A Portuguese map of about 1565 identified Sable Island as João Esteves' Island.[73] The presence of the livestock was a boon to the fifty convict-colonists left there by Troilus de la Roche de Mesgouez (1540?–1606) in 1598 to maintain surveillance over the route of the fishermen and fur traders so as to protect his monopoly.[74] When the supply ship failed to bring adequate provisions for the settlement, eleven of the stranded men were able to survive by slaughtering livestock until they were rescued in 1603.

The Portuguese rather than the French were the first to attempt permanent settlement in Canada. There is considerable uncertainty as to

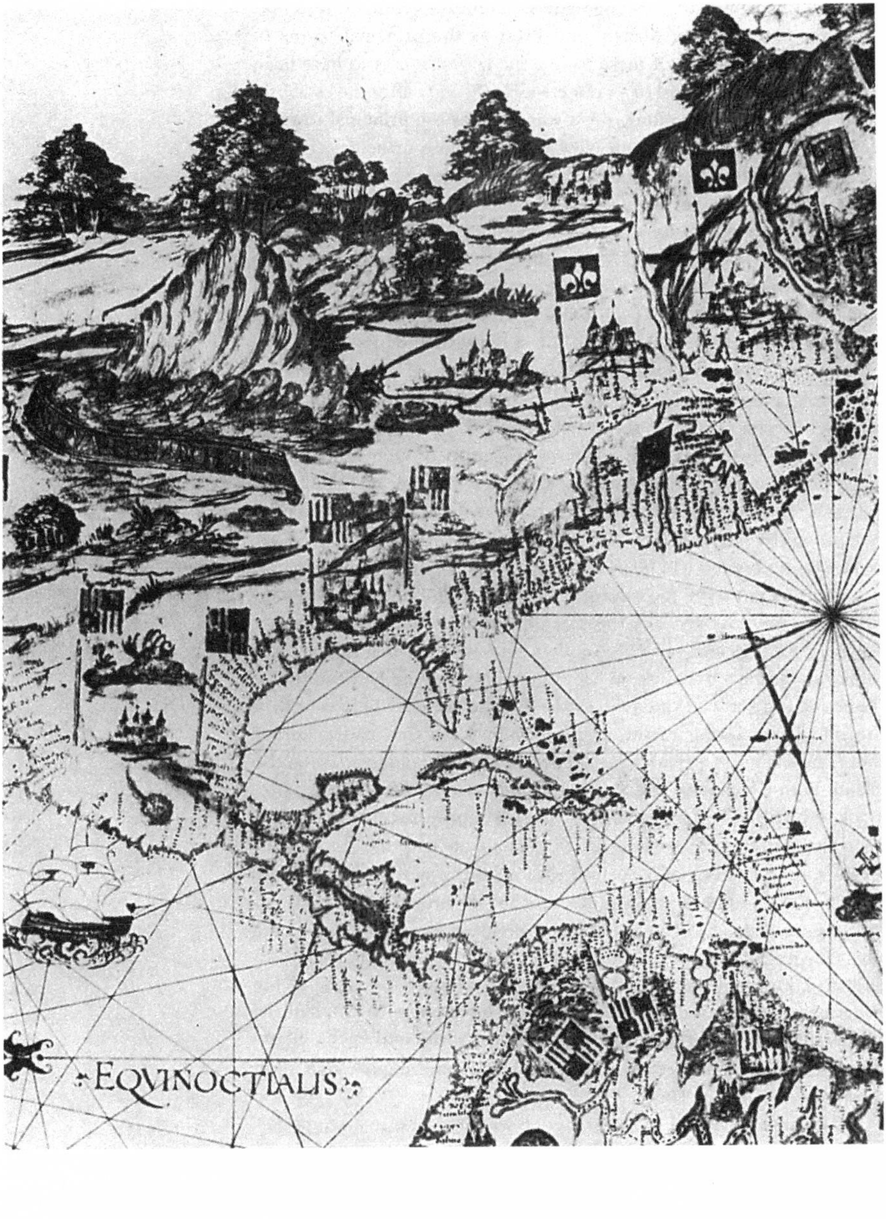
EQVINOCTIALIS

the exact location: Cape Breton or Prince Edward Island appear to be most likely, but no archeological evidence has been found. According to documentary evidence, João Fagundes attempted colonization somewhere in the general region between 1521 and 1525; there might have been a second attempt about 1553.[75] Fagundes may have been trying to capitalize on a grant of land he had received. Francisco da Sousa, writing in 1570, reported:

> the natives are submissive and the soil very fertile and good. . . . This is at Cape Breton, at the beginning of the coast that turns north in a beautiful bay, where there are many [native] people and goods of much value and many nuts, chestnuts, grapes and other fruits, whereby it is clear the soil is rich. And in this company went also some families from the Azores Islands, whom they took on board on their way out, as is well known.[76]

The Fagundes colonists established a works to make black and white soap[77] and modelled their colony on settlements of the Azores, which also depended upon agriculture and fishing. Basque fishermen who stopped by reported that the settlers were in need of a priest.[78] After the colonists lost their ships, contact between them and their mother country was broken. If available information is to be relied upon, such an establishment would have been in Micmac territory; however, the Micmac have no tradition of such.[79] Somewhat tenuous evidence is provided by a Portuguese map of about 1576, which illustrates Labrador by representing two figures of peasants, each prodding oxen-pulled ploughs.[80] Alfonce apparently believed a settlement had existed there because he reported that it had been destroyed by the natives.[81] Champlain said that it had been abandoned after one winter because of the rigors of the climate.[82]

Whatever the immediate reasons for the disappearance of the colony, Portugal in any case was not more than formally interested in asserting claims to those northern regions, occupied as she was in Brazil and the Orient. Neither was Spain, despite her stronger legal position, and her profitable whale oil industry in the Straits of Belle Isle. France was left to accept the challenge of colonizing the North, an undertaking in which she would rediscover in a new context what she had already learned in the dyewood trade in Brazil–the fundamental importance of cooperation and alliance with Amerindians.

Detail of map by Antonio Pereira, c.1545, shows two towns flying the French fleur-de-lis, one on the north shore of the Gulf of St. Lawrence, the other in the interior, perhaps Charlesbourg-Royal. The flag of Castile and Aragon indicates territories claimed by Spain.

CHAPTER 8

The French on the St. Lawrence

Beaver building a dam (left) and being hunted (right). From Chatelain's "Carte tres curieuse de la Mer du Sud," *Atlas Historique* VI, 1719. National Map Collection, C-17159 Public Archives Canada.

FRANCE'S FIRST reaction to Spain's and Portugal's moves to keep the New World for themselves had been to develop commercial enterprises in the restricted regions. France lost no time in establishing relations with the Tupinambá of Brazil in order to exploit coastal stands of brazilwood.[1] There were also the North Atlantic fisheries off the coast of Newfoundland and in the Gulf of St. Lawrence; from these developments the French became acquainted with coastal Amerindians and were able to verify what Corte-Real had observed in 1501, the potential for trade in furs. The attempt of the Portuguese to secure their northern claims by means of permanent settlement spurred François I to defy openly the papal division of the New World. In 1524, he sent an official expedition to explore the North Atlantic coast to determine commercial potentialities as well as those for colonization.

France's first official explorer in North America, Giovanni da Verrazzano, probed the coast from the Carolinas to Cape Breton.[2] He named this northern territory "New France," an appellation that was widely accepted, despite earlier Portuguese, Spanish, and British voyages to the region. None of them had matched Verrazzano's for thoroughness and scope.

In his report to François I, the explorer confirmed the region's wealth. He also told of the amazement of the natives on seeing Europeans:

> We saw many people who came to the edge of the sea and who fled on seeing us approach. Sometimes they stopped and turned to look at us with great astonishment. Reassured by signs, some of them approached the sea, displaying great joy at the sight of us, marvelling at our clothes, at our faces and our whiteness. They showed us by signs the place where we could land our barque most easily and they offered us what they had to eat.[3]

Nowhere in his account is there a suggestion of the awed reactions that Columbus and Vespucci had reported. Neither did Verrazzano meet overt hostility, although he found the people to the north less than cordial.[4] Sometimes, however, Europeans had difficulty in ascertaining the intentions of the natives. Verrazzano reported an incident in which a young sailor daringly began to swim from the ship to a group of people on the shore. As he drew close he lost his courage, threw some articles to the waiting natives, and began to swim back to the ship. But a large wave reversed his course and tossed him ashore. In his fear he cried out, and his bewildered hosts, apparently to reassure him, cried out also. They built a fire and stripped him in order to dry his clothes; the sailor was sure they were preparing to eat him. After he was warmed and dried

A seventeenth-century impression of the teeming bird life of eastern coasts. Du Creux, *Historiae Canadensis*, 1664. C-99222 Public Archives Canada.

he parted from the Amerindians on good terms and returned in a shallop that had been sent out by the ship.[5]

Verrazzano's account leaves an impression of a well-populated land; he was met by crowds of people whenever he ventured ashore.[6] As usual with early explorers, he depended upon Amerindians for supplies of fresh food; he found them generous, often expecting nothing in return. However, as he proceeded north, the people became more exacting. They were also less approachable:

> they came out on certain rocks at the shore where the surf was the strongest, and while we remained in our boat they sent out what they wanted to trade by means of a rope, continually shouting at us not to approach and demanding an immediate exchange. They would only accept knives, fishhooks and metal for cutting. They have no appreciation of amiability, and when we left, having nothing more to trade, they mocked us with shameful gestures such as would be used only by creatures lacking humanity and courtesy.[7]

Finally, Verrazzano reported, the people became "so barbarous that by no signs that ever we could make, we could have any kind of trafficke with them."[8] This supports the case for an established familiarity with Europeans in those areas, probably as a result of fishing activities.

Verrazzano found that all along the coast the Amerindians preferred the colors red and blue, being particularly fond of blue beads and other "baubles for ears and neck."[9] They also liked little bells, but displayed no desire at all for cloth of silk or gold; as for the explorer, his eye was caught by the embroidered skins worn by visiting chiefs, "skilfully worked like damask."[10] He wondered about the type of settlements the northerners lived in, and thought their dwellings would probably be of wood, but as far as he could judge many of these people slept out in the open air. Further south he witnessed the manner of taking down and putting up dwellings instantly. Unable to identify either temples or houses of prayer in their villages, he concluded that the inhabitants lived in complete liberty without religion.[11]

The land impressed Verrazzano, who compared it to the "wild wasteland of Scythia," adding that in his opinion, "it was not without some propperties of value, since all the hills showed signs of minerals."[12] Such speculations fed rumors of distant "Golden Kingdoms," similar to those of the Mexica, recently conquered by Cortés. This is suggested by the action of the French king who, finally in a position to follow up on Verrazzano's work, advanced 6,000 livres for Cartier "to discover certain islands and lands where they say are great quantities of gold and other rich things to be found."[13] Visions of great riches for France did not survive after Cartier's return with a load of fool's gold from his third voyage, an episode which confirmed growing doubts as to the existence of gold so far north.[14]

In 1534, however, the lure of gold was strong when Cartier made the first of three official voyages to Terra Nova, or, as it was popularly known, Canada.[15] That year he reconnoitered the coast, particularly the Gulf of St. Lawrence; on the second voyage (1535–36), he continued his explorations up the St. Lawrence River, getting as far as Hochelaga (today's Montreal). His third (1541–43) was to deliver colonists under Lieutenant-General Jean-François de La Rocque de Roberval (c.1500–1560). The 1534 voyage apparently was not Cartier's first to the New World; d'Avity and Biard said his first trip had been in 1524, and comments in Cartier's reports imply that he had already been to Brazil. He made several references to the corn of Canada as being similar to the millet of Brazil,[16] and wrote that the northern Amerindians "live with almost everything in common, much like the Brazilians."[17]

Not only did Cartier have an idea of what to expect, but the Amerindians did as well: instead of greeting the French captain in fear and wonder, they sought him out in order to trade. It has even been theorized that some had come to the shore expressly to meet European ships.[18] In any event, Cartier offered the natives knives and iron goods, and a red cap for their chief. They expressed their joy by singing and dancing and throwing sea water on their heads.

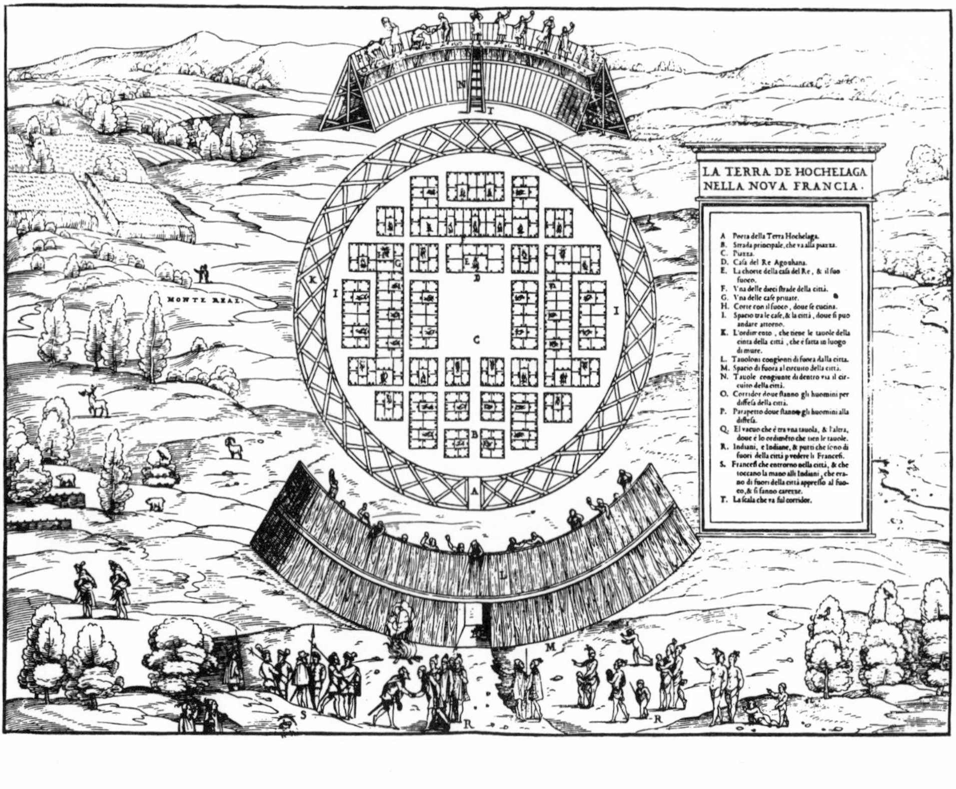

Hochelaga, as illustrated by Giacomo Gastaldi, in Ramusio's *Navigations et voyages*, 1556, showing cultivated fields of maize at upper left. Bibliothèque Nationale, Paris. p168

It is generally believed that the first group encountered by Cartier were Micmac. They welcomed him warmly, and convinced him of the sincerity of their friendship.[19] The second group he met were Iroquoians; Cartier noted that they spoke a different language from the first group, and had different customs. They were more reserved, and took the precaution of having their young women retire into the woods, at least at first.[20] These Iroquois could well have been from Stadacona (today's Quebec). Their lifestyle, based on hunting and fishing supplemented with agriculture, came somewhere in between that of the northern hunting Algonkians and that of the Huron or Five Nations. The Stadaconans went to live by the sea each summer, and so probably came into contact with Europeans at a very early date, perhaps almost as early as the Micmac. Their initial suspicions of Cartier had some justification, although not for the reasons they had anticipated. On the eve of his departure, Cartier erected a cross on Honguedo (Gaspé) to claim possession, following the established French practice. This immediately aroused Stadacona chief Donnacona, who apparently thought it was a ruse implying an attack. He came with armed men to ask Cartier if the French were trying to make themselves masters of the land.[21] According to his own testimony, Cartier replied that he intended the cross simply as a guidepost; that crosses were used as such is indicated by his later reference to a cross as a landmark at Lobster Bay on the north shore.[22]

However, cosmographer Thevet, who referred to Cartier as his "great and good friend,"[23] reported that the French told the Amerindians they wanted to help them against their enemies, for which purpose he proposed to establish a colony.[24] To the Iroquois, this would have meant offering an alliance, and accordingly, they brought food. Cartier's actions in kidnapping the two sons of Donnacona, Taignoagny and Domagaya, after such a commitment must have seemed the grossest treachery to the Stadaconans. One can but wonder if the two were as pleased as Cartier seemed to believe when the French dressed them in shirts and ribbons and put red caps on their heads and brass chains about their necks.[25] While Amerindians wandered about a great deal in their own lands, they were not at all interested in going to foreign places.[26]

The brothers were luckier than many of their fellows in similar circumstances. Surviving their stay in France, they returned with Cartier in 1535 to guide the French ships up the St. Lawrence. At the Saguenay, the party encountered four canoes of Stadaconans who, upon recognizing the French, displayed distrust and fear: obviously they remembered the events of the previous year. Later, near Stadacona, Cartier encountered a similar reaction. The Iroquois showed a tendency to flee, and at first did not recognize the two interpreters, probably because they would have been dressed and coiffed in the French manner. But when they realized who the interpreters were, the Stadaconans were transformed into welcoming hosts.

The rediscovered good will did not entirely dissipate the cloud of suspicion that hung between the French and the Stadaconans. This was manifested in the change of attitude of Taignoagny and Domagaya after their return. They no longer wanted to come aboard the French ships. It does not take a great effort of the imagination to appreciate what had happened. In France, the brothers had probably acted as they thought would best ensure their survival. In describing their homeland to the French, it is likely they embellished its attractions to the extent they thought necessary to assure their return.[27] They would have encouraged Cartier's desire to visit Stadacona and even Hochelaga with promises of guiding the French captain wherever he wanted to go along the St. Lawrence, even though they knew perfectly well that such an action would contravene Amerindian custom. According to that custom, the Stadaconans, as the first to encounter the French, would have acquired the exclusive right to trade with them, and to be middlemen between this new source of trade and the peoples of the interior.[28] The French, even though trading partners of the Stadaconans, required the latter's permission in order to cross their territory and penetrate its hinterlands. Domagaya and Taignoagny, back in Canada, could not implement the promises so easily made in France; the Stadaconans firmly opposed Cartier's desire to explore the river. If Cartier knew of the Amerindian trade convention, he showed no inclination to respect it, and he regarded as treachery his erstwhile guests' reluctance to honor their promise. When he finally sailed up the river to Hochelaga without benefit of guides, he was of course joyously welcomed by all whom he met. The upriver people were delighted at this bypassing of Stadaconan trading privilege, and did everything they could to encourage the French to return.

The French presence at Stadacona must have been profoundly disturbing to Chief Donnacona and the elders of the village. For although the French brought trade goods, they also brought an incomprehension of the Amerindian way of life, displaying little desire to tailor their behavior to its exigencies. For instance, the French went about fully armed even when the Stadaconans did not. When Donnacona objected, Cartier drily replied that such was the custom in France, as Domagaya and Taignoagny well knew.[29] Such an attitude on the part of the French is surprising, particularly as they already had colonization on their minds. In the south they had adapted to Amerindian ways, successfully facilitating Brazilian trade despite determined Portuguese opposition. Back on the St. Lawrence, there is no record as to whether Donnacona continued the discussion, pointing out that in Stadacona such French customs were not necessarily appropriate, and in this case certainly not diplomatic. The stories told by Domagaya and Taignoagny aroused curiosity about the artillery bristling on the French ships, and the Stadaconans asked Cartier to fire a cannon. The result, of course, was terror among the villagers, followed by a false rumor that two Amerindians had been killed in the episode.

It is revealing of the Stadaconan attitude that Cartier and his men were not invited upon their arrival to visit the village, which was back from the river by about half a league.[30] In fact, such an invitation was not forthcoming until Cartier's return from Hochelaga; and then it was carried out with a formality and a restraint that contrasted sharply with Cartier's reception by the Hochelagans.[31] Cartier made his call at Stadacona accompanied by an armed escort of fifty men "under strict orders."[32]

In the meantime, the Stadaconans displayed a spirit of compromise in their efforts to accommodate their difficult new allies. In a presentation designed to dissuade Cartier from going to Hochelaga, they offered him a girl, the daughter of Donnacona's sister, and two small boys, of whom one was Taignoagny's brother. The gravity of this gesture is evident, considering the Amerindians' great attachment to their children. Later, when the girl ran away, Donnacona, after some prodding from the French, brought her back, underlining the importance of his gift. The exchange of children was one of the traditional means by which Iroquoians, as well as other Amerindians, cemented the alliances.[33] Cartier accepted the children only on the understanding that it did not commit him to give up his Hochelaga visit. The Stadaconans persisted in making the gesture in the face of this position; they were doing everything they could to win the French to their side. In a manner characteristic of Amerindians generally, the Stadaconans tried to win over angry spirits (or difficult humans) with gifts.

The efforts of the Stadaconans to reach an accord with the French did not stop. They offered to permit Taignoagny and Domagaya to guide Cartier to Hochelaga if the French would leave a hostage at Stadacona. But Cartier was not inclined to negotiate; he refused to leave a hostage, ignored other Stadaconan attempts to dissuade him from his project, and went up the St. Lawrence without guides. His growing conviction that the Stadaconans were unreliable, to say the least, was reinforced by warnings he received from the chief of Achelacy (Hochelay, today's Portneuf) against Donnacona and his two sons.[34]

The implication of those warnings, that there was rivalry between the Stadaconans and the people of Achelacy and Hochelaga, was corro-

Cartier being greeted by Hochelagans. Detail of Gastaldi drawing, 1556.

Laurentian Iroquois carrying French as a gesture of hospitality. Detail of Gastaldi drawing, 1556.

borated by Cartier's reception upriver. The chief of Achelacy immediately sought to establish an alliance with the French by presenting them with an eight-year-old girl; Cartier refused a boy of about two or three years as being too young. That Cartier understood at least some of the ramifications of this gesture is suggested by his action on his third voyage in 1541, when he left two small boys along with other gifts with the "Lord of Hochelay."[35] His purpose was to have these boys learn the language and customs of the Amerindians and thus be able to act as interpreters and intermediaries in future dealings. It was a more limited goal than that of the Amerindians, who sought to forge blood ties that would help to bind an all-embracing alliance. There is no indication that Cartier left any children with the Stadaconans.

Similarly, the warmth of Cartier's reception by the Hochelagans, and his response to them, are in striking contrast to what happened at Stadacona. On his way up the river, Cartier at one point was carried by a big Amerindian "who took the Captain in his arms and carried him ashore as easily as if he had been a six-year-old child." On arrival at Hochelaga, the French were also carried ashore.[36] This might have been misread by the visitors as Amerindian acknowledgement of French superiority, where in fact it seems to have been a ceremonial gesture of deference that was widely practised in the Americas. In the region then known as Florida, Laudonnière and some of his men were also carried on the shoulders of their Amerindian allies on a war march.[37] Vespucci had reported of South Americans: "What greater wonder can I tell you than that they thought themselves fortunate when, in passing a river, they could carry us on their backs?"[38]

That this physical gesture of deference was not a sign of submission was demonstrated at Stadacona during the winter of 1541–42, when the French, not used to the cold, were limited in getting about. "The barbarians, large and powerful, had pity on them and carried them on their shoulders wherever they wanted to go." One of the French, a gentleman from Anjou, several times asked a certain Amerindian to take him in this manner for a walk. On the last such occasion, the Amerindian, with the Angevin on his shoulder, slipped on a rocky path, and the gentleman beat him with his cane. The Amerindian approached the shore, took the Angevin by the collar, strangled him and threw him in the water. Another Frenchman drew his sword, and the Amerindian gave him the same treatment. This frightened the company, according to Thevet, who said he received his information from the explorer in his house at St-Malo.[39]

The story of Cartier's first winter at Stadacona (1535–36) is one of mounting tensions. In the matter of trade, the Stadaconans became more exacting as Domagaya and Taignoagny told them they could get better value for their goods. The pair had probably heard stories in France of the great profits to be made in the New World because the Amerindians were content with so little in exchange for their goods. The French accordingly found that they had to pay better prices for their daily needs, such as fresh meat and fish, or else the Amerindians would refuse to trade.[40] Cartier complained of the niggardliness of the Stadaconans. The account of such churlishness, when contrasted with the usual stories of Amerindian hospitality at this period, strongly suggests that the French had displeased their hosts.

In another case, it was French suspicions that were aroused. Unfamiliar with the pattern of Amerindian winter activities, they did not believe Donnacona when he said he was going off on the winter hunt, and asked how long he would be absent. Domagaya replied, with typical Amerindian vagueness about time, that it would be about two weeks. When the chief's absence stretched into two months, Cartier began to wonder whether Donnacona was collecting a force to attack the French in their weakened condition.[41] Upon Donnacona's return, the French became aware of an unusual number of Amerindians in the village. Although they had gathered for winter ceremonies, in which myths were ritually recreated, Cartier mistakenly concluded that trouble was brewing for the French.

The French presence could well have exacerbated the factionalism that apparently existed in Stadacona. Taignoagny implied as much when he asked Cartier to take a rival chief, Agona, to France, a request that incidentally revealed how the young man felt about having been taken to Europe. Cartier's refusal did not ease relationships between the French and Donnacona's people. The culmination of this growing interplay of distrust occurred in 1536, when Cartier, on the eve of his departure, seized Donnacona, his two sons, and two other headmen. Ironically, the erection of a cross again marked the occasion. Ostensibly it had been set up in celebration of the feast of the Holy Cross; that there were political implications is evident from its size (it was thirty feet tall), as well as from the fact that it was emblazoned with the arms of France and the words, "Franciscus Primus Dei Gratia Francorum Rex Regnat" (Long live François I, by God's grace King of France).[42]

However the Stadaconans felt about the French in the New World, François in the Old was pleased enough with the results of the two voyages to present Cartier with one of the second expedition's ships.[43] Also, Cartier's reports crystallized the colonization plans that had been largely responsible for his reconnaissance of the St. Lawrence.[44] After delays caused by the war between Charles V and François I, Cartier sailed in 1541 with more than 250 people as part of Roberval's project to establish France in North America. The expedition split into two parts, with

Gastaldi's map of Canada, illustrating a sixteenth-century European view of the Canadian lifestyle. From Ramusio, 1556.

Cartier spending the winter of 1541–42 at Charlesbourg Royal, the French establishment near Stadacona, and Roberval wintering there the following year.

What little is known of Cartier's stay indicates that the French captain never achieved a satisfactory working arrangement with the Stadaconans. He told them that apart from Donnacona, who had died about two years previously, the other Iroquois he had taken on his previous voyage were happily settled in France as grand seigneurs and had refused to return to their native land. Although Cartier reported that this was accepted, one wonders if the Stadaconans were so easily fooled, particularly after what they must have heard from Taignoagny and Domagaya. Cartier's own testimony indicates that they had grave doubts:

> And when we arrived at our Fort [Charlesbourg Royal at the mouth of the river of Cape Rouge], wee understoode by our people, that the Savages of the Countrey came not any more about our Fort as they were accustomed, to bring us fish, and that they were in a wonderful doubt and feare of us.[45]

Hostilities became overt as the French attempted to establish themselves, and the Amerindians killed some carpenters who had been put ashore to start construction.[46] That this was followed by reprisals is indicated by the Stadaconan plot to set fire to the French ships that was foiled by Cartier. The Amerindians had been provoked, according to Thevet:

> When we landed, some of our brainless young bucks cut off arms and legs from several of these poor people, just to see, they said, if their swords cut properly. This was in spite of the fact that these barbarians had received them well, in friendship.[47]

Something of this is suggested by Christopher Carlysle, who said that the seizure of Donnacona as well as disputes during Cartier's second winter and during Roberval's stay had "put the whole country into such dislike with the French, as never since they would admit any conversation, or familiarities with them."[48] On his way back to France, Cartier told Roberval that he could not withstand the Amerindians, who went about daily to annoy him.[49] A seventeenth-century cosmographer wrote that Cartier had abandoned his part of the colonization attempt "because he saw no hopes of subduing the Savages with so small Forces as he had brought with him from France."[50] Thevet put it even more strongly: "And so ever since that time, they do not permit any Christians to approach or to put foot on their shores or within their boundaries, nor will they trade."[51] Amerindians told fishermen they had killed thirty-five of Cartier's men at his fort on the St. Lawrence.[52]

That this enmity was directed against Cartier and his group rather than against the French in general is suggested by the fact that Roberval did not at first encounter overt hostility when he arrived at Charlesbourg Royal in 1542. In fact, trading began, and at one point the Amerindians brought a "great store" of fish.[53] But Roberval does not seem to have been any more diplomatic than Cartier had been; from accounts of his character, he was inflexible and autocratic. The story of the courageous Marguerite, whom he abandoned with her lover on an island on the St. Lawrence because he disapproved of the romance, would indicate as much.[54] His method of governing his colonists was described by Montchrestien as leading only to disorder, quarrels, and fatigue.[55] Roberval made liberal use of the whip for both men and women, did not hesitate to put people in irons and even to hang one.[56] The lieutenant-general had obviously thought such measures were necessary to keep his convict-colonists in line; but they must have shocked the Amerindians, who could not endure physical restraint and who killed their enemies rather than their own compatriots.

Roberval made matters worse by mistreating Amerindians; this, along with other factors led to the "ruin of his plans."[57] Reports of this lack of success may have led to his recall, although the reason usually given is "the important affairs of the King." Expensive as Cartier-Roberval's colonization project had been, it needed still more reinforcements and supplies to keep going. The King could not afford this, and so the project came to nothing.[58] That official disillusion had set in is indicated by an inscription on a Descellier map of 1550, which reads, "As it was not possible to trade with the people of this country because of their aloofness and the intemperance of the land and small profits, they had returned to France and hoped to come back when it pleased the King."[59]

The experiences of Cartier and Roberval suggest that the widely acclaimed French skill in finding accommodation with Amerindians, which in New France was to come into its fullest flower toward the end of the seventeenth century and during the first half of the eighteenth, was an ability that had been developed through sometimes painful experiences.

The failure of the Cartier-Roberval colonization attempt gave France pause. The successes of Spain and Portugal had proved that Europeans could establish colonies in these new lands; had France not planned her venture properly, as Champlain was to claim?[60] Were Montchrestien's charges of maladministration justified, in regard to the colony itself as well as to relationships with Amerindians? Perhaps the location of the attempted colony had been to blame; was the St. Lawrence too far north for a successful European plantation?

The charges that France neither conceived nor planned her early colonization projects properly have, of course, the benefit of hindsight. At the time, her goals seemed clear enough. The official purpose of the Cartier-Roberval enterprise, according to a statement issued during the planning stages, had been to

> establish the Christian faith in a savage land far from France . . . even though [the King] knew full well no gold or silver mines were to be found there, nor any other gains save the conquest of souls for God,

> to deliver them from the tyrany of the infernal Demon, to whom they sacrifice even their children.[61]

This highly political declaration indicates the scope of the intentions of François I: he was challenging the papal demarcation of the New World and insisting on the right of France, a Catholic power, to share in the labors of evangelization. In one move, François sought to out-maneuver Spain in the New World, establish France as a missionary power, and create a New France overseas.

François, however, was clearer about his political goals than he was about the procedures of colonization. While he spared neither resources nor money in preparing for the expedition, he had no appropriate model upon which to pattern his efforts. Neither Spanish nor Portuguese colonies provided suitable prototypes, first of all because they were in areas where the climate did not demand great adaptation; and secondly—in the case of the Spaniards at least—empire in the New World had been largely based on the conquest of high civilizations. There was also the fact that it simply never occurred to the French, any more than to any other European colonizing power, to question the appropriateness of the cultural model they were seeking to establish under New World conditions.

Nor were their techniques the most efficient. For just one example, the custom of bringing kidnapped Amerindians to France in order to obtain information about the country to be colonized resulted in the accumulation of information that was at the very least dubious.[62] Amerindians quickly detected what the Europeans wanted to hear, and did their best to oblige. If some solidly based facts filtered through, it would have been in spite of, rather than because of, this particular method of gathering data.

To say that the planning and preparations were inappropriate or even inadequate is not to imply that great efforts were not made. What appear to be official recommendations in 1538 for a French colonizing expedition to Canada, apparently that of Cartier-Roberval, had suggested that it count six ships and 276 men: 120 sailors, forty soldiers, and the rest representing the trades deemed necessary for such an enterprise. Provisions for two years would be needed, and members of the crew should be paid their salaries before departure in order to sustain the families they were leaving behind in France. The expedition should leave by mid-March at the latest in order to give the colonists as much time as possible to settle into their new homes before the arrival of winter. The total cost was calculated at 33,120 livres, a sum comparatively large in the terms of the day. As the expedition was being fitted out, a Spanish spy reported that it consisted of six ships for Cartier at St. Malo and four for Roberval at Rouen and Honfleur.[63] Cartier finally sailed in May 1541 with five ships provisioned for two years, and Roberval followed a year later with three ships and 200 colonists. The final cost of the expedition was reported to have been 45,000 livres.[64]

Cartier's descriptions are the first to give details about Amerindians of the St. Lawrence. He was an accurate, if not profound, observer, slipping only on occasion perilously close to propaganda in order to promote his colonization project. For instance, in his dedication to the king in *Brief Recit*, he refers to Amerindian "goodwill and gentleness."[65] One wonders if he were not making use of le bon sauvage stereotype. In any event, the tone of his ingratiating comment is at variance with the asperity with which he reported his dealings with the Stadaconans. One gets the impression that although he had at first believed that they, as well as other Amerindians, "could easily be moulded in the way one could wish,"[66] he had come to realize that their complaisance was deceptive. To Cartier as well as to many of his contemporaries, this apparent pliancy appeared to be masking treachery; however, it could have been a defensive mechanism, masking instead anxiety lest one give offense. In an uncertain world in which he depended primarily upon himself, the Amerindian did not feel that he was in the position to take such unnecessary risks as would be incurred in openly contradicting others.[67]

Amerindians, for their part, were not favorably impressed by the elaborate courtesies the French often displayed toward avowed enemies. Conventional hypocrisies are acceptable only when one is familiar with the guidelines; neither the French nor the Amerindians were familiar enough with each other's social code to understand the nuances. In general, Cartier's tone indicates that he accepted the European consensus of his day that the Stone Age technology of the Amerindians implied that they were also inferior as humans. On one point he held aloof from popular belief: there were no monsters in his bestiary. However, he did report without comment Amerindian tales of pygmies, unipeds, and people who did not eat.[68]

Roberval's pilot, the celebrated Alfonce of Saintonge, was more credulous. In 1559 he published his *Voyages Avantureux*, the first routier or navigational guide to appear for certain parts of Newfoundland.[69] Less successful as an ethnographer than as a seaman, he attributed porcine characteristics to the people of Labrador, apparently reflecting the general European antipathy for the Beothuk and coastal Inuit.[70] Similarly, when Alfonce wrote of the people of the St. Lawrence in his "La Cosmographie," he reflected the attitude of Cartier's reports:

Diamond-shaped snowshoes are used by Canadian hunters. Thevet, *Singularitez,* 1558. NL-7090 National Library of Canada.

> Hochelaga is a much better land than Canada, and its inhabitants more reasonable. However we do not know which gods any of them worship. In this land much corn is grown, which the people eat with fish from the river and the sea. They are great fishermen and also hunt seals and porpoises nearly as big as whales.[71]

Information from the Cartier-Roberval voyages can be found in the publications of the cosmographers who flourished toward the end of the sixteenth century. Most informative are Thevet's *Les Singularitez de la France Antarctique* (1557), and his *Cosmographie universelle* (1575). His "Le Grand Insulaire et Pilotage," never published as such, may have been written earlier than either of these, perhaps as early as 1550.[72]

Thevet, although a Cordelier, was more interested in travelling than in practising the monastic disciplines of the Franciscans. As the King's cosmographer, he took advantage of his position to meet as many travellers and explorers as possible. In his techniques for collecting information, he was in fact a journalist. His bustling activity did not impress some of his contemporaries; Léry called him a liar.[73] Historian de Thou was equally harsh, claiming that the Cordelier was motivated by a "ridiculous vanity" to compile extracts from various authors and easily available guide books:

> In fact, he is ignorant beyond anything one can imagine, having not knowledge of literature or of antiquity... he uses the uncertain for the certain, the false for the true, with an astonishing assurance... therefore I cannot help but complain about several people who although versed in the sciences, do not perceive the foolishness of this charlatan, but cite him with honor in their writings.[74]

The trouble with such a criticism, of course, is that it can be so easily turned against the person who makes it. De Thou, for all his scholarly eminence, could no more escape being a man of his time than could Thevet. In his works, de Thou noted a rain of grain in Carinthia (part of the Holy Roman Empire, north and east of Venice) in March 1548; for 1560 he listed such signs as fires and horsemen in the sky as well as a comet as the "most sure announcer of death to the king." For 1572 he reported a flying dragon.[75] Such statements would lead one to believe that de Thou shared the naiveté of which Thevet has been so often accused. It must be admitted that Thevet, however, added his own dimension to the foibles he shared with his age. He was not above faking evidence, as when he concocted a conversation with words borrowed from Cartier's Iroquois vocabulary and attributed the result to people of the Penobscot;[76] also, he claimed visits to lands that his own descriptions would lead one to believe he had never seen. He was possibly trying to justify his own statements to the effect that the testimony of those who had been there was more valuable for use in writing about the New World than the speculations of stay-at-home scholars. "Experience," he wrote, "is the mistress of all things."[77] Cartier had also said as much;[78] it was a cliché of the period.

Thevet, in spite of his wide travels and official position, was neither learned nor sophisticated, and could not resist trying to sound more authoritative than he actually was. In all fairness to him, it should be pointed out that not all his contemporaries were as harsh as his own countrymen. Martin Frobisher, for one, set sail on his first voyage to the Arctic in 1576 with copies of two of Thevet's works.[79] It should be further noted that collecting information from explorers and travellers was standard procedure for cosmographers and geographers of the time, who seldom knew at first hand the areas they described. Belleforest, for example, relied on Cartier's materials just as Thevet did. The difference, of course, was that Belleforest did not claim to have gone to New France himself.

Thevet's version of his first visit to New France was a compound of fact and fancy:

> on my first voyage, returning from the southern lands, we had difficulty meeting barbarians. A kinglet in animal skins, accompanied by several persons, thinking that we were worried and that we feared them, spoke to us in a friendly manner in his language.... "Come, come, my brothers and friends. Come and drink of what we have. We swear to you by the heavens, by the earth, by the moon and the stars, that you will suffer no more harm than we ourselves." Seeing the goodwill and affection of this old man, we stayed with him the whole day, and the next took the route of the Gulf of Canada.[80]

On the other hand, one could also wonder if this was Donnacona's version of his first encounter with Cartier. Thevet met Donnacona in France; it could well be that the cosmographer could not resist telling the chief's story as his own.

With reservations of this sort kept in mind, it can be stated that Thevet's ethnographic accounts have stood up well under the test of time.[81] His descriptions of the Tupinambá of Brazil are comparable with, and supplementary to, those of the widely acclaimed Léry. When Thevet deals with New France, he is the source of information that is not otherwise available. He described cradleboards;[82] snowshoes, which he said were used for hunting;[83] and the making of maple syrup, which he apparently believed to be a French development.[84] He reported that

Warfare along the St. Lawrence, according to Thevet, 1575. Smoke is being used to overcome the enemy (lower right), while longhouses are being fired (background). C-17653 Public Archives Canada.

Amerindian houses were covered with snow and ice during the winter and sometimes collapsed under such weight, calamities which he took to indicate bad construction.[85] In war, Canadians smoked out their enemy[86] and used poison arrows. (Was Thevet thinking of the Tupinambá of Brazil? Later, Jesuits were to attribute the same practice to the Erie, but the report is considered doubtful.) The weapons of the Canadians were such that they fought wars in the manner of the ancients.[87] Thevet cited vengeance as the principal cause of war, as Amerindians did not fight for land. He did not see that they could be blamed for indulging in vengeance when Christians could not resist it.[88] Moreover, he did not think the northern people were cannibals.[89]

On the whole, Thevet would sooner trust Amerindians than Moors or Turks. He added that on the subject of courtesy toward strangers, he would like to say that there was no one more hospitable than New World peoples.[90] One looks in vain in Cartier's writings for such an appreciation of Amerindian hospitality; Alfonce was also silent on this matter.

Thevet easily ranks with Léry and Staden as the period's leading source of New World ethnographic material. But he casts his net wider than the other two, who confined their attentions to Brazilians. Thevet not only added flesh to the bare bones of Cartier's published observations, but also pondered entrepreneurial prospects of New France that Cartier must have considered but did not record.

As for the Amerindians of New France, they faced problems as the fur trade increased in volume and importance. Throughout the sixteenth century, Tadoussac was the principal center for trade on the Gulf of St. Lawrence for Europeans, and perhaps for Amerindians as well. As European goods spread into the interior, rivalries for direct access to the trade intensified. This could have been a factor in the disappearance of the Laurentian Iroquois from the St. Lawrence River, which may have occurred as late as 1600, if Lescarbot's account is accepted.[91] The Laurentian Iroquois may have been driven out by the Algonquin, who in their turn were pushed inland by the Five Nations.[92] The Stadaconans may have been dispersed earlier than the Hochelagans; perhaps by about 1580, which could account for the penetration of French traders as far as Lachine Rapids after that date.[93] The continued presence of Hochelaga on maps of the later sixteenth century could mean that it was still in existence at that time.[94] On the other hand, the fact that Cartier did not mention it in his fragmentary 1541 account has been construed by some to mean that it had already disappeared by that date.[95] But neither the silence of Cartier nor the conservatism of cartographers provide conclusive evidence in this regard. The story of war along the St. Lawrence appears in d'Avity, who obtained his material from Lescarbot:

> the Hurons, who were at war with the inhabitants, chased them away. There had been towns filled with many savages, but because of enemy raids, some retreated toward the land of the Abenakis, others to the Iroquois and some to the Hurons themselves.[96]

War tales are also found in Micmac legends[97] and in the *Jesuit Relations*.[98]

At the same time, New France was attracting attention. Once they recovered from the shock of the long winters and the accompanying low temperatures, the French began to note advantages for farming, mining, and lumbering. Thevet was enthusiastic: "the Canadian soil is well constituted and fertile, like that of Gascony, good to produce all sorts of grains." Such was the natural wealth of the country that "if it were inhabited, it could produce as much wealth for France as the Kings of Scotland and Denmark receive from their islands, the Hebrides and Orkneys."[99] In the domain of mining there was cause for optimism as Thevet repeated reports of copper, iron, and lead mines in Norumbega (roughly, New England). An abundance of salt was foreseen in the new land "as the country is flat and very clean."[100] Fish could be stockpiled, as this was true fishing country. Forests could provide for a shipbuilding industry. The air was benign and although far north, the climate allowed

Canadians killing eastern woodland buffalo. Thevet, *Cosmographie* (Chaudiere), 1575. C-99345 Public Archives Canada.

for habitation.[101] However, the land was subject to earthquakes;[102] and it had not been found to contain gold or silver. But its potentialities far outweighed its disadvantages in the eyes of Montchrestien, who urged his compatriots to work with "a good conscience" in order to support the mercantile enterprises and to justify the royal grants needed to realize the colonial dream.[103]

The character of the natives was also presented as an advantage, despite Cartier's troubles: "The people here are good, benevolent, and gracious, concerned about winning the friendship of strangers." Still, Thevet tacitly admitted difficulties when he recommended the fortification of Assumption Island (Anticosti) "to bridle the savages of Baccalaos and Norumbega; Canadians as well as others." The French were on hostile terms with the Beothuk of Newfoundland (Baccalaos); the Armouchiquois of New England (Norumbega); and the Stadaconans (Canada). Thevet apparently had the difficulties of Cartier and Roberval in mind when he observed that any prince or great lord who wanted to make a colony would have to fortify a post besides taking possession of the land.[104] French fisherman along the Atlantic coast and in the Gulf, in contrast to Cartier and Roberval, had succeeded in establishing working arrangements with such coastal sea-going people as the Passamaquoddy. According to one impressed observer, the effect had been salutary for the Amerindians, who now "not only practice good civility but also our religion, and no longer eat human flesh, unless very secretly."[105] The English expressed a lively appreciation of the economic benefits to be derived from such arrangements:

> the French and Biscaynes report them [Amerindians] to be ingenious and tractable people (being well used): they are ready to assist them with great labour and patience, and in the killing, culling and boyling of whales; and making the Train-oyle, without expectation of other reward, than a little bread, or some such small hire.[106]

Montchrestien was of the opinion that all things considered, Amerindians had a natural sympathy for the French. He advised his compatriots to learn from past experience; rather than despising Amerindians, it would be far more useful to turn them into Frenchmen. He added that the Greeks and the Romans would have done as much.[107]

CHAPTER 9

The French in Brazil and Florida

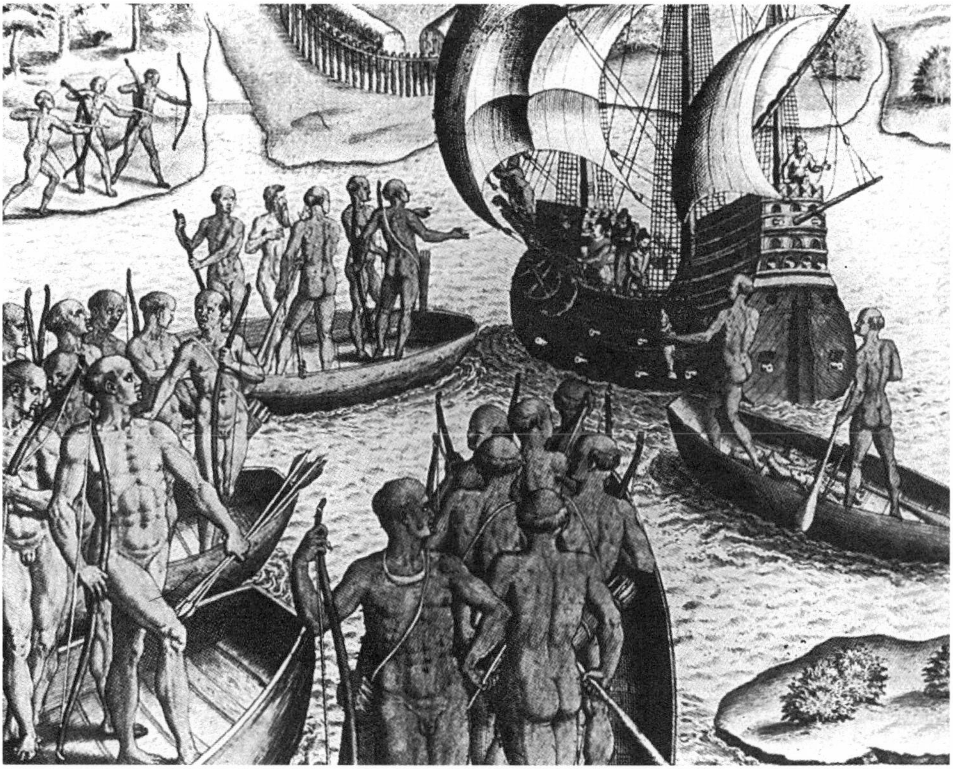

A French ship welcomed by a delegation of Tupinambá. Theodor de Bry, 1592, after Staden.

FRANCE'S NEXT major attempt at colonization was made in Brazil, between 1555 and 1560, in lands claimed by the Portuguese. By that time France's flourishing brazilwood trade[1] had expanded to include other products, such as peppers, jaguar skins, and parrots; and alliances with her trading partners, principally the Tupinambá and Potiguar, were on a solid footing.[2] The French had been aided by the vastness of the land in thus entrenching themselves; the Portuguese had been able to do no more than to harass them, despite the fact that they had moved quickly to establish their suzerainty. The situation seemed to be made to order to challenge both the papal demarcation and the Portuguese expansion, as well as to establish the French presence in America.[3]

Chevalier Nicolas Durand de Villegaignon (c.1510–71) launched the Brazil project with royal approval and the services of two armed ships of 200 tons each, with whose captains he negotiated agreements.[4] His skills as a propagandist, reinforced by the religious tensions of France at the time, caused many people to be attracted to his project, particularly as it was to be under the protection of the French flag. The king's approval was motivated by a desire to ease tensions, as well as by expectations that the expedition would bring "honor, glory and profit" to his kingdom.[5]

Such expectations and hopes were encouraged by the fact that Brazil had become a sort of promised land, particularly for the commercial classes and the lesser nobility. For many of them, the New World meant

Maize is among the items being carried by feather-skirted Tupinambá in the Triumph of Maximilian I. Woodcut by Hans Burgkmair, 1517–1518.

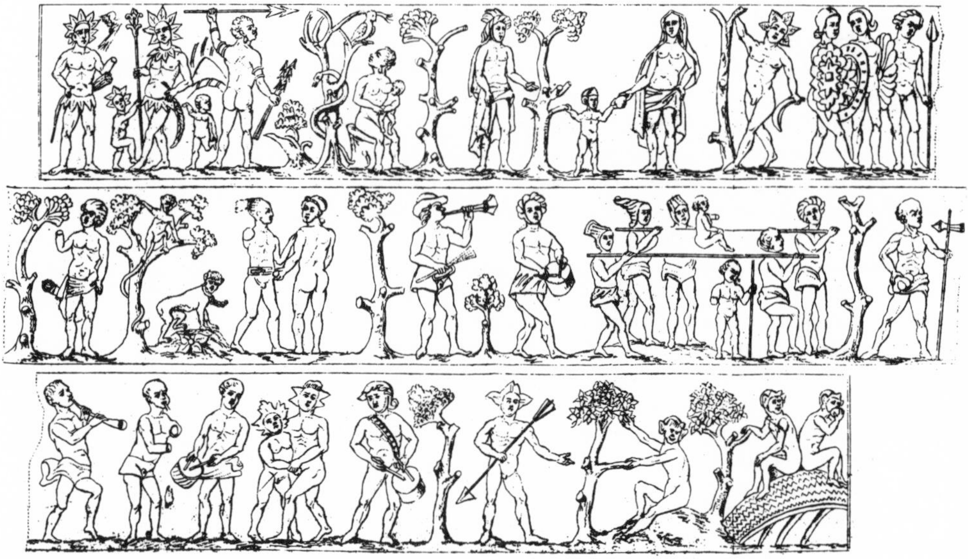

This frieze in Saint-Jacques Church, Dieppe, France, shows the people from around the world visited by Jean Ango's ships. The first family group is Brazilian. L'Église Saint-Jacques de Dieppe.

Brazil. Henry II's entry into Rouen in 1550 had provided an occasion for a poem to be addressed to the king, asking him to expel the Portuguese from Brazil.[6] Almost all the illustrations featuring New World people in sixteenth-century French-language geographical books were of Brazilians. This was true of other types of publications as well, such as the devotional *Les Heures à l'usage de Paris* (1551), which was bound in brown leather, embossed with a design that included Brazilian heads decked with feather headdresses, painted in green, pink, and black, and edged in gold.[7]

The first Amerindian known to come to France, Essomericq, had been a Carijó of the Tupinambá-Guaraní, who occupied most of the coast of Brazil at the arrival of Europeans. The Amerindians interviewed by Montaigne in Rouen toward the end of the sixteenth century had been Tupinambá,[8] whose people occupied the lands from the São Paulo region northward. Although fragmented into a bewildering variety of warring tribes, all of the Tupinambá-Guaraní displayed similarities in language and lifestyle that attested to the recency of their occupation of the coastal regions. Semi-sedentary and practising slash-and-burn agriculture, their staple crop was manioc (a root which in its natural state was poisonous, requiring lengthy preparation to make edible). Maize was secondary, and they also grew cotton and tobacco. (Later, in the Canadian fur trade, "Brazil tobacco" was highly prized.) Moving their villages every five years or so, they lived in communal buildings large enough to house as many as thirty families, perhaps as many as 200 individuals. As did Iroquoian farmers of the St. Lawrence, they exploited the resources of both inland waters and the ocean. Although Brazilians had domesticated fowl of their own, they quickly accepted those brought over by Europeans. They also adopted dogs for hunting. The migrations of the Tupinambá, in particular, seem to have been part of a messianic movement, a search for paradise, interrupted by the appearance of Europeans. Some of this movement occurred afterward, such as the Tupí descent on Maranhão toward the end of the sixteenth century.[9] Several branches of Tupinambá soon developed a trading relationship with the French, principally as suppliers of brazilwood.

It was partly because of the commercial success of this relationship that Brazil appeared so attractive to France at this time. Rapidly incorporated into French were Brazilian words for New World items previously unknown in France, such as *ananas*, *hamac*, and *tapir*. François I may have turned to the North in the Cartier-Roberval attempt for political reasons, but by far the greater part of the attention of his subjects was firmly fixed on the gentle prospects of the Brazilian coast.

The charismatic personality of Villegaignon also contributed to the interest aroused by the Brazil project. Having distinguished himself in the king's service against the Turks, he had been made a Knight of Malta.[10] As Vice-Admiral of Brittany, he had been one of those chosen to bring

The Amerindian custom of smoking tobacco quickly attracted European attention. Brazilians, standing beside a tobacco plant, demonstrate. Thevet, *Les Singularitez*, 1557.

Bas-relief in wood of Amerindians cutting brazilwood (top); carrying it to waiting ships (middle); and loading it (bottom). Mid-sixteenth century bas-reliefs in wood, Musée des Antiquités, Rouen. Lauros-Giraudon, Paris.

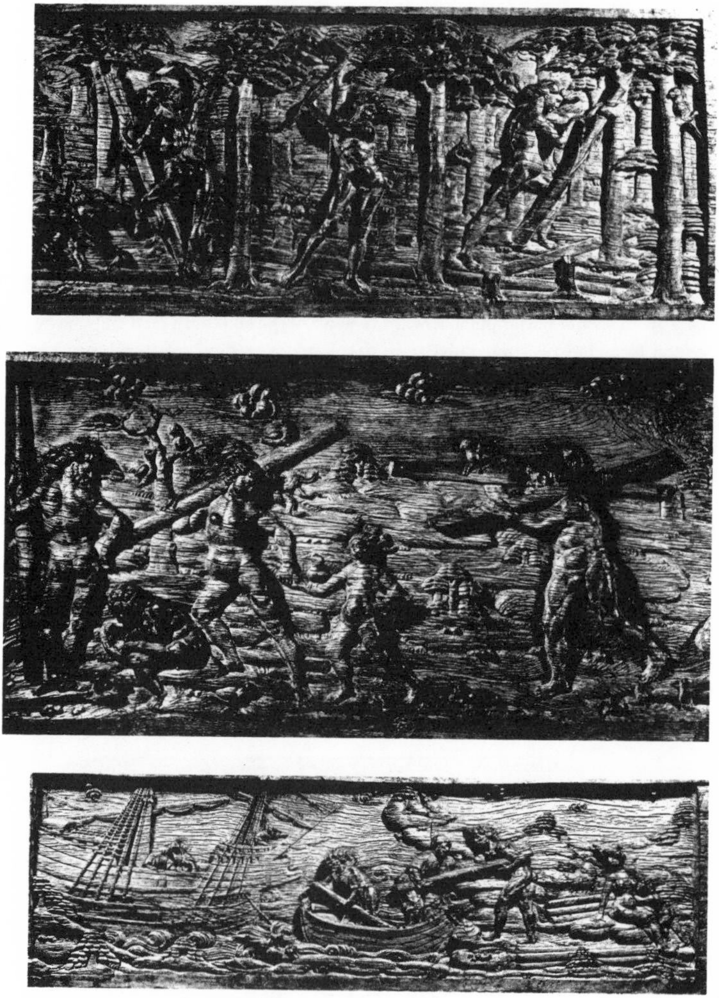

Mary Stuart from Scotland to France, where she was to marry François II. His quarrel with the governor of Brest drew the attention of Henry II, who supported not Villegaignon, but the governor.[11] Such a rebuff spurred the tempestuous vice-admiral to plan his colony, envisioning it as a haven for the persecuted of France and elsewhere, a haven where religious tolerance would reign. He was able to get sympathetic support for his vision from an influential cross-section of society; public interest, apparently, was high.[12]

Villegaignon tried to ensure the ecumenical character of his venture by taking out Catholic clerics (one of whom was Thevet, who stayed but three months) and later, by bringing out Protestant ministers (one of whom was Léry, who stayed about nine months). As it was mainly Protestants who volunteered as colonists, however, and as Coligny later became a major backer, the project came to be identified with Protestantism.[13] Belleforest charged that Villegaignon had really aimed at planting Calvinism "in the hearts of these barbarians [Brazilians] who have no knowledge of God nor of law or order" and so cause division in those lands.[14] When the colony's Fort Coligny fell to the Portuguese Governor Mem de Sá in 1560, the only Catholic object found within was a defaced missal.[15]

Even the well-advertised cannibalism of the Brazilians did not deter enthusiasm for the expedition. In his promotional campaign, Villegaignon said that if Europeans were sometimes eaten by Amerindians, it was because they had offended and outraged them with their boundless avarice and ambition. The fact that cannibalism was still practised was presented as proof of the previous lack of missionary zeal on the parts of both French and Portuguese, who "had never spoken a single word about our Lord Jesus Christ to the poor people of that country."[16] However, apart from his recruiting campaign, Villegaignon displayed very little concern for the souls of the natives. Both of the best known religious figures connected with the colony, Thevet and Léry, were more active in writing about Amerindians than they were in converting them.

In one vital area, that of obtaining rank and file colonist recruits, the chevalier's blandishments were unsuccessful: in spite of his best efforts, he drew practically no response from tradesmen and laborers. Finally, in desperation, he had to resort to convicts to make up the colonial complement that sailed in 1555. One of the reasons given for this lack of interest was the fear of being stranded in the New World without means of returning.[17] Apparently, prospective settlers preferred familiar evils at home to the fabled perils of the New World, particularly if they were to stay there permanently. Villegaignon sought to solve this problem in his second recruiting campaign in 1556 by instructing his agents to promise subsistence to the colonists until they were established, as well as to guarantee passage back to France if required.[18] This time so many applied that the three ships provided by the king could not accommodate them all.[19] But they were all men, except for half a dozen women who sailed with the second group. Far from being interested in permanently establishing overseas, they came without proper or sufficient equipment; most of them were bent on making a quick fortune in the New World and then returning to the wives and families they had left behind. The haven for the persecuted became instead a Mecca for treasure-hunters. Not only did ambivalent attitudes hamper Villegaignon's scheme, but they remained to bedevil later colonization projects.[20]

Villegaignon's first group, wan from the rigors of the crossing, arrived at Guanabara Bay to be joyously greeted by the Tupinambá, who lit bonfires and turned out "in large numbers to welcome them with gifts of food and curious things in order to enter into perpetual alliances with them."[21] But Villegaignon sought to keep as much distance as possible between his colonists and the Amerindians, and so he established his group on an island, off what is now Rio de Janeiro. His reasoning seemed to be supported when a pestilence brought by the colonists spread to the Brazilians, killing more than eight hundred of them. They, not unnaturally, blamed the French and their friendship turned into belligerence, but they were deterred from hostile action by the colony's island location.[22]

Villegaignon's success as a propagandist was not matched by his record as an administrator. He did not sufficiently provide for an agricultural base for his colony; its second convoy arrived without even the necessary implements. Villegaignon made arrangements with the natives to supply the colony with food, paying them with knives and fish hooks and other trade goods.[23] However, when he began to insist that the Brazilians help with the construction of the French fort, instead of letting them volunteer as they had been doing, they disappeared into the woods.[24] The colonists depleted the supply of bread and wine they had brought from Europe; their rations became so little that "it was pitiful to see."[25] Villegaignon modified his demands and was able to renegotiate with the Brazilians for provisions; however, the arrangement was far from satisfactory, and was strained by the difficulties of the French in adapting to native food.

The chevalier's efforts at isolating his people proved to be no better advised. The island location complicated supply problems and did not encourage the colonists to begin agriculture. Villegaignon's prescription of the death penalty for extra-marital unions with Brazilian women[26] was more successful in inciting conspiracies and desertions to the Amerindians than it was in guarding French morals. It resulted in the decamping of twenty-five Norman interpreters, all men who had been established in the country before the arrival of the colony – one for as long as nine years.[27] This desertion was a serious blow to the colony, as the interpreters had provided the principal liaison between the French and the Brazilians.

Like Roberval, Villegaignon was heavy-handed with his discipline, although presumably with less reason as he was dealing largely with volunteers. He overworked and underfed *engagés* often to the point of death,[28] treating them with the callousness characteristic of an age in which the masses were despised.[29] When religious quarrels were added to the dissensions that were tearing the colony apart, Villegaignon sought to confirm his authority by means of executions, including the drowning of some of the dissidents. Such disorder and repression, along with Villegaignon's falling out of favor with the king and his departure for France in 1558, left the colony vulnerable to the Portuguese attack of 1560.[30] It is surprising that Fort Coligny (as the French called their settlement) lasted as long as it did; the Portuguese had standing orders to sink all French vessels that ventured into Brazilian waters.[31] Villegaignon's efforts to raise a retaliatory force against Portuguese settlements in Brazil failed because his colony had been of no more than marginal interest to the Catholics, and he had betrayed the Protestants. Voices were raised to claim that the colony's destruction had been the work of God, who was thereby indicating he did not want a false faith implanted in Brazil.[32]

Villegaignon was no more successful with Amerindians who came under his control than he was with his own colonists. Lacking manpower for the work of his fort, he purchased prisoners of war from the natives. When they were recalcitrant about wearing clothes, he had them whipped.[33] The prisoners reacted by claiming they preferred to be eaten by their Amerindian captors to being bought as slaves by the French.[34] Villegaignon also upset the allies, the Tupinambás and Tamoyos, by insisting on ransoming their captives, thereby depriving them of more than half of those they would have eaten otherwise. The only ones pleased with the new arrangement were the Portuguese prisoners, whom the French leader conscientiously tried to locate and ransom from the Amerindians.[35] For all the disruptions they caused, Pay Cola (as the Brazilians rendered Villegaignon's Christian name, Nicolas) and his colony did bring trade to the natives, resulting in the establishment of a Brazilian village close to the French fort.[36]

In spite of the sympathetic picture he drew of Amerindians in his recruitment propaganda, Villegaignon did not have a high opinion of his

Brazilian allies. He wrote to John Calvin in 1557: "They were a fierce and savage people, far removed from courtesy and humanity, very different from us in learning and in doing. So much so that it has occurred to me to wonder if we had fallen among beasts in the form of humans."[37] He was careful, however, not to push matters to the point of disrupting the alliance of the French with the Tupinambá and Tamoyos, by Villegaignon's time an association of long standing. The importance of this alliance to the French is illustrated by an episode that concerned a German, Hans Staden, who had been a prisoner of the Tupinambá from 1547 until 1555, immediately prior to the arrival of Villegaignon's colony. According to his own account, Staden was repulsed by French sailors when he attempted to escape aboard their vessel; they told him that if they took him in against the will of the Brazilians, the latter would become their enemies and rise against them. When another French vessel finally agreed to rescue the German, the crew played an elaborate game to convince the Amerindians that he was a relative, and by this stratagem avoided antagonizing them.[38] Conversely, the fact that Staden survived his captivity because of doubts as to his nationality even though he was with the Portuguese when taken–his beard was red rather than black, and he protested that his native Germany was friendly with France–indicates the importance the Tupinambá placed on their French alliance. The Amerindians were not at that point regretting the benefits of the civilization being brought to them by the French, as Ronsard had wondered whether they might do some day.[39]

The French, for their part, used the occasion of Villegaignon's colony to continue sending lads to live with the Brazilians to learn their languages and way of life. For the purpose six boys were sent out with the second convoy of colonists.[40] It is not known exactly when the French started to do this, but by the time Villegaignon and his colonists arrived, there were two dozen or more "interpreters" living in the Rio de Janeiro area alone, some of them for many years. In the Americas, the custom can probably be dated back to Cabral, who in 1500 had left behind condemned convicts to live with the newly discovered Brazilians. Although one of these ex-convicts was later to prove very useful to the Portuguese in trade,[41] it was not surprising that most of them antagonized their New World hosts to the point of getting themselves eaten.[42] But the French were the most active in developing go-betweens; later, in Canada, they were known as *coureurs de bois.*

It is a testimony to the skill with which they nurtured their alliances that the French were able to continue trade in Brazil until the end of the sixteenth century, in spite of the dispersal of Fort Coligny. Five years after that event, there were still about thirty French known to be living

A Frenchman reciprocates as he is welcomed in a Brazilian weeping ceremony. From Jean de Léry, *Histoire d'un voyage fait en la terre du Brésil*, 1580.

in the vicinity of Rio de Janeiro, "men of base condition, living with the savage Indians."[43] Trade with France also continued. The Portuguese Jesuits José de Anchieta and Manoel de Nóbrega, who organized the first Brazilian mission, found that they had often been preceded in Amerindian villages by French traders who had been lavish with their gifts.

Villegaignon's colony provided the occasion for two major French works on the Brazilians: André Thevet's *Les Singularitez de la France Antarctique* and *Histoire d'un voyage* by Jean de Léry, not published until 1578 but written twenty years earlier. The two works present much the same picture of the Tupinambá, although they are complementary in some respects. However, of the two, Léry's has the most depth; today his work is considered the classic on the Tupinambá at the time of contact.[44] Although his work went through five printings between 1578 and 1609, Léry, in his time, was far from being the most popular writer on distant places. Atkinson noted that the reading public preferred Villamont,[45] who wrote on travels in the Middle East.

While sharing his age's astonishment at learning that men, women, and children lived their whole lives naked as when they were born, Léry presented this custom as resulting from simplicity and innocence rather than from the curse of Ham, whom he was inclined to think of as the ancestor of New World people.[46] He admired their good looks and health as well as their restrained habits of eating, reporting that they ate first and drank afterward. This habit caused Europeans to observe, "Are they then like horses?" The Amerindians for their part mocked Europeans for drinking during their meals. Generally, Léry found the Brazilians' food good[47] and their domestic habits clean.[48] He implied that European mothers would do well to follow the example of New World women in the matter of nursing their babies; then, observing that Amerindians had straight legs despite their never having been swaddled as infants, he suggested that Europeans imitate them, at least in summer, as swaddling must be a Gehenna for the babies. In almost a year in Brazil, Léry saw disputes among Amerindians only twice. Danger to Europeans from Amerindians was often the result of ignorance of their customs. Personally, wrote Léry, he would entrust himself more willingly to Amerindians than to Frenchmen in certain parts of France; Thevet also expressed similar sentiments. Those Europeans who recoiled from the cruelty of "savages" should think of the practices of usurers in Europe; such avarice and miserliness as theirs was despised by the Amerindians. As for cannibalism, Léry had observed it in Europe after the St. Bartholomew's Day massacre.[49] Amerindians made war only against their enemies.[50]

Although Léry agreed with his contemporaries that Amerindians had no religion, he did not use this as a base from which to argue that they did not have the use of reason. Quite to the contrary, he reported that they spoke better than most peasants, and that some of them could be very eloquent.[51] He illustrated his point with an anecdote. Noting that Amerindians were frightened of thunder, Europeans took the occasion to tell them that it was God speaking, in order to prove his strength and power to shake heaven and earth. To this the Amerindians replied that if he had to frighten them so to prove that, his position could not be very secure.

If the Amerindian way of life resembled that of classical antiquity, then it must be possible for these people to rise to civility as Europeans had done; all they needed was to be taught. But if, as Léry was inclined to believe, they were descended from the accursed Ham, would education be effective? Léry did not pronounce himself on this point, but he did not hide his appreciation of those attainments of the Tupinambá culture he considered worthwhile. For instance, he collected the music of the Amerindians, and even published some melodies in the 1585 and 1586 Geneva editions of his work.[52] In this he exemplified that strain of tolerance toward Amerindians and their ways that ran through sixteenth-century European thought, culminating in Montaigne. This viewpoint never dominated, yet was never entirely absent. Early in the eighteenth century it found expression through Lahontan, to be at last refined by Rousseau.

Quite apart from the writing of Léry and Thevet, Villegaignon's attempt at establishing "La France Antarctique" in Brazil aroused a great deal of interest. Accounts were published on the colony itself, as well as on the religious issues involved. The only other French colonial effort to arouse comparable interest during the sixteenth century was that of Ribault-Laudonnière in "Florida" (including parts of today's South Carolina), 1562–65, which also inspired several accounts.[53] Here, the point at issue was not so much religion as politics: specifically, rivalry with Spain.

The Ribault-Laudonnière expeditions, launched two years after the dispersal of Villegaignon's colony, were made in territory claimed, but not effectively occupied, by the Spanish.[54] The French king, in making his stand against such claims, encouraged the Huguenots to attempt to establish colonies in the "vacant" regions.[55] Roberval, Villegaignon (wavering Calvinist at one point), Ribault and Laudonnière, Mesgouez de La Roche, Chauvin de Tonnetuit, de Monts—all were Protestant. The king's policy led Belleforest to observe sourly that France's first overseas fortresses were established to protect colonies that were retreats for heretics. Coligny, however, was as much motivated by a patriotic rivalry

Timucuan widows, grieving for their dead husbands, ask their king to avenge them while the French look on. Theodor de Bry, 1591, after Jacques Le Moyne de Morgues. C-116139 Public Archives Canada.

with Spain as he was by religious concerns in his second attempt to establish a New France overseas. He selected Florida at least partly because the Spaniards had managed to antagonize the Amerindians to such an extent that it was their "cemetery,"[56] which he hoped could be turned to French advantage. The Englishman Sir John Hawkins later reported that Spaniards called Amerindians of the area *gente triste* (bad people), "yet here the French found them so witty in their answeres, that by the Captain's own report, a counsellor with us could not give a more profound reason."[57] They were Timucuans, the "Thimogoa" or "Tymangoua" of the French.

These Muskhogean-speaking peoples formed an eastern outpost of the Mississippian mound-builders. They lived in communities organized around public squares, practising an agriculture based on corn, beans, and squash. Their societies are usually classed as chiefdoms, although there are those who claim that they had the characteristics of states. In any event, in their cultural orientation, they displayed an affiliation with the city-states of Mexico. Elaborate burials testify to their social hierarchies, platform mounds to directed rituals, and central squares to organized administrative systems. In their beliefs they shared some of the characteristics of New World religions in general, such as the four-part division of the world and the importance of celestial phenomena. They appear to have had active and far-flung trading networks.

These were the peoples who were hostile to Juan Ponce de León when the Spaniard came exploring in 1513. Pánfilo de Narváez had passed here in 1528, Hernán de Soto eleven years later, both at least partly inspired by the fabled Seven Cities of Cibola.[58]

In his new project Coligny demonstrated that he had learned from the Villegaignon failure. More carefully thought out than the earlier attempt, Coligny's enterprise consisted of three voyages. The first (1562), under navigator Jean Ribault of Dieppe (c.1520–65), was a voyage of reconnaissance[59] and of territorial claims; the second (1564), under René de Goulaine de Laudonnière, sought to establish the French presence, while the third voyage (1565) was to reinforce the colony by bringing out a "great number" of entire families.[60]

The French, arriving within sight of "New France," as they now called Florida, were greeted with sweet odors wafted out to them by offshore breezes.[61] They found the Amerindians hospitable and hopeful that the newcomers would become allies in their wars against neighboring tribes. The French, under instructions from Coligny to maintain good relations with the caciques, hoped to get information as to the location of gold and silver mines as well as to obtain food. (The people of the Florida Coast had the reputation of being liberal in trading provisions with visiting ships.) There was an element of arrogance on each side: the least valet among the French thought himself superior to the most prestigious cacique;[62] such an attitude almost certainly found its counterpart among the Floridians,[63] as reports on the behavior of Amerindians at Versailles would suggest. In spite of their covert convinctions, both sides looked for help against the Spanish.

French diplomatic relations with the Floridians involved receiving and sending embassies, and listening to long discourses, which were even more boring because of language difficulties. But the gifts were often beautiful: on a typical occasion a cacique, Satouriona, welcomed the French with a crest of aigrette plumes, a cunningly woven basket, and a great skin on which wild animals were so well painted they seemed alive. The French were impressed with the dwelling of another cacique, Onadé, which was hung with feather tapestries. Onadé, seeing the admiration of the French for this work, presented them with six tapestries, woven with white feathers in ingenious compartments, and fringed with scarlet.[64]

When Ribault symbolically took possession of the land by erecting columns bearing the arms of France, Amerindians were in attendance, although not aware of the full significance of the act.[65] But they considered themselves allies, and accordingly built a new house for the French when the latter were burned out. When Ribault had to return to

France for reinforcements, Floridians kept those he left behind supplied with food and invited them to feasts.[66] Ribault reported in Europe that the Amerindians were

> of a good and amiable nature, which willingly will obay: yea be content to serve those that shall with gentleness and humanitie goe about to allure them, as it is needful for those that be sent thither hereafter so to doe, as I have charged those that be left there to do, to the end they may aske and learne of them where they take their gold, copper, and turquesses, and other thinges yet unknown unto us. . . . For if any rude or rigorous meanes would be used towards this people, they woulde flie hither and thither through the Woods and Forests, and abandon their habitations and countreys.[67]

But it did not take long for the *entente cordiale* to develop complications. At least some of the French accepted Amerindian hospitality somewhat cavalierly; one cacique found it necessary to ask some of the French vistors to leave during a native ceremony because they were laughing at it.[68]

More seriously, the French discovered that their dependence upon the Amerindians for food and services implied in the eyes of the latter that they were allies and that they were expected to behave as such in local wars. This was not acceptable to Laudonnière, who did not envision the

French become involved in Timucuan wars, and join Outina against their former ally, Satouriona. Theodor de Bry, 1591, after Jacques Le Moyne de Morgues. C-116144 Public Archives Canada.

French as playing a secondary role in Amerindian politics. He expressed this all too clearly when Satouriona announced his intention of paying the French a formal visit, and Laudonnière responded by refusing to accord him the expected honors. The Frenchman then broke his pledge to Satouriona when he refused the latter's request for help in his campaign against another cacique called Outina. When Satouriona returned victorious from the expedition, Laudonnière forced him to give up his prisoners to the French. As if that were not enough, the French leader then returned the prisoners to Outina and entered into an alliance with him, in the belief that Outina's land contained deposits of gold and silver. But this new-found alliance did not last either, as the Amerindians tired of the Frenchmen's continual requests for food and had the bad grace to mock them in their difficulties. The French reacted by seizing Outina as a hostage in order to reinforce their demands. Laudonnière later said this never would have happened if the French had been properly provisioned.[69] Sir John Hawkins, coming upon Laudonnière's fort, found that the French, "in extremity" for want, had

> made the inhabitants weary of them by their daily craving for maiz, having no wares left to content them withall, and therefore were forced to rob them, and to take away their victuals perforce, which was the occasion that the Floridians (not well contented therewith) did take certain of their company in the woods, and slew them; whereby there grew great warres betwixt them and the Frenchmen.[70]

More than half a century later, Lescarbot, upon observing the good results from gardens at Port Royal in Acadia, wrote, "I cannot wonder enough how it is possible that they which have been in Florida have suffered so much famine."[71]

Although the French this time had come equipped to establish an agricultural colony,[72] they apparently could not settle down to working the land that Laudonnière recognized as being fertile. Hawkins attributed this failure in farming to the fact that most of the men were soldiers who "desired to live by the sweat of other men's browes." They would not even make the effort to procure fish: as long as they could depend upon their Floridian allies, they had sufficient; but when they had a falling-out, "then would not the Frenchmen take pains" to construct new weirs to replace those taken away by the Amerindians.[73]

The French colonists' preoccupation with amassing wealth was exemplified by Pierre Gambye, who established himself in a village, married the cacique's daughter, and proceeded to go to all lengths to acquire gold and silver. However, most of what he found among the Amerindians came from wrecks cast upon the shore; none of the precious metals were native to the region. He was finally killed by the disenchanted Amerindians, who by this time had begun to wonder whether there was much to choose between the French and Spaniards.[74] The gold of the Spanish Main was still exercising its unfortunate influence, as it had done in the cases of Roberval and Villegaignon. Neither Coligny's patriotism nor his ability to plan in the light of past mistakes was sufficient to overcome the gold fever of the colonists. Such a deficiency, coupled with lack of support from France because of the civil war, meant that the colonists were unable to cope with New World conditions.[75]

A defensive Laudonnière, upon being recalled to France to explain his actions, reported:

> Neither should wee have had the occasion to offend the Indians, which with all paines in the world I entertained in good amitie . . . that although I was sometimes constrained to take victuals in some few villages, yet I lost not the alliance of eight Kings and Lords my neighbors. . . . Yea, this was the principal scope of all my purposes, to win and entertain them. Knowing how greatly their amitie might advance our enterprise.[76]

As a leader, Laudonnière was not consistent; with the Amerindians, he vacillated between a desire for friendship and the desire to dominate, and he could not bring himself to trust them.[77] He described them as traitors and dissemblers, and expressed annoyance at the high prices they asked for food.[78] Neither had Laudonnière been able to control his own men. Unrealistic expectations had given rise to much discontent, so that in 1564 a group of men deserted to go privateering against the Spaniards. When they ran out of food, they ate one of their own members before returning to the French fort, where the ringleaders were hanged. That may have reestablished discipline, but it did little for the esprit de corps. As in Brazil, the destruction of the colony was almost a foregone conclusion.

Yet, in spite of everything, Le Challeux's pessimistic comment about the Amerindians preferring the Spaniards was not borne out. One French lad, a native of Havre-du-Grâce, escaped the slaughter of the colonists by Spanish colonial governor Pedro Menéndez de Avilés in 1565 and was sheltered by Satouriona;[79] he was one of about two hundred French survivors who were thus taken in by various Amerindians.[80]

The boy acted as interpreter during negotiations between Amerindians and French when the Gascon captain Dominique de Gourgues came on his own initiative and at his own expense in 1567–68 seeking to avenge his nation's honor. The Amerindians' welcome to the French on this occasion probably reflected the fact that Gourgues's motives coincided with their own desire for revenge. After the elimination of the French in Florida, the Spaniards had proceeded to alienate the Timucuans by kidnapping forty of them for shipment to the mines as forced labor. With the exception of one man, known to the Spaniards as Charles of Ciquola, who had been baptized and presented to Charles V, members of one such group reacted by starving themselves to death. As a result of such experiences, Satouriona was ready to forget past differences with the French by the time Gourgues appeared. An alliance was formally sealed by an exchange of gifts. Gourgues presented such objects as daggers, knives, mirrors, axes, rings, little bells, and shirts for ceremonial occasions and for burials; Satouriona gave the French two strands of silver grains, hanging them around Gourgues's neck; and each of the chiefs profferred decorated deerskins. There was also an exchange of hostages, Satouriona sending a son and his favorite wife, aged eighteen, dressed in tree moss.[81] Amerindians and French drank cassine to seal the contract (cassine, brewed from leaves, had the effect of removing thirst and hunger for twenty-four hours). Gourgues, however, made only a pretense of drinking. Such a sealing of an alliance, Amerindian fashion, which had also been done by Ribault at the beginning of his enterprise, was already standard in French-Amerindian diplomatic relations. In Canada, Gravé Du Pont would follow the Amerindian custom when he confirmed the French alliance with Anadabijou at Tadoussac in 1603. The practical basis for such a procedure lay in the fact that alliances, to be effective, had to be negotiated in terms the Amerindians could understand.[82]

His pliability before Amerindian custom paid handsome dividends for Gourgues; his new allies informed him of the Spanish disposition of forces in their three forts, indicating the weak points in the fortifications. He destroyed all three; the Spaniards, routed, preferred to die at the hands of the French rather than at those of the Amerindians. The Floridians hailed the French as liberators. At one point, so many pressed about the French that Gourgues became uneasy, and he called forty sailors armed with pikes to ensure the safe return of his men to their ships.[83] As had been the case with Cartier, Villegaignon, and Ribault-Laudonnière, distrust was never far below the surface of their diplomacy when the French found themselves in these faraway lands. This was perhaps to be expected, as they were conscious of being invariably far outnumbered. Gourgues, in taking his leave from the Amerindians, promised to come back in twelve months with presents, a promise he failed to keep. An adventurer rather than a colonizer or an empire-builder, he had served as a galley slave for both Spain and Turkey, and in 1582 he was in the pay of the Portuguese fighting the Spaniards.[84]

The Ribault-Laudonnière episode marked the end of French attempts to colonize in areas actively claimed by the Spanish or the Portuguese. Le Challeux put it succinctly:

> Qui veut aller à la Floride,
> Qu'il y aille j'y ay esté[85]

The British could not resist the opportunity to jibe at their rivals:

> There is no wonder that the French being so slightly planted, did not take deeper roote in America . . . for they . . . affecting more by making a needless ostentation, that the World should know that they had been there, then that they did continue still to inhabit there like them, they were more in love with glory than with vertue, then being always subject to divisions among themselves, it was impossible that they could subsist, which proceeded sometime from emulation or envie, and at other times from the laziness of the disposition of some who (lothing labor) could be commanded by none, who would impose more upon them then was agreeable with the indifferencie of their affections and superficial endevours.[86]

One of the few positive results of the Ribault-Laudonnière attempt for the French was the introduction of sassafras to European medicine.[87] Le Challeux moralized that what happened in Florida was probably divine punishment for having encouraged so many men to abandon their families while they went off seeking a fortune.[88] As for the Spaniards, their reaction to the French challenge was to establish the first permanent European colony in Florida, San Augustín, in 1565.

Apart from precipitating Spanish colonization in the region, the principal legacy of the French to the Timucuans seems to have been Calvinist songs. According to Le Challeux, the French had taught the Timucuans to sing certain psalms, which they later used as an "endearing greeting," a "watchword, [for] are you French or not?" Two centuries later, settlers reported the tunes being faithfully rendered by the natives.[89]

French attend a Timucuan execution. Theodor de Bry, 1591, after Jacques Le Moyne de Morgues. C-116125 Public Archives Canada.

In the meantime, Timucuans continued harassing the Spaniards, eating their missionaries. The latter reported that the Floridians were "worse than heretics, as they had no scruples about eating meat during Lent, even that of a missionary, whom they treated with no more respect than they would a wild beast."[90] The Spaniards responded with more suppression, with their usual charges that the natives were bestial, irrational, and incapable of learning Christian ways. Such views prevailed and it came to be accepted in Europe that the Floridians were not only barbarous, they were "dirty and savage beyond anything human. They lived on vermin, serpents and other poisonous and foul creatures. That is why the French and Spanish attempts to settle the region have been in vain."[91]

Their Florida failure spurred the French to do some serious reassessment of their techniques of colonization. Montchrestien thought the French had performed poorly because their "rude and tyranical" behavior had risked transforming their Amerindian allies into irreconcilable enemies; nevertheless they had welcomed Gourgues with open arms and had made possible his mission against the Spaniards.[92] Montchrestien's point was clear: the key to success in these new lands was cooperation with their original inhabitants. Another opinion held that such cooperation, while helpful, was not in itself enough. Rather, colonization, to be successful, depended upon cohesive leadership backed by sufficient military and naval force.[93] Neglect in these areas had led to the failures in

Canada, Brazil, and Florida. As the two courses of action did not seem to be incompatible, the French adopted both. *La douceur*, that is, cooperation with Amerindians, was brought to the fore; but armed support, never far in the background, sometimes overwhelmed humane intentions.

It proved simpler to dissect the anatomy of colonial failure than it was to construct a new corpus of colonial procedure. The French continued to expect the European model of civilization to function under all circumstances,[94] an attitude that exacted a high toll in lives and money.[95] This expectation was particularly evident in agriculture, which did not make the same immediate demands for accommodation with Amerindian ways as did trade. French colonists tended to ignore Amerindian techniques; the result was that colonists often suffered from famine in the midst of potential plenty.[96] The trouble was not so much that the colonists were anti-Amerindian as that in these matters they did not take the natives into account: in the European-style communities they sought to erect, there was no place for Amerindians or for their particular fund of knowledge.[97] This attitude was later pushed to its ultimate conclusion by agricultural English colonists.[98]

But in concerns of war and trade, the situation was quite otherwise. Even in this regard, of the two colonial attempts considered here, only that of Ribault-Laudonnière moved toward active cooperation with the Amerindians. Whereas Villegaignon had largely stayed aloof from native affairs, Ribault-Laudonnière had become deeply embroiled; in neither case did French-Amerindian relations tip the balance in favor of the survival of the colonies. The Florida episode, however, marks a definite stage in French colonialism, as it was the first time that a French colony became involved in Amerindian politics to the point of joining in its wars. In the case of Gourgues, Frenchmen actively sought an Amerindian alliance in order to wage war on other Europeans, in this case, the Spanish. The policy of douceur here received a new dimension.[99] Not only was friendship of the Amerindians seen as being useful in providing a basis of power in the New World, it could be employed in attacking European rivals. It would no longer be enough merely to get along with Amerindians; their active cooperation was required wherever possible. In the northern regions where New France was finally established, such cooperation would be essential to the survival of the colony.

CHAPTER 10

Amerindians in Europe

Brazilian tableau staged for the entry of Henry II and Catherine de Medici into Rouen, 1551. Fifty Brazilians were reported to have been brought to France for the occasion. Anonymous, French.

THE FIRST contact that most sixteenth-century Europeans had with Amerindians was not in the New World but in the Old. A survey of the cosmographies and travel accounts of the period, as well as those for the succeeding century, gives the distinct impression that Amerindians were seen more frequently in Europe than documented instances would indicate. This could be at least partly explained by the fact that they were first looked upon as little more than curiosities and their visits were reported, when they were noted at all, in much the same vein as the arrival on a Dutch ship of a live walrus from Canada for display in Flemish towns.[1]

These trips to Europe, particularly in the beginning, were not usually voluntary on the part of the Amerindians. Early explorers were accustomed to kidnapping New World men and bringing them to Europe as proof of where they had been. This tradition led to the practice of taking Amerindians home to train as interpreters and guides for subsequent voyages. Very early, the French added their own dimension to this usage, and sought to circumvent Spanish and Portuguese claims by bringing over Amerindians to request the protection of His Most Christian Majesty.

Similarly, France asserted her right to evangelize and, by extension, to colonize, by staging some spectacular ceremonies for the baptisms of New World visitors. On a smaller scale, missionaries brought Amerindians to Europe for public appearances to enlist support for their particular projects; and as colonization developed, children and young people were sent across the Atlantic for indoctrination in European ways. France became particularly active in this regard. She also encouraged chiefs and headmen to come to court in order to strengthen alliances, and tried to transform enemies into friends by sending over prisoners of war. When the court sought to solve a manpower problem by using a group of such prisoners as galley slaves, the outcry was such that the project was dropped. The expense of the visits proved to be high in proportion to the results obtained, and eventually they were discouraged. By the latter part of the seventeenth century visits were becoming rare and all but ceased during the eighteenth.

Columbus began the movement of Amerindians to Europe when he presented six islanders to the Spanish court. Of the original ten, one had died at sea and three others had been too ill upon landing at Seville to proceed further; the six who survived were baptized at Barcelona. One stayed in Spain with Don Juan of Castile and learned Castilian, but died two years later.[2] Of the others, three lived long enough to return with Columbus on his second voyage. Upon his arrival in the West Indies, the admiral released one in the hope he would act as an ambassador. The other two escaped.[3] On his second voyage, Columbus brought thirty Amerindians as prisoners of war from Hispaniola; they were sold in Seville as slaves.[4] The extent of the resistance that the Spanish were meeting from the Amerindians in the West Indies is indicated by the report that 600 others were sent as war captives that same year (1494), also to be sold as slaves at Seville.[5] In 1495, the number brought over was given as 500.[6] In 1496, Don Bartholomew Columbus, brother of the admiral, sent 300 islanders to Spain for having taken arms against the Spanish;[7] that same year, Columbus estimated that he could export as many slaves as could be sold, about 4000.[8] Vespucci reported that on his first voyage to the West Indies, 250 Amerindians were taken as prisoners of war, of whom 222 survived the transatlantic crossing to be sold at Cadiz.[9]

However, such traffic quickly dwindled to a trickle, probably owing to the rapidity with which Amerindians died in the Old World. Sometimes they starved themselves to death when first captured; many others died during the Atlantic crossing.[10] Also, the source of supply was dwindling; of an estimated 300,000 Amerindians on Hispaniola, two-thirds had disappeared within a few years after the Spanish Conquest.[11] In view of such considerations, official sentiment in Spain veered against importation of Amerindians. This was illustrated by the cool reception accorded Esteban Gómez when he returned from his voyage in 1525 along the coast of New England and Cape Breton with his ship's hold filled with Amerindians, "people of both sexes, all innocent and half-naked, who had lived contentedly in their huts." Gómez's action was in contravention of express instructions he had received before setting out on his search for the Northwest Passage.[12] His return to Spain was marked by an incident that was to become a favorite with sixteenth- and seventeenth-century chroniclers. In the confusion of his arrival, the report ran through the streets to the court that he had brought back "clavos" (cloves) rather than "esclavos" (slaves). When Charles V learned the truth he was not at all pleased, and ordered the captives to be set at liberty. Their subsequent fate is unknown. Not until 1550 was an ordinance issued forbidding the bringing of captive Amerindians to Spain.[13]

In the meantime, a spectacular group of Mexica musicians, singers, dancers, eight jugglers, and twelve ball players, accompanied by two princes, arrived in the entourage of Cortés in 1528 for presentation to the court of Charles V. They proved to be so successful that the enterprising conquistador, seeking to legitimate his natural children, sent the jugglers to entertain the pope.[14] The sensation was such that a Polish magnate, famous for his vanity and predilection for the exotic, asked diplomat Jan Dantiscus to intervene with Cortés to make him a gift from

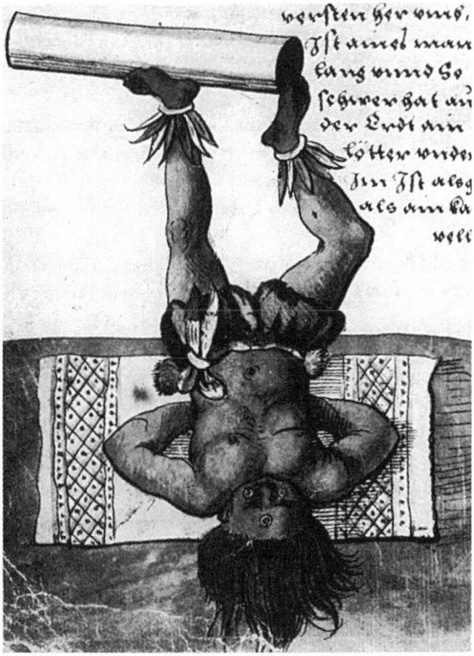

Mexican jugglers and acrobats were brought to Europe by Hernán Cortés. Drawn by Christoph Weiditz, 1528. Germanisches Nationalmuseum.

the New World–even if it were just an Amerindian.[15] On another occasion Martire invited Amerindian Francisco Chicorana to dinner, and found him not unintelligent. Francisco for his part entertained his host with ingenious recipes for producing giants; a custom which he said was practised in the New World for making kings who could be looked up to. Martire was dubious, but reported it anyway.[16]

The earliest account of Amerindians from the northern regions of North America in the Old World concerns the Portuguese Gaspar Corte-Real (c.1450–1501), who later disappeared on a voyage to Greenland and the mainland coast in 1501.[17] These Amerindians aroused considerable interest, including that of an Italian diplomat, in Lisbon:

> The hair of the men is long, just as we wear ours, and they wear it in curls, and have their faces marked with great signs, and these signs are like those of the (East) Indians.... Their manners and gestures are most gentle; they laugh considerably and manifest the greatest

> pleasure.... In fine, except for the terribly harsh look of the men, they appear to me to be in all else of the same form and image as ourselves.[18]

The reaction of another observer was that the king of Portugal would be pleased at this new source of slaves, fit for every kind of labor, as according to reports their land was well populated.[19] Two years later, 13 July 1503, four Portuguese ships returned to Lisbon loaded with dyewood and Amerindians.[20]

Earlier, three men had been brought from Newfoundland to England, according to an entry in Stow's *Chronicle* which begins "18. Henry VII A.D. 1502":

> This yeere were brought unto the king three men taken in the new found Island, by Sebastian Caboto, before named, in anno 1498, these men were clothed in beasts skins, and eat raw flesh, but spake such a language as no man could understand them, of which three men, two of them were seene in the kings court at Westminster two yeeres after clothed like Englishmen, and could not be discerned from Englishmen.[21]

If the evidence of this account is to be credited, these New World men must have been very adaptable indeed. In another instance, the adaptation worked another way; when Sir Martin Frobisher (1535?–94) brought Inuit along with a kayak to England in 1577, Queen Elizabeth allowed them to hunt on the Thames and did not exempt swans from their attentions, to the amazement of the English public.[22] Henry VIII had previously been visited by a Brazilian cacique, who had agreed to come over with William Hawkins in 1531 on condition that one of the English captain's men stay in Brazil as a pledge for his safe return. At the sight of the cacique, Henry and

> all the Nobilitie did not a little marvaile, and not without cause: for in his cheekes were holes made according to their savage manner, and therein small bones were planted, standing an inch out from the said holes, which in his owne Countrye was reputed for a great braverie ... his apparel, behaviour, and gesture, were very strange to the beholders.[23]

After a year in England the cacique set sail for his own land, but he died at sea, reportedly from the change of air and diet. His people back in Brazil believed Hawkins and yielded up the hostage to return to England.

The first New World visitor to France of whom there is a record appears to have flourished. Essomericq came over from Brazil in 1505 with Captain Binot Paulmier de Gonneville of Honfleur. De Gonneville had gone to the New World in 1503 to trade, taking a selection of merchandise that indicated that he had a clear idea of items that would interest the natives.[24] He had remained with the Carijó (Guaraní) in southern Brazil for six months; upon his departure, his host, Arosca, had agreed to send over his son on the understanding that he would be returned in approximately twenty months. De Gonneville was not able to fulfill this promise because he lost everything as a result of two attacks by pirates in the Channel. When he finally got to France, the young Brazilian apparently took to his new life. During the voyage he had already indicated his willingness to try out French ways by accepting baptism after nearly dying of scurvy. This disease had claimed the life of his relative and companion, Namoa, as well as those of several members of the crew. In any event, Essomericq was reported to have married a relative of de Gonneville's, to have established a family, and to have lived in France until 1538.[25]

Essomericq's great-grandson, Abbé Jean Paulmier de Courtonne, canon of Lisieux (d. c.1669), wrote a memoir to Pope Alexander VII in which he argued for the establishment of a French mission in the "third world," as he referred to the Americas, also known as "Terres Australes."[26] He asked that he be sent as a missionary, both because of his birth and of his calling.[27] In recounting his ancestor's story, the Abbé said that de Gonneville had arranged Essomericq's marriage "which made him an ally" in order to recompense him for the good treatment the French captain had received among the Amerindians.[28] In his arguments in favor of the missionary enterprise, the Abbé showed himself well informed about the New World, as well as about procedures for founding missions.

There is no record of the fate of the next Amerindians known to have arrived in France, seven homines sylvestres who in 1509 came to Rouen equipped with a bark canoe so light that a man could easily lift it to his shoulder.[29] The French noted that these men ate dried meat and drank water, and were not acquainted with wine, bread, or money. It is usually assumed that they were brought to France by Captain Thomas Aubert, one of Jean Ango's pilots, known to have sailed from Dieppe in 1508.[30] The Jesuit missionary Biard wrote that Captain Aubert brought some natives "whom he exhibited to the wonder and applause of France."[31] However, there is no proof that these were the same as the seven men of Eusebius's account. A curious contemporary report tells of a French ship encountering a bark canoe off the English coast in which were seven men whose wide, bronze faces were marked with tattoos like "livid veins" outlining their jaws. They wore sealskin clothes and their "multicolored coiffures" were styled to look like seven ears. These men ate raw meat and drank blood.[32] Six of these men quickly succumbed on arriving in Normandy, but the seventh was sent to the court of Louis XII as an object of curiosity.[33]

A few years later, the story was told of a young Amerindian woman successfully resisting capture. The incident occurred during the voyage of Giovanni da Verrazzano along the coast of North America in 1524. The young woman raised such a fuss that the sailors let her go; however, they kept a boy whom they brought back to France.[34] Among the French, such incidents seem to have continued on a desultory and individual level, although there were exceptions to this, of which Cartier provided the most notable examples. On his 1534 voyage he brought back the Stadaconans Taignoagny and Domagaya. As their names indicate, they were not baptized; it can be speculated that Cartier took them to act as guides and go-betweens for his second voyage which he was even then hoping to make. In this he was successful; the pair learned French and were able to act as interpreters upon their return to Stadacona. It is also possible that Cartier was able to use them in order to procure his second commission. In any event, this was not his first such action; in 1527, he had brought a girl from Brazil, who was then baptized 30 July 1528 at Saint-Malo with Cartier's wife, Katherine Des Granches, acting as godmother.[35] There is no indication as to what prompted him to bring over the girl.

On his second Canadian voyage, Cartier's kidnappings increased in scale, as he retook not only Taignoagny and Domagaya, but also their father Donnacona and other head men, a total of about six.[36] On this occasion Cartier appears to have wanted spokesmen of stature to appear before the French king to tell him about their land. Apparently a colonization project was already in the wind. Donnacona was at least partly responsible for being taken, as he had been telling Cartier tales of white men on the Saguenay who wore woollen clothes and who possessed immense quantities of gold.[37] Donnacona may have been trying to tell Cartier what he thought the explorer wanted to hear; but he also may have been recounting reports of Spaniards to the south that had filtered through native trade routes. The chieftain was only too successful; Cartier took him to tell his stories to François I. Spanish historian Barcia said that Cartier arrived back in Saint-Malo 9 July 1536 with his guests, "who were travelling contentedly in the hope of returning quickly to Canada with a good share of wealth."[38] About two years later, three of the men were baptized in Saint-Malo.[39] However, none of the group survived to accompany the French on their first colonizing attempt in North America. A little girl, apparently one of the children who had been presented to Cartier, seems to have lived to reach adulthood, but as there is no indication that she was ever brought back to her native land, it is reasonable to assume that she spent her life in France.

That François I approved of Cartier's action is indicated by his payment of fifty écus for the maintenance of the Amerindians during two years at Saint-Malo.[40] There is also a hint of this in the wording of François's commission dated 17 October 1540 for the establishment of a colony in Canada:

> from which land we have brought several men whom we long maintained in our kingdom, instructing in the love and fear of God, in the holy faith and Christian doctrine, with the intention of taking them back to the said country with a good number of our subjects of goodwill to help influence the peoples of these lands to believe in the holy faith... in consideration of which... we have decided to send Cartier back again.[41]

By this time Saint-Malo had become a center of activity for bringing in Amerindians, probably as an adjunct to the developing fur trade. If they survived, they usually returned home within a few months to act as go-betweens in trade. A Newfoundland native was baptized there in 1553, and named Jehan.[42] Jacques Noël, a nephew of Cartier, was among those who carried on this practice. In applying in 1587 with sea captain Etienne Chaton de La Jannaye for a monopoly of the Canadian fur trade, Noël claimed to have brought several Amerindians to France to be trained as interpreters.[43] The custom of preparing for colonization by bringing natives of the area concerned to the metropolis to learn European ways and above all the language, was well established before the birth of New France.[44] This formula also proved useful to Sir Ferdinando Gorges and the English colonies.

Rouen, as the center for the brazilwood trade, had many New World visitors; a house at 17 rue Malpalu, now demolished, may have served as a residence for them.[45] One of the most unusual of the Brazilian visitors was not a native-born, but a shipwrecked Portuguese who had been adopted by the Tupinambá of Bahia. He was Diogo Alvares, known by his Tupí name of "Caramuru." Married to Paraguaçu, daughter of a paramount chief, he had become influential in both Amerindian and Portuguese circles. In 1547 he accepted a French invitation and brought his wife to the court of Henry II and Catherine de Medici. The couple was showered with honors and the queen bestowed her name on the lady. The pair, however, remained loyal to Portugal, and two years later, back in Bahia, founded the city of Salvador.[46]

By mid-sixteenth century, it was fashionable in France for both royalty and wealthy nobles to have Amerindians in their entourages, a custom that was to continue until well into the next century. For instance, some boys taken captive by the Tupinambá and sold to Villegaignon were sent by the latter to Henry II, who in his turn made gifts of them to various nobles.[47] Similarly, François Gravé Du Pont, a naval captain turned merchant who was associated with Champlain, presented Henry IV with Amerindians from Canada in 1602. One of these was the young son of Begourat, a Montagnais captain, sent on the strength of favorable reports of two fellow tribesmen who had previously accompanied Gravé Du Pont to France.[48] The lad was installed as a companion to the dauphin in the Château Saint-Germain, where he died the following year.[49]

The role of Amerindians at court is indicated by a news report from Paris dated 23 March 1668 to the effect that Louis XIV had gone to Versailles "where he intends to divert himself upon the Lake with several guilt [*sic*] boats which are there provided for him; where there are also Hiroquois with their Gondolas brought from the Indies, made of one entire piece of Bark, in which they Row with extraordinary swiftness."[50] Though Amerindians were kept as curiosities, there was a certain interest in their particular skills. Their deftness with canoes was much admired, as was their technique for making fire with two dry sticks. Mocquet reported a demonstration of their fire-making before Henry IV at Fontainebleau in 1605.[51]

The Renaissance love of pageants, however, was the most effective means of bringing Amerindians to the attention of the public. Indeed, on occasion they were expressly brought over to participate in such events, as in the celebrated entry of Henry II and Catherine into Rouen in 1550. This was a pageant so lavish that books were published about it, beginning with one the following year.[52] One of its most important tableaux illustrated life in Brazil; fifty natives were supplemented with 150 sailors who had frequented the New World sufficiently to be able to speak a native language as well as to enact tribal customs and manners. In spite of the lateness of the season (it was the beginning of October), a park on the banks of the Seine was transformed into Brazilian woodland by the addition of artificial trees with trunks painted red to indicate brazilwood, although the tree actually has grey bark. There were Brazilian fruits *imitans le naturel* (imitating the natural), with birds, monkeys, squirrels, and other fauna from Brazil. In the midst of this sylvan setting were houses built in Brazilian style. Naked Brazilians and sailors-turned-Brazilian pursued activities of daily life, shooting at birds and animals, lying in hammocks, chopping dyewood and carrying it to a fort near the river where a French ship in full sail waited for its precious cargo. A battle was staged, during which the mortuary and "fortress" of the defeated group was burned. Some of the sailors had lived so long in Brazil that their impersonations seemed real.[53] Others who had lived in Brazil testified to the accuracy of the presentation.[54] The spectacle so pleased Catherine de Medici that she came back to see it a second time.

The entry of Charles IX into Troyes, 23 March 1564,[55] also featured Amerindians; the chief was mounted on a horse masquerading as a unicorn.[56] Bordeaux honored the same monarch on 9 April 1565 with a procession of captives from a dozen nations, including "sauvages américains et brésiliens."[57] Each group made submission to the king in its own language, which was then interpreted to the king. The political motivation behind such displays is obvious: France was seeking to establish her right to colonize in the New World. At a royal wedding pageant in 1619, where appropriately enough the theme was love rather than conquest, the American entry was entitled "Heureux de l'Amérique" (The Happy Ones From America).[58] Costuming *à l'amériquaine* was also popular for special occasions. For instance, in 1524 Seweryn Boner, governor of Cracow, sent two trumpeters dressed Amerindian fashion in parrot feathers to salute Elizabeth of Hapsburg, wife of the king of Poland.[59]

Not unexpectedly, Renaissance Europe combined its fondness for display with its concern for souls. Usually the New World men who were brought to France were baptized as soon as possible.[60] One could consider as symbolic the experience of the Amerindian whose first view of Louis XIII was in "the house of prayers"; Louis's reaction was to ask the visitor if he were baptized.[61] This concern for souls, genuine enough in itself, became an instrument in France's campaign to establish her right to evangelize (and, by extension, to colonize) in the Americas, and baptisms of visiting Amerindians tended to become affairs of state. The most spectacular of such occasions, if one is to judge by the popular interest aroused, occurred in 1613 when François de Razilly (1578–1622)[62] brought a group of six Tupinambá to France under the care of the Capuchin Claude. The Amerindians had agreed to come as a delegation to present their homage to the French king, and to ask for help in the form of missionaries and soldiers, artisans, and merchandise.[63] The occasion was considered important because the French were attempting to establish a colony on the island of Maragnan off the northern Brazilian coast in territory claimed by the Portuguese. The attempt was to be short-lived, as the Portuguese were to destroy the colony in 1615.

Six Brazilians from Maragnan (Maranhão) were brought to France in 1612 by Claude and Razilly. Here one is illustrated in his native costume, showing his tatoos. Claude, *Maragnan*, 1614.

In the meantime, the excitement generated by the arrival of the delegation was intense. There was a reception at Havre-de-Grâce, marked by a church service during which the Tupinambá recited aloud the "Pater Noster" and "Ave Maria" in their own language. Their entry into Paris almost a month later took on the aspects of a triumph, with the Amerindians dressed after their fashion in feathers, and shaking maracas. They were accompanied by twenty-six Capuchins. Fashionable Paris turned out in such numbers for the event that the press of the crowd forced the Capuchins to retreat with their exotic charges into their convent. But still the visitors came, so that the king was constrained to send pro-

The same Tupinambá in his baptismal finery. His baptismal name is Louis Marie. Claude, *Maragnan*, 1614.

tecting guards; even so, the quiet walks of the convent became something of a public hall. "Who would have thought," mused Claude, "that Paris, used to the strange and the exotic, would have gone so wild over these Indians?"[64] However, at least one contemporary Frenchman was not so impressed. François de Malherbe (1555–1628), poet and critic, observed the exotic figures later in Rouen:

> they were dressed in the French manner because according to their own customs they go naked except for a black rag they place before their shameful parts; the women wear nothing at all. Their dance was

> a sort of oscillation without holding hands or moving from one spot; their violins were gourds such as pilgrims use for drinking and in which they had placed something such as nails or pins. One of them had one and the interpreter, a Norman from Dieppe, the other. I do not believe that this booty will stir up much envy among those who have not gone to their land.[65]

The ceremonies surrounding the entry of the Tupinambá into Paris included their formal submission to the King. They referred to their people, before the arrival of the French, as living "a miserable life, with-

One of the six Brazilians as he appeared when he adopted French dress, but still retaining his own ceremonial headdress. Joachim Duviert, 1613. *L'Amérique historique*, 1638, pl. 187. Bibliothèque Mazarine, Paris.

out law, without faith."[66] One could wonder if the Brazilians believed the words put into their mouths by the enterprising Capuchins; in any event, they provided the king with the occasion to consent publicly to the sending of twelve Capuchins, as well as soldiers, to the New World, as duly reported in *Le Mercure François*.[67] Three of the Tupinambá quickly succumbed under the pressures of an unaccustomed lifestyle; the remaining three were prepared for baptism, scheduled for Saint Jean-Baptiste day at the church of the Capuchins, which was richly decorated for the occasion.[68] The Tupinambá were dressed in white taffeta, each being led by two white-robed priests to the baptismal font obscured by yards of white taffeta billowing to the floor against a backdrop of gold and silk tapestries. The Bishop of Paris officiated, and the king and queen regent were godparents; Claude interpreted. Sacred song and music accompanied the ritual. In the concluding procession, the Brazilians carried lilies and hats decorated with feathers. Cloistered nuns were allowed to see them.[69] Claude's description of the entry into Paris was included in his book (1614) on the Maragnan expedition, and was frequently reproduced in the anthologies so popular at this period. The Brazilians also became a favorite with illustrators, particularly in their baptismal finery or wearing French dress.[70]

Another spectacle was orchestrated in 1637 when two Montagnais girls were baptized in the great convent of the Carmelites of Paris. As with the Tupinambá, the occasion was attended by a host of fashionable and important participants and guests, including the princesse de Condé as godparent.[71] The social glitter of such occasions emphasized the importance of the political point that was being made, even though it was not overtly expressed.

Amerindians go to School in France

With the establishment of colonies in Acadia and along the St. Lawrence early in the seventeenth century, such visits gained a new dimension as emphasis shifted to sending over Amerindian children to be educated in the French manner to transform them into French men and women. The Jesuits, in embarking upon this policy in New France in 1634, were following in the footsteps of the Recollets, who had begun sending over lads in 1620.[72] Even though aware of earlier failures with Amerindians who had lived in France, and who had been baptized there, only to revert to their traditional ways as soon as they returned home, the missionaries were not yet shaken in their faith as to the program's essential validity.[73] Not only would such children be able to live like the French in

France, the theory went, but given the proper conditioning, they should also achieve the admittedly more difficult feat of doing so in their native lands. To quote Father Le Jeune:

> I see no other way than that which your Reverence suggests, of sending a child every year to France. Having been there two years, he will return with a knowledge of the language, and having already become accustomed to our ways, he will not leave us and will retain his little countrymen.[74]

In 1635 the missionary noted optimistically that "the Savages are beginning to open their eyes and to recognize that children who are with us are well taught." The next year, in 1636, he wrote concerning a lad he was sending over as a "gift" to M. De Noyers, secretary of state: "I have great hopes that so good a hand will return him to us some day, so well educated that he will serve as an example to the people of his nation."[75] In 1637 five Amerindians were sent over, including a young Iroquois woman.

Although the program began with the boys, the *Jesuit Relations* give the impression that on the whole it involved more girls. The rationale behind this was expressed by Le Jeune when a girl was sent to Madame la Princesse:

> If someone would give her a dowry, when she is of marriageable age, and then send her back to these countries, I believe that much would be accomplished for the glory of our Lord. For a little Savage girl, comfortably settled here, and married to some Frenchman or Christian Savage, would be a powerful check upon some of her wandering countrymen. This is the point to be aimed at, if this nation is to be effectually succored.[76]

What is known of the behavior of the children while they were in France seemed to endorse these high expectations. A girl taken in 1635 to live with the Hospitalières in Dieppe was described as winning

> the love of all; she was very obliging, very obedient, and as careful as a Nun not to enter forbidden places; and when it was desired to make her enter, either through inadvertence or to test her obedience, she answered very sweetly, "I have not permission; the Mother Superior does not wish it" . . . She already knew the Catechism and a great deal of French . . . she could say very well the Manitou was good for nothing; that she no longer desired to return to Canada.[77]

A boy who had been baptized Bonaventure was reported transformed in France, becoming "quite different from what he was. He has become quite obedient, astonishingly enough."[78] Even more surprising, "he was neither a liar, nor a scold, nor a glutton, nor lazy." The change in Bonaventure confirmed Le Jeune in his belief that "education alone [was] lacking to the Savages." The transformation aroused his expectations: "I am hoping he will be of great service to us in our seminary."[79] But the hazards in the way of such hopes were many; the girl died of smallpox, and Bonaventure died as the result of being lost in the woods following an accident, for which the missionary feared reprisals from his relatives, even though his parents were dead. However, as colonial officials had offered gifts to find the lad, his people were appeased.[80] The French behaved similarly when the young Iroquois woman died in France. Her relatives had petitioned with gifts for her return; upon learning the news of her death, Charles Huault de Montmagny, lieutenant-general and first governor of New France (1636–48), replied to the Iroquois with gifts so that "her bones might be laid to rest in her own country, or that she might be brought back to life by making some other woman bear her name."[81]

More disturbing were the early failures to remold Amerindians into the French pattern. These were at first explained away on the grounds that the Amerindians, "not being sufficiently instructed, and finding themselves without shepherds as soon as they returned to these shores, immediately resumed their former habits and traditions."[82] The pill of failure had been particularly bitter in respect to the Huron Louis Amantacha and the Montagnais Pierre-Antoine Pastedechouan. Louis had been sent to France in 1626, baptized as Louis de Sainte-Foy and returned a little over two years later.[83] Pierre for his part had practically grown up in France, so that he had all but forgotten his native tongue. Both of these men were in New France when it fell to the English in 1629. Upon their repossession of the colony in 1632, the French found their two neophytes to have reverted to their traditional ways. Louis, however, had not lost all interest in his new religion, and actively worked with Champlain and the Jesuits to promote the French-Huron alliance. He was eventually captured by the Iroquois while on a raid in their country, and was heard of no more. Pierre had become a misfit in both European and Amerindian society. Le Jeune observed sourly, "I may add that I have not seen a savage so savage and so barbarous as he is," and blamed Pierre's exposure to the English for the failure. In the end, only the priests were prepared to endure Pierre, and then, only for the sake of learning his native language. Finally, in 1636, he was reported to have died of starvation, alone in the woods.[84] Thus were dashed the high hopes the French had entertained at his baptism, when the prince de Guémenée had stood as his godfather.

That the French were finding the task of remolding the "savages" far less simple than they had at first anticipated is amply documented in the frustration apparent in their admissions. "It was 38 years, as I have heard, before anything was accomplished in Brazil," Le Jeune had observed in 1633.[85] Such unrealistic expectations mirrored the persistent French belief that Amerindians were in an "untutored" state of nature, ready to accept the teachings of the civilized French. When this turned out not to be the case, it was easy to attribute the failures to the perversity of the Amerindians or perhaps to their alleged devotion to the devil.

Yet, Amerindians could and did cooperate with the French. For example, Louise, a Montagnais, wrote that she was glad to be in France; and the superior of the hospital at Dieppe where she was staying reported:

> Our little Louise is doing very well. She is very sweet, compliant, obedient and devoted. When there is some small act of devotion to be performed in the class of the little Seminary girls, she is the first to ask to do it; she is so modest and attentive... she puts our little French girls to shame; for my part, she inspires me with devotion.[86]

Louise said she did not want to return to Canada except as a nun; there is no record that she realized her ambition. Cooperation had also been found on the part of the parents, as in the case of another girl, brought up in French fashion, going to visit her natural parents in their bark lodge not far from Quebec. Her father, Mantoueabeouichit, "very happy to see his daughter well clothed and in very good condition," would not allow her to stay for long, and sent her back.[87] In this connection it should be pointed out that there is no sure way of gauging the success rate of these efforts at assimilation; on this point, existing records are silent. One can reasonably assume, however, that successful cases would disappear from view as the individuals concerned passed as French; the resistant ones drew attention, and were therefore likely to be reported.

When boys or men were sent over, the occasion could assume some of the aspects of a diplomatic mission, as had occurred with Claude's Brazilians. In 1638, the son of Iwanchon, a Montagnais captain, laid his "crown of porcelain beads" (wampum) at the feet of the French king "as a sign that he recognized the great Prince, in the name of all the nations, as their true and lawful monarch." The king and queen responded by showing him their dauphin, and making him a present of six suits of clothing "entirely of cloth of gold, velvet, satin, silk, plush, scarlet and everything else in keeping." Back in Quebec the young man displayed these gifts to Montmagny, "who deemed it advisable to distribute them among several of the nations present. Therefore, three splendid suits were given to this young Savage–one for himself, one for his son, and the third for his father. The three other suits were presented to Christian captains of different nations." They were worn in a procession for the feast of the Assumption of the Virgin, with the men wearing the six suits leading the Amerindian section. These chiefs responded by sending an Amerindian costume for the dauphin. They explained, "It is not a present that we make him, for his riches are far greater than ours; but it is a *metawagan*–a small toy to amuse his little Son, who may perhaps take pleasure in seeing how our children are dressed."[88]

Such gift exchanges continued throughout the period of New France, if one is to judge by the collection of "Les Enfants de France" at the Bibliothèque de Versailles. Two "porcelain collars" at Chartres Cathedral are mute testimony of another exchange, this time of a religious nature.[89]

War Prisoners

The French custom of sending war prisoners to France was described by an Englishman as "the great and most effectual means they have taken for confirming of their Indians, and for the subverting or corrupting of ours." According to John Nelson, a Scottish merchant who was at one point a prisoner at Quebec and who reported on his observations,

> they have from time to time transported into France some of the most eminent and enterprizing Indians (not only of their own, but of ours whom they have happened to take their prisoners) for no other intent, than to amaze and dazzle them with the greatness and splendour of the French Court and Armie where the King hath so thought it worth his countenancing as to send them into Flanders, where the Armies have been expressly mustered before them, to show their greatness.

As a matter of fact, added Nelson, "there are actually at this instant now at Versailles six Sagamos or chiefs sent from Canada, Hudson's Bay and Nova Scotia to sollicite such help and assistance against us."[90]

By the time Nelson penned his observations, the French had been sending Amerindian war prisoners to France for more than half a century. One of the most noted of these was the Mohawk Honatteniate who arrived at Havre-de-Grâce on 7 December 1649. Known to the French as Le Berger, he had several years before been ransomed by Montmagny from Pieskaret, the Algonquin captain who waged his own private war against the Iroquois with such success that he had become a legend in his own time.[91] Le Berger had returned to his own people, but did not forget that he owed his life to the French. He had opposed the killing of Father Isaac Jogues in 1646. Two years later he decided to give himself up to the French, which he did while on a hunting expedition near Trois-Rivières. The French were convinced that he had come to spy, and did not believe him when he showed a scar on his arm where he claimed to have taken a blow intended for Jogues. They shackled his feet. To prove his sincerity, he arranged for some fellow Iroquois to be captured by the French. All of the prisoners managed to escape, except Le Berger, who determinedly remained. The French, fearful that he might one day return to his own country with information he had gathered while at Trois-Rivières, decided to send him to France. On board the ship, the sailors bound him for fear he would escape; in the morning he would be found free of his fetters. This happened several times, so that the sailors began to wonder if he were a sorcerer.[92] The sight of Havre-de-Grâce so astonished him that he did not speak for two hours. Although it was in December, he refused to wear a hat, and preferred to go barefooted rather than to confine his feet in French shoes and stockings. Injuring his foot in consequence, he was lodged in the hospital at Dieppe where the nuns reported that "he took his repast, not as a Barbarian, but as a temperate man; for, although he was tall and powerful, he ate rather sparingly." Eventually, he was taken to Paris, where he was lodged in a house for recent converts; there he died. The concluding remark about Le Berger was to the effect that it was estimated that he had eaten fifty men in his day.

The most celebrated incident in the history of New France concerning Amerindians in Europe occurred when Denonville transported thirty to sixty Iroquois war prisoners for service as galley slaves.[93] A terse note in *Mercure Galant* reported the arrival of the Iroquois destined for galley service, to see if they would be useful for it.[94] The experiment–if that is what it can be called–aroused bitter criticism at the time. Jesuit Jean de Lamberville (1663–1714), for one, felt that it threatened his work among the Iroquois, particularly as the prisoners included "some who had been to France often."[95] Lahontan also had some sharp words on the subject.[96] As early as 1663 it had been proposed to destroy the Iroquois either by killing them or by sending their best men to serve in the galleys.[97] Talon three years later wrote in a similar vein;[98] in 1684, La Barre was urged to take as many Iroquois prisoners as possible for service in the galleys.[99] One can only speculate as to the fate of the Iroquois once they got to France. That at least some of them were sent to Marseilles is suggested by an account that concerns the expenses of four Iroquois travelling from Bordeaux and Castelnaudary to that city.[100] Perhaps the cries of outrage from the colony had their effect, or perhaps the Iroquois died too quickly to be of much use as galley slaves. Or perhaps it was pressure exerted by allies; in any event, the survivors were released more than a year later, in 1689.[101] According to de Lamberville, only thirteen returned to Canada; he claimed the rest died from "destitution."[102] A nineteenth-century historian listed the names of twenty-one he claimed had been sent to Rochefort for return to Canada.[103] This episode is unique in the history of New France. When Frontenac returned for his second term as governor, he brought three of the Iroquois with him.[104] One of these, Orecone (whose name also appears, in the casual seventeenth-century French orthography, as Oreacona, Orcoué, or Oréouache), was Frontenac's inseparable companion.[105] He became renowned for his exploits in the French cause, which he explained "with a modesty rare among Indians, that he still had not done enough to repay his father Onontio."[106]

The English, in the meantime, remained convinced that the French policy of sending influential Amerindians to France was producing better results than it actually was. Nelson makes this clear:

> In regard to our Indians, no better methods can be taken, than by imitating the French, both as to their encouragements at home, as also to have some chiefs of the diverse nations of the Indians to be sent into England whereby to give a counterpoise unto the French reputation and greatness.[107]

But the French had slowly become convinced that the policy had produced nothing but useless expense, at least as far as Amerindian chiefs were concerned.[108] First of all, Amerindian delegates displayed a tendency to consider themselves as equal even to the French king, in spite of all the pomp and circumstance with which he was surrounded. Secondly, even when they were suitably impressed with French might, they were seldom able to fully convince their fellows in the New World of what they had seen in the Old. So it was, that in terms of gaining new alliances or cementing existing ones, such visits proved ineffective, finally leading the French to discourage the practice.[109] Unofficial or casual visits also came to be discouraged, particularly during the eighteenth century. In 1740, the unauthorized passage to France of a Micmac and his interpreter drew severe official displeasure on the head of the captain involved.[110] The Micmac, Denis d'Esdain, was given red cloth, gold braid, gold fringe, beads, and ribbon in assorted colors and the missionary Jean-Louis Le Loutre was instructed to impress upon him the value of the gift from the king, and to assure him that His Majesty would have treated him even better if he had come to France with proper authorization.[111]

Such reactions on the part of the French accorded with the attitudes of Amerindians who, during the sixteenth and seventeenth centuries, seldom regarded going to Europe with any particular enthusiasm, to say the least. European explorers and colonizers reported, with apparent surprise, that while Amerindians travelled much in their own countries they were not eager to go to Europe. Ribault had discovered this in "La Floride" when under instructions from the French queen to bring back two Amerindians, presumably for her court. Ribault obtained the consent of an Amerindian "king," who named two men; these, at first, felt they were being honored over their fellows, and so were happy to consent. But the two quickly changed their minds when they realized that they would be leaving their homeland. The best efforts of the French to cajole them in accepting their lot proved fruitless, and they escaped, carefully leaving behind the clothing and other items their hosts had given them.[112] Similarly, the king's geographer, Jean Mocquet, told of a young Caribbean Indian who had indicated a willingness to go to France under the impression that it was the ship in which the French were sailing. Upon learning the truth, he sought to escape; the French tied him, but he freed himself from his bonds. By that time the ship was too far out at sea for him to swim back to shore. The frustrated young man vented his fury on a shipmate, an Amerindian belonging to an enemy tribe. The captain ordered the belligerent one to be whipped, to which his only reaction was to tense his shoulders and shroud himself in silence, even as the lash raised welts on his back. Eventually Mocquet presented him to the king.

The loneliness that Amerindians probably experienced in Europe was suggested by Mocquet's story of Yapoco, whom he saw in Paris with Claude's group. Mocquet had known Yapoco in Brazil; the latter, upon seeing a familiar face from his homeland, ran and embraced him about the neck, and recounted his adventures.[113] Some Amerindians went to extraordinary lengths to return home.[114] Occasionally, particular circumstances modified this attitude, at least in the case of some individuals; one little girl cried so hard to join her companions, who were being sent to France, that she was allowed to go along, too. Noël Negabamat (c.1600–1666), the Montagnais captain who was a firm friend of the French, expressed a wish to go to France, but instead was sent to Boston on an unsuccessful embassy in 1650 with Jesuit Gabriel Druillettes (1607–85) to seek an alliance with the English against the Iroquois.[115]

Europe Through Amerindian Eyes

Outside of Montaigne's celebrated interview with three Brazilians in Rouen, in which they expressed surprise at the social inequalities they saw in French society, there are very few reports of Amerindian impressions of Europe from the sixteenth or even the seventeenth centuries. Already noted were the accounts of Amerindians who had gone over with Gravé Du Pont, and had influenced Begourat to allow his son to go. Obviously, impressions must have been expressed in terms of cultural experiences; thus the son of Iwanchon told of "rolling cabins drawn by moose."[116] In another case the visitor, seeing the street of metal workers' shops in Paris, wondered if the coppersmiths were not relatives of the king, and the copper trade a privilege of the seigneurs.[117] Back in the New World, reports of such masses of people and houses seemed incredible. "They have bribed you" was an understandable reaction.[118] It is also entirely possible that the Amerindians, once they recovered from their first astonishment, were not so overwhelmed by European cities as Europeans would have liked to assume. From the very beginning, Amerindians were loyal to their own cultural values and displayed a preference for their own way of life. Typical was Louis of Dominique, who after some time in France wanted only to return to his own people. Asked if he was happy to be returning to the "desert" of Dominique after staying in Paris, where he had lived in beautiful houses and associated with princes, he replied simply that he loved his own country best.[119] As soon as he was back home, he took great pleasure in discarding his French clothes and putting on his native garb.[120]

Europeans were misled by their own preconceptions of Amerindians as "poor savages" who could not help but be impressed by a sophisticated civilization. The Montagnais of Tadoussac were not alone in conceiving things "only in their own manner."[121] The truth, of course, was that Amerindians had a sophistication of their own.[122] The French began to perceive this when they observed that the Amerindians were quite as devoted to their own self-interest as were the French, and were as willing to avail themselves of every means at their disposal to gain their own ends. Thus those chiefs who were impressed with French power reacted by trying to win it to the service of their particular interests. The French found themselves not over-awing simple savages, but negotiating with accomplished diplomats. There is little wonder that their initial enthusiasm for bringing chiefs to France cooled.

The Europe that visiting Amerindians saw was not what Europeans expected them to see. The French concentrated so intensely on the undeniable glories of their civilization that they quite naturally tended to minimize its less attractive side. For instance, Cartier, in bringing his reluctant Iroquois guests to the court of François I, would quite reasonably have expected them to be impressed with France's royal splendors without taking into consideration the beggars outside the palace walls. Yet the sight of those beggars very likely shocked the Iroquois as it was later to shock the Brazilians interviewed by Montaigne. The Paris in which the court was held was a fortress city. Public executions were at times daily occurrences and could hardly have been avoided by visiting Amerindians. In fact, the year after Cartier's Iroquois arrived, 1535, was that in which the practice of public burnings, tortures, and mutilations of heretics was being stepped into high gear.[123] The accounts of some of these executions are so horrifying that one could wonder whether

A young Inuit woman and her seven-year-old daughter, brought to Antwerp in 1566 and put on exhibition. Woodcut from handbill advertising the occasion.

visitors from the northeastern woodlands of North America, where torture was practised, did not learn a thing or two. It was an age, for one mild example, when counterfeiters were boiled in oil by being ever so slowly dipped into the bubbling liquid.[124] The filth and confusion of the crowded Paris streets could not be avoided by those who ventured out, unless they were rich enough to afford sedan chairs. By contrast, Le Jeune, in seeking to escape from the smoke and crowded conditions of an Amerindian lodge, found solitude and cleanliness in a snowbank, although it was a cold comfort.[125]

Amerindian visitors to Europe during both the sixteenth and seventeenth centuries saw a young population; a study of 3,700 children of all classes born in Paris at the end of the seventeenth century indicates an overall life expectancy of twenty-three years.[126] The average life expectancy for ruling classes in Europe was twenty-eight years for a man, thirty-four years for a woman. More than half the children who were born alive died before their seventh year. At the end of the sixteenth century, France counted 230 cities and towns, and a population of 16,000,000 that consisted of ninety percent peasants, eight percent bourgeoisie (who were mostly small merchants), and two percent nobility.[127]

Epidemics were still recurrent. Paris and Marseilles had been hit in 1580; in 1630, the plague took nine out of ten inhabitants in Pignerol,[128] while Naples and Genoa lost nearly half their populations in 1565. Other diseases could be just as devastating; in 1599, dysentery took 2,500 of the 3,000 people of Santander, Spain. Epidemics were often followed by famines; when poor crop conditions coincided with an outbreak of disease, the results could be particularly severe, as with the famines of 1594–97 and 1659–62. In 1661 young Louis XIV gained political advantage by appearing as a benevolent ruler when he distributed free grain and bread.[129]

The economic crisis of the first half of the seventeenth century led to a series of popular revolts; in fact, the peasants could be described as being in a state of perpetual revolt.[130] There were riots in which wheat merchants, corrupt officials, and usurers were killed by mobs. One such incident occurred in Dauphiné in 1588. Its leader, Jean Servé or Paulmier, apparently took the time during carnival to participate in festivities by dressing in a bear's skin and eating what passed for Christian flesh while sitting in the mayor's chair, while the people danced in the streets crying, "Christian flesh for sixpence!" According to one historian, the ceremonial eating of human flesh on such occasions represented the overturning of social values.[131] In Saintonge, a tax collector was cut to pieces alive in 1636. Between 1590 and 1630, witch hunting was at its

On a prison wall at Gisors, France, an imprisoned Frenchman wiled away his time engraving scenes from his memories of America. Amerindians and Europeans dance together in what may be a marriage celebration. In the upper right corner, a European holds a banner with a cross while another holds what may be a cross of possession. The date is about 1561.

height in France.[132] The sixteenth and seventeenth centuries also saw France torn by extensive and extremely damaging wars. The Wars of Religion, 1559–98, were marked by the 1572 massacre of St. Bartholomew's Day, in which 3,000 Protestants were killed in Paris, and 20,000 in all of France. The anarchic upheavals known as the Fronde, 1648–53, caused a population loss of twenty percent in some areas.[133] It was the worst crisis of the Ancien Régime, which Louis XIV sought to remove from memory by destroying all public documents relating to it.[134]

In other words, visiting Amerindians did not find in Europe a society in which living conditions were generally more comfortable than those they had been used to. Cold was such a hazard in Renaissance Europe that people frequently died of exposure. (It was during this period that chimneys were perfected, so that the nuisance of smoke was eliminated, at least for those who could afford such luxury.)[135] Neither did Amerindians find a society with less violence than their own; rather they found one in which for all practical purposes it was the prerogative of a privileged group.[136] Amerindians found this unacceptable, as they were accustomed to considering each man his own master, whether in trade, warfare, or religion. They were astonished to see poverty in the midst of opulence; it did not accord with their practice of sharing, which, if not always even, was always inclusive.[137]

What the Amerindians saw in Europe only confirmed them in the belief that they were at least equal, if not superior, to the French, both as individuals and as a separate civilization. The people in France, for their part, continued to regard Amerindians as curiosities; apart from Montaigne, few Frenchmen seem to have considered that there was anything to learn from these exotic visitors. From the viewpoint of their contribution to the development of understanding and sympathy between the two worlds, the visits can only be considered as failures; in any event, bringing about understanding was a secondary aim. More important were the international considerations, involving as they did challenges to Spain, to Portugal, and to papal authority. Here the French displayed considerable skill, and developed diplomatic techniques for dealing with Amerindians that were to stand them in very good stead in staking out their New World empire.

Terres Arctic
Nouveau Danemarcq.
Mer Christiane
New North Walles
New South walles.
Buttons Bay.
Hope Check
Port Nelson
New Severne R.
Golfe de Hudson, ou Hudson Bay.
Mansfeild I.
Nottingham
Salisbury I.
C. Charles
Estotilande, ou
Terre de Laborad
Nouvelle Bretag
la Grande Baye ou Deli
Lac Superieur
Lac de Puans
Karegnon di.
Ontario, ou Lac de St. Louys
Erie, ou du Chat
Nou velle France
Le Sague nay.
Quebecq
Tadoussac
Iroquois
Nouvelle Angle terre
Nouveau Pays Bas
Lange Eyland
Vir ginie
Floride Fran cois
Floride
La Floride Espagnole
Apalacy
Occident
Midi
Septentrion

PART III

Iron Men and True Men in New France

Sanson's map of New France, 1656.
Association of Canadian Map Libraries,
Facsimile No. 86, Public Archives
Canada.

CHAPTER 11

Traders Pave the Way

The interplay of French and Amerindian into the early history of New France is symbolized in the cartouche on Franquelin's map of northern America, 1699. National Map Collection, C-15791 Public Archives Canada.

THE SUCCESSFUL establishment of New France in the land that was popularly known as Canada was the culmination of a century of contact with the New World. The broad lines of the policy of douceur had already been worked out and remained only to be developed in specific points by traders disseminating material goods and missionaries spreading the gospel.

By the beginning of the seventeenth century, French officialdom was familiar with those northern regions where French ships had long resorted to fish, to whale, and to trade with the natives. Although their notions about Amerindians were still vague and even confused, officials understood very clearly how "fruitful, opportune and useful for us" this trade could be. Those were the words of Henry IV's commission of 8 November 1603 to Pierre Du Gua, Sieur de Monts (1558?–1628), the man who brought out Champlain.[1] According to popular rumor, de Monts found that the Basques had been in the area for so long that the Amerindians were using the Basque language for trade; a Spanish historian corroborated that Montagnais and Basques were able to converse with each other.[2] "The merchants trade with the Savages of the country," Thevet remarked more than once.[3] The sight of Amerindians dressed in martens (marten being of the sable family) obviously impressed hierarchy-conscious Europeans, for whom the wearing of such furs was the privilege of rank backed by sumptuary laws. According to a seventeenth-century description, the people of Labrador "painted their bodies to appear beautiful, wore silver and copper rings in their ears, and dressed in marten and other furs."[4] Verrazzano had reported marten being worn as breech clouts.[5] Personal fortunes had already been made in the fur trade, as the king implied when he referred to "the apparently great profits" his subjects had amassed in those regions.[6]

Furs were, of course, only some of the items in which Europeans had found profit trafficking in the New World, as the following report from Brazil indicates:

> Trade will serve to win the spirit of the Savages, who love nothing more, and without it you will be very badly received. Through them you will be able to establish a commerce yielding almost incredible profits, because with baubles such as bells, brass rings, trumpets and horns, strings of beads . . . you will be able to obtain a variety of precious merchandize.[7]

One century later, Europeans were still expressing surprise at the Amerindian attitude that made such profits possible:

> It is well known that prodigious profits can be made from the savages with cheap trinkets. These peoples . . . in truth seem to have a singular philosophy . . . if they decide that the effort to obtain certain commodities is disagreeable, they remain in a pure animal indolence, living like hares or deer in the woods. They regard us as fools . . . because we endure so many hardships for frivolities such as clothing and houses. . . . [8]

It was a different scale of social values rather than a lack of commercial perspicacity that created such a situation. As Cartier had long before discovered, Amerindians were perfectly capable of raising their prices if they thought the situation warranted it.[9] Nicolas Denys attested to the fact that the natives often outwitted ships' crews in trade;[10] and a Jesuit, bargaining for a goose to make broth for some patients, found himself paying what he considered to be an exorbitant price. In general, Amerindians considered Europeans to be lacking in judgment because they were prepared to risk so much for a trade that was not essential for the support of life.[11] The importance Amerindians attached to trade concerned the accumulation of goods in order to honor community obligations, based on status and reciprocity. Trade was part of the apparatus for the redistribution of goods within a particular group that functioned without reference to cost or price in the Western sense. Amerindian social and economic institutions were not separated and they were in Europe.[12] External trade conducted by "tribal" societies was not necessarily a guide to its material well-being. Vespucci had observed something of this when he had reported that Amerindians neither bought nor sold, "for they are quite content with what nature freely offers them. . . . Of their friends, they are just as eager to ask and to receive." Northern Amerindians as well as Brazilians, however, were active traders, and knew very well how to make a profit in their external dealings.[13]

The interplay of attitudes of these two profoundly different ways of life–the Amerindian and the European–provided the background against which the fur trade developed so as to become "the best profession in the world for self-enrichment within a short time."[14] Exploitation soon began; during the first decades of the sixteenth century a typical summer of trading yielded 15,000 to 20,000 furs.[15]

Prehistorically, Tadoussac had been a trading rendezvous for hunters from Hudson Bay as well as for agriculturalists from New England. That Europeans recognized the importance of pre-existing networks is suggested by such comments as "Canadians are always trading"[16] and "most Canadians have been trading between themselves since time immemorial."[17] In 1603 Champlain encountered a band of Montagnais between Tadoussac and Gaspé on their way to barter arrows and moose meat with Etchemin, Algonquin, and other Montagnais.[18] Maps of the middle of the sixteenth century have Micmac names on Cape Breton, implying active contact with native populations.[19] One of the names the Micmac were known by, Tarrantines, may have meant traders.[20] "The greatest riches and treasures of Florida, Canada and Baccalaos are in their peltries and fisheries of cod and whales," wrote Thevet in 1575.[21] This was not mere theorizing; between 1550 and 1570, Prince Edward Island saw as many as two hundred ships a year, probably attracted by walrus and seal as well as the fisheries and fur trade.[22] Thevet placed the figure at a hundred ships a year for fishing.[23] In 1578, 150 French ships were noted at Newfoundland, as well as 100 Spanish, fifty Portuguese and fifty English.[24] La Court de Pré-Ravillon's 1591 trip on the *Bonaventure* was to acquire train oil, tusks, and walrus hides on the Magdalen Islands in the Gulf.[25] When David Ingram walked up the coast from Mexico in 1568–69, he claimed to have been finally picked up by a French vessel, *Gargarine* of Le Havre, commanded by a Captain Champagne, that had come to Cape Breton to trade.[26] The English became exceedingly interested when they heard that ships were leaving New France laden with furs reported to be worth 8,000 pounds;[27] they estimated France's annual revenue from the trade at 30,000 crowns.[28]

Flensing whales in the New World, sixteenth century. From a very early period, coastal natives assisted Europeans in their whaling operations. De Bry, 1602. National Maritime Museum, Greenwich, London SE10 9NF.

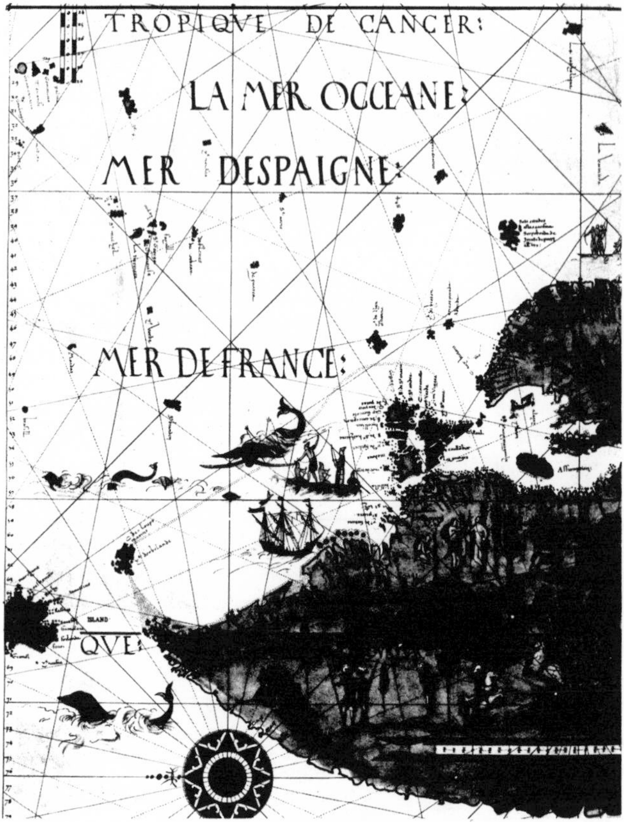

Europeans whaling off the northern end of the Straits of Belle Isle, as illustrated on the world map by Pierre Descelliers, 1546.

This activity was along the coast and in the Gulf. On the upper St. Lawrence, Cartier's voyages appear to have been followed by a hiatus in trading activity; contact does not seem to have been reestablished until 1581:

> drawen on by gifts of many trifling things, which were of great value with them, they are . . . within these two or three yeeres, content againe to admit a traffique, which two yeeres since [1581] was begunne with a small barke of thirtie tunnes, whose returne was found so profitable, as the next yeere following, being the last yeere, by

> those Merchants, who meant to have kept the trade secret unto themselves, from any others of their owne Countreymen.

Apparently the profits to be had from this trade were great, as the French were reported to be obtaining "fourteene or fifteene hundreth for every one hundreth."[29]

The same year that Carlysle made his report, 1583, "a man of St. Malowe" discovered the sea on the backside of Hochelaga.[30] This may have been an exaggerated version of the statement of Cartier's nephew, Noël, to the effect that he had heard of a great lake to be found ten days' journey westward, beyond the Lachine Rapids. This immediately aroused speculation that it could be the sea that would lead to the Orient.[31] Also in 1583, a major French expedition headed by Etienne Bellenger, a Rouen merchant who had previously been twice to the Acadian coast, traded at Cape Breton and in Norumbega. Under the auspices of the archbishop of Rouen, Charles Cardinal de Bourbon, and of Anne de Joyeuse, the duc de Joyeuse and admiral of France, the expedition was more than a trading trip, being also concerned with reconnaissance for colonization.[32] About one hundred leagues south of Cape Breton, Bellenger found "a towne of fourscore houses covered with the barkes of trees, upon a river side."[33] If this was a Micmac summer village, it was an unusually large one. Generally, he found the Amerindians good to deal with, "But those about Cape Briton and threescore or fowerscore leagues Westward are more cruell and subtill of norture than the rest." In that region he lost two of his men and a small pinnace "which happened through their owne follye in trusting the salvadges too farr."[34] In spite of that incident, he brought back enough "beastes skynnes, as bevers, otters, marternes, lucernes, seales, buffs, dere skynnes, all drest and painted on the innerside with divers excellent colours" to have made the expedition a profitable one. The next year, 1584, five ships of St. Malo returning from "Canada and the Contries upp the Bay of St. Laurence," were reported to "have founde suche swete in that newe trade that they are preparinge tenne shippes to returne thither on January nexte."[35]

By the last two decades of the sixteenth century, trade had reached such a volume that France decided to establish a monopoly in order to bring it under control. Accordingly, one was granted to Cartier's nephews, Noël and Chaton de La Jannaye. In his application, Noël said he had been engaged in the Canadian trade for some years; this could indicate that Cartier had recognized the trading potential of the region and had encouraged his nephew to take advantage of it, in spite of his own failure with the Stadaconans.[36] However, so violent was the reac-

A French view of a Canadian beaver. From Bacqueville de la Potherie, *Histoire de l'Amérique septentrionale*, 1722.

tion of rivals that the monopoly lasted only about four months before free trade was reestablished. Commercial competition assumed the aspects of a war in which the French fought each other almost as ardently as they fought other nations. Nevertheless, there was some differentiation of trading zones, with the Rouennais and Malouins frequenting Tadoussac and the Rochellais going to the Gaspé.[37] During free-trade days, as many as twenty vessels would be seen at one time at Tadoussac during the summer; but after the Company of New France became operative in 1627, these were reduced to two a year, and then only in summer.[38] In Europe, Amsterdam became the center of the fur trade during the seventeenth century, acting as an intermediary between the New World, Moscow, and the Orient. Moscow was the principal market, though from the Far East there came a steady demand for otter. This demand, coupled with the need of European felters for New World beaver, as those of the Old World had been hunted out, resulted in a boom for furs that lasted until the 1670s, when oversupply resulted in the collapse of the Moscow market. The fur trade was not only the midwife for the birth of New France, it also played a primary role in maintaining England's Plymouth colony for about thirty years.[39] For New France, the fur trade was to be the major commercial activity throughout the French regime.

This competition had encouraged de Monts to petition for a monopoly in New France, "land of the long cold where the bears are white."[40] In presenting his case he said he could see no better way to serve his country

> than by applying himself to discover distant coasts and lands either unpeopled or else inhabited by Savages innocent of religion, law or civility. There he would establish and fortify himself, attracting Christians and developing commerce, all under the authority of the French flag.[41]

De Monts, in winning his mandate to colonize New France, received a commission that was drawn up along lines similar to those that had been granted previously to Roberval and Villegaignon.[42] In other words, French thinking in this regard had remained constant since the first attempts at colonization. In the case of de Monts, Henry IV named him lieutenant-governor of New France and proposed a monopoly in return for bringing out 100 colonists a year. De Monts was less sanguine. He had seen what had happened to Chauvin, who had not been able to honor such a commission. But de Mont's voyage of reconnaissance of

1603, in which he had been accompanied by Gravé Du Pont and Champlain, had confirmed him in his belief that the prospects for settlement were good. Because of this he agreed to take out sixty colonists annually, whom he thought he could recruit from among vagabonds. Either de Monts was familiar with the reluctance of French workers and peasants to hazard unknown but vividly imagined dangers (particularly in Canada with its disagreeably non-French climate), or else he believed that colonies could be established by using people who for one reason or another were having difficulties in the Old World. Perhaps he shared something of both opinions, as he was evidently a pragmatist.

De Monts's project aroused considerable interest in France, if one is to judge by the amount of space it received in *Le Mercure François*.[43] This could be an indication of the growing pressures in French official circles for the successful establishment of a New France overseas. While officialdom was concentrating on grand colonial designs, however, public attention had been distracted by the weather. Europe was experiencing a period of severe winters, when rivers were so frozen that loaded wagons could drive on them, and the citizens of Antwerp saw the river Scheldt frozen as it had not been since 1563. Individuals had died of the cold or were crippled by it–many hands and feet had suffered cruelly.[44] Little wonder, then, that *Le Mercure François* paid particular attention to Canadian winters. De Monts's colonists spent their first winter in Canada (1604–5) on Ile Ste. Croix in Eastern Etchemin territory. According to *Le Mercure François*, they found that the Amerindian type of housing was the best in order to survive the cold.[45] Such an adaptation seems to have been fairly frequent during the first days of colonization.[46] The hard winter at Ile Ste. Croix had brought a strange malady believed to have been caused by drinking water from melted snow.[47] The malady, of course, was scurvy. As the French were not familiar with the use of melted snow, they were understandably suspicious of it. Lescarbot, in describing the first winter, when about thirty-five colonists had died out of a total of eighty, implied that one of the causes had been bad water: "many idle and sluggish companions dranke snow-water, not willing to take the paines to cross the river."[48] Champlain also referred to being obliged to drink melted snow that winter,[49] but was not convinced it was the cause of the malady, particularly after his first winter at Quebec when he noted that an Amerindian, living with the French and sharing their diet of salted meat, died.[50] More than twenty years later Champlain wrote positively that the disease was entirely due to eating salted food and to the lack of fresh provisions.[51] In spite of their reservations as to the snow, the French seemed to have regarded the climate as healthful,

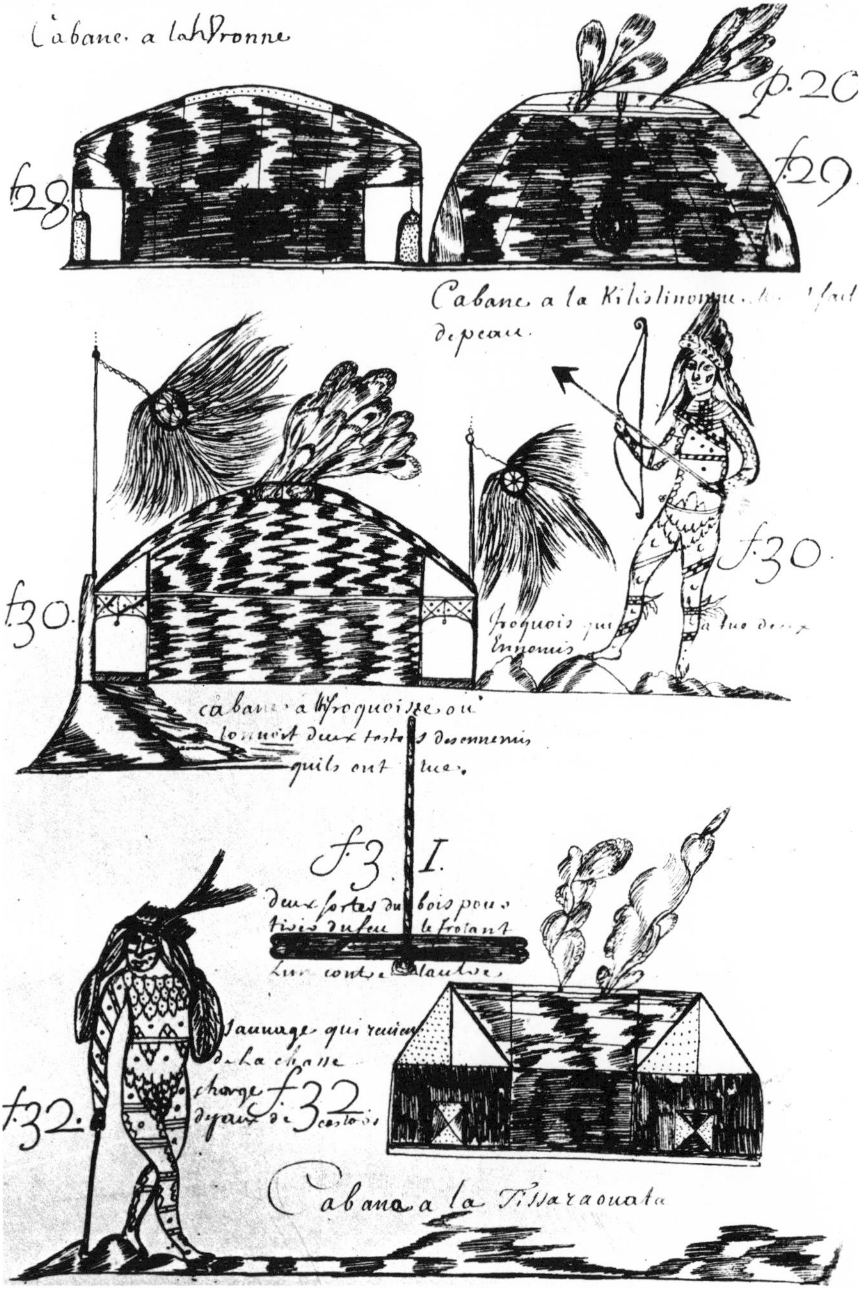
Cabane a laHronne
p. 20
f.28
f.29
Cabane a la Kilistinonne
depeau
f.30.
f.30
Iroquois qui
a tue deux
Ennemis
cabane a l'Iroquoise ou
lonvoit deux testes desennemis
quils ont tue.
f.31.
deux sortes du bois pour
tirer du feu le frotant
Lun contre lautre
Sauvage qui revient
de la chasse
charge
depeaux de castors
f.32.
f.32
Cabana a la Tissaraouata

as they attributed the good health and long life of Amerindians to it. Later, second-generation colonists were seen as being healthy for the same reason.[52]

If the aim of the establishment of New France was the extension of commerce, as Montesquieu observed,[53] there can be no doubt that it was successful. So much so, in fact, that early colonists often displayed a preference for trading to the hard work of farming. It was a tendency colonial officials strove to counteract, for while such enterprise led to the rapid penetration of the new lands, it was not helpful in developing the agricultural basis so desperately needed for permanence. It was a perennial problem for French colonial administrators. What little is known of Roberval's effort indicates that he was more interested in finding the fabled golden kingdom of the Saguenay than in establishing farms; de La Roche sought primarily to maintain a post to detect violations of his trading monopoly; and Chauvin de Tonnetuit concerned himself so exclusively with trade that he did not properly provide for the sixteen men he left to winter at Tadoussac in 1600, who had no choice but to live off the charity of the Amerindians. That he had made no attempt to honor his commitment to establish 500 colonists on the St. Lawrence in order to secure France's claim to the country was widely known.

The founding of Quebec (Montagnais territory, as was Tadoussac) altered the pattern of the fur trade.[54] In the days when it was carried on from ships, Amerindians made annual trips from far in the interior to such seaboard rendezvous points as Tadoussac, Miscou, and the mouth of the St. John River. At the arrival of the first ships they lit bonfires along the coast,[55] a signal for those in the area. As permanent posts developed along the coast, the immediate effect was to extend the trading time available to Amerindians. The establishment of Quebec and later of Trois-Rivières and Montreal shifted the location of rendezvous points into the interior. Annual trade fairs developed, the one at Montreal being particularly important. The posts also provided bases from which the French could send their agents into the interior instead of waiting for the Amerindians to come to them. This in turn affected the role of the Amerindian middleman.[56]

The requirements of this trade were variations of what had been needed in Brazil where, in the words of Staden, the French "had been obliged to conform to Amerindian customs and manners."[57] Realizing the importance of wampum to the people of the northeastern woodlands, the French adapted very quickly to its use in both trading and diplomacy.[58] For the Amerindians, the fur trade affected subsistence patterns as the northern Indian hunters concentrated on winter trap-

Various types of Amerindian dwellings, as interpreted by Bécard de Granville, *Les Raretés des Indes*. In the second row, scalps hang from poles before and behind an Iroquois cabin. The man at lower left carries a beaver pelt on his shoulder. C-16852 Public Archives Canada.

ping, thereby becoming more dependent upon the agriculturally produced foods of the Huron.[59] In their turn, the Huron grew more corn to meet this new demand. This move away from self-sufficiency toward interdependence increased the danger of famine, a consequence of the trade which had been experienced very early by the Micmac.[60] In spite of this, the trade brought material benefits the immediate effect of which was to encourage an efflorescence of the cultures of the northeastern woodlands during the seventeenth and early eighteenth centuries, a sort of swan-song before their submergence by the tidal wave of European immigration.[61]

Competition between Europeans for the fur trade put Amerindians in a strong position, providing them with the opportunity of playing off one trader against another. The initiative of the French in being first in the field did not free them from such unwelcome competition. Rather, it encouraged the aggressive attentions of the English and the Dutch. Henry Hudson, exploring the coast for the Dutch in 1609, learned from the natives that they were already trading with the French. A group "brought many Beaver skinnes, and other fines Furres, which they would have changed for redde gowns. For the French trade with them for red Cassockes, Knives, Hatchets, Copper Kettles, Trevits, Beades and other trifles." Robert Juet, a member of Hudson's crew, added in his journal, "they desire Cloathes, and are very civill."[62] Later the *Warwick*, on a trading journey up the Potomac, encountered Anacostans, "who trade with Canadian Indians." The English were near the site that was to become Washington:

> On the 11th of July 1632, there came from another place seven lusty men – they had red fringe and two of them had beaver coats. They had two axes, such as Captain Kirke traded in Cannida, which he bought at Whits of Wapping, and there I bought mine, and think I had as good as he . . . They called themselves Mostikums, but afterwards I found they were of a people three days' journey from these and were called Hereckeenes, who, with their own beaver, and what they get of those that adjoin them upon them, do drive a trade in Cannida, at the plantation, which is fifteen days' journey from this place. These people delight not in toys, but in useful commodities.[63]

About two years later the Dutch, on an exploratory trading mission among the Mohawk, were told by the latter that the French had already been there and had offered better value than the Dutch: besides, they had also distributed gifts.[64] Up in Huronia, at this same time, the French were also distributing gifts in order to pave the way for evan-

Huron women were also fond of personal adornments, referred to as "matachias" in early accounts. Difficult porcupine quill work soon gave way to easier beadwork in many areas. Du Creux, *Historiae Canadensis*, 1664. C-99228 Public Archives Canada.

gelization. In the words of Jean de Brébeuf, "This is a small thing in detail, but on the whole it exerts a great influence and is of great importance in these regions."[65] The Dutch were impressed with the quality of the French goods they saw among the Amerindians, "very good axes to cut the underwood, and French shirts and coats and razors."[66]

As for the Amerindians whose territory was concerned, they were willing to go along with de Monts's project insofar as they realized its implications, as they expected benefits for themselves. Besides, by this time they liked the French who, following the Cartier-Roberval failure, had made efforts to respect Amerindian formalities and ways of doing things. The French had by now worked out a general policy concerning Amerindians:

> If one is amiable and gentle with them, they will reciprocate in kind. It is extremely important to abide by this from the beginning, taking

> great care in small matters as well as in large, in order to lead these people along the paths of friendship and salvation.[67]

Perhaps most importantly of all, continued *Le Mercure François*, it should be remembered that Amerindians "are not concerned about those things for which we torment ourselves so much."[68] This, of course, was more easily said than realized in practice. The colonial society as finally achieved by the French never made more than a minimum allowance for the values of Amerindians. However, in New France at least, Frenchmen did respect the Amerindian ideal of personal liberty. For instance, Poutrincourt,[69] commander of the first permanent settlement in Acadia, instead of using Amerindians as servants or enslaving them, followed the instructions he had received from the king and sought to evangelize them.[70] Distinctions between French and Amerindians were to be suppressed by persuading the latter to adopt the manners and customs of

Pipe-smoking Huron wearing elaborate embroideries and painted designs. Du Creux, *Historiae Canadensis*, 1664. C-99229 Public Archives Canada.

France and to change the "spirit of libertinage which is natural to a savage into that of orderly humanity which expresses the higher nature of man."[71] This approach, for all its self-conscious righteousness, contributed to the handsome dividends received by the French when the Amerindians fought so effectively beside them during the colonial wars.

The Huron called the French "iron men," which Champlain says they expressed as *adoresetoüy*, and Sagard said as *agnonha.*[72] "Iron men" was a name that the people of the Northwest Coast in their turn applied to the English and Yankees during the eighteenth and nineteenth centuries. The Montagnais name for the French meant "men who are workers of wood," or "men who are in a vessel of wood"; Sagard said the term was *mistigoche*, wooden canoe or boat. In the days of de Monts, Amerindian impressions of their first view of the French in their "floating islands" were still vivid.[73] The French, they observed, were masters of iron and of merchandise. The Amerindians, welcoming them with their traditional hospitality–"they owe us nothing and we stay with them at their expense," Sagard had observed–soon found that the French did not respond in kind.[74] Later, an Amerindian was to tell a missionary that he did not want to go to the French heaven, as he would get nothing to eat there.[75]

More commonly, Amerindians reacted by offering their hospitality only if the French would live with them in their manner; otherwise they asked for payment.[76] Charles Lalemant (1587–1674), first superior of the Jesuits at Quebec, found the Amerindians not at all hospitable; on the contrary, they expected food or payment from the French, although they continued to exercise their traditional hospitality toward each other.[77] It was a case of each side expecting the other to conform to rules about which it knew nothing: the French, for instance, finding that the Amerindians had no notion of paying debts European-style, refused to grant them any more credit.[78] The process of accommodation and adaptation between the "iron men" and "the people" was already well on its way.

CHAPTER 12

Missionaries Accept the Challenge

Title page of Sagard's *Le Grand Voyage du Pays des Hurons,* 1632, showing Recollet missionaries. C-113480 Public Archives Canada.

THE HIGH NOTE of optimism about the prospects for colonizing this new land, where wheat and oats grew as well as they did in France,[1] was particularly evident in French hopes for evangelizing the natives. France's New World experiences had entrenched her officialdom more firmly than ever in its conviction that conversion of Amerindians was essential for the realization of a New France along the St. Lawrence. Accordingly, when the French returned to Quebec after their temporary eviction by the English, 1629–32, they prepared for an all-out offensive against the religious beliefs of their Amerindian allies. The Jesuits, soldiers of Christ, were at first assigned the task. Paul Le Jeune was their superior in Quebec from 1632 to 1639.

Early estimates of the ease with which Amerindians could be expected to be converted were already being modified. The natives, so eager to enter into trading and military alliances, displayed much less interest in adopting a new religion. If the French were to proceed by persuasion rather than by force, the best approach would be by obtaining the affection of these people through learning their languages. Such a procedure would take time; in fact, warned Charles Lalemant, the first six or seven years would seem unproductive to certain people. Perhaps, he continued, even ten or twelve years would be needed.[2] Le Jeune, basing his estimate on the experiences of the Jesuits in Brazil,[3] thought a generation would be a realistic estimate. He wondered if an "imposing" presence on the part of the French would facilitate the process.[4] By 1642 Charles Lalemant's brother, Jérôme (1593–1673), superior of the Huron mission who in 1645 became superior for Canada, confessed that early impressions of easily converting Amerindians were totally mistaken:

> experience has shown us that they [the Amerindians] are full of Diabolical Superstitions, looking upon their Dreams as their Divinities, upon whom the happiness of their lives depends. Besides that, we see that they acknowledge more powerful Genii who settle Public affairs, who cause Famine, who control Wars and give Victory to those who become most obedient to their will.[5]

The Jesuits by that time had come to realize that changing religious beliefs meant changing a whole way of life:

> the greatest opposition that we meet . . . consists in the fact that their remedies for diseases; their greatest amusements when in good health; their fishing, their hunting, and their trading; the success of their crops, of their wars, and of their councils, – almost all abound in

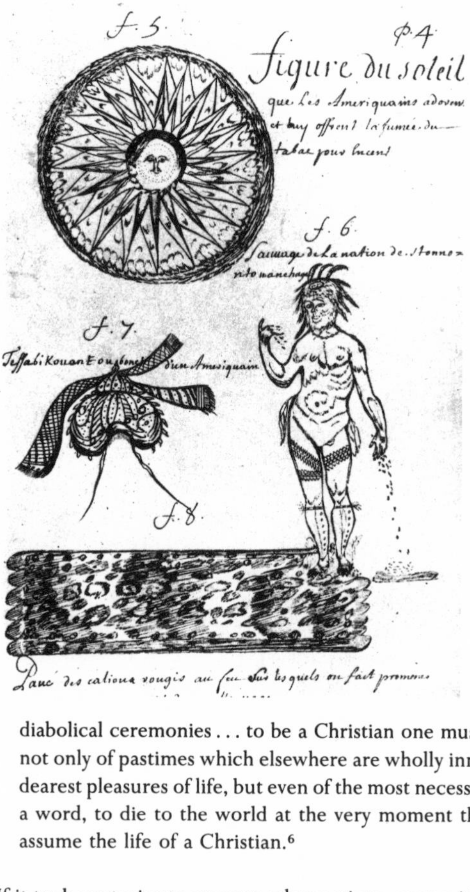

The sun was widely revered by Amerindians throughout the Americas. This representation, drawn by Bécard de Granville, is from Iroquoia; the Iroquois at lower right is walking on a bed of red-hot stones. C-21117 Public Archives Canada.

> diabolical ceremonies . . . to be a Christian one must deprive himself not only of pastimes which elsewhere are wholly innocent, and of the dearest pleasures of life, but even of the most necessary things, and, in a word, to die to the world at the very moment that one wishes to assume the life of a Christian.[6]

If it took centuries to convert other nations, even with the aid of miracles, why were immediate results expected without miracles in the New World?[7] But back in France, officials found it difficult to believe that "simple savages" could be so hard to convert, and the pressures continued.[8] In the New World, a backlash developed in the form of a growing conviction on the part of some officials that preaching was useless.[9] The missionaries were feeling the pressures of the meeting between two worlds.

This dilemma was perhaps best demonstrated by the spirit in which Amerindians accepted baptism. Donnacona, for instance, had formally

A Huron with two suns tattooed on his chest. Du Creux, *Historiae Canadensis*, 1664. C-99224 Public Archives Canada.

requested it of Cartier at Stadacona during the Frenchman's second voyage. Membertou and his family were pleased to be accorded the honor in 1610, which the French were equally pleased to give them to satisfy official pressures in France. Observing the importance the French attached to their religion, the Amerindians reacted by assuming that participation in this ritual would cement an alliance with the Christians.[10] When Biard and Ennemond Massé arrived at Port Royal in 1611, they found that the baptized Amerindians considered themselves allies of the French, "already nearly Normans," but had very little knowledge of Christianity. Biard was particularly incensed to find one such "Christian" with eight wives.[11] Later, baptism was regarded sometimes as a cause of death; as one Huron reasoned, if baptism were the path to heaven as the Jesuits claimed, then he would die as soon as the ceremony was performed.[12] Alternatively, it was seen as an aid to health;[13] Le Jeune was shocked to discover that some believed that the more water used, the more healthful the consequences.[14]

Learning to Speak Their Languages

Could it be, wondered the Jesuits, that such misapprehensions had been caused by the language barrier?[15] Amerindians showed little inclination to learn French; if the program of evangelization was to be realized, it would be incumbent upon the missionaries to learn native languages.[16] This was given top priority by Le Jeune in the four-pronged plan he devised to attack the kingdom of Satan. He placed language-study ahead of the establishment of seminaries for Amerindian children, the erection of a hospital, and the encouragement of a sedentary mode of life.[17] Long before the founding of New France, it had been realized that the use of interpreters for evangelization was not satisfactory. The second Council of Lima (1567–68) had ruled against the use of interpreters for preaching sermons and hearing confessions, a ruling that contravened royal decrees ordering that instruction be in Spanish.[18] Besides, missionaries were not long in discerning Amerindian admiration of rhetoric, of the man who had the power of words.[19] To gain supremacy among the Amerindians, it was necessary to master their language: "Anyone who knew their language perfectly would be powerful among them," Le Jeune observed.[20] He therefore accorded to language learning a paramount role, even liberating missionaries from other duties to undertake such studies. His tactics were simple and direct: "first we take steps to go and attack the enemy on its ground with its own terms, that is, by the knowledge of the Montagnais, Algonquin, and Huron languages."[21]

A course of action was quickly decided upon: to follow the example of Jean de Brébeuf (1593–1649), the Jesuits' outstanding linguist in New France, who had wintered with the Montagnais in 1625–26 to gain an understanding of the people and of their language. Le Jeune had done the same during the winter of 1634–35. Both Brébeuf—who soon turned his attention to Huron—and Le Jeune quickly discovered that learning these languages would not be the work of a day, or even of a season.[22] The missionaries soon discovered that the Amerindian languages were not simple or only partially developed, as was generally believed,[23] but exactly the opposite. These "excellent systems"[24] were fully formed and complex in their structures, and in a manner that was seldom compatible with European patterns of thought. "The astonishing thing," Brébeuf wrote of the Huron, "is that all their words are universally conjugated . . . we find ourselves hindered from getting them to say properly in their language, 'In the name of the Father, and of the Son, and of the Holy Ghost.' Could we say, for instance, 'In the name of our Father, and of His Son, and of their Holy Ghost'?"[25] Later Bressani lamented that the mere sign of the cross had cost the mission a year of

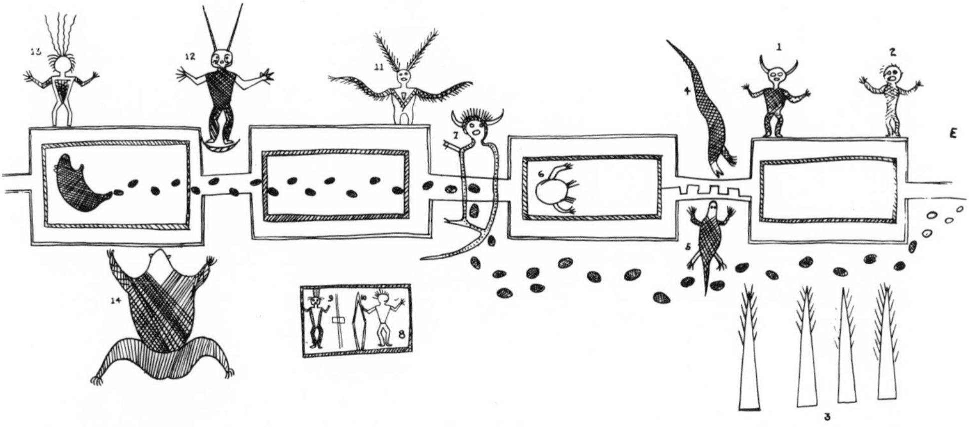

An Ojibway medicine lodge parchment, described as "very old" when it was collected by the Canadian Ethnology Service, National Museum of Man early in the twentieth century. According to its former owner, "the things it represents have been always". The "E" at right indicated east, from which Mugwa (bear), in the medicine lodge at far left, has come, as indicated by his tracks. The other figures: 1) manido; 2) medicine man, who instructs people how to "make medicine"; 3) medicine trees of the earth shelf below this one; 4) snake manido watching that no bad person enters the earth shelf below this one; 5) frog manido, doing the same thing; 6) shell with hands, which lives in a wigwam next to the earth shelf; 7) lynx manido, who watches the road to the other world as well as entrance to the lodge; 8) wabeno wigwam, which, although a bad practice medicine lodge, contains two medicine men who dance to make people good; 9) medicine man with cross signifying he has danced four times; 10) medicine man with post signifying he has danced and made medicine; 11) chief manido, who lives in the third world below this one; 12) manido standing on snake, watching the entrance to his lodge; 13) medicine man, watching medicine wigwam; 14) bear manido also watching.

study.[26] Even the talented Brébeuf had needed four years to discover the key to mastering Huron.[27]

Amerindian fondness for metaphor added to the missionaries' difficulties. "Unless you accustom yourself to it, you will understand nothing in their councils," Brébeuf warned. On the other hand, biblical metaphors were meaningless to Amerindians, abounding as they did with "sheepfolds" or "kingdoms," which had no counterpart in the native cultures.[28] In spite of such hazards, the missionaries-turned-linguists found Montagnais not as ambiguous as French;[29] eventually the priests learned to use metaphor in the Amerindian way to aid in their preaching.[30]

When the fathers wrote of the "poverty" of Amerindian languages, they were attributing the difficulties they found in translating Christian concepts to supposed defects in those tongues.[31] Another "defect" was discovered in the lack of words to express commonplaces of France or Europe. But the same missionaries soon came to recognize the wealth of Amerindian languages within their own cultural frameworks: "they have so tiresome an abundance that I am almost led to believe that I shall remain poor all my life in their language," Charles Lalemant complained of the Montagnais.[32] Brébeuf echoed those sentiments for the Huron when he wrote, "I shall have to go a long time to the school of the Savages, so prolific is their language."[33] The letter on Montagnais in Le Jeune's Relation for 1634, attributed to Lalemant, is the first known sustained discussion of a Canadian language.[34] Lalemant was impatient with his incapacity in Montagnais, not being able to say what he wanted; for Le Jeune, it was a triumphant day when he gave a speech in Montagnais fol-

Colonial officials and missionaries used pictures to get their message across to Amerindians. This was most effective when related to an already familiar idea or thing. The picture the officials are displaying to the Huron shows the Christian God in the heavens with the sun and other celestial bodies. From Lahontan, 1728. C-99231 Public Archives Canada.

lowing an Amerindian-style feast at which the governor had distributed gifts. By 1644 the Jesuits were speaking of the ease with which the missionaries were expounding the truths of the faith, "which at the beginning seemed to us most difficult to explain." Eventually missionaries were able to improve greatly the effectiveness of their preaching by adopting the special idioms and mannerisms of famous orators, making use of a tactic also employed successfully by French officials and envoys.[35]

The eloquence of Amerindians in their own tongues was so frequently noted as to have become axiomatic. The Jesuits considered that it was of a caliber that would have done justice to the finest minds of France. Typical was the remark of Sebastian Râles (1652–1724): "I fully believe that if I had written down what this Savage said to us, offhand and without preparation, you would readily acknowledge that the most able Europeans could scarcely, after much thought and study, compose an address that would be more forcible and better arranged." Brébeuf had observed that there were hardly any Amerindians "incapable of conversing or reasoning very well, and in good terms," on things with which they were acquainted.[36] He thought that the custom of their holding daily councils, in which each person had the right to express his opinion, allowed them to develop this fluency, as well as to learn how to speak with moderation even when the subject was highly charged.[37] They mocked those who stumbled in their speech, but with the missionaries they discreetly overlooked language blunders. When Le Jeune stuttered in Montagnais, it was passed off in laughter.[38]

With increasing proficiency in Amerindian languages, the Jesuits became aware of the limits of office for even the most respected of orators. Eloquence might give the power to persuade, but not to compel: "All the authority of their chief is in his tongue's end; for he is powerful in so far as he is eloquent; and, even if he kills himself talking and haranguing, he will not be obeyed unless he pleases the Savages."[39] In other words, mastery of language was merely a powerful aid rather than the pass-key to supremacy for which Le Jeune yearned. He sighed for someone who "could stop the wanderings of the Savages, and give authority to one of them to rule the others. . . . "[40] Still, he was impressed with the willingness of the New World men to accept the leadership of a knowledgeable person in a specific situation.[41]

The unreasoning savage of European folklore was giving way to the subtle savage of Jesuit experience. In the words of François Du Peron: "They nearly all show more intelligence in their business, speeches, courtesies, intercourse, tricks and subtleties, than do the shrewdest citizens and merchants in France."[42] This, of course, was more far-reaching than the usually quoted remark that Amerindians equalled European peasants in intelligence. It was, moreover, disturbing in its implications for controllability.[43]

Capturing Young Minds

As they wrestled with the languages, the French also launched themselves upon an educational program "to capture the minds" of the young, the second part of Le Jeune's program.[44] Day schools had been started very early both in Acadia and at Quebec, by the Recollets, Capuchins, and Jesuits. When Le Jeune arrived at Quebec in 1632, he soon acquired two Amerindian boys, whom he set about rearing *à la française*.[45] By the following year he had more than twenty students attending his day school.[46] He found the children apt and eager to learn, and encouraged them by the distribution of little gifts as well as by awarding prizes for lessons well learned.[47] But this was not enough; to win over the children to the French way of life, it would be necessary to put them into boarding school, away from the home environment. Champlain had expressed ideas similar to this in 1621 when he had appealed to Louis XIII for funds for such a purpose. Help had been forthcoming and a seminary had been built at Notre Dames des Anges,[48] but before the Recollets had been able to solve the problems of acquiring Amerindian children and keeping them in school, they had been driven out by the English in 1629. When the French regained Canada in 1632, only the Jesuits returned immediately; the Recollets were not allowed back until 1670. The Jesuits lost no time in reopening the abandoned school at Notre Dame des Anges. But in five years' time it was closed again, for want of pupils, and also because the missionaries had decided to concentrate on another seminary they had just opened in Quebec.[49]

Enlisting Amerindians as pupils had proved to be a major problem. Faced with parental reluctance to part with their children, the French resorted to diplomatic pressures. When a delegation arrived seeking the aid of the French in war, the latter replied,

> you have not allied yourself up to the present with our French people, your daughters have married with all the neighboring Nations, but not with ours... you have not offered them [your children] to the French for instruction. If you had done this from the time of our first arrival in the Country, you would all know by this time how to handle arms as we do, and your enemies would not exist in your pres-

> ence—you would not die every day as you are doing. . . . Not that we have need of your daughters or your children; we are as populous as the leaves of your trees.[50]

Le Jeune added that it was obvious that the Amerindians did not care to be one people with the French, as they did not hesitate to send their children to other allies.[51] This drew the exasperated retort that the French were continually asking for Amerindian children but never offering to give any of their own (apparently they had discontinued the practice of sending boys to grow up with Amerindians). The French placed the utmost importance upon the acquisition of Amerindian children, not only to evangelize them and educate them in French ways, but also because the children would serve as "so many hostages . . . for the safety of the French who are among them, and for the strengthening of our commercial relations."[52] In this, the Jesuits were speaking remarkably like the Amerindians they were determined to "civilize"; exchanging of hostages for such a purpose was characteristic of native diplomacy.

In the end, the Fathers had to resort to giving presents to the parents in order to get children for their seminary. In other words, instead of the parents paying the school to educate their children, the school paid the parents in order to acquire pupils. To make matters worse, those students who did not run away showed a distressing tendency to sicken and die. Realizing that the switch to the French diet was probably a factor, the priests compromised, and tried feeding the children half in the Huron way, half in the French. This improved things a little,[53] but two years later the Jesuits were admitting sadly that it was difficult to keep Amerindian children alive out of the homes of their kindred.[54] As could be expected, such consequences increased the resistance of the parents. Another factor contributing to this resistance was the dismay of Amerindians at the French custom of physically punishing children, so contrary to their own way of never scolding or refusing anything to a crying child.[55]

Besides the seminary, which was for boys only, the Jesuits experimented with placing both boys and girls to live with French families. Le Jeune's pleasure was undisguised when he reported, in 1636, that an Amerindian had of his own accord brought him a gift of a little girl: "That greatly rejoiced us, for heretofore there had been great difficulty in obtaining girls." The Father arranged for her to be boarded with a family and had her dressed as a French child.[56] The Fathers had high hopes for this procedure, particularly as far as the Christianized girls were concerned, as they would marry either Frenchmen or baptized natives and would "draw as many children from their nation as we would desire."[57] In the absence of reports to the contrary, it may be assumed that these children had a better chance of survival than did the seminarists. They were also assimilated more readily. It was reported of some that they "do not look at the Savages except to flee from them, or make sport of them."[58] Such results could be achieved, however, only when the children had been raised in French centers of population. This realization encouraged Father Le Jeune to develop his program of sending children, particularly girls, to France for their education.[59]

When the Ursulines arrived in Quebec in 1639 along with the Hospital nuns, their specific purpose was to teach Amerindian girls. They began with Marie, the ten-year-old daughter of Noël Negabamat, the Montagnais chief who had settled at Sillery and who was the first neophyte of importance in the colony. Marie was also the godchild of Marie-Madeleine de Chauvigny de La Peltrie, the wealthy patron of the Ursulines who had come out with them to live at Quebec. Four days after Marie's arrival at the convent, she tore up the dress the nuns had given to her and ran off to join her family. Upon her father's telling her to go back, she changed completely and became so docile that "no sooner did she commit a fault, than she demanded pardon on her knees."[60] The complete submission of this gesture is evident when one considers that kneeling was not a posture that was used in this way by Amerindians;[61] in fact, at one point, when distrust of the Jesuits was at its height, such gestures were highly suspect.[62]

Both the Jesuits and the Ursulines reported examples of changes from defiance to total compliance among their difficult new charges, particularly the girls. There were even those who, once they reached such a point of acceptance, no longer displayed any overt desire to return to their families: "they seem to regard the sisters as mothers."[63] Those who did not adapt and who fell into a melancholy were allowed to leave for fear that otherwise they would die. The nuns were wise enough to observe that it was better to make concessions than to insist too much on certain points; little was to be gained through the use of force or fear.[64]

More than twenty years later, in 1663, after much labor and unexpectedly high expenses, Marie Guyart, *dite* Marie de l'Incarnation (1599–1672), foundress of the Ursuline order in New France, was able to write of some success in her educational efforts, although she found that in general Amerindian girls were not amenable to convent life. The nuns had succeeded in teaching a few how to read and write, and some of their charges had been married to Frenchmen. Just the previous year two had been provided with trousseaux; one of these girls had been with the Ursulines for seven years, another for four.[65] Both were skilled housekeepers, with judgment and poise that matched those of Frenchwomen. In fact, "one could easily take them for French because their pronounciation is so good."[66] A high point for the Ursulines was the visit of an Iroquois embassy in 1655 to see how students were "trained in the French manner." One of the girls read before the visitors in Latin, French, and Huron, and also sang in the three languages. Marie de l'Incarnation reported that the Iroquois were impressed, as they left promising they would not fail to send their children to so good a school.[67]

Such a result, while modest enough, had called for plenty of resources, as in New France thirty students were more work than double the number in France. Maintaining Amerindian girls à la française was costly, amounting to a minimum of 200 livres per student, according to Marie de l'Incarnation's estimate. An ever-present problem was the conflict between the needs of the parents and the aims of the seminary. The nuns found that there were times when they could not refuse to let their students join their families on the hunt, particularly if the parents were Christian. But that, of course, entailed absence from the sacraments.[68] Although the nuns devoted everything they had to the project, they succeeded only with those children whose parents were solidly behind the school, or else with orphans who had no alternatives. By the end of 1668, the convent had only one Amerindian student in residence. Of the girls the nuns educated, about eight adopted French ways and were adjudged suitable for religious vocations, but all were prevented from taking the vows for one reason or another. The Ursulines, for all their labors, did not succeed in having an Amerindian girl enter their order during the seventeenth century.[69]

Most of the students returned to their people and their traditional lives, although some remained good Christians: "Savage life is so attractive, because of its liberty, that it is a miracle to get them to act in the French manner, which they consider to be unworthy of themselves. . . . Judge, then, if it is any easy task to change habits so engrained since childhood that they have become natural to them."[70] Besides, the young had no prestige in Amerindian communities, nor any voice in the councils. In one case, the Jesuits hesitated to baptize a boy because of his lack of influence; if he had been living in a French community, there would have been no doubts.[71]

Very soon the Fathers realized the necessity of dealing with elders,[72] whose voices were heard in the community. But the family was the important unit; accordingly, in 1638, the priests decided to aim for heads of families, and called a meeting in Huronia to make an announcement to this effect.[73] Such a meeting was in itself an adaptation to the Amerin-

Huron praying to the Christian God. From Bressani's map of New France, 1657. National Map Collection, C-71502 Public Archives Canada.

dian way, and was called in order to engage the cooperation of the chiefs. It took more than two weeks to organize the required assembly of 150 captains,[74] at which the Fathers gave a feast. Brébeuf announced the plans and one of the captains gave a supporting speech. It was a successful move. The immediate result was a noticeable improvement in the attitude within the cabins the Jesuits went to visit. "There were even some who made feasts expressly to announce that all their family desired to embrace the faith."[75] But such gestures were marked more by good intentions than by actual results, particularly in the face of community pressures. Still, the policy of proselytizing heads of families was being continued two years later.[76] Later, as the Jesuits started work among the Iroquois, they began with the "slaves,"[77] a choice that proved successful in gaining converts if not in influencing the community. Slaves, of course, were outside the community, and so had no voice in its affairs.

The House of Death

The third part of Le Jeune's four-pronged program was the provision of medical care to the Amerindians. Early accommodation for Amerindian patients at the French hospital was in bark cabins, particularly during times of epidemic when space was at a premium. Facilities and medical knowledge being what they were, the mortality rate was so high that the hospital became known as a house of death and was consequently shunned at first by Amerindians, particularly as their traditional medical practices were at least as effective, if not better, than those of Europeans. But against the imported diseases they were helpless; and so in the face of these strange epidemics, they eventually accepted the nuns' offer to care for the sick. In fact, they took advantage of it by leaving infants, the aged, and the infirm at the hospital, pleased not to be faced with the necessity of killing, or leaving behind to die, those who could not follow them in their wanderings.[78]

But adaptation and accommodation had its limits, as the nuns discovered. The hunters returned with *boucan,* smoked meat as a gift for their benefactors. The nuns feigned pleasure in accepting it, "but, as we are not accustomed to that sort of diet, we would have died of hunger rather than eat it."[79] They gave it to their workers, along with wine to help mask the flavor. The nuns even found objectionable the odor of smoke that hung about the Amerindians: "the odor of the savages greatly inconvenienced us; it seemed as though everything we touched, even the bread, was penetrated with it."[80] That the French eventually accommodated themselves to boucan is evident from the rise of the *boucanniers*–buccaneers–in the West Indies during the seventeenth century.

As the selfless devotion of the Hospital nuns impressed the Amerindians, the nuns in their turn admired the charity with which the natives cared for each other and the patience with which they endured illnesses.[81] Sometimes this led to inconveniences as when they shared medicines the nuns had so carefully doled out. Not surprisingly, the Hospital nuns received the first Amerindian girl to take vows in New France, in 1657. She was Geneviève-Agnès Skannudharoi, a Huron who had been educated by the Ursulines. She died within hours of the ceremony, at the age of fifteen.[82] The only other Amerindians to become nuns in New France during the seventeenth century were accepted into the Congregation of Notre Dame, founded in 1671 in Montreal by Marguerite Bourgeoys (1620–1700). They also died young.[83] It should be noted, however, that mixed-bloods very early became nuns. For instance, two of the daughters of Charles de La Tour entered religious orders.[84]

As for ordaining Amerindian men into the priesthood, the church in New France appears to have been constrained by the doubts of Rome on the subject. In any event, such a possibility was not even raised in the *Jesuit Relations,* although it is difficult to believe that it had not been discussed, and probably at some length. The Mexican synod of 1555 had ruled against such a step on the grounds that Amerindians, mestizos, and Negroes were unable to acquire a full understanding of the mysteries of the faith; neither were they judged capable of the monastic life.[85] Even if an Amerindian did achieve such an understanding, he would not be able to preach to his fellows as he could not have the required authority over them.[86] In other words, the egalitarianism of Amerindians was viewed as being incompatible with anything other than a simple acceptance of Christianity. The synod reversed the stand of an earlier assembly, which had judged that Amerindians could well become priests, although none had yet been permitted to rise to that degree.[87] Eventually, during the seventeenth century, some Amerindians were permitted into the priesthood in Mexico, but haphazardly, and into humble positions in rural parishes.[88] That the Jesuits in Canada were ambivalent toward the issue can easily be read into their frequent comments upon the intelligence of Amerindians and upon the profound fervor that characterized some of the converts.[89] What the Jesuits did do was to use their converts, both men and women, as catechists. They were defined by Bishop de Saint-Vallier (1653–1727) as "masters of prayer and chant" (*dogiques*),[90] assisting in the work of evangelization and conducting prayers and certain portions of the services in the absence of the missionaries.[91] A Huron dogique even founded a church 500 leagues from Quebec.[92] These catechists proved to be extremely useful as intermediaries between converts and the unconverted.[93]

Encouraging Sedentary Life

The fourth part of Le Jeune's program, the adoption of a sedentary mode of life, was transmuted into the idea of establishing reserves, as was being done in central and South America.[94] It was based on the belief that nomadism was contrary to the laws of the church and incompatible with Christianity.[95] Inspired by that conviction, Recollet Denys Jamet had envisioned a village for nomadic hunters-turned-farmers at Quebec in 1615.[96] The Jesuits, with the founding of Sillery in 1637, hoped that their wandering charges would settle down voluntarily.[97] Le Jeune thought that such a project would become self-continuing once one hunting family had agreed to take up farming;[98] in the Relation of 1639, two families were reported established in Sillery,[99] with the French going to considerable trouble and expense to launch them on their new path. For the next six years, progress was encouraging; by 1645, there were 167 Christian Amerindians in residence. But traditional life patterns soon reasserted themselves, and these combined with warfare and disease to prevent Sillery's founders from realizing their hopes. Eventually there were no more Amerindian residents in the settlement. Title to the land was finally transferred from the Amerindians to the Jesuits, a move the ethics of which have been questioned.[100]

But the idea of reducing nomadism did not die, particularly as the Jesuits had become convinced that the failure was caused by the attempt to settle Amerindians next to French. Contact with Europeans, instead of inspiring Amerindians to become good Frenchmen, seemed to have the opposite effect. Therefore, reasoned the Jesuits, it would be best to segregate the Amerindians as much as possible. On this basis, Prairie de la Magdelaine (Kentaké) was established in 1667, and in 1680 was moved to Sault St. Louis (Kahnawaké); two moves later it reached its final location, today known as Caughnawaga. This was a radical departure from the original idea of "one people" to which French officialdom still clung. The royal government was to become increasingly critical of the slowness with which the "humanization" of Amerindians was proceeding, and it eventually decided to curtail the Jesuit dominance of missionary work by the reintroduction of the Recollets in 1670.[101] Even before they had lost ground with officialdom, Jesuits had begun to modify their ideas about nomadism sufficiently for some of them to join their flocks in the northern forests, as Le Jeune himself had done during the winter of 1634–35. Alternatively, as French settlements increased in numbers, nomads in their wanderings could be encouraged to camp near such a village or town. Thus even if the Indians did not become sedentary, there would always be French around to continue instruction.[102] In the growing turbulence of colonial rivalries, the French found that reserves had several uses, such as serving as buffer zones as well as places of refuge for those dislodged by wars. The latter provided the reason for the founding of St. François de Bécancourt south of Trois-Rivières in 1680 for the Abenaki allies, who, before the arrival of the Europeans, had lived in the region of Maine, "land of the rising sun."

Problems of Acculturation

The problems considered so far represented only a small part of those facing the missionary church during the seventeenth century. Extremely difficult ones were presented by the pagan practice of polygyny and by the Christian doctrine of restitution. The 1524 Mexican synod had ruled that converts with more than one wife had to choose one and dismiss the rest, or else keep them as servants.[103] Attempts to regulate which wife should be chosen were finally given up, as churchmen had not arrived at the necessary understanding of Amerindian marriage customs. So the convert was left free to make up his own mind. As can easily be imagined, abuses were not long in appearing, with converts developing ingenious ways of evading the rules. In New France, the church very early realized that polygyny was an integral part of the Amerindian social fabric. Biard recognized this in Acadia, when he wrote that a chief needed several wives

> in order to retain authority and power by having a number of children; for in that lies the strength of the house, in a great number of allies and connections; the second reason is the entertainment and service, which is great and laborious, since they have large families, and a great number of followers, and therefore a number of servants and housewives; now they have no other servants, slaves or mechanics but their women.[104]

Similarly, in Huronia, the work of the wives provided the agricultural products needed for a chief's household. Also, they played a substantial part in village affairs, particularly while their husbands were away on trading missions or at war.[105] In the Hudson Bay region, Charles Albanel came across still another native rationalization for such a custom: when a woman lost her husband, it was up to the nearest male relative to take care of her and be seen as "holding her not as a slave but as a wife."[106] Earlier, Le Jeune had reported that it was the women who had resisted when he preached monogamy: "since they are more numerous than the men, if a man can only marry one of them, the others will have to suffer."[107]

The missionaries sought to counter such situations by providing special privileges for the converts, such as the cherished one of possessing guns;[108] converts also made up a high proportion of the Huron trade delegations.[109] Later, as missionaries gained authority, they were able to order chiefs openly to give up their extra wives[110] and to exert social pressure to get them to conform to the Christian pattern.[111] They used similar tactics against serial monogamy, which struck them as being an even greater danger.[112] Amerindians could not conceive how persons could tie themselves indissolubly to one marriage partner.[113] The battle provoked by this was not a simple one, for while the missionaries were struggling to get the Amerindians to conform to Christian standards, French traders and even officials found it only too convenient to adopt the Amerindian way. Not only was this true of coureurs de bois, whose social position was ambiguous, but also of envoys on official missions who found that it could greatly facilitate matters during negotiations to take the daughter of a leading chief to wife, according to Amerindian custom, even though the delegate already had a wife at home whom he had married in the Christian way.[114]

Equally as thorny, but in a different way, was the problem of restitution. According to this custom, the convert was called upon to make good the injuries he had done before baptism. It was soon realized that such a doctrine had been less difficult to implement in Europe than it was in the totally different social atmosphere of the New World. An Amerindian, in order to be baptized, must "despoil himself, his wife and his Children to repair an injury that he did to others at a time when he thought he was free to do anything."[115] And yet converts made such gestures, which in some cases entailed serious hardships.

The Jesuits achieved the conversions they did by a judicious accommodation and adaptation to the ways of the people among whom they were working. They recognized perhaps as clearly as anyone of their time that too much was made of the distinction between "savage" and "civilized"; that the Amerindians possessed a viable culture which, while it did not always correspond to the French way, still had its own logic that worked very well; however, this realization aroused considerable debate both within the order and within the church. The Jesuits made great efforts to adopt a pattern of behavior that would accord with that of Amerindians without compromising their own principles; for example, in Huronia, they found that the best way to get good attendance at their meetings was to go through the village making the announcement "according to the custom of the country for general assemblies" instead of ringing a bell.[116] At the arrival of a delegation in 1642, in which canoes were drawn up in line with the chief standing in his craft to state the purpose of the visit, the French displayed their gifts along with those of other nations. Their purpose was to be allowed to evangelize.[117] The early hesitancy of the French to participate in gift exchanges had vanished and they became skilful at this type of diplomacy. Father Simon Le Moyne (1604–65), for instance, on his mission to Iroquoia, approached an Onondaga village calling by name all the captains, families and persons of importance, speaking slowly and using the tone of a captain. When the chiefs assembled, he presented two gifts: the first to wipe their faces, "that I may never see any sign of sadness on their brows"; and the second, to remove any gall remaining in their hearts.[118] That was far removed from the occasion in 1636 when the French had come empty-handed to a parley and had been rebuked by an Old Man as a result.[119]

The variety of the hazards in the way of creating "one people" was very great. In the "Instruction for the Fathers of our Society who shall be sent to the Hurons,"[120] the neophyte missionary was advised, among other

Getting ready for a feast, Iroquois are preparing themselves à la française. Bacqueville de la Potherie, *Histoire de l'Amérique septentrionale*, 1722.

things, not to indulge in French civilities when offered anything by their hosts as "these ceremonies offend them."[121] A few years later at Tadoussac the priests were somewhat taken aback when their converts began to practise such courtesies, as they now considered themselves French in all things:

> The Savages and the French, in the manner of compliments, hold the two extremes: the former are insipid and boorish in the little respect which they bear for one another; and the French are annoying in the excess of their ceremonies, and [are] very often deceptive in the too great demonstrations of their friendship. Rustic candor is preferable to a feigned courtesy; excess was never good, in whatever it be; if these good Neophytes adopt it, they will soon be weary of it.[122]

At other times the priests were strongly reminded that there were certain French customs they would prefer that their charges not adopt. For instance, during the epidemics of the 1630s, when the Huron were desperately looking for the reasons for the disease that was decimating their ranks, their suspicion focussed on the Jesuits, in accordance with their belief that such disasters as epidemics were not impersonal, but were caused by someone. At a meeting to discuss the issue, a Jesuit tried to turn the situation into an occasion to preach. A captain cried out that the missionaries were forever trying to speak about their oki (Spirit); the issue was the cause of the contagion. Would it not be more to the point if one of the priests were tortured to get at the truth?[123] Such a suggestion must have been particularly disturbing to the missionaries, as it was uncomfortably close to contemporary French practice back in Europe.

The forces marshalled by France in her assault on the cultures of her Amerindian allies in New France were formidable. Her efforts were particularly intense during the seventeenth century: the wealthy shared in the expenses, all classes contributed manpower, and the bureaucracy orchestrated the campaign. The seven or eight years originally envisaged for transforming Amerindians into Frenchmen stretched into generations and through the whole century. In spite of some genuine efforts at cooperation on the part of the Amerindians, the two world views never became one.

It is not that the missionaries' labors were without result. On the contrary, the Amerindians were profoundly affected by these exotic and not

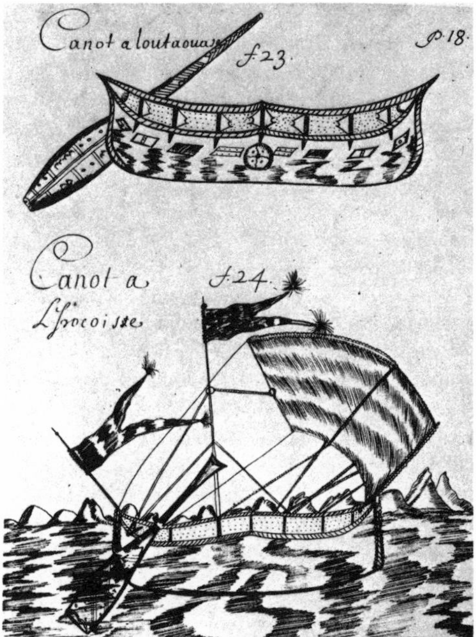

An aboriginal Ottawa canoe (above) and one that has been subjected to French influence (below). Envisioned by Bécard de Granville, late seventeenth century. C-33288 Public Archives Canada.

readily comprehensible visitors who stayed to take over their land.[124] For instance, there was their horror at the idea of compatriots, perhaps even blood relatives, suffering the tortures of the damned. According to anthropologist A.G. Bailey, this "struck many into a blind coma in which the will to live was submerged in ubiquitous despair." It is certain that it inspired terror.[125] On the lighter side, Huron mothers immediately took to tonsuring their infants in imitation of the early missionaries.[126]

Inevitably, Amerindians identified the Christian God with the most powerful of their own spiritual beings: a good example of this is seen in the transformation of Gluskap of the Micmac, Malecite, and Abenaki. According to Mircea Eliade, "despite the immense historical distances involved, the experiences of the monotheistic prophets can be repeated in the most backward and primitive tribes."[127] Such perception indicated the healthy reaction of a viable culture seeking to incorporate new concepts into its ideological framework, which in the case of Amerindians allowed much latitude. As Hennepin observed, America was no place for European missionaries to seek religious martyrdom: "The Savages never put any Christian to death upon the score of his Religion; they leave everybody at liberty in Belief."[128] What did disturb Amerindians was the withdrawal of converts from traditional community offices, rituals, and practices, threatening the very basis of their societies. The result could be persecution, ostracism, and sometimes even death.[129] It is now recognized that the modal personality fostered by a particular culture is by its very nature highly resistant to change.[130] This is as true of Europeans as it is of Amerindians or any other peoples.

Very quickly, then, the French faced a crisis in their school program: while educating the young was deemed essential for the long term, more immediate results seemed to call for another course of action. Even if France had been able to sustain her efforts, it is unlikely that she would have succeeded. Both missionaries and officials became aware that it was easier to cause disorientation and disintegration than it was to reform a culture arbitrarily into another mold.

But the balance sheet was by no means all negative as far as France was concerned. Out of such tensions as inevitably arose in the realm of trade, as well as in that of religion, were forged the alliances of French and Amerindians that became legendary during the colonial wars. New France's first intendant, Jean Talon, might scold the Jesuits for not having civilized the Amerindians,[131] but the loyalty and friendship of many of them had been engaged. The Amerindians' first major campaign as allies of the French was that of Tracy and Courcelle's against the Iroquois in 1666.[132] This set a pattern that was to endure for a hundred years, until the downfall of New France.

CHAPTER 13

Conclusion

The hairy hunter Esau, as interpreted in Johann Jacob Scheuchzer, *Kupfer-Bibel*, 1731.

IT WOULD BE difficult to overestimate the effect of Europe's classification of New World men as hommes sauvages, whether "bons" or "cruels." The French, for all their policy of douceur toward Amerindians, never officially accepted that they were anything other than "sans roy, sans loy, sans foy." Like the Wild Men of the Woods, Amerindians represented anti-structure, man before the acquisition of culture had differentiated him from animals. It mattered little whether these savage New World men were perceived as living in a Golden Age or as wallowing in unrelieved bestiality. The fact was that in the European folk imagination, denizens of the New World, like the Wild Men, were living metaphors for antisocial forces that could be brought under control only by evangelization and assimilation; transformation into the spiritual and cultural conformity that Europeans acknowledged as the condition of being civilized.

The European approach was doomed to failure because it assumed a cultural dichotomy between "savage" (lack of order) and "civilized" (order) that did not, in fact, exist. Whatever the differences may be between "tribal" societies and "civilizations," the presence or lack of order is not one of them. The people of the New World all led highly structured lives, with or without agriculture and whatever their degree of nomadism. But this was not evident to Europeans in the first years of contact.

The terms in which the French conceived their association with New World peoples are readily apparent in what may be their earliest novel to be set in Canada, Antoine Du Perier's *Les amours de Pistion*. Actually, it is a European fantasy in which the Amerindian characters resemble nothing so much as Wild Men of the Woods, a romance that includes "Amerindians" described as possessing a rustic grace. However, they were "poor men having nothing human but the form; living with beasts like beasts . . . I only call them men because they spoke. . . . Living without delights in this world, they will be suffering in the next because of the devils they worship."[1] Du Perier then forgets his description, and makes his Amerindians act like Europeans; an instant transformation into civilized man. This novel was adapted by Jacques Du Hamel into a play entitled *Acoubar ou la Loyauté trahie*, first published in 1603.[2] Another revealing glimpse of the French self-image in the New World is provided by Sieur de Cõbes in his imaginary *Coppie d'une Lettre envoyée de la Nouvelle-France*. He represents Amerindians as wanting to adore the French as gods and install them as emperors; "but our people replied that they were only men, even as they."[3]

In the realm of the politics of the age, such views implied a mandate to colonize these new territories. The duty of Christians, as the children of

Amerindian canoes impressed Europeans with their speed and maneuverability. The word "canoe" derives from Taino, spoken by inhabitants of Hispaniola. This one-man version of the craft, which notably fails to suggest the canoe's outstanding characteristics, is from Oviedo's *La hystoria generale de las Indias*, 1547.

God, was clear: legally to claim non-Christian territory in order to implant the faith and to lead the inhabitants into civilization. In spite of Vitoria's defence of the sovereignty of Amerindians and the papal stand in favor of their proprietary rights, neither the French nor Europeans generally considered that Amerindians, as savages, possessed either. The French in New France sometimes negotiated alliances with Amerindians whose territories they claimed, but this involved neither acknowledgement of aboriginal rights nor payment of compensation.

The full implications of such attitudes never came into play in New France, however, as the French did not become so numerous as to disbar their allies from their lands. In general, they sought to avoid doing so: in 1665, Louis XIV instructed Governor Courcelle "not to usurp the lands on which they [Amerindians] habitually reside on the pretext that they would be improved by the French."[4] When an Amerindian was converted to Christianity, he was legally considered to be a French citizen, with full rights, including the privilege of living in France without any further declaration of naturalization. But whatever land he received was granted either by the French Crown or by French individuals, and not by mere assumption of aboriginal right.[5] Thus, by the process of evangelization and assimilation, the Amerindian would become *humanisé* as well as *francisé*, and France would have taken a step toward realizing the missionary ideal of one world, one God, and one faith.[6]

This exalted concept gave an enormous impulse to the missionary movement by opening up what seemed to be unlimited new fields at a time when missionary work had come to an end in Europe. The process was reinforced by the speed with which New World civilizations were conquered: on the one hand it confirmed Europeans in the belief that they were savage, otherwise they would not have fallen so quickly; and on the other hand, Europeans interpreted these easy conquests as signs of divine approval of their actions. In that theocratically minded age, the lure of creating a New Jerusalem was as powerful as the lure of gold and silver. Missionary work was a privilege and a sought-after honor; nuns and priests vied to be sent to New World missions, particularly those of New France.[7]

Missionaries soon recognized the error of their initial belief that the Amerindian was a tabula rasa awaiting the Christian imprint. This realization complicated evangelization, as it meant that existing cultures had to be destroyed, or at least radically altered, to allow for the acceptance of Christianity. The limits of accommodation with pagan beliefs and practices were outlined by Gregory XV when he reformed the Sacred Congregation of Propaganda in 1622. The alternative of leaving Amerindians to work out their own destinies was never seriously considered by either missionaries or government officials. But the extent to which Amerindians should be expected to change their customs was a troublesome issue. Finally, during the last decades of the seventeenth century, the matter was resolved against the syncretists—those who believed in working as much as possible within the frameworks of native cultures—in favor of those who believed that such cultures should be totally supplanted by Christianity. The Jesuits had been the chief exponents of syncretism; in New France, they had used this technique to establish a native Christian church in Huronia, until the project was destroyed by members of the Five Nations in 1649.

But even in Huronia, which had held out such promise, missionaries had encountered unexpected difficulties as natives displayed loyalty to their own ideals and lifestyle. The Huron had been astonished at first that missionaries should suggest that they change their ways. Their stock

The "wonderful" manner of Virginians making their canoes. Theodor de Bry, 1590, after a description by Hariot.

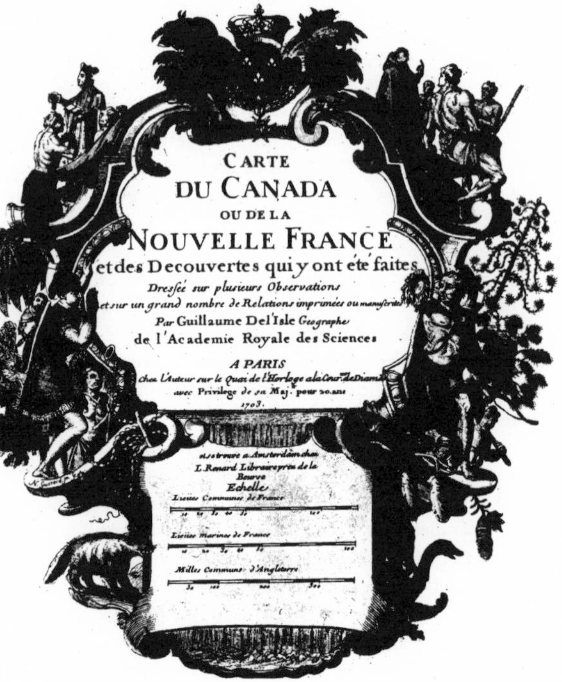

Canada, as symbolized by geographer Guillaume Delisle in the cartouche for his map, 1703. Clockwise from lower left, the fur trade is represented by an Amerindian family and a beaver; evangelization by a baptism and a sermon; and warfare by a warrior holding up the scalp of the enemy at his feet. National Map Collection, C-27099 Public Archives Canada.

response initially was "we have our own ways of doing things, and you yours, as well as other nations."[8] The frequency with which the Jesuits mentioned such conversations in their *Relations* suggests that they were disturbed by them. They reported that the Huron believed not only that their country was different from France, but that they possessed a different God and another paradise: "the God who created . . . [your world] did not create ours." Furthermore, they continued, their ways were not those of France, and they were entitled to their own customs.[9] In one case the Fathers used the Amerindian line of argument for their own ends. When they finally succeeded in getting the Huron to accept being barred from the priests' quarters at certain times (such a refusal being unheard of among the Huron), the Fathers observed, apparently with unconscious irony: "they are reasonable, and are not surprised that our ways are different from theirs."[10]

In other areas, such as trade and war, the French soon realized that it was in their best interests to work out means of cooperation and accommodation rather than to insist that Amerindians become Frenchmen. In trade, they sought to engage Amerindian self-interest.[11] In war, their network of tribal alliances testified to their skilful manipulation of the Amerindian love of honors and prestige.[12] To put it in different terms, as the missionaries labored to transform Amerindians into Christians and Frenchmen, practical politics demanded that Frenchmen adapt to the ways of the Amerindians.[13] In the pull and haul of these processes, a few French began to appreciate that Amerindians had a civilization of their own; but such an appreciation, when it did occur, remained an individual matter. Occasionally, such a conclusion was reached by fairly important officials, as when an eighteenth-century commissioner, sent to report on the colony in Cayenne, noted that "the savage life, which appears to us to be so miserable, is civilized to the degree that is acceptable to these people, and is sufficient for their happiness."[14] He elaborated:

> First of all, they have a society and live in families; they have a national cohesion, as their village is their city; they have magistrates or chiefs who represent them in negotiations with others, and who lead them in war. They do not need a civil code, as they have neither individual ownership of land nor lawsuits, but the usages and customs of their forebears are carefully observed . . . Thus, all things considered, they have the knowledge and industry necessary for their individual and social existence. Their customs are gentle, hospitable and inoffensive.[15]

He thought that perhaps the difference between Amerindian and European forms of society lay in the fact that the former was natural while the latter was political. Both forms interfered with the happiness of mankind, the former by submitting to nature, the latter by outraging it.

Such an intellectual tolerance of Amerindian civilizations found little reflection in the politics of colonization. The French, being a practical people, determined to make their colony function, adapted and accommodated wherever necessary in the fur trade, in evangelization, and in the exigencies of war. But at no time did they lose sight of their perspective of themselves as a civilized Christian nation whose mission it was to lead backward native peoples to a better life. The adaptations they found necessary in the beginning when they were founding their colonies were modified as their establishments became more secure. Perhaps the best known illustration of this was intermarriage, which at

Canadian going to war on snowshoes, with belt pouches decorated à l'indienne. Bacqueville de la Potherie, *Histoire de l'Amérique septentrionale*, 1722.

first was proposed to the not particularly interested Amerindian allies, then was made official policy, and was finally discarded in favor of a stand against such marriages. By the end of the French regime in Canada, active measures were being taken to discourage such alliances. In other words, the successes of the French in finding working arrangements with Amerindians reflected the pragmatic necessities of colonial politics rather than any compromise with *la mission civilisatrice.* Throughout her stay as a colonial power in the New World, France took very seriously her self-imposed task of bringing order to the anti-social forces represented by l'homme sauvage.

The final irony was that la douceur could not validate the fundamental misconception of viewing Amerindians as hommes sauvages. La mission civilisatrice, for all its good intentions, meant disaster for Amerindians just as surely as the ostensibly less accommodating policies of other colonizing nations such as England or Spain. It was an example of a general phenomenon. The rise of states has inexorably led to the subordination of non-state societies, usually resulting in their disappearance or their incorporation to a greater or lesser degree into the dominant group. Non-state societies had once been in a position to live and let live because of their ability to fragment; but that asset proved to be a fatal liability in the face of the agglomerative tendencies of institutional and territorial states. Intentionally or unintentionally, when men from antithetical cultures have encountered each other, they have not refrained from disinheriting their brothers, as the pastoralist Jacob did the hunter Esau, or even from killing them, as the city-building farmer, Cain, did the shepherd, Abel.

Appendices

I Origin of the Name "Canada"

DURING THE sixteenth and seventeenth centuries, the generally accepted version of the origin of the name "Canada" was that it derived from the Spanish "el cabo de nada" (cape of nothing) or "aca nada" (nothing here). That was how Canada was reportedly assessed by Juan de Agramonte, who in 1511 was sent by Spain, along with two Breton pilots, to check on the location as well as the potentialities of the new land discovered fourteen years earlier by Giovanni Caboto under the auspices of Henry VII of England.[1] Nothing more was heard of Agramonte's reconnaissance, even though Canada was considered to be on the Spanish side of the Line of Demarcation. The currency of the "el cabo de nada" and the "aca nada" stories suggests that Spain had established her proprietary right in the north even though she failed to discern its exploitable potentialities; however, she was too occupied with her budding empire to the south to do more than establish a formal claim. The early popularity of this explanation of the name reflected the first impression that Canada was "a poor, unsought-after country,"[2] or, as Cartier said of Labrador, "the land God gave to Cain."

Thevet thought "Canada" derived from "Segnada Canada," which he said meant men hunting land.[3] Charlevoix also gaves a variation of this.[4] Another version was presented by Belleforest, who thought the word signified "land" and could apply to any land in the world.[5] He elaborated as to its location: "Canada is bordered on the north by the high mountains of *Saguenai*; to the east lies the Gulf of St. Lawrence; to the west the land of *Hochelaga*, and to the south the land of *Nurumbeg.*"[6] (Other geographers had different ideas as to its situation, and Canada wandered on sixteenth-century maps, although always in the northeastern part of North America. At first it was shown separately from New France, but later in the century the two became identified. Cartier's was probably the most authoritative voice, and he reported that Canada began about eight leagues above Isle aux Coudres.[7]) According to Cartier, when he asked the Iroquoian natives what they called their land, they had replied *ka-na-ta* (village), which today has come to be widely accepted as the origin of the name.[8] The old Huron form is *Andata*. One of the Iroquoian towns upstream from Stadacona may have been called "Canada."[9] Arent Van Curler, in his journal for 1634–35, listed "Canadaghi" as the Mohawk word for "castle," the early English way of referring to an Amerindian town or village.[10]

Lescarbot held that both Belleforest and Cartier were wrong, and that "Canada" really meant "province."[11] One of the more tortured explanations of the derivation of "Canada" was that of Thomas Jefferys, to the effect that it meant "mouth of the Country" from *can*, "mouth," and *ada*, "country."[12] This appears to refer to the country being accessible by the St. Lawrence River; in this context, some believed that Canada received its name from the word used by the Portuguese to identify the river, which translates as "narrow road" or "narrow street."[13] This explanation has not received wide acceptance.

Amerindians of the North Shore claim that "Canada" derives from a Cree word meaning "clean land." Interestingly enough, Thevet described Canada as "flat and very clean."[14] In the sixteenth century, the term "Canadian" (or "Canadeen" as Belleforest spelled it) was generally used to signify the people of the North Shore.[15] The region's inhabitants were Montagnais, who spoke a variety of Cree; they were among the first trading partners of the French in what is today's Canada.

In light of all this, Sauer's claim that Labrador is the geographic name to have persisted the longest north of the West Indies should be treated with caution.[16]

II Vartan's View of the Celestial Hierarchies

THE HIERARCHICAL concept of the universe, which shaped the outlook of sixteenth- and seventeenth-century geographers, explorers, and men of science generally, came down to the Renaissance from classical writers, especially Aristotle and Pseudo-Dionysius (fl. c. 500), a Byzantine Christian mystic strongly influenced by Neoplatonism. The latter's works were translated into Latin in the late fifteenth century by the celebrated humanist, Marsilio Ficino. A striking expression of this world-view may be found in this passage of the Armenian geographer-historian Vartan (d.1271) from Saint-Martin, *Mémoires historiques et géographiques* 2:407:

> D'abord c'est le tabernacle où est le trône de la Divinité qui est au dessus de tout ce qui existe. Aucun être creé ne peut entrer ni voir dans ce tabernacle. La sainte Trinité seule y habite dans une lumière inaccessible. Après sont les demeures des anges; d'abord sont les ordres des séraphins, des chérubins et des trônes, perpétuellement occupés de glorifier Dieu. Ils lui sont enchaînés par l'amour, et ils ne veulent pas s'en éloigner: ce n'est pas par stabilité, mais par attachement et par amour. Comme ils sont incorporels, on ne peut pas dire qu'ils sont dans un lieu, mais les désirs et les amours sont comme leurs lieux, et c'est parce qu'ils le veulent qu'ils sont là. Ces trois ordres n'en font qu'un par le rang et la gloire. Après eux sont les *Dominations*, les *Vertus* et les *Puissances* (potestates) qui forment les hiér-

archies moyennes. Enfin aprèsceux-ci sont les *Principautés* (principatus), les archanges et les anges qui forment les dernières hiérarchies. Ces six ordres ont des places et des degrés de gloire différents, de même que les hommes tous d'une même nature, sont de divers rangs, que l'un est roi, tandis qu'un autre est prince, chef de ville, et ainsi de suite. Les cieux fixes et sans mouvement sont leurs demeure. Ensuite est une ceinture aqueuse placée par la volonté du Créateur qui est toujours en mouvement et qui par cette raison est connue sous le nom du *Premier Mobile*. Après cela on rencontre les cieux du firmament où se trouve une grande quantité d'astres qui se meuvent circulairement. Au dessus sont les deux pôles des astres qui tournent entièrement en vingt-quatre heures et ne sont pas semblables à la ceinture aqueuse. Ensuite est la zone des Sept Planètes placées l'une audessus de l'autre; on trouve ensuite les quatres éléments qui s'enveloppent les uns les autres sphériquement. D'abord la *Sphère du Feu* qui environne tous les autres éléments, on trouve ensuite *l'air*, puis *l'eau* et enfin la *Terre* qui est le dernier des quatre et qui *est au milieu de tous les autres* (Santarem, *Essai sur la Cosmographie* III:XXVI-XXVIII).

Notes

The following are common abbreviations used throughout the notes:

AC	Archives des colonies
BN	Bibliothèque Nationale
JR	R.G. Thwaites, ed., *Jesuit Relations*
NYCD	E.B. O'Callaghan and J.R. Brodhead, eds., *Documents Relative to the Colonial History of the State of New York*, 15 vols. (Albany, 1853–87)
PAC	Public Archives of Canada

Preface

1. A recent definition of civilization distinguishes seven characteristics: subsistence based on agriculture; relatively large and dense population; efficient system of distribution; diversity of settlement types; centralized state structures; intensive social stratification; and extensive occupational specialization (Lanning, *Peru Before the Incas*, 3). Lanning arrived at this definition by listing ancient and modern societies considered civilized, and determining what they had in common. According to Lanning, "tribal" societies may have one or more of these characteristics, but only civilizations possess them all. *See also* Renfrew, *Before Civilization*, 212–13.
2. Thwaites, ed., *JR* 13:74.
3. Exceptions to this included peoples of the Southeastern Ceremonial Complex, such as the Timucuans of Florida.
4. Thwaites, ed., *JR* 1:285. Jouvency never visited Canada; he compiled his *Canadicae Missionis Relatio* in Rome from missionary reports as part of a history of the Jesuits.
5. According to Joseph Campbell, all of our world's civilizations share the same concept of cosmic order, which was first formulated in ancient Mesopotamia on the basis of long observations of the heavens (*Mythic Image*, 72ff.).
6. Perceptual biases are not peculiar to Europeans. The Chinese, in extending their sway over the "barbarians" of Nam-Viet were also the "prisoners of their ecological lexicons" (Schafer, *Vermilion Bird*, 42).
7. Chinard makes the point that the French conception of the New World was influenced first by Italy, then by Spain (*L'Exotisme américain*, 219).

1 Some First Reactions

1. Columbus, *Spanish Letter*, 12–13.
2. Martire, *De Orbe Novo* (MacNutt) 1:67. Columbus also speculated in his journals as to whether or not he had found Paradise (*Four Voyages*, 137–38).
3. Between 1450 and 1550 an immense number of antiquities were unearthed in Rome and its neighborhood, filling many palaces and wealthy homes and giving impetus to the development of museums (David Murray, *Museums* 1:13).
4. Elliott, *Old World*, chap. 1. It is interesting to note that France's *littérature de colportage* (popular literature) was

silent on the subject of New World discoveries (Mandrou, *De la Culture populaire*, 66).

5. Hirsch, in Chiapelli, ed., *First Images* 2:538. *See also* Columbus, *La Carta de Colón* and *The Columbus Letter of 1493*. The three Paris reprints of the letter are all presumed to date from 1493, although the year is not indicated on the title pages. According to Harrisse, printer Guyot Marchant had ceased to publish after 1501 (*Bibliotheca Americana* 1:9).

6. Tazbir, "La Conquête de l'Amérique," 6. On the role of the printing press in the geographical distribution of the news of discovery, *see* Chaunu, *L'Expansion européenne*, 235–37.

7. These are a relation of Columbus's second voyage published in Pavia in 1494–95; Martire's first decade (Venice, 1504); and an account of Columbus's fourth voyage (Venice, 1505). *See* Hirsch, in Chiapelli, ed., *First Images*, 553–60.

8. Chapelain, *Lettres*, 2:340–41. Hale says that voyage accounts began to receive significant readership about mid-sixteenth century (*Renaissance Europe*, 53).

9. Brant (1458–1521) had first published *Das Narrenschiff* in Basel in 1494. It was reprinted in Latin in 1497 and 1498, and in French in 1497, 1498, and 1499. *See* Winsor, *Narrative and Critical History* 2:58.

10. Winsor, *Narrative and Critical History* 2:58. Brant was not the first to characterize travels to strange lands as a folly. Dante, in describing Ulysses' voyages, had used the terms "il folle volo" and "il varco folle" (*Inferno* 26.125, *Paradiso* 27.82–83. *Divina Comedia*); his consignment of the wanderer to the eighth circle of the Inferno, however, had nothing to do with travel, but with Ulysses' false counselling.

11. The English version of Brant's work, *The shyppe of fooles*, published in 1509, portrayed the men of the New World living "as beestes." Harrisse maintained that this was the first reference to the New World in English (*Bibliotheca Americana* 2:45, no. 33). However, *Of the newe lādes* may have been earlier.

12. The initial burst of publicity given to Columbus's voyages was followed by what has been called "a conspiracy of silence." Columbus's letter drops from sight during the sixteenth century; it has been suggested that its report of gold and other riches in abundance in the New World had caused Spanish officials to impose a belated censorship. Besides, as very little, if any, effort was made to preserve these early works at the time of their publication, the rate of their destruction has been substantial.

13. Hirsch, in Chiapelli, ed., *First Images* 2:540–41.

14. Jantz, in Chiapelli, ed., *First Images* 1:98–100; Trudel, *Vaines tentatives*, 39 n. 18.

15. *See* Burton's footnote, in Staden, *The Captivity*, 60; Sir Clements Markham, tr. and ed., *The Travels of Pedro de Cieza de Leon, A.D. 1532–50*, 2 vols. (London, 1864), 1:64.

16. Its full title was *Paesi novamente retrovati e Novo Mondo da Alberico Vesputio Florentino intitulato*. By 1521 it had also been through three editions in Milan and two in Venice, all in Italian, and six editions in French and two in German (Tilley, *Studies in the French Renaissance*, 26–29).

17. The facsimile of the 1515 Paris edition of *Sensuyt le nouveau monde*, published by Princeton University Press in 1916, is the one that will be cited.

18. At the time of contact, the Inca postal service of relay runners between the Peruvian coast and Cuzco took three days; the post-horse in seventeenth-century Europe took twelve days to cover the same distance (Kamen, *The Iron Century*, 9). On the effect of distance on European life in the sixteenth century, *see* Braudel, *La Méditerranée*, 309–47.

19. Santarem, *Essai sur la Cosmographie* 3:XIX.

20. Ibid. 3:XII–XIII, XVIII.

21. These "islands" have been identified as Burma. "Cryse" was the southern Burmese coast, including the Irrawaddy Delta, perhaps also part of the Malay Peninsula; "Argyre" was to the north, the Burmese coast along the Bay of Bengal. *See* J.E. Schwartzberg, ed., *Historical Atlas of South Asia* (Chicago, 1978).

22. The belief in legendary far-off islands of great wealth had the respectability of antiquity. Horace (65–8 B.C.), for instance, writing in his sixteenth epode about the Roman civil wars, opined that the best recourse for citizens was to flee to such islands reputed to lie in the Atlantic.

23. Hermann, *The World Unveiled*, 40.

24. Columbus, *Four Voyages*, 28.

25. Du Redouer, *Sensuyt le nouveau monde*, 123, 155.

26. Navarrete, *Quatres voyages* 2:469. In the Europe of Columbus's day, it was accepted medical practice to use parts of the human body for medicinal purposes. Egyptian mummies were preferred, but when they could not be had, which was most of the time, bodies of criminals were used. They were "mummified" by filling them with bitumen to which aloes and other ingredients were added, and baked in an oven until the embalming matter had penetrated so thoroughly that the flesh would keep and could be trans-

ported to wherever it was needed. Artificial mummies were advocated as being every bit as efficacious as the Egyptian product (Murray, *Museums,* 1:50–55; Brian Fagan, "Mummies, or the Restless Dead," 62–77).

27. The "great multitudes" of the New World peoples were consistently reported by European travellers of this period, beginning with Columbus (*Spanish Letter,* 11), and Vespucci, who found the land "very thickly populated" (Waldseemüller, *Cosmographiae introductio,* 111–13, 120). A century later it was being reported that "all this region is filled with an incredible number of inhabitants" (*Cinquième tome du Mercure François,* 165). Supportive contemporary estimates are presented by S.F. Cook and Woodrow Borah in two works, *Essays in Population History: Mexico and the Caribbean,* 2 vols. (Berkeley, 1974); and *The Aboriginal Population of Central Mexico on the Eve of the Spanish Conquest* (Berkeley, 1963). Europeans of the Age of Discovery were sensitive on this point, as they still had very vivid memories of the demographic disasters of the Black Death. Concerning the difficulties of estimating America's pre-Columbian populations, *see* H. Paul Thompson, "A Technique Using Anthropological and Biological Data," 417–49.

28. Du Redouer, *Sensuyt le nouveau monde,* 154.

29. Ibid.; Columbus, *Journal,* 24; Pigafetta, *Voyage et navigation,* 5.

30. Oviedo, *Natural History,* 13, 28. Oviedo spent thirty-four years in the Caribbean in various official capacities, including that of governor of the province of Cartagena. His history, published in part in Seville in 1535, did not appear in complete four-volume form until 1851–55.

31. Pigafetta, *Voyage et navigation,* 5.

32. Du Redouer, *Sensuyt le nouveau monde,* 155.

33. Ibid., 154. *See also* Macer, *Trois livres,* 78v. This particular item of misinformation was not only one of the earliest to be picked up, but became one of the most widespread. It was included in the caption for the cannibal scene illustrated in the much-reproduced Augsburg woodcut (Harrisse, *Bibliotheca Americana* 1:51, no. 20).

34. [Bembo], *L'Histoire du Nouveau Monde,* 17. The attribution of this work to Bembo is doubtful.

35. Cellère Codex, in Wroth, *Verrazzano,* 138.

36. Vespucci, *Letters,* 7. Later, Jesuit Charles Lalemant was to write from New France that the French were neither "as peaceful nor as patient as these barbarians" (Carayon, ed., *Première Mission des Jésuites,* 129).

37. Du Redouer, *Sensuyt le nouveau monde,* 154. Vespucci in effect was corroborating Columbus, who had reported that Amerindians had no creed (Columbus, *Journal,* 24, 33, 58).

38. Eating fish was seen as virtuous where eating meat was not. Ethiopian *Ichthyophagi* were considered to be models of virtue. *See* Bernheimer, *Wild Men,* 105–6.

39. Atkinson, *Nouveaux horizons,* 76–77; Cohn, *Pursuit of the Millennium,* 74; Thorndike, *History of Magic* 6:572. Thorndike pointed out that in Europe during the fifteenth century, the use of frogs was considered legal proof of sorcery (ibid., 4:301). *See also* infra, 66–67.

40. Barré, *Copie de quelques lettres,* 24; Fontaine, *Les Nouvelles,* Aiii(verso).

41. Columbus, *Select Documents,* 70.

42. Thorndike, "The Survival of Medieval Intellectual Interests," 156, citing Germain, ed., *Cartulaire de l'Université de Montpellier* 2:1912.

43. Léry, *Histoire d'un voyage* (1580), 127; Mocquet, *Voyages en Afrique,* 125. Reptiles inspired the largest single body of European folklore concerning New World fauna (Hand, in Chiapelli, ed., *First Images* 1:47–48).

44. Thwaites, ed., *JR* 5:97. In the early days of New France, French cuisine was proposed as a means of luring Amerindians into alliance with the French. *See* Huguet, *Jean de Poutrincourt,* 167.

45. Vespucci, *First Four Voyages,* 16.

46. Montaigne, *Complete Works,* 154; Hanotaux and Martineau, *Histoire des colonies françaises* 1:12; Cartier, *Voyages,* 147. As for chocolate, it remained an Amerindian drink until the end of the sixteenth century, when it began to gain popularity in Spain; by the end of the seventeenth century, it was the fashionable drink of Western Europe. *See* MacLeod, *Spanish Central America,* 242, 440 n. 19.

47. Cartier, *Voyages,* 269; Thevet, *Cosmographie* (L'Huillier), 1013v.

48. Hariot, *Merveilleux et estrange rapport,* 26. For a similar sentiment, *see* Saint-Michel, *Voyage des isles Camercanes,* 175. Marc Lescarbot in New France, 1606–7, reported no gluttony there to compare with that of Europe: "I have no evidence that our savages wax fat or that they have big bellies; rather, they are nimble and swift" (*History of New France* 3:172–73). Lescarbot apparently did not experience the Amerindian "eat-all" feast which was to later horrify missionaries, even as they admired the usual "continual Lent" of two meals a day and the capacity to fast for as long

as ten days without complaint, and with good humor (Thwaites, ed., *JR* 2:77; 6:233–37; 15:183).

49. Wood, *New England Prospect,* 70–71. Wood was in the colony during the early 1630s.

50. An eighteenth-century French surgeon was to wonder why the health of Amerindians did not appear to be affected by the vagaries of their diets, alternating as they often did between excess and starvation (Diéreville, *Voyage to Port Royal,* 175).

51. Ibid., 299. "Who would believe that they without/ Doctors could live to such an age?" (ibid., 175); Du Redouer, *Sensuyt le nouveau monde,* 155; Léry, *Histoire d'un voyage* (1580), 96. Thevet, *Cosmographie* (Chaudiere), 1004, reported that Amerindians lived as long as 250 years. The "coarse" foods of Amerindians caught the attention of Robert Burton (1577–1640) in reference to their long lives. He pointedly observed that such diets were not favored by European physicians. The Europeans' impression of the longevity of New World peoples could have reflected their own short life expectancy. Today, in Canada, Amerindians have a life expectancy one-third shorter than the average (Baker, "Color, Culture and Power," 3).

52. "Nothing new here," reported a Rome newsletter of Febuary 1558, "except that people are dying of hunger." According to Mandrou, hunger was the great preoccupation of the French peasantry during this period. He wrote that meat or fish rarely found its way into the peasant diet, which was based on bread and wine, in contrast to the conspicuous consumption of the privileged classes (*Introduction à la France moderne,* 20–35).

53. Yves, *Voyage dans le Nord du Brésil,* 109.

54. Herrera, *General History* 1:139. Herrera's ten-volume *Historia General de los hechos de los Castellanos* had first appeared in 1603–13; a three-volume French adaptation followed in 1659–71. The author was historian to the king of Spain.

55. Herrera, *Histoire générale* 1:191; Columbus, *Oeuvres,* 44.

56. Sauer, *Sixteenth Century North America,* 296.

57. *Description de l'Amérique,* 2; Thwaites, ed., *JR* 2:77; 5:181; 68:93.

58. An exception was the Jesuit Pelleprat (*Relation des missions,* 73). In listing the tasks of the men, Pelleprat included hunting and fishing, as well as repairing the houses and making furniture.

59. Claude, for example, noted that Brazilian archers could fire six arrows for a Frenchman's three (*Maragnan,* 289). There were even reports that Amerindians were better archers than the English, considered by Europeans to be the best. Such an observation in "Extracts of the Historie of John Lerius [Jean de Léry], a Frenchman," drew the retort from Samuel Purchas, "bee it spoken by the Englishmen's leave, who are yet accounted the most skilfull Archers" (*Hakluytus Posthumus* 16:544). Purchas (1577?–1626), an English clergyman, carried on the work of Hakluyt as compiler of voyage accounts after the latter's death.

60. Wroth, *Verrazzano,* 139.

61. Columbus, *Spanish Letter,* 14. Later, Fontenelle (1657–1757) was to belittle Amerindian dugouts on the grounds that not only did they take a long time to make, but they were so easily capsized that only good swimmers could use them (*Dialogues des Morts,* in *Oeuvres diverses* 2:101–2).

62. Columbus, *Four Voyages,* 84–85.

63. European perception of Amerindians as expressed in pictorial arts was the subject of an exhibition (1975–77) in honor of the American bicentennial. It was highly acclaimed at its opening in Washington, D.C. as was its catalogue, *The European Vision of America,* by English historian Hugh Honour.

64. Léry, *Histoire d'un voyage* (1580), 180; supra, 10.

65. Vitet, *Histoire des anciennes villes* 1:121.

66. This painting is in the Cathedral of Viseu (Honour, *European Vision,* no. 4 in the section, "Savages and Men of Ind").

67. Josephy, *American Heritage Book of Indians,* 102–3.

68. Hale, in Hay, ed., *Age of the Renaissance,* 322.

69. Deserpz, *Recueil de la diversité des habits,* 394–95,382–83. The hairy homme sauvage is discussed in Chapter 4.

70. This was particularly true for cartographers. *See* Cortesão and Teixeira da Motá, *Portugaliae Monumenta Cartographica* 1, pls. 22; 4, pls. 490, 397; 5, pl. 616(A); Le Testu, *Cosmographie universelle,* fol. XLVI.

71. The bas-relief came from the facade of a house that once stood at 17 rue Malpalu in Rouen. The sculpture is now in the Musée des Antiquités de Rouen. One of its scenes is reproduced in Honour, *European Vision,* no. 8 in section "Savages and Men of Ind."

72. Staden, *Warhafftiger kurtzer bericht.* An edition with the wording of the title changed somewhat also appeared that same year in Marburg; a facsimile was published in Frank-

furt in 1925. The illustrations in Oviedo's *Natural hystoria de las Indias* (Toledo, 1526) are sketchier.

73. The painting is in the Museu Nacional de Arte Antiga at Lisbon.

74. The definitive work on this artist is that of Hulton and Quinn, *American Drawings of John White.*

75. Comparisons of Amerindians with the men of classical antiquity can be dated to Martire, whose reports of Columbus's discoveries began to be published in Latin in Seville in 1511; his first decade, which had appeared in Venice in 1504, had been in Italian. Martire's first three decades were adapted into French as *Extraict ou recueil des isles.* Comparisons with ancients were preferred over those with contemporary peoples, as classical antiquity was considered the only "true" reality as far as civilization was concerned. The point could also be made that Europeans, in relating Amerindians to their own classical antiquity, were in effect relating them to themselves. *See* Elliott, *Old World,* 50.

76. Léry, *Histoire d'un voyage* (1580), 108. Glaser has collected early illustrations from voyage accounts in *Engraved America.*

77. Dacos, "Présents américains," 57–64.

78. For contemporary references to this "vertige de curiosité," which reached such proportions among the literate during the sixteenth and seventeenth centuries, *see* Belon de Mans, *Les Observations* 1:1; Saint-Michel, *Voyages des isles Camercanes,* au lecteur. A recent discussion of the same phenomenon is found in Hodgen, *Early Anthropology,* 111ff.

79. Tazbir, "Conquête de l'Amérique," 7 n. 13; Rowe, "Ethnography," 3.

80. Murray, *Museums* 1:28–29, 82.

81. Rowe, "Ethnography," 2–3; Trigger, "Sixteenth Century Ontario," 206–8.

82. For examples of this type of description, *see* Hodgen, *Early Anthropology,* 177–201.

83. For example, the works of Bernard de Sahagún, Cristóbal de Molina, etc. (Rowe, "Ethnography," 2–3; Elliott, *Old World,* 35–37).

84. It should be remembered that the New World as revealed in the sixteenth century was more strongly differentiated from the Old World in its flora and fauna than it is today. *See* Crosby, *Columbian Exchange.*

85. Cartier, *Voyages,* 86–87.

86. Thorndike, *History of Magic* 6:276; idem, "The Survival of Medieval Intellectual Interests," 148–59.

87. Columbus, *Spanish Letter,* 14–15. Ironically, 150 years later, Recollet missionary Louis Hennepin (1626–c. 1705) was to hear reports from Amerindians that Europeans had tails, and that European women had only one breast but bore five or six children at one time (*A New Discovery* 2:84).

88. Hand, in Chiapelli, ed., *First Images* 1:52. He is citing Friederici, *Der Charakter der Entdeckung* 1:409. *See also* Friedman, *Monstrous Races.*

89. Columbus, *Spanish Letter,* 17.

90. Columbus, *Journal,* 143. Mermaid sightings continued up until the twentieth century; a number were reported by solid citizens of Victorian England (Carrington, "Mermaid," 129–30).

91. Columbus, *Spanish Letter,* 16.

92. "The Relation of David Ingram . . ." in Hakluyt, *Principall Navigations* 2:558. Dog-headed men were called *cynocephali,* a term also applied to baboons. A Chinese legend attributed the origin of cynocephali to an emperor who promised his daughter to anyone who would kill a hated subordinate. The palace dog showed up with the head, and the emperor kept his word. The dog took the princess to a remote mountain area, where their descendants were "fond of living in high altitudes and averse to plains" (Gossett, *Race,* 4). Aulus Gellius (fl. second century A.D.), *Attic Nights* 9.4.6–10, placed dog-headed men in the mountains of India, and reported that they barked and fed upon birds and wild animals. European mapmakers of the twelfth and thirteenth centuries tended to place them in the north (Santarem, *Essai sur la Cosmographie* 3:XXII). Their physical resemblance to the Egyptian Anubis is obvious, and indeed North Africa (Libya, specifically) was also reported to harbor such beings. In the Christian context, St. Christopher, the patron of travellers, was a converted cynocephalus. The classical term for cannibals is *anthropophagi.*

93. Augustine, *City of God,* bk. 16, chap. 8.

94. Vadianus, *Epitome trium,* 275. *See also* infra, Chapter 3, n. 108.

95. Thorndike, *History of Magic* 5:248; 6:408.

96. Ibid. 6:275. Unfamiliar varieties of animals were sometimes transformed into monsters by the time their descriptions reached Europe. One such case is that of a scaly crea-

ture with a second head at the end of its tail. It may have been inspired by an armadillo, or perhaps an alligator. It is illustrated in Fontaine, *Description des terres trouvees,* B4. Medieval and Renaissance fascination with imaginative animals is evident in statuary, as well as in manuscript drolleries. *See* Post, comp., *Atlas of Fantasy.*

97. Hanke, *Aristotle,* 5.

98. "Description du Voyage de l'Amerique fait par M. de Gabaret," in *Le Mercure Galant* (1683), 180–81; PAC, AC. C11A 122:82, Lettre pour Monsieur de Brouage, n.d.

99. Lafitau, *Customs of the American Indians* vol. 1, pl. 3. According to Pliny, such monsters roamed the Libyan desert. He called them "Blemmyae."

100. La Calancha, *Histoire du Perou,* preface; Saint-Michel, *Voyages des isles Camercances,* au lecteur. The idea for such people had come from Pliny's *Natural History.* Aulus Gellius had described a people living in farthest India who had bodies "that are rough and covered with feathers like birds, who eat no food but live from inhaling the perfume of flowers" (*Attic Nights* 9.4.6–10). Reports that Brazilians covered themselves with feathers could have led to the conclusion that they also lived on odors, as the ancients had written.

101. *Troisième tome du Mercure François,* 266–73. *See also* Murray, *Museums* 1:46.

102. Huizinga, *The Waning of the Middle Ages,* 97.

103. *C'est la deduction,* 40v–41.

104. Infra, 50–51; Belleforest, *Cosmographie universelle* 2:2087. This work is a revamping of Münster's *La Cosmographie universelle* (1568); Münster, for his part, had followed Johann Boem (infra, 35).

105. Martire, *De Orbe Novo* (MacNutt), 1:102–3.

106. Atkinson, *Nouveaux horizons,* 63ff.; Hale, in Hay, ed., *Age of the Renaissance,* 335.

107. Mendoza (1545–1618), *Histoire du grand royaume,* 243v; Du Tertre, *Histoire générale des isles,* 452; Herrera, *Description des Indes Occidentales,* 15.

108. Purchas, *Hakluytus Posthumus* 16:252.

109. Fontaine, *Description des terres trouvees,* A6; [Bembo], *L'Histoire du Nouveau Monde,* 11. Eliade, *The Sacred and the Profane,* 100–102, makes the point that among early peoples, one becomes truly a man by conforming to the teachings of myths, that is, by imitating the gods, and the gods practised cannibalism. For a general study of the subject, *see* Loeb, "Cannibalism."

110. A lad left by the Basques with the people of the Gaspé early in the seventeenth century was reported to have been eaten during a famine (Thwaites, ed., *JR* 8:29).

111. Gerbi, *Dispute of the New World,* 38. Oviedo noted that the surface temperature of the soil in tropical America was temperate, which he saw as explaining why the root system of New World trees spread horizontally rather than vertically. Down below, said Oviedo, the earth in the New World was too hot to sustain life (*Natural History,* 30). *See also* Hemming, *Red Gold,* 25.

112. Pigafetta, *Voyage et navigation,* 4v.

113. Dassié, *Description générale,* preface. The Greeks had had a similar reaction at their first encounter with mounted men from the north, who entered their legends as centaurs.

114. Giovio, *Histoires de Paolo Jovio* 2:324. Another version has the Mexica worshipping a sculptured horse. Later Chauveton theorized that it was not Spanish arms or artillery that conquered Amerindians, as they had quickly adapted to that new technology, but rather the latter's fear of horses (Benzoni, *Histoire nouvelle,* 474–75).

115. Fontenelle, *Oeuvres diverses* 2:103. This theme was picked up by Shakespeare in *The Tempest:* Caliban asks Stephano, "Has't thou not dropped from heaven?" *See* R.R. Cowley, "Shakespeare's Use of Voyagers," *Publications of the Modern Language Association of America* 41 (1926):717.

116. Levi-Strauss has described those efforts as scientific (*Tristes Tropiques,* 68). *See also* his *Race et histoire,* 21–22. Voltaire had found it difficult to believe that Amerindians had really looked upon Europeans as gods; he conjectured that perhaps they had also believed them to be monsters (*Essai sur les moeurs,* in *Oeuvres complètes* 12:380).

117. Hanke, *Aristotle,* 24–26; Benzoni, *Histoire nouvelle,* 27–28.

118. Ramusio, *Navigations et Voyages,* 74.

119. Acosta, *Histoire naturelle et moralle,* 372v–73. Acosta had gone to Peru as a missionary in 1570, and had spent seventeen years in the Indies.

120. Martire, *Extraict ou recueil,* 22–22v.

121. Hanke, *Aristotle,* 104.

122. Compare this attitude with that expressed in I Corinthians 14:10–11 (Confraternity text): "There are, for example, so many kinds of languages in this world and none without

meaning. If then, I do not know the meaning of the language, I shall be to whom I speak, a foreigner; and he who speaks, a foreigner to me."

123. *See* Jones, "The Image of the Barbarian," 376–407.

124. Lurie, in J.M. Smith, ed., *Seventeenth-Century America,* 58. This legend was first reported from Mexico. According to Séjourné, Cortés arrived at a time when the Mexica were at the end of a religious cycle. They were expecting Quetzalcoatl's second coming, which would have implied the advent of a new spiritual order (*Burning Water*). Apparently this expectation was not shared by the Inca; instead an oracle had warned them against bearded beings who would topple the empire. But the Inca Atahuallpa was told by his personal oracle that he was invincible, and so he agreed to meet the invaders.

2 What Manner of Men are They?

1. Hodgen, *Early Anthropology,* 34–35, 56ff. For a discussion of the Greek concept of *oikoumene, see* Penrose, *Travel and Discovery in the Renaissance,* 1–6.

2. A persistent early report had St. Thomas preaching in the New World, usually in Brazil or the Caribbean (Purchas, *Hakluytus Posthumus* 1:163; 16:227; Hemming, *Red Gold,* 46–47, 57, 87).

3. Herrera, *General History* 1:6–7. The story of the dying pilot, returning from an extraordinary voyage and passing on his information to Columbus, is told by Oviedo, *Historia General* 1:16; and by Benzoni, *History of the New World,* 14–15. Purchas did not consider it necessary to look beyond Columbus's "piercing Wit, judicious Observation of Occurents, learning in Mathematikes," aided by Divine Providence, to explain his success (*Hakluytus Posthumus* 1:20).

4. Alexander actually issued four bulls in 1493 relating to the discovery of the New World, two of them called *Inter Caetera.* The texts and bibliographies of all four are reproduced by Davenport in *European Treaties* 1:56–83. *See also* Streit, *Bibliotheca Missionum* 2:1–4.

5. Augustine, *City of God,* bk. 16, chap. 8.

6. Cited by Elliott, *Old World,* 48.

7. Crone, *The Discovery of America,* 81.

8. Cartier, *Voyages,* 186. Such sentiments had come to be applied to Amerindians generally. For instance, in a letter dated 27 August 1612 and published the following year, similar ideas were expressed concerning Brazilians (Arsène, *Dernière lettre,* 11).

9. "Libellus ad Leonem X pontificem maximum," a church reform project prepared by two Venetian noblemen turned hermits, Paolo Giustiniani and Pietro Quirini. *See* O'Malley in Chiapelli, ed., *First Images* 1:185–200. O'Malley makes the point that in spite of such an expression of concern, and of the fact that representatives of the missions in the New World were present, not a single mention of the Americas is to be found in the acts and orations of the Fifth Lateran Council, which met in Rome from 1512 to 1517. This could be an indication of Rome's lack of direct control of the missions in the New World, faced as she was with the overriding power of the Spanish king, and later that of the French king. The Americas came in for somewhat more attention at the Council of Trent (1545–63), although the situation vis-à-vis Spain was essentially unchanged (Mateos, "Ecos de América," 559–605).

10. Hanke, "Pope Paul III and the American Indians," 68–69.

11. Ibid., 96; Hanke reproduces the text of the retraction in app. 1, 97–98.

12. Thevet, *Singularitez,* 135.

13. Gómara, *Histoire generalle,* chap. 27, 27. Earlier Oviedo had reported that certain highly respected Amerindians called *tequina* were masters of communication with the devil (*Natural History,* 33–35).

14. *L'Histoire de la Terre Neuve du Pérou,* Cij(verso). The perfectly preserved body of a boy, apparently a sacrificial victim, was found entombed near an Inca shrine at 5,399 meters on El Pomo peak in Chile (McIntyre, "The Lost Empire of the Incas," 733).

15. Postel, *Des Merveilles du Monde,* 31; Macer, *Trois livres,* 29v. Later, Amerindians of New France were reported to have sorcerers called *pillotoas (pilotuas)* who conversed with devils (de Laet, *L'Histoire du Nouveau Monde,* 50; Champlain, *Works* 1:117).

16. Drake, *Le Voyage,* 14.

17. *Martire, De Orbe novo* (Gaffarel), 65; Friederici, *Der Charakter der Entdeckung* 1:43–46. Oviedo reported the contrary: "every Christian should contemplate the fact that everywhere Holy Communion has been celebrated, these hurricanes and terrific storms have not occurred in large numbers, nor are they as destructive as they used to be" (*Natural History,* 37).

18. Cicero, *De Natura Deorum* 1.16.43.

19. Campbell, *Mythic Image*, 170–75. Later, missionaries would be astonished to find the cross being used among the Micmac (infra, 104).

20. Acosta, *Histoire naturelle et moralle*, 248v, 260–65.

21. Ricard, *Spiritual Conquest of Mexico*, 31–33; Benzoni, *Histoire nouvelle*, 308–9.

22. Perhaps the most colorful exponent of this view among New England Puritans was the Congregational minister, Cotton Mather (1663–1728). *See*, for example, his *Magnalia Christi Americana*.

23. Hanke, "Cultural Contribution," 276–277. Hanke compiled these observations from the first part of Oviedo's *Historia general* (1535).

24. Cited by Levi-Strauss, *Tristes Tropiques*, 67–68. Also in Martire, *De Orbe Novo* (MacNutt) 2:274–75; and Herrera, *Histoire généralle* 2:661–63.

25. Hanke, "Pope Paul III," 72. A bibliography of the bull, also known as *Excelsis Deus* and *Veritas Ipsa*, is in Streit, *Bibliotheca Missionum* 2:281 and 24:3. The bull had been preceded by an edict addressed to Juan Cardinal de Tavera, Archbishop of Toledo, granting him full powers to take whatever measures he deemed necessary to protect Amerindians (Pastor, *History of the Popes* 12:518–19).

26. Pastor, *History of the Popes* 29:262; Alden, "Black Robes Versus White Settlers," 30.

27. Boem, *Omnium gentium mores leges et ritus ex multis clarissimis rerum scriptoribus*. . . (Augsburg, 1520).

28. Boem's work went through numerous editions in several languages, the first appearing in French in 1540 under the title, *Recueil de diverses histoires touchant les situations de toutes regions & pays contenuz es trois parties du monde, avec le particuliers moeurs, loix, & ceremonies de toutes nations & peuples y habitans.*

29. Marco Antonio Coccio (called Sabellico), *Enneades* (Venice, 1498). According to Rowe, Boem also used the Venice edition of 1504, *Secunda pars enneadum* ("Ethnography," 4).

30. Boem, *Recueil de diverses histoires* (1542), i–ii.

31. Ibid., iii.

32. Boem, *Recueil de diverses histoires* (1540), 3.

33. In one case mentioned in the *Jesuit Relations*, a Huron shaman was misshapen (13:101). The Armouchiquois of the Atlantic coast were also described as malformed (infra, 106).

34. For one example, Magnus, *Histoire des Pays Septentrionaux*. Here we have the bon sauvage in a northern European setting.

35. Sir William Alexander, first Earl of Stirling (1567–1640), a Scottish colonizer, observed that the division of the world between Noah's three sons had been accomplished without taking "any notice of natives" of the New World (*American Colonization*, 156).

36. Bissell characterized the sheer bulk of this "pseudo-scientific" theorizing during the sixteenth and seventeenth centuries as "amazing" (*American Indian in English Literature*, 6). A good résumé of the debate is found in Charlevoix's *Histoire et description* 5:1–64.

37. One cosmographer went so far as to postulate that in that case "the inhabitants of the New World are descended from us" (d'Avity, *Estats*, 262).

38. La Calancha, *Histoire du Perou*, 13; Du Bartas, *Oeuvres poetiques et chrestiennes*, 167–67v; Postel, *Des Merveilles du Monde*, 41v; Macer, *Trois livres*, 31v.

39. Aristotle, *Nicomachean Ethics* 7.5.2; Huddleston, *Origins of the American Indians*, 73–74, 92–93. George Horn, in a major work, *De originibus Americanis* (The Hague, 1652), maintained that the Americas had been peopled by Phoenicians from the west, Chinese from the east, and Scythians from the north. A latter-day argument holds that certain stone constructions and inscriptions in the Americas indicate the presence of Celts, Phoenicians, Egyptians, and Norsemen during the Bronze Age (Fell, *America B.C.*, *Bronze Age America*).

40. Martire, *De Orbe Novo* (MacNutt) 1:161.

41. Acosta, *Histoire naturelle et moralle*, chaps. 20, 21; Benzoni, *Histoire nouvelle*, aux lecteurs. *See also* Huddleston, *Origins of the American Indians*, 50–51, 101–2. A latter-day echo of this can be discerned in the detection of Scytho-Siberian influences in some motifs found in Inuit designs (Snow, *American Indians*, 228–29). In 1975, the Metropolitan Museum of Art held a much-acclaimed exhibition, "From the Land of the Scythians," in which the gold work of these early nomads was featured.

42. Le Mascrier, *Memoires historiques* 1:120.

43. Thwaites, ed., *JR* 22:35. Mather had his own version of the resemblance between Scythians and Amerindians when he wrote that the difficulties of Xerxes and Tamburlaine in

finding the Scythians in order to conquer them was paralleled by the experiences of the English against New England tribes (*Magnalia Christi Americana* 1:166–67). Later he described Amerindians as "worse than Scythian wolves" (ibid., 1:193).

44. Léry, *Histoire d'un voyage* (1580), 206; Langenes, *Thrésor,* 42; Gómara, *Voyages et conquestes,* au lecteur; Boem, *Recueil de diverses histoires* (1540), 2v.

45. Benzoni, *Histoire nouvelle,* aux lecteurs; 192.

46. Couillard, *Antiquitez,* 97.

47. *See,* for example, Bourne, *Treasure for travailers.*

48. La Peyrère, *Prae-Adamitae* (1655). *See* McKee, "Isaac de La Peyrère," 456–85. The eighteenth century saw a revival of speculations that Amerindians were descended from Adam but not from Noah, as they had been missed by the Flood, which had not been universal. *See* Engel, *Essai;* Bendyshe, "History of Anthropology," 353–54.

49. Boem, *Recueil des païs* (1558), 28. To Homer, the Ethiopians had been the happiest of men, tall and beautiful, living peacefully according to the laws of nature; in other words, a Greek version of the bon sauvage. *See* Hodgen, *Early Anthropology,* 475.

50. Virgilio, *Notable works,* vi.

51. Le Roy, *De la Vicissitude,* 25.

52. Münster, *La Cosmographie universelle* (1556), 3. Münster (1489–1552), a Catholic turned Protestant, was renowned as a Hebrew scholar and geographer. The term "honnesteté" in the sixteenth century meant conventional integrity, polite respectability, and decent social behavior.

53. Boem, *Recueil de diverses histoires* (1542), iv(verso).

54. Thevet, *Singularitez,* L. "These savages are inhuman, and we read with horror, pity and anger about their great cruelties. Yet I also praise the simple goodness of some of their practices and policies."

55. Ibid., XLV. "These barbarians walk naked while we do disguised behind our make-up and masks. These people, strangers to pity, do not range themselves against others; we despise, entrap, betray and dissemble. These barbarians have less to justify in their conduct than we do, in spite of all the reasons that we marshal in support of our position."

56. Louis Nicolas, "Histoire naturelle; ou la fidelle recherche de tout ce qu'il y a de rare dans les Indes occidentales," unpublished eighteenth-century manuscript (BN Fonds français, 24225, fol. 126).

57. Bruzen de la Martinière, *Le Grand Dictionnaire géographique* 2:88, s.v. "Canada."

58. Cortés, *Correspondance,* 100–101.

59. "Civilization" was a word that was not current until the end of the seventeenth century. In the sixteenth century, "civility" also meant good citizenship, which implied familiarity with the ethics and political theory of Greek and Roman philosophers (Rowe, "Ethnography," 7).

60. The ramifications of this attitude in missionary work are discussed by Freeman, "The Indian Convert," 113–27.

61. *L'Histoire de la Terre-Neuve de Pérou,* preface.

62. Chinard, *Rêve,* 223.

63. Atkinson, *Nouveaux horizons,* 10–11.

64. In assessing the interest in the Orient compared with that in the New World, M.P. Gilmore found that the latter was "slighted" in favor of the former: "It remains surprising that on the eve of the great French colonization of Canada, there was not a popular demand for more information on the newly discovered lands" (Chiapelli, ed., *First Images* 2:520). However, as Rowe noted, a "surprisingly high proportion of the ethnographic data published in the sixteenth century relates to the New World" ("Ethnography," 2). There was also a considerable increase in the amount of space devoted in official publications to Canada at the time of the de Monts-Champlain colonization and the first Jesuit missions.

65. Atkinson, *Nouveaux horizons,* mentions some of these considerations without going into their full implications. A seventeenth-century memoir noted instances when Illinois women had trouble in childbirth: "even though savage, they were as sick as French women" (PAC, AC, C11A 122:147, lettre 61, n.d.).

66. La Croix, *Nouveau Cynée,* 81. La Croix (Emeric de Crucé), a monk, was a pioneer advocate of international arbitration. Gonnard, in *La Légende du bon sauvage,* 11, cites Louis Hébert, the first farmer of New France: "I crossed the seas more to come and help the savages than from private interest."

67. Oviedo, *L'Histoire naturelle,* 39v.

68. Genesis 6 (Confraternity text) says in part: "When the Lord saw the wickedness of man on the earth was great, and that man's every thought and all the inclination of his heart were only evil, he regretted that he had made earth and

was grieved to the heart. Then the Lord said, I will wipe from the earth man whom I have created–man and beast, crawling creature and bird of the air as well–for I regret that I made them."

69. Gómara, *Histoire generalle,* 252v.

70. *The principall navigations, voiages and discoveries of the English nation, made by sea or over land, to the most remote and farthest distant quarters of the earth at any time within the compass of these 1500. yeeres*. . . (London, 1589). The edition used for the most part is entitled *The Principal Navigations, Voyages, Traffiques and Discoveries of the English Nation* (1903–5).

71. Hakluyt, *Original Writings* 2:503, document 89, "Epistle Dedicatory to the Council of Virginia," 1609. Hakluyt also expressed the same idea in "Epistle Dedicatory to Sir Walter Raleigh, 1587," reproduced in this work as document 58, 2:377.

3 To Each a Place and Rank

1. Hale, *Renaissance Europe,* 53.

2. Marcel, *Sur quelques documents peu connus,* 6; Morison, *Portugese Voyages,* 71.

3. Saint-Martin, *Mémoires historiques et géographiques* 2:407. Also cited by Santarem, *Essai sur la Cosmographie* 3:xxvi–xxviii. For the complete text as cited by Santarem, *see* Appendix II. The idea of the "chain of being" enjoyed its widest popularity during the eighteenth century (Lovejoy, *Great Chain of Being,* 183ff).

4. Lovejoy, *Great Chain of Being,* 228.

5. Ibid., 187.

6. Ptolemy, *Tetrabiblos,* 121–27.

7. Thorndike, *History of Magic* 5:34.

8. Petit, *De ignis et lucis.*

9. Le Roy, *De la Vicissitude,* 9v–14.

10. [Poncelin de la Roche-Tillac], *Almanach américain,* 18–19. This uniformity had been noted very early (supra, 10–11). I am citing an eighteenth-century source because of its apt phraseology.

11. Martire, *De Orbe Novo* (MacNutt) 1:133; a similar but more realistic observation is in "The Second Voyage to Guinea," in Hakluyt, *Principal Navigations* 6:176.

12. Lescarbot, *History of New France* 3:139–40. Acosta devoted considerable space to the subject of the temperature and humidity of the New World's Torrid Zone. *See also* Garcilasso de La Vega, *Royal Commentaries of the Yncas* 1:18.

13. Belknap, *A Discourse,* 127.

14. Bodin, *Republique* (1577), 541.

15. Montesquieu, *Oeuvres* 2:114.

16. Thevet, *Singularitez,* 408–9.

17. Charron, *De la Sagesse,* 217.

18. Bodin, *Republique* (1577), 406.

19. Postel, *Des Merveilles du Monde,* 92–92v.

20. Maffei (1533–1603), *Histoire des Indes,* 96; [Nóbrega], *L'Institution des loix,* 5v.

21. Langenes, *Thrésor,* 165.

22. De Brosse, *Histoire des Navigations* 2:374.

23. Thorndike, *History of Magic* 5:577.

24. This idea was to be given its classic formulation by Montesquieu (*Oeuvres* 2:133). However, it was implicit in the writings of such sixteenth-century figures as Oviedo and Acosta. The eighteenth-century produced a large body of writing on the effects of geography and climate on the human condition, following the paths indicated by writers of the previous two centuries.

25. Herrera, *General History* 1:17.

26. De Brosse, *Histoire des Navigations,* 376.

27. Bodin, *Republique* (1577), 540.

28. Ibid., 198.

29. Agrippa von Nettesheim, *Of the vanitie and uncertaintie,* 71v.

30. Estienne, *L'Introduction au Traité,* 3–4v.

31. Estienne, *Apologie pour Hérodote* 1:149–50. However, Saint-Michel was later to view travel as a means of recouping lost virtue and refinding the faith of our fathers (*Voyages aux isles Camercanes,* au lecteur).

32. Hodgen, *Early Anthropology,* 264. On the general Renaissance fascination with mutability and decay, "the dance of death," *see* ibid., 257ff.

33. Marconville, *Traicte,* 48.

34. Bodin, *Methode,* in *Oeuvres* 3:315.

35. Hodgen, *Early Anthropology* 378. *See also* Charlevoix, *His-*

toire et description 5:55–58, 63; and Lafitau, *Moeurs des sauvages amériquains.* Toward the end of the seventeenth century, geographer Nicolas Sanson d'Abbeville theorized continual wars and consequent lack of communication had contributed to the New World's luxuriant array of languages (*Atlas nouveau* 1:16).

36. La Popelinière, *Trois Mondes,* bk. 1:38; bk. 2:26v. This was also the theme of Rochas, *La Physique réformée.*

37. Le Roy, *Considerations,* 404–5.

38. Le Roy, *De la Vicissitude,* 98v.

39. Ibid., 26v.

40. Ibid., 98v.

41. Charron, *Les Trois Vérités,* 367.

42. Charron, *De la Sagesse,* 401–3.

43. At the time that Charron wrote, the Catholic Reformation was restricting sexual freedom in France as well as elsewhere. A century or so earlier, attitudes had been more relaxed, approximating those that had aroused Charron's wonder. *See* Ladurie, *Montaillou.*

44. [Nóbrega], *L'Institution,* 6v. Observations about the Amerindian belief in a universal Deluge are to be found in, among others, Gómara, *Histoire generalle,* 142; and Lescarbot, *History of New France* 3:101. A pre-Columbian Mayan pictorialization of the Flood myth is reproduced by Morley in *The Ancient Maya,* 215.

45. Garimberto, *Les Problemes,* 115.

46. Charron, *De la Sagesse,* 112–13. Such philosophizing had little, if any, influence on missionaries who were astonished to note that Amerindians, when they wore European garments at all, did so to adorn themselves rather than to conceal their nudity. For example, *see* Claude, *Maragnan,* 273–74.

47. Charron, *De la Sagesse,* 330–31. Later, Gabriel de Foigny was to push the argument further, claiming that the nudity of Amerindians was an infallible proof that clothing meant loss of innocence (*La Terre australe,* 105).

48. Herrera, *Histoire générale* 3:662.

49. Hale, in Hay, ed., *Age of the Renaissance,* 335. Martire told of Columbus's men, cutting wood in a dense forest, imagining they saw natives dressed in immaculate white tunics. The Spaniards ran to tell the admiral, who was "delighted finally to discover a civilized nation." But the mysterious natives were never seen again (*De Orbe Novo* [MacNutt] 1:99).

50. For one example, Mendoza, *Histoire du grand royaume,* 244. Concerning God's "singular" affection in elevating Europeans to clothed civility, *see* Thevet, *Singularitez,* 135.

51. Léry, *Histoire d'un voyage* (1580), 107. Another objection, reported by Thevet, was that clothes interfered with freedom of action (*Singularitez,* 142). Once converted, Amerindians could develop excessive modesty (Thwaites, ed., *JR* 19:51). Northern Amerindians, already clothed for reasons of climate, also found European styles restrictive.

52. Léry, *Histoire d'un voyage* (1580), 107. The Christian concern about wearing clothes long puzzled Amerindians (*see* for example, the questioning reported in Thwaites, ed., *JR* 13:51). A pictograph at Meyers Springs, Texas, attributed to the Lipan Apaches, reveals that these people were under the impression that wearing clothes was one of the Christian Ten Commandments (Martineau, *The Rocks Begin to Speak,* 132–33).

53. Garimberto, *Les Problemes,* 19–21.

54. Coréal, *Voyages* 2:164. Earlier, Claude had reported an amusing story of a Brazilian woman finding herself the only person naked at a baptism (*Maragnan,* 128). Missionaries were sometimes embarrassed by the nudity of their charges, as when a group barricaded itself behind locked doors to prevent the entry of a Tupinambá delegation because its members were innocent of clothing. The annoyed Brazilians broke down the door (*Nouvelles des choses,* 13).

55. Charron, *De la Sagesse,* 176; Du Choul, *Discours de la religion,* 191.

56. Bodin, *Republique* (1577), 55; [Bembo], *L'Histoire du Nouveau Monde,* 10; Martire, *De Orbe novo* (Gaffarel), 55; Vespucci, *Letters,* 10; Fontaine, *Les Nouvelles,* Aiii(verso). Some attributed the introduction of the distinction between "mine" and "thine," which they saw as instrumental in undermining the sentiment of fraternity, to Roman and Canon law (Cohn, *Millennium,* 119). As late as the nineteenth century, Russian priests were reported to have found a tribe on a Bering Sea island leading lives reflecting so well the teachings of Christ that the priests confessed the people were better left alone (Hanke, *Aristotle,* 26).

57. Oviedo, *L'Histoire naturelle,* 39–42; d'Avity, *Estats,* 316–17; Belleforest, *Cosmographie universelle* 2:2081, among many others.

58. Hanke, *Aristotle,* 5. Another island believed inhabited by evil spirits was Ile aux Démons off the Labrador coast (Thevet, *Cosmographie* [Chaudiere], 1018v). An extension of this was to place the land of the barbarians Gog and

Magog, descendants of Japhet, in the New World. *See* Anderson, *Alexander's Gate.*

59. Du Redouer, *Sensuyt le nouveau monde,* 154. For a discussion of this negative form of description, *see* Hodgen, *Early Anthropology,* 196–201. For latter-day examples of such Amerindians, *see* James Walker, "The Indian in Canadian Historical Writing," 21–47.

60. Gómara, *Histoire generalle,* chap. 92.

61. Frobisher, *La Navigation,* no pagination.

62. Fontaine, *Les Nouvelles,* Aiii(verso).

63. Girava in Apianus, *Cosmographie,* 166.

64. D'Avity, *Estats,* 261. D'Avity also said they did not have dogs, which was true for the Tupí-Guaraní along the Brazilian coast; however, Peruvians had dogs, as did the peoples of Central and North America. *See* Alfred Métraux, in *Handbook of South American Indians* 3:100, 102.

65. [Bembo], *L'Histoire du Nouveau Monde,* 13.

66. Thevet, *Cosmographie* (L'Huillier), 1011v.

67. Barré, *Copie de quelques lettres,* 23.

68. Pierre de Ronsard (1524–85), "Discours contre Fortune à Odet de Colligny Cardinal de Chastillon," in Le Moine, ed., *L'Amérique et les poètes français,* no. 95.

69. Coppier, *Histoire et voyage,* 33.

70. Dassié, *Description générale,* preface.

71. Chevillard, *Desseins de cardinal Richelieu,* 171.

72. Coppier, *Histoire et voyage,* 146.

73. That was how Jesuit missionary Pierre Biard (1567?–1622) described his flock in Acadia (Carayon, ed., *Première Mission des Jésuites,* 31). In Renaissance Christian eyes, the conduct of pagans, no matter how exemplary, could not be classed as moral (Thwaites, ed., *JR* 6:240).

74. Hobbes, *Leviathan,* 62. The work was published in Latin in Amsterdam in 1668. Hobbes's position was a logical development of that of Sepúlveda during the Valladolid debate of 1550. Hanke deals with the debate in *The Spanish Struggle.*

75. Myres, *Influence of Anthropology,* 8–12.

76. Claude, for one, reported that the Brazilians addressed each other as if they all belonged to one family (*Maragnan,* 284v).

77. Cited by Myres, *Influence of Anthropology,* 38.

78. Hallowell, *Culture and Experience,* 249. For an eighteenth-century argument against Hobbes's theory of early man in a continual state of warfare against his own kind, *see* Gerdil's *Discours philosophique.* Tylor surveyed individuals who had been found living in a state of nature in "Wild Men and Beast Children," 21–32. A twentieth century case is described by Gabriel Janer Manila in *Marcos: Wild Child of the Sierra Morena* (London, 1982).

79. Martire, *Extraict ou recueil,* 23.

80. Claude, *Maragnan,* 265v.

81. Fernandes de Queiros, *Copie de la Requeste,* 4–12. In spite of discovering the Marquesas, Tahiti, and other islands, he failed to interest the kings of Spain in colonizing them.

82. Boyer, *Veritable Relation,* 273.

83. Carayon, ed., *Première Mission des Jésuites,* 31.

84. For just one example, cosmographer Petrus Bertius wrote that the people of the New World were stupid because they did not value gold and silver as did Europeans (*Description d'Amerique,* 246).

85. Heyns, *Miroir du Monde,* 2. Acosta had the horses being shod with silver (*Histoire naturelle et moralle,* 134).

86. Berquen, *Les Merveilles des Indes,* 108.

87. *L'Histoire de la Terre-Neuve de Pérou,* preface.

88. Manso, "The Quest for El Dorado," 59–65; Friederici, *Der Charakter der Entdeckung* 1:410.

89. Manso, "The Quest for El Dorado," 59–65. Berquen reported another story of Amerindians dumping gold into a bottomless lake. This concerned a gold chain so heavy that a hundred men were needed to carry it; it was being transported as ransom for Atahuallpa, but was thrown into the lake when the Amerindians heard of the Inca's death (*Les Merveilles,* 80). One can but wonder if this tale is not a fantastication of Inca bridge-building procedures. The Inca spanned rivers with *keshwa chaca,* bridges of gold-colored straw, the cables of which were braided and carried by long lines of men to the construction site. Such bridges had to be renewed every year.

90. Biet, *France Equinoxiale,* 154.

91. Lescarbot, *Nova Francia,* 197.

92. Du Val d'Abbeville, *Memoires geographiques,* 13.

93. Among those who made this identification were Thevet, *Singularitez,* 424–25; Bodin, *Republique* (1577), 37–50; Martire, *Extraict ou recueil,* 46v.

94. Burke, *European Settlements* 1:167.

95. Glacken, *Traces on the Rhodian Shore,* 117. Ronsard also saw the bon sauvage simply as an unevolved being, the slave to his own nature ("Discours contre fortune," in Le Moine, *L'Amérique et les poètes français*). Acosta calculated from the evidence of the traditions of Amerindians concerning their origins, that they could not be more than 400 years old as a people, even as he noted the belief of the Peruvians that they had originated in their country (*Histoire naturelle et moralle,* 50). Geographer John Ogilby (1600–1676) argued that the New World's multiplicity of languages proved that "America was Peopled presently after the Confusion of Tongues at Babel." However, they had been there long enough (perhaps a thousand years) to develop arts (*America,* 12–13).

96. Hallowell, *Culture and Experience,* 311. A.E. Jensen holds that "progress" is a term of limited value in considering the essence of a culture. Knowledge of physical reality and cognitive values may accumulate, but that does not diminish such achievements as the invention of pottery, the insights of a Newton, or the creations of a Beethoven within the terms of their contemporary cultures (*Myth and Cult,* 34).

97. Montaigne, *Complete Works,* 693.

98. Pasquier, *Lettres,* 62v.

99. Maffei, *Histoire des Indes,* 98–99; Mastrilli, *Relation,* epistre. According to Eliade, cannibalism was not practised at the oldest–i.e., the earliest–levels of culture (*The Sacred and the Profane,* 100–104).

100. Montaigne, *Essais,* 214. Although Montaigne's comments on the New World and its peoples can be found dispersed throughout his works, most of them are in his essays "Des Coches" and "Des Cannibales." The latter was a source for Shakespeare's *The Tempest* (Kermode, ed., xxxiv–xxxviii).

101. Europeans of this period had an undisguised appetite for horrors, as witness the popularity of public torture. For example, a mob in Bruges in 1488 asked that such a spectacle be prolonged as long as possible; and the people of Mons purchased a brigand for the pleasure of seeing him quartered (Hale, *Renaissance Europe,* 27).

102. Atkinson said that the favorable notices received by the Amerindians far outweighed the unfavorable, in spite of which the image of Amerindians as "thieves, liars and idolators" persisted (*Nouveaux horizons,* 147, 211). Chinard wrote that from the mid-seventeenth century onward, there was only praise of the "good savage" in travel accounts (*Rêve,* 38–39). Hodgen flatly disagrees; during the sixteenth century, she said, "misrepresentation of the savage was at its height" (*Early Anthropology,* 367).

103. Pasquier, *Lettres,* 63.

104. Ternaux-Compans, *Bibliothèque américaine.*

105. White, in Chiapelli, ed., *First Images* 1:125.

106. Scaglione, in Chiapelli, ed., *First Images* 1:63–70, makes the point that Italy, in spite of its early involvements in the voyages of discovery, did not develop such a tradition.

107. Mayer, *The Crusades,* 220–22.

108. O'Gorman argued that Renaissance Europeans did not accept appearance as a criterion of humanity, but rather looked to ideals and habits. If these did not conform to the "supreme and absolute" standards of Christianity, then the newcomer appeared as monstrous, possessing no true human significance (*Invention of America,* 134). *See also* supra, 19–21. Thus François I, after the burning of six heretics, publicly claimed that "France was the only Power which had not nourished monsters" (Seward, *Prince of the Renaissance,* 186). An attenuated form of such ideas persists; there are still those who see Amerindians as "villains desperately in need of Europe's civilizing hand" (E. Bradford Burns, *A History of Brazil* [New York, 1970], 15).

109. Villey, *Les Sources* 2:157. For a survey of how such attitudes influenced Quebec historians, *see* D.B. Smith, *Le Sauvage.*

4 L'Homme Sauvage

1. The information in this chapter was published in a somewhat different form as an article, "The Concept of *l'homme sauvage* and early French Colonialism."

2. Fenton discusses the concept of savagery in his introduction to Lafitau's *Customs of the American Indians,* li–liv, as does Jennings, *The Invasion of America,* 74–80.

3. Larousse (1817–75), *Grand Dictionnaire Universel.* Similar definitions are given by Oxford and Webster. The latter adds another meaning, that of "a man holding radical political views."

4. Maffei, *Histoire des Indes,* 98. Münster, in his *Cosmographie universelle* (1556), placed barbarians, savages, and monsters all in the same category.

5. La Curne de Sainte-Palaye, *Dictionnaire historique.*

6. Richelet, *Dictionnaire françois.*

7. Furetière, *Dictionnaire universel.*

8. Columbus, *Oeuvres*.

9. Waldseemüller, *Cosmographiae Introductio*, 123–26.

10. Cartier, *Voyages*, 60.

11. Supra, 15. This "frayeur subite" was later presented as one of the reasons why the Spanish were able to conquer Amerindians so rapidly (Coréal, *Voyages* 2:132; Imhof, *Grand théâtre historique* 3, bk. 4, 176).

12. Martire, *De Orbe novo* (Gaffarel), 55.

13. Vespucci, *Letters*, 9.

14. Le Moyne, *Les Peintures morales* 2:620–29.

15. Ibid. *Le Mercure François*, France's official newspaper during the first part of the seventeenth century, described Amerindians thus:

    > As for the behavior of the Savages, it is enough to say that it is altogether savage. From morning until night they have no other care than to fill their bellies. They are beggars if ever there were, yet they are inordinately proud . . . the vices of the flesh are frequent among them . . . one cannot speak of their cleanliness, as they are very dirty in their eating habits and in their cabins. (*Treizième tome*, 16)

    Jesuit Charles Lalemant had written to that effect from New France in 1625 (Thwaites, ed., *JR* 4:197–99). During the nineteenth century, Brinton was to theorize that a hunting culture bred a disregard for human suffering, a vindictive spirit, a tendency to sanguinary rites, and an inappeasable restlessness: "The law with reason objects to accepting a butcher as a juror on a trial for life; here is a whole race of butchers" (*Myths of the New World*, 21–22).

16. D'Avity, *Estats*, 315.

17. PAC, AC, C11A 1:10. The task of the missionaries was to render "the savages reasonable," to enable them to become Christian and sedentary. *See also* C11A 3:210, Description du Canada, 1671.

18. La Croix, *Nouveau Cynée*, 26. In the Spanish colonies, the term *gente de razón* was reserved for whites and mestizos (Ricard, *Spiritual Conquest of Mexico*, 291).

19. Oviedo, *L'Histoire naturelle*, 68v.

20. The view of the savage as a retrograde figure was given scientific impetus by George Louis Leclerc, Comte de Buffon (1707–88), and reached its greatest popularity during the nineteenth century. For example, Pierre-Simon Ballanche (1776–1847) wrote: "The state of savagery is simply one of degeneration of which we do not know the cycles, but which is certainly neither natural nor primitive" (*Essai*, 224). It derives somewhat obliquely from Aristotle, who argued that although bestiality was not frequently found naturally in man, it could develop through habitual wrongdoing (*Nicomachean Ethics* 7.5.1–4).

21. Montchrestien, *Traicté*, 269.

22. D'Avity, *Estats*, 315.

23. Herrera, *General History* 1:58. The suspected connection of Amerindian diet with devils has already been noted (supra, 11).

24. D'Avity, *Estats*, 316. Recently, Baron James de Coquet in *Lettres aux Gourmets, aux Gourmands, aux Gastronomes et aux Goinfres sur leur Comportement à Table dans l'Intimité* (Paris, 1977), told of his mother, who was convinced that certain foods made gentlemen of little boys.

25. D'Avity, *Estats*, 316. This belief eventually faded before the necessity to adapt to Amerindian ways, including Amerindian diet, in order to survive in the New World. In 1687 an aide-de-camp to Denonville wrote that the Jesuits were hospitable enough "although the food is very bad, including neither bread nor wine nor meat, but only some ground maize boiled in water with a little fish" (Baugy, *Journal*, 181). The reader will recognize the Amerindian recipe for *sagamité*. The term "sagamité" is a French adaptation of the Algonkian *tchi sagamiteou*, "the broth . . . is hot" (Thwaites, ed., *JR* 5:97; 68:91). The role of the control of fire and of cooking in the development of man is a subject of speculation. *See* Leakey and Lewin, *Origins*, 131.

26. Hennepin, *A New Discovery* 2:84; *see also* Thwaites, ed., *JR* 19:97. The same accusations were used by the Huron against the French in an attempt to obstruct the efforts of Recollet Joseph de La Roche Daillon to establish a mission among the Neutral in 1626 (Le Clercq, *First Establishment* 1:267).

27. Thevet, *Cosmographie* (L'Huillier), 930.

28. Vespucci, *Letters*, 7. In the seventeenth century, the Jesuits, after smugly reporting that Amerindians had learned not to eat from the ground in their presence, later ruefully admitted that for "want of a table and household utensils, we sat on the ground and drank from the bark of trees" (Thwaites, ed., *JR* 5:101; 18:17).

29. Hennepin, *Louisiane*, 55. A Dominican reported that Amerindians of the Caribbean thought nothing of defecating while eating (Du Tertre, *Histoire générale des isles*, 429). Thevet, on the other hand, wrote of the Brazilians that they

ate "very carefully," not like Europeans, who devoured their food (*Singularitez*, 148). The Jesuits gave mixed reports for the people of New France (Thwaites, ed., *JR* 10:215; 5:99–101; 6:267).

30. D'Avity, *Estats*, 316–17.

31. Ibid., 317–18.

32. Acosta, *Histoire naturelle et moralle*, 287v–88. Acosta discerned three classes of barbarians: those who were not far from reason, had governments and cities (Chinese, Japanese); those who did not have writing but who still had government (Mexicans [*sic*] and Peruvians); those who lived in the woods without fixed abode (Caribs). The latter, Acosta believed, should be constrained to civility (Acosta, *De procuranda salute indorum*, proemium, 115–23).

33. It is now being speculated whether Amerindian pictography, based on sign language, was a precursor of writing. It was once used throughout North and South America, and was apparently universally understood, as it was associated with sight rather than sound. *See* Martineau, *The Rocks Begin to Speak;* and Jesuit Sebastian Râle's comments from Narantsouak (Thwaites, ed., *JR* 67:227). Fell claims to have detected a variety of Old World scripts in the inscriptions (*America B.C., Bronze Age America*). Alexander Marshack holds that the creation of a symbol system was at least as important as the development of tools in the rise of civilization ("The Message of the Markings").

34. Thwaites, ed., *JR* 1:11,13; 3:193–97; 20:71. For a Spanish view of this subject, *see* the letter of Friar Domingo de Betanzos, written in 1544, which argued that the limitations of Indian languages could easily lead to gross errors in explaining Christian doctrine. It is reproduced by Hanke in "Pope Paul III," 102. Two centuries later, the same point was being argued. *See* Loskiel, *History of the Missions*, 20–21.

35. Maffei (Maffée) in Duret, *Thresor de l'histoire*, 945; Greenblatt, in Chiapelli, ed., *First Images* 2:568.

36. PAC, AC, C11D 10, Mémoire de Lamothe Cadillac, 1693. Also, Eckstorm, *Old John Neptune*. However, Jesuits reported that the Montagnais used "r" instead of "l" (Thwaites, ed., *JR* 7:31).

37. For instance, Frobisher's sailors, acting on the assumption that New World natives mated indiscriminately at first encounter, brought together an Inuit man and woman who had been captured separately, and watched in anticipation. The sailors were disappointed (Hakluyt, *Principal Navigations* 7:306–7).

38. D'Avity, *Estats*, 318.

39. Henry Hawks, in Hakluyt, *Principal Navigations* 9:397. Du Tertre noted in the Caribbean that as soon as the Amerindians awakened in the morning, they went down to the river to bathe (*Histoire générale des isles*, 421). Yves made similar observations concerning Brazilians (*Voyage dans le Nord du Brésil*, 106). Toward the end of the seventeenth century, Henry de Tonty was impressed with how successfully Amerindian mothers kept their babies "very clean, very neat," without cloths (*Dernières decouvertes*, 25).

40. Léry, *Histoire d'un voyage* (1580), 118. Cortés was struck by the fact that Tenochtitlan streets were tended by squads of cleaners. In 1607 a Paris physician suggested that the plague could be reduced in that city by keeping the streets clean. Nothing came of the suggestion (Lewis, *Splendid Century*, 202).

41. Elias, *Civilisation des moeurs*, 78–83.

42. Thorndike, *History of Magic* 2:207–8. However, contrarily enough, medicinal baths were approved. And at least one Renaissance writer wondered if the superior health of Amerindians was not due to their habit of bathing frequently (Saint-Michel, *Voyages des isles Camercanes*, 175).

43. Saint-Michel, *Voyages des isles Camercanes*, 143; Hennepin, *Louisiane*, 53; Thwaites, ed., *JR* 6:261–69.

44. The casual use of the word "cruel" is illustrated by Dassié's comment, "The Iroquois are cruel, the Hurons [and] Algonquins are friends of the French" (*Description générale*, 253). A contemporary English ballad was entitled, "The crueltie of ye Spaniardes toward th[e] Indians" (Arber, *A Transcript of the Registers* 2:2086).

45. For instance, Bodin, in speaking about the cruelty of Brazilians, is referring to cannibalism and not to torture (*Republique* [1577], 528).

46. Later writers sometimes extended this, and reported that Amerindians were more humane than Europeans in general. Françoise Froger, for one, wrote that black slaves often preferred Amerindians to Europeans as masters for that reason (*Relation d'un voyage*, 148–49). An eighteenth-century missionary at Kaskaskia observed that "The Savages, especially the Illinois, are of a very gentle and sociable nature" (cited by Good, *Guebert Site*, 47). Such reports have been reinforced by the discovery in 1971 of the Tasaday, a small group of Stone Age people who had been living in isolation in southern Mindanao Island in the Philippines for six centuries. Their outstanding characteristic is a lack of aggressiveness; they have no words for weapons, hostility,

anger, or war (L.S. Stavrianos, "Basic Myths of our Time," *The Globe and Mail* [Toronto], 26 May 1976, 7). A report on these people by Kenneth MacLeish, "Stone Age Cavemen of Mindanao," appeared in *National Geographic*, vol. 142, no. 2 (August 1972): 219–49.

47. Thorndike, *History of Magic* 5:577, citing Cardano (1506–76), *De Rerum Varietate*, bk. 8, chap. 40.

48. An exhibition, "The Wild Man: Medieval Myth and Symbolism," was held by New York's Metropolitan Museum of Art from October 1980 to early January 1981. Its catalogue, by Timothy Husband, recapitulates the history of this figure. In 1963, Hamburg's Museum für Kunst and Gewerbe held an exhibition on the same topic, entitled "Die wilden Leute des Mittelalters."

49. Pausanias, *Description* 1.23.13. In another case reported the following century, a satyr caused panic among village women (Philostratus, *The Life of Apollonius*, bk. 6, chap. 27).

50. Janson, "A 'Memento Mori'," 248.

51. Chevalier, *Dictionnaire des Symboles*. *See also* Grimal, ed., *Larousse World Mythology*.

52. Silenus began as a woodland deity who presided over springs and running streams. According to Pausanias, *Description* 1.23, the name "Silenus" at one point was applied to all satyrs. In any event, he was shaggy and full-bearded, had horse's ears and was extraordinarily wise. In the sixth century he became associated with Dionysus.

53. White, in Dudley and Novak, eds., *The Wild Man Within*.

54. Bernheimer, *Wild Men*, 1–33.

55. Merlin, the master of nature, was descended from an incubus in the guise of Wild Man. *See* Robbins, *Encyclopedia of Witchcraft and Demonology*, 462.

56. Spenser, *The Faerie Queene* 4.7. In the English folk imagination of the day, the hairy man was considered to be green, hair and all.

57. Plinius Secundus, *Historia Naturalis*, 156. Another candidate is China's golden monkey; the animals are known locally as "wild men" (Boris Weintraub, "Scientist believes 'Wild Man' of China really golden monkey," *The Globe and Mail* [Toronto], 5 November 1982).

58. Janson, *Ape Lore*, 337.

59. Yerkes, *Great Apes*, 12; Janson, *Ape Lore*, 351 n. 47. In Greek mythology, the trickster figures known as *cercopitheci* (a term which has been applied to a genus of long-tailed African monkeys), were bandits whom Zeus, in a moment of irritation, had transformed into monkeys. According to Chevalier, Trickster corresponds to the most primitive level of human life, having the mind of an infant and no control over his appetites. He is cruel, cynical, and insensitive, but capable of becoming human. Such figures are found in Algonkian myths–for instance, Nanabozho of the Ojibway. *See* Chevalier, *Dictionnaire des Symboles*. Mayan myths also characterize monkeys as men who were not satisfactory as human beings. Munro S. Edmonson, tr., *Popol Vuh* (New Orleans, La., 1972).

60. Janson, *Ape Lore*, 83, citing Albertus Magnus, *De animalibus*.

61. Topsell, *History of Foure-footed Beastes*, 2–3.

62. Bernheimer, *Wild Men*, 92.

63. Janson, *Ape Lore*, 270, citing Cardano, *De subtilitate*, bk. 10.

64. Yerkes, *Great Apes*, 18, citing George Edwards, *Gleanings of natural history....* 3 vols. (London, 1758–64). Edward Tyson in 1699 published an essay in which he held that satyrs were monkeys or baboons, but not men ("A Philological Essay Concerning the Satyrs of the Ancients," in *Orang-Outang*).

65. Janson, *Ape Lore*, 86. Buffon took the reverse view and saw the ass as a degraded horse, the ape as degraded man.

66. Ibid., 80, citing Thomas Cantimprensis, *Liber de natura rerum*, 1240.

67. Creeney, *A book of Fac-similes*, 21.

68. To this day, the sign "In dem Wildemann" is a favorite for inns and taverns in Belgium and The Netherlands.

69. Such a figure, cast in iron, is to be seen in the Musée Le Secq des Tournelles in Rouen.

70. Sandars, *Epic of Gilgamesh*, 60–92.

71. Van Gennep, *Folklore* 4:622.

72. Bernheimer, *Wild Men*, 65. Hellekin or Harlequin was also associated with *la chasse sauvage*, or, as it was known in Saintonge, *la chasse-galerie*. A bibliography of this mythical activity of the "wild horde" is found in Van Gennep, *Folklore* 1:632–41.

73. Bernheimer, *Wild Men*, 84. For an illustration indicating how this might have come about, *see* the Breugel woodcut reproduced in Bernheimer, fig. 16. According to Chevalier, Arlequin (Harlequin) symbolized a malicious buffoon of unstable personality, a being who was not yet individualized. He was a stock character in *la commedia dell'arte*.

74. Bernheimer, *Wild Men*, 51, 58.

75. Ibid. Also, Barber and Riches, *Dictionary of Fabulous Beasts,* 154.

76. Van Gennep, *Folklore,* 1:924.

77. Ibid., 923. This could have been a survival of the Bacchanales of classical times; ecclesiastical authorities banned the practice on several occasions during the seventeenth century.

78. Bernheimer, *Wild Men,* 120; Hale, *Renaissance Europe,* 174.

79. Van Gennep, *Folklore* 1:923. *See also* Gerbi, *Dispute of the New World,* 70.

80. Cloulas, *Catherine de Medici,* 195. The previous year, 1563, Brazilians had been among the nations who welcomed Charles IX when he had formally entered Bordeaux (ibid., 207).

81. *Le Dix-huitième tome du Mercure François,* 59.

82. PAC, AC, C11A 7:90. Denonville au ministre, le 13 novembre 1685.

83. Bernheimer, *Wild Men,* 177. For a discussion of Amerindians as heraldic figures, *see* Swan, "American Indians in Heraldry." Two of Canada's provinces, Nova Scotia and Newfoundland, have Amerindians as supporting figures in their coats of arms.

84. Weismann, *Mexico in Sculpture,* 27, fig. 19.

85. For example, the colonization tract of Sir Robert Gordon of Lochinvar, *Encouragements for such as shall have intention to bee Under-takers.* It was reproduced in Lehner, *How They Saw The New World,* 151. The first book to be printed in French in Paris, *Chroniques de France* (1477), started with an account of how the French were descended from the Trojans, illustrating this with an illumination of a hairy man and woman holding banners.

86. Bernheimer, *Wild Men,* 43.

87. Plinius Secundus, *Historia Naturalis* 7.2.24.

88. Nordenskióld, *Periplus,* pl. 39.

89. Pigafetta, *Voyage et navigation,* sec. 11:54. Another contemporary reference is found in Molinet, *Faictz et dictz,* cvii.

90. Biggar, *Precursors,* 66: Letter of Pietro Pasqualigo, 18 October 1501.

91. Eusebius Pamphili, *Epicscopi Chronicon,* s.a. 1509. This chronicle had been begun by Eusebius Pamphili of Caesarea (260?–340?).

92. Kermode, ed., *The Tempest,* xxxviii–lix; Fiedler, *Return of the Vanishing American,* 45–49. Fiedler says *The Tempest* represented Europe's judgment and rejection of the Amerindian. *See also* J.E. Hankins, "Caliban the Bestial Man," *Publications of the Modern Language Association of America* 62 (1947):793–801. Other authorities feel that Caliban represents the fickle mob in any society (e.g., Jorgenson, in Chiapelli, ed., *First Images* 1:85). Incidentally, *cauliban* is a Romany word meaning "blackness."

93. Ptolemy, *Opus geographiae.*

94. *Le Mercure Galant,* April 1681, 143. This could have been a reference to the Beothuk of Newfoundland or the Labrador Inuit, who had become hostile to European fishermen.

95. The confusion exists even today. When I encountered the hairy man while researching in Paris, my first reaction was to regard this figure as being somehow derived from early reports of Amerindians. A recent edition of the memoir of Nicolas Perrot, that of Editions Elysée, Montreal, 1973, has figures of the Wild Man and Wild Woman on its endpapers; obviously the editors were under the same impression.

96. Thevet, *Singularitez,* chap. 31. Amerindians practised depilation by using fingernails as well as certain shells. Metal pincers very quickly became an item Europeans offered in trade. Later, Thevet, in his *Cosmographie,* again stressed that Amerindians "do not have any hair except on the head" ([Chaudiere], 1001v). Exceptions to this hairlessness were to be found later among Amerindians of the Pacific Coast.

97. Thevet, *Singularitez,* 413.

98. Léry, *Histoire d'un voyage* (1580), 60, 97.

99. Ibid., 100. Theodor de Bry, who in 1592 published Léry's account in his series *Grands Voyages,* included among the illustrations a cannibal scene in which one of the Brazilians is covered all over with down as the author described. The idea of covering one's body with feathers or down was picked up in Europe and such masquerades were seen in pageants and carnivals until the nineteenth century (Van Gennep, *Folklore* 1:923). Claude Haton (1534–1605) noted in his *Memoirs* concerning Brazilians: "they are neither furred nor shaggy as are other types of Savages, who are covered with hair like beasts; but they are barbarous, eating one another, especially if they are enemies" (1:39).

100. Lescarbot, *Nova Francia,* 200.

101. Sagard, *Long Journey,* 138. The incident occurred in 530 B.C. (Hermann, *Conquest by Man,* 79–80). Le Clercq also referred to it (*New Relation,* 82). The Gorgades Islands are

today's Arquipelago dos Bijagos off the coast of Guinea-Bissau.

102. Laon d'Aigremont, *Relation du voyage,* 90.

103. Thwaites, ed., *JR* 38:257.

104. Manesson-Mallet, *Description de l'univers* 5:280.

105. Lahontan, *Voyages dans l'Amérique septentrionale* 2:95 and 1:47. Lahontan's comment dismissing the European belief that Amerindians looked like bears was repeated word for word by Bruzen de La Martinière, *Le Grand Dictionnaire géographique* 2:88, s.v. "Canada."

106. Le Clercq, *New Relation,* 92. Charlevoix in his turn observed, "the idea which was formerly held in Europe of Savages, when they were represented as hairy men, not only did not conform to reality, but actually represented their impression of us, because they believe that we are as hairy all over our bodies as we are on our chins and chests" (*Histoire et description* 6:17).

107. Du Tertre, *Histoire générale des isles,* 396, 398.

108. D'Aleyrac, *Avantures militaires,* 36. My thanks to Mme. Marie Gerin-Lajoie, Ottawa, for pointing out this reference to me. Another aspect of the European iconography of Amerindians drew much less attention, but indicated even more surely the identification of New World man with the Wild Man. This was the depiction of Amerindian women with sagging breasts, a characteristic of the Wild Woman. *See* Bernadette Boucher, *La sauvage aux seins pendants* (Paris, 1977).

109. Bernheimer, *Wild Men,* 102.

110. Chaulmer, *Le Nouveau Monde,* 8.

111. Boas and Lovejoy, eds., *Documentary History,* 289. Tacitus's descriptions of Germans as noble savages in *Germania* (first century A.D.), which follows a similar description by Caesar in *De Bello Gallico* (51 B.C.), is a well-known expression of this concept. However, during the sixteenth and seventeenth centuries it was the Scythians and Tartars with whom Amerindians were compared, not the Germans.

112. Boas, *Essays on Primitivism,* 137.

113. Thevet, *Singularitez,* 135. In the words of Jeremy Bentham, "If we suppose the least agreement among savages to respect the acquisitions of each other, we see the introduction of a principle to which no name can be given than that of law" (cited by Hallowell, *Culture and Experience,* 245).

114. Claude, *Maragnan,* 311–11v.

115. Du Tertre, *Histoire générale des isles,* 396–97; Thwaites, ed., *JR* 21:55; 50:171. Explorer Louis Jolliet and Jesuit Jacques Marquette, the first white men to encounter many of the tribes of the Mississippi Valley, found these people, on the whole, to be civil, liberal, and humane (*Voyages et découverte,* 20). This was echoed more than a century later by Louis Vivier, missionary to the Illinois: "Let us consider the Savages in particular. Nothing but erroneous ideas are conceived of them in Europe; they are hardly believed to be men. This is a gross error. . . . They have wit . . . as much, at least, as most Frenchmen. . . . I found in them many qualities that are lacking in civilized peoples" (cited by Good, *Guebert Site,* 47–48).

116. Bissell, *American Indian in English Literature,* introduction.

117. For one of the earliest examples of the use of the Amerindian bon sauvage as an instrument for criticizing European society, *see* Martire, *Extraict ou recueil,* 68v–69. Among the French writers who were inspired by Amerindians to create literary ideal societies were Fénélon, *Les Aventures de Télémaque;* Vairasse d'Alais, *Histoire des Sévérambes;* and Foigny, *La Terre Australe.*

118. *L'Histoire de la Terre-Neuve du Pérou,* preface.

119. Garcilasso de La Vega, *Royal Commentaries* 1:47; Acosta, *Naturall and Morall Historie,* 497.

120. Sieur de La Borde, "Relation des Caraïbes," in Justel, comp., *Recueil de diverses voyages,* 15.

121. Waldseemüller, *Cosmographiae Introductio,* 92–93.

122. Dr. Louise M. Jilek-Aall did a comparative study of European and Amerindian attitudes toward the Sasquatch in "What is a Sasquatch–or, the Problematics of Reality Testing," in *Canadian Psychiatry Association Journal* 17 (1972): 243–347. Recent publications are those of Don Hunter with Rene Dahinden, *Sasquatch* (Toronto, 1973); and John Willison Green, *The Sasquatch File* (Agassiz, B.C., 1973). *See also* Halpin and Ames, eds., *Manlike Monsters on Trial.*

123. Thevet, *Singularitez,* 135.

124. Levi-Strauss, *Structures,* particularly the introductory section; and Hallowell, *Culture and Experience,* 248–49. Voltaire also did not believe that human nature was capable of the solitary, rootless life implied by the concept of l'homme sauvage ("Essai sur les moeurs," in *Oeuvres* 11:19–20).

125. Levi-Strauss, *Structures,* 30; Leakey and Lewin, *Origins,* 162, 224–29. Similarly, tattooing, body painting, and rites of passage are uniquely human institutions. Yves, while recognizing that tattooing was practiced by "civilized na-

tions," thought that the custom must be founded in nature, as barbarous Brazilians "invented and practised it without being in contact with any civilized nations" (*Voyage dans le Nord du Brésil,* 44). *See also* infra, 94–96.

126. Leakey and Lewin, *Origins,* 148.

127. Levi-Strauss, *Structures,* 9.

128. Sightings included an eye-witness account from Mecca (Belleforest, *Cosmographie universelle* 1:279), although Boem held that unicorns were to be found only in India (*Recueil de diverses histoires* [1540], 65). Pilot Jean Alfonce wrote of Norumbega (New England): "And the Savages say there are unicorns" ("La Cosmographie" in *Recueil de voyages,* 497). Ogilby corroborated this by describing a wild animal to be found on the borders of Canada which he did not name but whose identity he indicates beyond doubt (*America,* 172). Sir John Hawkins, following his visit to the Ribault-Laudonnière colony in Florida, reported that the French had obtained pieces of unicorn horn from the Floridians, who wore them about their necks (Hakluyt, *Principal Navigations* 10:59).

129. Thevet, *Cosmographie* (Chaudiere), 19, 114; Mendoza, *Histoire du grand royaume,* 306. Atkinson's praise of Thevet as the only author to doubt the existence of the unicorn is thus overly enthusiastic (*Nouveaux Horizons,* 279).

130. Thwaites, ed., *JR* 12:181.

5 Amerindians of New France

1. Jaccard, *Sens de la direction;* also, Hallowell, *Culture and Experience,* 190–200. The question has been asked whether humans may, under certain circumstances, orient themselves by means of the earth's magnetic field, as bees and birds appear to be able to do. *See* Lisa Yount, "Some animals move in mysterious ways," *National Wildlife* (Oct.–Nov. 1981): 21–23.

2. The Jesuits told of a Huron, in strange country, climbing a tree to reconnoiter (Thwaites, ed., *JR* 46:35). Le Clercq described being lost for three days while travelling with an Amerindian guide and his wife (*New Relation,* 167–73). Jesuit Gabriel Druillettes was accused of bewitching Amerindians so that they lost their way (Eckstorm, *Old John Neptune,* 104–5, footnote).

3. Lescarbot, *History of New France* 3:146.

4. "Wilderness" is not an Amerindian concept; there is no word for it in New World languages.

5. Apianus, *Quatres parties du Monde,* 166. All human skeletons that have been recovered in the Americas have been of Homo sapiens sapiens; also, the discovery of worked stone points contemporaneous with long-extinct megafauna indicates the antiquity of man in the New World. This antiquity is being extended as archaeology and biogeography reveal new evidence; there is little serious doubt now that man has been in the Americas for at least 20,000 years and probably much longer.

6. Thevet, *Singularitez,* 419; however, Thevet qualified his observation by adding that Canadians had "much more civilitie than inhabitants of America [Brazil]" because they covered themselves with animal skins, whereas the latter went totally naked (Thevet, *New Found worlde,* 126). Later, Cluvier reported that Canadians were exceedingly ingenious in the mechanical arts (*Introduction à la géographie universelle,* 487).

7. It has already been indicated that to the Renaissance mind this suggested degeneration (supra, 48).

8. For arguments in support of Algonkian affiliation, *see* John Hewson, "Beothuk and Algonkian: Evidence Old and New," *International Journal of American Linguistics* 34, no. 2 (1968): 85–93. Not all authorities are convinced.

9. Champlain, *Works* 4:301.

10. Lescarbot, *History of New France* 3:252.

11. H. T. Lewis, "Fire technology and resource management in Aboriginal North America and Australia," in *Resource managers: North American and Australian hunter-gatherers* (Washington, 1982). Kroeber said the long-range effect of European contact was to entrench Amerindians more firmly as hunters (*Cultural and natural areas,* 95–96; Snow, *American Indians,* 83–155). Similarly, in South America, the flourishing herds of horses and cattle, descended from animals introduced by the Spanish and turned wild, caused whole groups of Amerindians to give up agriculture and take to the saddle (Crosby, *Columbian Exchange,* 102). This was ironic, in view of the stated purpose of colonial powers to stabilize the migrants.

12. "Cabot Legends," 446.

13. Thwaites, ed., *JR* 48:119–21.

14. Dreams in general were considered to be of first importance by most Amerindian peoples. The Iroquois went to considerable lengths to interpret dreams and to act out their messages. According to A.F.C. Wallace, they considered that dreams expressed suppressed desires, which, if given satisfaction, would relieve psychic and psychosomatic stresses. In this understanding of psychodynamics,

Iroquoians were far ahead of Europeans of the seventeenth and eighteenth centuries (*Death and Rebirth of the Seneca*, 63).

15. Tooker, *Ethnography*, 120–21.

16. Andreas Cesalpinus (1519–1603) was of the opinion that bezoars from the New World were less efficacious than those of Persia and the Orient (Thorndike, *History of Magic* 6:275, 335). This was also the opinion of Acosta, who ranked bezoars of Peru second to those of the Orient, but above those of New Spain (*Histoire naturelle et moralle*, 207). Bezoars were highly regarded in China for medicinal purposes (Schafer, *Golden Peaches*, 191–92).

17. This is also known as the windigo psychosis. The fear of this type of cannibalism among the hunters of the north contrasts with the ritual cannibalism practised by the agriculturalists to the south. Wihtiko could also be a cannibal giant. *See* Paredes, "A Case Study of 'Normal Windigo'," 97–116; and Preston, in Halpin and Ames, eds., *Manlike Monsters on Trial*, 111–31.

18. The first mention of the triple-crop complex is found in Cabeza de Vaca's account of the Narvaez expedition in Middle America in 1528 (Sauer, *Sixteenth Century America*, 42). The first representation of corn in European art is in Hans Burgkmair's woodcut, "People of Calicut," which shows it being carried in a triumphal procession that includes Amerindians (*European Vision of America*, no. 5 in the section "Savages and Men of Ind"). All plants cultivated by natives of North America were of Mexican origin, except for the Jerusalem artichoke, tobacco, and sunflowers.

19. Joseph B. Walker, "The Valley of the Merrimack," 417.

20. Thwaites, ed., *JR* 62:55–57. Archaeological evidence indicates that early town occupation could be for periods up to seventy years (Tuck, *Onondaga Iroquois Prehistory*, 214). Vespucci reported from his visits to the Caribbean and South America that the people of those regions changed residence every eight to ten years, because of the soil, which became corrupted and unhealthy (Vespucci, *First Four Voyages*, 11).

21. Sagard, *Long Journey*, 92. The farmers of the pueblos of the Southwest and of Mexico and Peru were more sedentary.

22. This cyclical pattern probably influenced the Huron to identify the seasons of the year by wild beasts, fish, birds, and vegetation (Thwaites, ed., *JR* 15:157; Tooker, *Ethnography*, 71).

23. Thwaites, ed., *JR* 5:133; 6:233–35.

24. Levi-Strauss, *Tristes Tropiques*, 191–203; and supra, Chapter 4, n. 125.

25. Cited by Sir Anthony Wagner, *Heralds and Ancestors*, 1; Diéreville, *Voyage to Port Royal*, 169–71; Denys, *Description and Natural History*, 413; Le Clercq, *New Relation*, 97–98.

26. Levi-Strauss, *Tristes Tropiques*, 191.

27. Thwaites, ed., *JR* 38:253. Some of this was expressed in letters attributed to Antoine Silvy, but which seem to have been written by Intendant Jacques Raudot, *Relation par lettres*, 204–5. Oviedo had noted that in the Caribbean, tattooing indicated rank (*Natural History*, 44).

28. Levi-Strauss, *Tristes Tropiques*, 194–95.

29. Cooper, in Johnson, ed., *Man in Northeastern North America*, 280ff.

30. Ibid., 279; also Flannery, *Analysis of Coastal Algonquian Culture*, 182ff.

31. The Ojibway, who inhabited the central boreal forest south of the fifty-fourth parallel of latitude, had clans, but they were of less structural significance than those of southern groups. *See* R.W. Dunning, *Social and Economic Change Among the Northern Ojibwa* (Toronto, 1972), 80.

32. Levi-Strauss, *Pensée sauvage*, 77.

33. Levi-Strauss, *Structures*, 95–96.

34. Levi-Strauss, *Pensée sauvage*, 95.

35. Mauss, *Sociologie*, 264.

36. Ibid., 275; Levi-Strauss, *Structures*, 66.

37. Mauss, *Sociologie*, 275.

38. Le Clercq reported a Micmac as saying: "It is necessary . . . to be content . . . and to endure with constancy the misfortunes of nature, because the sun, or he who has made and governs all, orders it thus" (*New Relation*, 243).

39. Levi-Strauss, *Pensée sauvage*, 219.

40. In fourteenth-century southwestern France, households preserved locks of hair and fingernail parings from ancestral heads of family in order to preserve good fortune (Ladurie, *Montaillou*, 288).

41. Cartier, *Voyages*, 22–23.

42. Alfonce, *Voyages avantureux*, 27v. Alfonce's comment is the only record we have of the name "Tabios" (B.G. Hoffman, *Cabot to Cartier*, 168). The term "Beothuk" did not appear until the end of the eighteenth century when it was also re-

ported as the people's name for themselves (Reynolds, in *Handbook of North American Indians* 15:107).

43. Ramusio, *Navigations et Voyages,* 111. Similar references are found in Thevet, *Singularitez,* 348; and Apianus, *Cosmographie,* 77, 166. Lescarbot also seemed to be referring to the Beothuk when he wrote of "a Savage tribe which carries on perpetual war with our sailors who are engaged in fishing" (*History of New France* 1:59). Another reference is in Le Blanc, *Voyages fameux,* 65. Jean and Raoul Parmentier were among the better-known captains who sailed for Dieppe shipowner Jean Ango.

44. Barkham, "A note on the Strait of Belle Isle," 53.

45. Le Tac (1649?–99) *Histoire chronologique,* 34–35; and Georges Musset, manuscript for the second edition of *Les Rochelais à Terre Neuve,* pt. 2:27 (this manuscript is at La Bibliothèque de la Rochelle, Ms 2556). Another version of the story is given in Le Clercq, *New Relation,* 267. As hostilities continued, the town of St. Malo in 1610 sent out two armed vessels against the Newfoundland natives in retaliation for the killing of two sailors (Biggar, *Early Trading Companies,* 194–95, and Cartier, *Relation originale,* pt. 2:34–35).

46. Whitbourne, *Discourse and Discovery,* 4. Hakluyt described a Beothuk attempt to take some small boats from the *Grace* of Bristol; the sailors were able to recover their property (*Principal Navigations* 8:164–65).

47. Thevet may have been referring to the Beothuk when he wrote of a people living by the sea, "with little kind of other meate than fishe . . . whereof they take a great multitude & chiefly sea wolves, of which they eat the flesh, which is very good. With the fat of this fish they make a certain Oyle, that after it has come to . . . perfection, hath a redde colour, which they drink at their tables as we do wine or beere." Identification becomes even more uncertain when he describes their war customs:

> their principall guide the which they honour as a King, shal goe the first, being armed with faire skins and fethers, sitting on the shoulders of two mighty men, to the end that every one should see him, and know him also to be ready to obey him, whatsoever he shall commaund. And when they obtaine victory, he shall lacke no honor, so they returne joyfull to their houses with their banners displayed, which are braunches of trees garnished with feathers of swannes wavering in the aire, and wearing the skin of the face of their enemies spred in litle circles in token of victorie. (*New Found worlde,* 133v–36)

He also reported similar behavior among Canadians (*Cosmographie* [Chaudiere], 1013). However, his description tallies more closely to the manner in which the Timucuan chiefs were carried into battle.

48. Hakluyt, *Principal Navigations* 8:58; Patterson, "Beothiks or Red Indians of Newfoundland," 123–71.

49. Whitbourne, *Discourse and Discovery,* 2.

50. Lahontan, *Voyages en Amérique septentrionale* 2:33–34. Earlier, in 1583, the Hungarian Stephanus Parmenius had looked for natives about St. John's but had found none (Quinn and Cheshire, *The New Found Land of Stephen Parmenius,* 56).

51. Swanton, *Indian Tribes of North America,* 549. However, Swanton's figures tend to be low. Reynolds does not even attempt a general estimate for pre-contact days ("Beothuk," in *Handbook of North American Indians,* 15:106–7).

52. Silvy, *Relation par lettres,* 208–9; also, Whitbourne's "A Relation of the New-found-land" in Purchas, *Hakluytus Posthumus* 19:438.

53. "Roucou" is also known as urucum; the seeds are those of the annatto or annatta tree (*Bixa orellana*), found as well in the West Indies and along the Caribbean coast. George Percy, with the English expedition of 1607 to establish a colony in Virginia, observed of West Indians: "their bodies are all painted red to keep away the bitings of Muscetoes" (*Hakluytus Posthumus* 18:404). *See also* Oviedo, *Natural History,* 33; Crouse, *French Pioneers in the West Indies,* 4. A recent discussion of the Archaic Red Paint culture of the Eastern Woodlands is that of Snow, *American Indians,* 34–37.

54. Jenness, *Indians of Canada,* 266.

55. For a recreation of the last days of the Beothuk, *see* Such, *Riverrun.* F.G. Speck's claim to have found a Beothuk woman in 1911 remains debatable (Reynolds, in *Handbook of North American Indians,* 15:107).

56. Tuck, "Summary of Newfoundland Prehistory," 25. Also Howley, *Beothucks.*

57. Thwaites, ed., *JR* 1:177, 3:105–7; Denys, *Description and Natural History,* 444–50. Charges of poisoning, so frequently made by Amerindians against Europeans during the seventeenth century, may have stemmed at least partly from poor keeping methods of ships' supplies. However, Biard reported seeing arsenic and sublimate in the possession of Amerindians, which they said had been supplied by French surgeons (Thwaites, ed., *JR* 3:105).

58. B.G. Hoffman, "Historical Ethnography," 230. Bock places the figure at 4,000 ("Micmac," in *Handbook of North American Indians* 15:109).

59. Quinn, "Voyage of Etienne Bellenger," 332.

60. Thwaites, ed., *JR* 2:73; 3:111.

61. B.G. Hoffman, "Ancient Tribes Revisited," 27. Concerning "Megumaage," *see* the map compiled and drawn by G.T. Bates (PAC, Map Division, V_1/202–1965).

62. Bradford, *Of Plymouth Plantation*, 79. Later, the Tarantines were confused with the Abenaki.

63. B.G. Hoffman, "Historical Ethnography," 130.

64. Denys, *Description and Natural History*, 405–6. Thwaites, ed., *JR* 3:77; Le Clercq, *New Relation*, 100.

65. Lescarbot, *History of New France* 3:194–95.

66. Bourque, in Johnson, ed., *Man in Northeastern North America*, 3–11. Consequences of contact for the early Micmac are discussed by Calvin Martin, "The European Impact," 3–54.

67. Lescarbot, *History of New France* 3:219–20; B. G. Hoffman, "Historical Ethnography," 151.

68. Thwaites, ed., *JR* 45:65–67.

69. B.G. Hoffman, "Historical Ethnography," 145.

70. Lescarbot, *History of New France* 2:309; Thwaites, ed., *JR* 7:5. An illustration of a Peruvian sailing vessel with a figure painted on the sail is in Gottfried's *Newe Welt und Americanische Historien*, 499.

71. De Laet, *L'Histoire du Nouveau Monde*, 36. Whitbourne, *Discourse and Discovery*, 2, makes a similar observation, apparently referring to Micmacs on Newfoundland.

72. B.G. Hoffman, "Historical Ethnography," 705–8.

73. PAC, Map Division, V_1/202–1965. *See also* Bock, in *Handbook of North American Indians* 15:110.

74. B.G. Hoffman, "Historical Ethnography," 530–31, 569. Also, Lescarbot, *History of New France* 2:354–56; 3:81–82, 104, 265.

75. Le Clercq, in particular, wrote at some length on the subject (*New Relation*, chaps. 10 and 11). Earlier, Spaniards had been taken aback to find the cross in use among the Maya.

76. Gustave Lanctot used it to support the theory of a ninth-century colonization of Gaspesia by Irish monks (*Histoire du Canada* 1:50–51). He also used as support the reference in the Icelandic sagas to the people of the mainland holding processions and carrying white banners. That description tallies very closely to Thevet's account of Amerindian war customs (supra, Chapter 5, n. 47).

77. Cartier, *Voyages*, 177.

78. B.G. Hoffman, "Souriquois, Etechmin, and Kwedech," 77; Cartier, *Voyages*, 178.

79. Hadlock, "War Among the Northeastern Woodland Algonkians," 216. Lescarbot, besides making numerous references to these hostilities, wrote a poem entitled "La Deffaite des Sauvages Armouchiquois" (*History of New France* 3:497–508). *See also* Morrison and Goetz, "Membertou's Raid," 141–79.

80. [Maillard], *Customs and Manners*, 33.

81. Ibid., iv. Maurault, *Histoire des Abenakis*, included the Malecite as one of seven Abenaki tribes.

82. Champlain, *Works* 1:269, 272–73, 297; Charlevoix, *History and General Description* 1:275–76. The terms "Etchemin," "Eteminquoi," and "Etheminqui," may have included some eastern Abenaki.

83. Thwaites, ed., *JR* 2:71–73. He also estimated the total population from Newfoundland to Chouacoet (Saco, Maine) at 10,000 (ibid. 3:111).

84. B.G. Hoffman, "Souriquois," 69–72. Biggar, *Early Trading Companies*, 119, said the disease had been introduced by a French trader. *See also* Heagerty, *Four Centuries of Medical History* 1:57.

85. White-tailed deer were not present in Maine and New Brunswick at the time of contact. Early settlers recorded the disappearances of caribou and the appearance of deer (Byers, in Johnson, ed., *Man in Northeastern North America*, 24. Also B.G. Hoffman, "Historical Ethnography," 122).

86. Eckstorm, *Old John Neptune*, 76; Erickson, in *Handbook of North American Indians* 15:123. After the Peace of Paris of 1783, the Passamaquoddy moved to the American side of the border (ibid., 124–25).

87. Purchas, *Hakluytus Posthumus* 19:400–405; Snow, in *Handbook of North American Indians* 15:138.

88. B.G. Hoffman, "Souriquois," 80.

89. Silvy, *Relation par lettres*, 196; PAC, AC, C11A 122:223–26, lettre 82, "Des Sauvages Abenakis et des 4 villages qu'ils ont à l'Acadie."

90. Day, *The Mots loups*, 35–44.

91. Snow, in *Handbook of North American Indians* 15:138; B.G. Hoffman, "Souriquois," 68.

92. D'Avity, *Description générale,* 30. "Malebare" (Mallebare, Malabar) today is Nauset Harbor, Mass.

93. Cayet, *Chronologie septenaire* 2:423. This description was repeated by Lescarbot, *History of New France* 2:169. This was also how the Tartars were described.

94. Corneille, *Dictionnaire universel* 1, s.v. "Armouchiquois"; Thwaites, ed., *JR* 2:73.

95. Day, in *Handbook of North American Indians* 15:150.

96. During which they bore the brunt of the Seneca ambush (Mauralt, *Histoire des Abenakis,* 189). More peacefully, a group of Sokoki and Penacook accompanied René-Robert Cavelier de La Salle down the Mississippi in 1682 (Day, in *Handbook of North American Indians* 15:151).

97. Day, *Handbook of North American Indians* 15:150–52; Dickason, "Louisbourg and the Indians," 45.

98. Jenness, *Indians of Canada,* 271–72. The early French took this casualness to mean lack of technical knowledge. It would be nearer the truth, however, to say that the Montagnais did not attach the importance to tailoring that the French did.

99. Thwaites, ed., *JR* 32:283.

100. D'Avity, *Description générale,* 30. Today Têtes-de-Boule have revived the name "Attikamègue" for themselves; in the seventeenth century, these people were probably included in the general term "Gens de Terre" by which the Jesuits referred to northern Algonkian bands.

101. Cartier, *Voyages,* 76. In 1625 Lope de Isasti described the Montagnais as friendly and the neighboring Inuit, who were hostile to Europeans, as inhuman (*Compendio Historial,* 154).

102. Rogers and Leacock, in *Handbook of North American Indians* 6:171.

103. D'Avity, *Description générale,* 42–43.

104. Etouat also liked to wear French clothes (*Journal des Jésuites,* 53).

105. Jenness, *Indians of Canada,* 274.

106. Champlain, *Works* 5:103. Champlain seems to have respected Amerindian feelings on this point, which was not often done by Europeans. According to J.-A. de Thou, Champlain, "seeing that his plan to sail up the Saguenay did not please his savage allies," "abandoned the project" (*Histoire universelle* 15:61). De Thou's monumental history, *Historiarum sui temporis,* the largest such project to have been undertaken up until his time, had first appeared in Latin in Paris between 1604 and 1620.

107. J.E. Murray, "Fur Trade," 71.

108. Sagard, *Long Journey,* 87, 99; concerning the Mohawk, *see* Hunt, *Wars of the Iroquois,* 34. The Algonquin also tried to intimidate the French when the latter passed through their territory by predicting that the Huron would kill the French, as they had done with Etienne Brulé (Thwaites, ed., *JR* 8:83).

109. Bauman, "Ottawa Fleets and Iroquois Frustration," 7–40; idem, "The Ottawa Trading System." Also, Feest and Feest, in *Handbook of North American Indians* 15:772–77.

110. Eid, "The Ojibwa-Iroquois War," 297–394. Hallowell has claimed that the Ojibway of the Great Lakes region (Saulteaux) never engaged in war either with whites or with other Amerindians (Hallowell, *Culture and Experience,* 278). However, besides the Iroquois, they also warred with the Dakota, which was at least one reason for the latter moving out of the woodlands onto the plains. *See* Harold Hickerson, *The Chippewa and Their Neighbors* (New York, 1970).

111. This was a fashion they shared with the Ottawa, whom the French called "Cheveux Relevez" (Raised Hair), describing their coiffures as "better combed" than those of French courtiers (*Cinquième tome du Mercure François,* 297).

112. Jenness, *Indians of Canada,* 289. Trigger says the appellations Cord and Deer are by no means certain (Trigger, *Huron Farmers,* 14). Heidenreich has translated the name for the Cord as "Barking Dogs" (*Huronia,* 28 and app. 1). For this sketch of the Huron, I have drawn on this work, but principally on Trigger's writings and Tooker's *Ethnography.* Trigger's major work, on Huronia to 1660, is *Children of Aataentsic.*

113. Tooker, *Ethnography,* 10. Although the move to Huronia was comparatively recent, the Iroquoian tradition in Ontario dates back to about 1,000 A.D. (J.V. Wright, *Ontario Iroquois Tradition,* 13).

114. Tooker, *Ethnography,* 11; Thwaites, ed., *JR* 10:31.

115. Trigger, *Huron Farmers,* 9; idem, "Sixteenth Century Ontario," 208.

116. Thwaites, ed., *JR* 8:115.

117. Sagard, *Long Journey,* 90. Two decades later, Dr. François

Gendron was equally impressed with Huronia's countryside. One of his letters was published by d'Avity, *Description générale,* 201–6; *see also Dictionary of Canadian Biography* 1, s.v. "François Gendron."

118. Thwaites, ed., *JR* 7:225; 8:115; 10:313.

119. Sagard, *Long Journey,* 92. These estimates, once considered too high, have been supported by archeological evidence; arguments are now being presented for a population as high as 50,000 (Schlesier, "Epidemics and Indian Middlemen," 137). The epidemic of 1635–40 reduced the numbers of the Huron by at least a half, and probably more.

120. Champlain, *Works* 3:122; Thwaites, ed., *JR* 8:115; 10:313; 11:7; and Sagard, *Long Journey,* 92.

121. Trigger, *Huron Farmers,* 113. However, Onondaga villages were usually located in pairs (Tuck, *Onondaga,* 3, 216). The longhouses of the Onondaga were the largest in Iroquoia–from 210 to 410 feet in length (ibid., 209).

122. Trigger, *Huron Farmers,* 23.

123. Trigger, "The French Presence in Huronia," 111ff.

124. Wright, *Ontario Iroquois,* 3.

125. Thwaites, ed., *JR* 8:57.

126. Witthoft, in Dale Morgan et al., eds., *Aspects of the Fur Trade,* 65ff.

127. Thwaites, ed., *JR* 8:115.

128. Sagard, *Long Journey,* 140.

129. Thwaites, ed., *JR* 20:19.

130. Champlain, *Works* 5:103; J.E. Murray, "Fur Trade," 71.

131. Thwaites, ed., *JR* 33:241–49. Killing for vengeance on the part of the relatives of the dead person could be considered a more serious crime than the original murder (ibid. 10:223).

132. Gosselin, *Nouvelles glanes historiques,* 33; Biggar, *Early Trading Companies,* 88.

133. Wood, *New England Prospect,* 67.

134. Thwaites, ed., *JR* 24:271–97. In this connection it is interesting to note that the Lateran Council of 1179 prohibited the sale to Saracens of arms, iron, wood for construction, and anything else useful for warfare (Davenport, *European Treaties* 2:11). Nicholas V, in his bull *Romanus Pontifex,* 8 January 1455, accorded Portugal the right to trade with infidels except in the prohibited articles. Thus the ban on trading guns with non-Christians had been in effect long before the discovery of America. For the text of the bull, *see* Davenport, *European Treaties,* 1:9–26.

135. Trigger, *Children of Aataentsic* 2:632–33.

136. Thwaites, ed., *JR* 33:243. *See also* Trigger, *Huron Farmers,* 57.

137. Champlain did not see that the Huron had an effective legal system (Champlain, *Works* 3:142–43); however, Jesuit missionaries disagreed, and found that the Huron did possess a system of law, which they strictly observed (Thwaites, ed., *JR* 10:215; 9:275).

138. Thwaites, ed., *JR* 8:121–23; 10:223.

139. Ibid. 15:177; 8:121. Amerindians were surprised that the French did not believe in dreams (ibid. 6:183).

140. Ibid. 23:171.

141. Trigger, *Huron Farmers,* 106–12; Sagard, *Long Journey,* 213–14. The Bear tribe at one point sought French participation in their Feast of the Dead so they could claim them as relatives, and were disturbed at the French refusal (Thwaites, ed., *JR* 10:311).

142. Thwaites, ed., *JR* 20:43. *See also* Garrad and Heidenreich, in *Handbook of North American Indians* 15:394–97.

143. Thwaites, ed., *JR* 21:181.

144. Ibid. 19:125; 21:177; 35:107–15; 40:15–19.

145. Ibid. 21:193–95; White, in *Handbook of North American Indians* 15:410.

146. Thwaites, ed., *JR* 27:27, 25; 21:195.

147. Mary K. Jackes, "Historic Neutral Burial Practices," paper presented to the Canadian Association for Physical Anthropology, Guelph, Ontario, November 1982. Dr. Jackes indicates that the Neutral were more distinct from the Huron than previously thought. Her monograph, *The Osteology of the Grimsby Site,* is scheduled to be published by the Royal Ontario Museum.

148. Le Clercq, *First Establishment* 1:267–68.

149. Thwaites, ed., *JR* 21:315; 41:81–83; 42:179.

150. Dickinson, "La guerre iroquoise," 45–46.

151. L.H. Morgan, *League of Ho-dé-no-sau-nee,* 226–28. Trigger, however, estimates that before the epidemics of the 1630s and 1640s, the Iroquois may have numbered 18,000 to 20,000 (*Huron Farmers,* 19). Even this may prove to be too conservative, as a recent study of the Mohawk places their pre-contact population between 10,000 and 13,000

(Staina, "Mohawk Iroquois Population: A Revision").

152. Thwaites, ed., *JR* 33:117.

153. At one point the Seneca came close enough to negotiating a peace of their own with the French to disturb the Mohawk (ibid. 41:201–3). The peace that was eventually agreed upon, in 1653, included the Mohawk. The treaty did not last.

154. Trelease, "Indian Relations," 32. *See also* Tooker, in *Handbook of North American Indians* 15:421. The Five Nations became the Six Nations when the Tuscarora joined in 1722.

155. A good résumé of possible dates is given by Tooker, *Handbook of North American Indians* 15:418–22. *See also* Tuck, "The Iroquois Confederacy," 32–42.

156. Witthoft, in Dale Morgan et al., *Aspects of the Fur Trade*, 56ff; Trigger, "Sixteenth Century Ontario," 212.

157. Witthoft, op. cit. Even lead bullets and shot occur on Seneca sites, and have been dated to the end of the sixteenth century.

158. Trelease, "Indian Relations," 37; L.H. Morgan, *League of the Iroquois*, 62–65.

159. PAC, AC, C11A 2:264–69, untitled memoir on the Iroquois, 1666. It is reproduced under the title "The Nine Iroquois Tribes, 1666," in O'Callaghan and Brodhead, eds., *NYCD* 9:47–51.

160. Goldenweiser, in R.C. Owen et al., eds., *North American Indians*, 566.

161. Iroquois medical skill early impressed the French (Thwaites, ed., *JR* 49:121).

162. Goldenweiser, in R.C. Owen et al., eds., *North American Indians*, 572.

6 The Old World Embraces the New

1. Particularly influential in their support of a strong monarchy were Bodin in *Republique*, and Le Roy in *De l'Excellence*. Le Roy especially exemplified the prevalent disdain for the masses, whom he saw as being unsurpassed in ignorance and insolence, unable to rise above their mean occupations, petty dishonesties, and poor business sense: "Their principal aim is liberty and equality, and to make sure that no one, no matter how superior, is raised above others, which is to the great advantage of the bad and the useless" (*De l'Excellence*, 10v). According to Atkinson, the prevalence of that attitude prevented the egalitarianism of Amerindians from being taken seriously (*Nouveaux Horizons*, 375). A good study of European political thought of this period is by Pierre Mesnard, *L'Essor de la philosophie politique*.

2. Supra, 43–44.

3. La Popelinière, *Trois Mondes*, bk. 2:26v.

4. De Saulx, in Petitot, ed., *Collection complète* 23:241. Huguenots, generally, deplored France's lack of aggressive enterprise in colonial matters.

5. Montesquieu, *Oeuvres* 2:321.

6. Morison, *Admiral of the Ocean Sea*, 90–91.

7. La Popelinière, *Trois Mondes*, avant-discours, bk. 2:50.

8. Taylor, *Two Richard Hakluyts* 2:290; and Newton, *European Nations*, 8. *See also* Linden, "Alexander VI," 1–20.

9. Parry, *Spanish Theory*, 13. An interesting work in this connection is that of John of Paris, *On Royal and Papal Power*, J.A. Watt, trans. (Toronto, 1971).

10. Folmer, *Franco-Spanish Rivalry*, 21; Parry, *Spanish Theory*, 320–21.

11. Folmer, *Franco-Spanish Rivalry*, 20. There is no doubt as to the authenticity of the bull *Laudabiliter*, which ostensibly armed Henry II with the required papal sanction; however, in 1171–72, the Irish accepted obedience to Rome and submitted to Henry, which, along with other supporting evidence, argues in favor of the papal donation. Luis Weckmann-Muñoz maintains that the justification for the papal donations was based on the doctrine of Saint Peter's Patrimony, in turn derived from the spurious Donation of Constantine, by which the pope claimed the right to dispose of islands lying off the western part of Europe. According to Weckmann-Muñoz, Alexander VI thought he was dividing islands between Spain and Portugal when he issued his 1493 bulls (*Las Bulas Alejandrinas;* "The Alexandrine Bulls of 1493," in Chiapelli, ed., *First Images* 1:201–9).

12. De Saulx, *Mémoires*, 238–39. This was, of course, an argument that could have developed only after the rise of Protestantism, which occurred after the European discovery of the New World.

13. It is conceivable that this pique with papal politics helped influence François to sign an alliance with Sultan Suleiman II of Turkey in 1536. France was the first western Christian power to enter into such an agreement with the infidel; Christendom – at least that part that was serious about

its religion–was outraged. The alliance was short-lived; two years later, François had joined forces with his erstwhile enemy Charles V against Suleiman the Magnificent (Seward, *Prince of the Renaissance*, 188, 197, 199). I am indebted to Nicholas Wickenden for this reference.

14. Alfonce, "La Cosmographie," 83.

15. Thevet, *Cosmographie* (Chaudiere), 965.

16. *Relation de l'Establissement*, 1.

17. Montchrestien, *Traicté*, 270.

18. Thwaites, ed., *JR* 8:9–13.

19. Parry, *Spanish Theory*, 18. Some historians have assumed that such reasoning implies that Medieval and Renaissance Christianity saw itself as *ipso facto* in a state of war with all infidels (Kimmey, "Christianity and Indian lands," 44).

20. Vitoria, *De Indis*, "On the Indians," II.3 and 6. Etienne Grisel surveyed Vitoria's thought in Chiapelli, ed., *First Images* 1:305–25.

21. Vitoria, *De Indis*, "On the Indians," II.4.

22. Ibid., II.1.

23. Ibid., I.24. The issue of sovereignty and proprietary rights was further complicated by doubts as to under what circumstances rights of conquest could be invoked. Strict interpretation of legal doctrine implied that such rights only applied in the case of states. This encouraged the search for other legal justifications for assuming sovereignty over peoples not recognized as belonging to the "family of nations." For some latter-day thoughts on the subject, *see* Green, "Aboriginal Rights," 219–24.

24. Vitoria, *De Indis*, "On the Indians," III.12.

25. Ibid., III.10.

26. Ibid., III.3 and 7. Compare this with the Amerindian custom of granting exclusive trading privileges to those who made first contact with a new source. *See* supra, 109, 112.

27. Ibid., III.12.

28. Ibid., III.15. Vitoria even argued that the king of Spain would have the right to intervene and compel obedience if the French people refused to obey their king (ibid., II.7).

29. Ibid., III.16.

30. Ibid., III.18.

31. Parry points to the prior work of Matías de Paz, a Dominican, and Palacios Rubios, a civil jurist. Both of these writers declared Amerindians to be rational beings and therefore possessing basic human rights. However, they did not see this as mitigating the Christian duty of bringing them within the fold of the church (*Spanish Theory*, 12–19).

32. Las Casas, *Histoire admirable*, 6. An anti-Spanish pamphlet entitled *Harangue d'un cacique Indien* estimated that the population of the West Indies had been five or six millions before the Spaniards had arrived and reduced it to 6,000. However, even today, estimates vary enormously as to the extent of population destruction following European contact; I have cited median figures.

33. Crosby, *Columbian Exchange*, 99. Some native American animals suffered a similar fate, and for some of the same reasons–disease and brutal exploitation. The llama and the alpaca both declined heavily in numbers after the Spanish arrival (ibid., 94).

34. Vitoria, *De Indis*, "On the Indians," II.7. This was also the position of the renowned jurist and statesman, Huigh de Groot (Hugo Grotius, 1583–1645) (Rose et al., *History of the British Empire* 1:192).

35. Keller, et al., *Sovereignty*, 148.

36. Gage, *Nouvelle relation* 1:epistre. This work had appeared originally in English in 1648.

37. Purchas, *Hakluytus Posthumus* 1:42.

38. Claude, *Maragnan*, 87v; *Troisième tome du Mercure François*, 7. The French, on planting their cross on Maragnan, told the Amerindians that it obliged them to abandon their "bad way of life, especially the eating of human flesh." They would now have to obey the laws of France, as well as her priests, and defend the cross with their lives.

39. Parry, *Spanish Theory*, 6–8. Palacios Rubios drafted the *requerimiento* in 1510; it was first used in Darien in 1514.

40. Keller, et al., *Sovereignty*, 150–51. That the English did not consider a purchase as implying recognition of Amerindian sovereignty is abundantly clear from the royal charters issued for the purpose of colonization. *See* Kimmey, "Christianity and Indian Lands," 44–60. The English also used evangelization as rationalization for the seizure of Amerindian lands. Trade was another means of peaceful occupation; in 1698, Governor Francis Nicholson of Maryland urged a policy of furnishing "the inland Indians with goods in such quantity and so cheap that they may take the trade from the French or prevent their increasing it, and may make settlements among the Indians, as the French do, and build vessels upon their lakes" (*Calendar of State Papers*, Colonial Series, Governor Nicholson to Council of Trade and Plantations, 20 August 1698, 392). Similar sentiments were expressed by Richard Coote, Earl of Bellomont, Gov-

ernor of New York (ibid., 547–48). However, quite another method of procedure was indicated by a colonization tract of the early part of the century, which not only had made no mention of Amerindian territorial rights, but had said the English assured peace "by killing the Barbarians" (Gordon, *Encouragements,* 20).

41. Muntz, "Race Contact," 81. This thesis was published in 1927. *See also* Leclerc, *Marquis de Denonville,* 214–26. Leclerc discusses French territorial claims without mentioning extinguishment of aboriginal rights.

42. The English, who followed the Dutch example and sought to purchase land in the European sense, were startled when Amerindians returned later for more payments. Hence the derisory epithet, "Indian giving" (Trelease, "Indian Relations and the Fur Trade in New Netherland," 48).

43. Le Challeux, *Brief discours,* 7–8; and Benzoni, *Histoire nouvelle,* au lecteur.

44. Supra, 32.

45. Hemming, *Red Gold,* 278–79. In 1741, Benedict XIV sent an encyclical to the bishops of Brazil, relying on his spiritual powers to forbid "enslaving, selling, buying, exchanging or giving Indians, separating them from their wives and children, despoiling them of their goods, leading them to strange places. . . depriving them of liberty in any way." Keeping Indian slaves was forbidden on pain of excommunication. Although apparently instigated by João V of Portugal, the encyclical was not published in Brazil for sixteen years (ibid., 451).

46. Lescarbot, *History of New France* 1:17.

47. Enciso, *Suma de geografía,* 220–21. Repeated by Gómara, *Histoire generalle* 233; similar sentiments were reported by Le Challeux, *Brief discours,* 7–8; Thevet, *Cosmographie* (L'Huillier), 964v; and La Popelinière, *Trois Mondes,* bk. 2:53v.

48. Benzoni, *Histoire nouvelle,* 498–99.

49. Amerindians have various stories to illustrate this point, such as that of the tribesman offering a European a seat on his log, and finally being shoved off (Sealey and Kirkness, eds., *Indians Without Tipis,* frontispiece). For another version of the same idea, *see* Turner, *Red Men Calling,* xiii.

50. Elliott, *Old World,* 60–61. A seventeenth-century writer set the amount at "66 millions" without specifying the unit of measure (Berquen, *Les Merveilles des Indes,* 107).

51. Kamen says the peak was reached during the decade of 1591–1600 when about nineteen million grams of gold and about three billion grams of silver reached Europe (Kamen, *Iron Century,* 79; *see also* Braudel, *La Méditerranée,* 374ff.). Geographer Pierre Du Val d'Abbeville estimated in 1674 that Spain's annual revenue from the New World totalled 10 to 12 million from various sources, such as pearls, cochineal, and sugar, besides gold and silver (*Memoires geographiques,* 13). Before the establishment of plantations in the Americas, sugar had been so scarce in Europe that it had been sold only in apothecaries (Maffei, *Histoire des Indes,* 91).

52. Acosta, *Histoire naturelle et moralle,* 118.

53. Saint-Michel, *Voyage des isles Camercanes,* au lecteur. The materialistic values of Christian Europe were later reflected by Bishop Saint Vallier of Quebec, when he repeated, with unconscious irony, that before they were Christians, the people of New France buried their dead with all their best things; but since becoming enlightened by the Gospels, they bury their dead with their worst things (*Estat present de l'Eglise,* 160–61).

54. Bodin, *Les Paradoxes,* gii(verso). I have made no attempt to work out equivalent values in currencies; Wyndham Beawes indicated its complexities when he wrote that making equivalencies was "not over difficult, as it only consists in making the Comparison between the intrinsic value of Gold and Silver Coins of each Country, and the Price they pass current at; it is therefore necessary that the exact Weight and Standard of such Monies be first known" (*Lex Mercatoria Rediviva,* 485).

55. Berquen, *Les Merveilles des Indes,* 88. A conquistador complained that after a division of spoils in Peru, more than 180,000 livres of gold and silver remained which were not, however, divided among the men (*L'Histoire de la Terre-Neuve de Pérou,* Niiij[verso]).

56. Masselman, *Cradle of Colonialism,* 72. It was told of Cortés that toward the end of his life he borrowed money at high interest for distribution to the poor in order to wipe out his sins in pillaging the New World and to purchase entry into heaven.

57. Elliot, *Old World,* 85.

58. E.J. Hamilton, "American Treasure," 338–57; idem, *American Treasure and the Price Revolution.* Paul Gaffarel makes the point that the influx of moveable riches into Europe shifted the emphasis from land, which had been formerly considered the measure of wealth. This in turn affected concepts of class structure and human rights (*Histoire de la découverte* 2:422).

59. Elliott, *Old World,* 68–78. On the trade between Spain and

America, 1500–1650, *see* Huguette and Pierre Chaunu, *Séville et l'Atlantique*, 8 vols. (Paris, 1956–60).

60. Ingrid Hammarström provides some pertinent insights in "The 'Price Revolution' of the Sixteenth Century: Some Swedish Evidence," *Scandinavian Economic History Review* 5, no. 142 (1957): 118–54. *See also* Braudel, *La Méditerranée*, 398–420; and Kamen, *Iron Century*, 64.

61. De Saulx, *Memoires*, 239.

62. Bodin, *Republique* (1579), 614. According to Hamilton, most Spanish observers did not link rising prices with imports of American gold and silver (*American Treasure*, 289).

63. Dent, "Historical Background of the French Renaissance"; and Braudel, *La Méditerranée*, 535.

64. Berquen, *Les Merveilles des Indes*, 89.

65. Martire, *De Orbe Novo* (MacNutt) 2:177, 196.

66. Diez del Corral, "L'Europe face à l'Amérique," *La Découverte de L'Amérique*, 325–35.

67. This conflict gave rise to the flamboyant corsair Guillaume Pépin de La Broussadière, noted for his taste in clothes. In red boots, black doublet, and cape, he sailed off to attack the Spanish fishing fleet (Umstead, "The French in the Americas," 40). For a contemporary account of some of this, *see* Benzoni, *History of the New World*, 96ff. Pirates and buccaneers have attracted considerable attention from historians, including Oexmelin, *Histoire des Avanturiers;* on the flibustiers, *see* Desjeans, *Relation;* Le Sage, *Les Aventures;* and Archenholtz, *Histoire des Flibustiers*. On the corsairs, *see* Marcel, *Les Corsaires français*.

68. Umstead, "The French in the Americas," 174; Folmer, *Franco-Spanish Rivalry*, 66. The importance of the fishing fleet to France can be gauged by the report, although possibly exaggerated, that it provided a living for 100,000 persons (Malapart, *La Prise d'un seigneur*, 13).

69. This was the second such defeat for France within a few years. At the Treaty of Vaucelles, 5 February 1556, Henry II had been forced to recognize Spain's exclusive right to the Indies (Folmer, *Franco-Spanish Rivalry*, 67).

70. Savelle, *Diplomatic History*, vii, viii.

71. The Portuguese had made similar use of religion against the Huguenots. In 1573, they burned a Frenchman as a heretic at Bahia, the first *auto-da-fé* on Brazilian territory (Hauser, "Les Huguenots français," 114). P.E. Hoffman touches on the situation in "Diplomacy and the Papal Donation," 151–83.

72. For instance, "A Good Speed to Virginia" in 1609 said "it is likely true that these savages have no particular property or parcell of that country, but only a general residence there as wild beasts have in the forest" (cited by Horton, "Relations in Colonial Virginia," 20). *See also* Jennings, "Virgin Land and Savage People," 519–41.

73. Mary Anna Joseph, "French and English Pressures," 94. However, the Virginia Assembly had recognized as early as 1622 that English encroachment on Amerindian lands was the chief cause of friction between the races (Horton, "Relations in Colonial Virginia," 21).

74. Thwaites, ed., *JR* 8:13.

7 Ephemeral Settlements and Unknown Hazards

1. Alfonce, "La Cosmographie," 495; Denys, *Description and Natural History*, 250; Diéreville, *Voyage to Port Royal*, 90. By mid-eighteenth century the forests were still being held responsible for the cold climate; "if America is colder than Europe in the same northern latitudes, the cause can be partly attributed to the lack of cultivation and to the vast forests which cover the land. These huge woods hold the fogs and the great degree of cold with which this country is too well furnished" (De Brosse, *Histoire des Navigations* 1:49).

2. Sauer, *Sixteenth Century America*, 278.

3. Thevet, "Grand Insulaire," PAC, BN, Fonds français 15452, f.110.

4. Bertrand, *Lettre missive*, 4–5.

5. Champlain, *Works* 3:13; Denys, *Description and Natural History*, 90, 106, 247–56.

6. Pierre Boucher, *Histoire veritable*, 2, 142. Another chronicler, Chaulmer, observed that where in Europe a draft in a house caused a person to catch a cold, in the New World, where the winters were long and the snow fell continually, the cold did nothing more than to stimulate the appetite (*Nouveau Monde*, 42).

7. Gregorio García had made this proposition in *Origen de los Indios de el Nuevo mundo, e Indias Occidentales* (Madrid, 1607). However, he modified his position by allowing that heredity was also a factor (Huddleston, *Origins of the American Indians*, 68–69).

8. Supra, 44–45. Also, Ptolemy, *Geography*, 31–32. Even Montaigne believed that climate affected personality and appearance (Villey, *Les sources* 2:314).

9. Because the body was viewed as the dress of the soul, black skin was taken to indicate moral depravity (Chinard, *Rêve*, 20). At best, it argued "à natural melancholy" (Burton, *Anatomy of Melancholy*, 181).

10. Du Choul, *Discours de la religion*, 297.

11. Cayet, *Chronologie septenaire* 2:249v.

12. Le Moine, *L'Amérique et les poètes français*, 189. "Not to wish to return to France until one sees Moors become white and Frenchmen so tanned they assumed the tint of a Moor."

13. *See* Jordan, *White over Black*, 14–15.

14. Vespucci, *First Four Voyages*, 7.

15. Cartier, *Voyages*, 268.

16. Corte-Real reported that the northern Amerindians were like the Brazilians, except that they were white. However, the cold caused them to turn sallow brown with age (Morison, *Portuguese Voyages*, 70). Pierre Boucher expressed that idea in *Histoire veritable*, 92. Other references to white Amerindians in the north are found in Martire, *De Orbe Novo* (MacNutt) 2:259; Sagard, *Long Journey*, 136; Le Blanc, *Voyages fameux*, 64; Girava in Apianus, *Cosmographie*, 166. White Amerindians were also reported from the south; *see* Alfonce, *Voyages avantureux*, 33. Geographer Guillaume Le Testu illustrated Brazilians as being white in his 1555 New World map. It was reproduced in *Horizon* 9, no. 4 (1972), 32. *See also* Jordan, *White over Black*, 250; and Wasserman, *Seventeenth century chronicles*, 36ff.

17. Lescarbot, *Nova Francia*, 182; "Rapport de Giovanni de Verrazzano," in Ramusio, *Navigations et Voyages*, 100. It was also sometimes reported of Inuit that they were nearly white, and that the men occasionally had beards. *See*, for example, [Poncelin de la Roche-Tillac], *Almanach américain*, 23; however, the author felt that this indicated that the Inuit were of a different race from Amerindians. Charlevoix doubted a report of a black people with thick lips, wide noses, and white, straight hair living in far northern Labrador on the ground that it would be strange indeed to find "black men so close to the Pole and in a climate where even the bears were white" (*Histoire et description* 1:27).

18. Wytfliet, *Histoire universelle*, pt. 1, 126.

19. D'Avity, *Description générale*, 30; Sagard, *Long Journey*, 136; Coréal, *Voyages* 2:36; Le Beau, *Avantures* 1:306. William Wood, after noting that Amerindians were born fair, attributed their smooth skins to their habit of annointing themselves with oils (*New England Prospect*, 71). That such ideas were present in Europe long before contact with Amerindians is witnessed by an observation of Marco Polo's while in southern India: "All the people of this Countrey be blacke, not because that they be so borne, but for that they would be blacke, they annoynt themselves with a kind of oyle, called oyle of Aioniolly, for the blackest are esteemed most fayre" (*The Travels of Marco Polo*, John Frampton, trans. [London, 1937], 110). This reference was pointed out to me by Nicholas Wickenden.

20. D'Avity, *Estats*, 262.

21. Thwaites, ed., *JR* 8:159.

22. Marie de l'Incarnation, *Ecrits spirituels* 3:374.

23. Claude, *Maragnan*, 266v, 315–15v.

24. Du Tertre, *Histoire générale des isles*, 398–99. Martin Frobisher also noted that the "tawny or olive" color of Amerindians was natural, "as appeared by their Infants, and seems [to be] the complexion of all Amerindians" (Crouch, *English Empire*, 20).

25. Cobo, *Historia del Nuevo Mundo* 3:13–14; Lahontan, *Voyages en Amérique septentrionale* 2:347–51.

26. Lechford, *Plain Dealing*, 103; Du Perier, *Amours de Pistion*, 9; and, during the eighteenth century, Navières, "Un voyage inédit," 11. Wasserman also noted the persistence of the belief that Amerindians acquired their color by choice (*Seventeenth century chronicles*, 36–41).

27. Du Perier, *Amours de Pistion*, 9; also Navières, "Un voyage inédit," 11. Recently, European presence in the Americas during the Bronze Age has been argued (Fell, *America B.C.*, *Bronze Age America*).

28. Such a defection could be an explanation for an Amerindian grave, if one is to credit a report attributed to the Pilgrim Fathers. The grave was described as "much bigger and larger than any wee had yet seene," and its contents listed as including a skull which had fine yellow hair on it. It had been "bound up in a Saylers Canvas Casacke, and a payre of Cloth Breeches" (Clarke, *Someone Before Us*, 91–92). Surprise was still being expressed during the eighteenth century at different types of men living under the same climate. *See* Brosse, *Histoire des Navigations* 2:376. For a general discussion of European notions about Amerindian color, *see* Jordan, *White over Black*.

29. Champlain said on at least two occasions that "our young men will marry your daughters, and we shall be one people" (Thwaites, ed., *JR* 5:211 and 10:27).

30. Yves, *Suitte de l'histoire*, 270.

31. Jordan, *White over Black*, 254.

32. Surlaville, *Les Derniers Jours,* 85.

33. An argument against this belief was presented by Sir Josiah Child in *A New discourse of trade.*

34. La Popelinière, *Trois Mondes,* avant discours; Elliott, *Old World,* 83–103. The reabsorption of armed forces into civilian life was generally an unsolved problem in Renaissance Europe. For instance, in 1477, a horde of young Swiss soldiers, discharged from the Burgundian wars, vandalized their way from Lucurne to Geneva (Hale, *Renaissance Europe,* 26).

35. Bodin, *Republique* (1579), 587.

36. Hospital, *Oeuvres inédites* 1:102–3.

37. Thévenot, *Relations de diverse voyages* 4:2. That the control of the metropolis was difficult to enforce across the Atlantic is evident from complaints and petitions from colonists to the king. For example, *Au roi sur la Nouvelle France;* and Clodoré, *Plaintes et griefs.*

38. La Popelinière, *Trois Mondes,* avant-discours.

39. Elliott, *Old World,* 76–77; *Memoire pour servir d'instruction,* 11. *See also* Saint-Michel, *Voyages des isles Camercanes,* au lecteur.

40. A recent thesis maintains that France's official enthusiasm for colonization never did succeed in arousing popular support. *See* Philip Boucher, "France 'Discovers' America."

41. G. Fournier, *Hydrographie,* 180.

42. Ibid. Eau-de-vie, which during the fifteenth century had been confined largely to medicinal use, during the latter part of the sixteenth and early seventeenth centuries came into general use as commercial techniques of distilling it from grain were developed. Before the Thirty Years' War its manufacture was already established as an industry. However, this was the object of some religious scruples on the grounds that it was a profane use of the ingredients of daily bread (E. Fournier, *Curiosités,* 61).

43. G. Fournier, *Hydrographie,* 180.

44. Yves, *Voyage dans le Nord du Brésil,* 215.

45. *Histoire des choses memorables,* 13v.

46. Cahingt, ed., "Documents sur le Canada," document 16, "Memoire de ce que les filles qui passent doivent fayre," 109.

47. Diéreville, *Voyage to Port Royal,* 241.

    How foul the Dishes and the Linen were!
    The Plates were never scoured; and to protect
    Them, if they fell, they were wrapped all about
    With greasy rags; that was my pleasure then,
    To see ten arms, in vain attempt
    To keep things on the board, while in
    Their mouths Men put the food, they picked
    From off the floor. (Ibid., 63)

48. Supra, 67.

49. La Barre, *Description,* 50–51.

50. Some typical tales are recounted in *Histoire véritable de plusieurs voyages.* A favorite myth was of an unkind people who profited from sailors by selling them wind. One author placed these opportunists in "Vinslande" (Signot, *La Division du Monde,* 52–53).

51. Diéreville, *Voyage to Port Royal,* 57–58.

52. Yves, *Voyage dans le Nord du Brésil,* 214.

53. Ibid., 214–17. This was corroborated by La Barre, *Description,* 52, and Boyer, *Veritable Relation,* 367–68, both of whom pointed to the usefulness of trade for gaining Amerindian good will.

54. Yves, *Voyage dans le Nord du Brésil,* 216.

55. Ibid., 215, 217.

56. Carayon, ed., *Chaumonot,* 29. Bread, of course, was in European eyes a symbol of civilization, and therefore an essential for the diet of a civilized person.

57. La Barre, *Description,* 48–49.

58. Yves, *Voyage dans le Nord du Brésil,* 216–17.

59. La Barre, *Description,* 46–48.

60. Champlain, *Works* 3:291–97.

61. La Barre, *Description,* 6, 46.

62. La Popelinière, *Trois Mondes* bk. 1:37, bk. 2:47v.

63. Langenes, *Thrésor,* 190. *See also* Henrion, *Cosmographie,* 894.

64. Buno, *Descriptio orbis,* 84. A curious letter datelined Brest, 13 February 1608, attributes a population of 50,000 to the settlement. The letter has been described by Atkinson as "imaginary . . . a little bit of fiction about Canada" (*Nouveaux horizons,* 311–12). He theorizes that the author took some of his details from Champlain's account; if so, it was a point of departure for a flight of imagination. The letter was included in the exhibition, "Canada," at the New York Public Library in 1935 (Sieur de Cõbes [Combes], *Coppie d'une Lettre*).

65. Manesson-Mallet, *Description de l'univers* 5:274.

66. *Privy Council, Judicial Committee. In the Matter of the Boundary between the Dominions of Canada and the Colony of Newfoundland in the Labrador Peninsula,* Courtemanche's Memoir (1705), 3686. *See also* the unpublished report prepared by Anick, "A History of the Fur Trade in Eastern Canada," 5–8.

67. Anick, "A History of the Fur Trade in Eastern Canada," 7–8. More likely, it was the fortified French settlement dispersed by the Basques in 1555. Five hundred survivors were sent back to France (Folmer, *Franco-Spanish Rivalry,* 66–67).

68. Robertson, "Notes on the Coast of Labrador," 32–44. Bowen believed that the settlement had been established by the Basques ("Social Condition of the Coast of Labrador," 338–39). That there were settlers from a very early date is supported by the traditions of the "livyers" of Newfoundland who have descended from these early residents, some of whom claim their families were established in the New World as early as the 1540s.

69. Lescarbot, *History of New France* 1:45. Various dates have been assigned to this enterprise, such as 1528, 1539, and 1553.

70. De Laet, *L'Histoire du Nouveau Monde,* 39.

71. Bergeron, *Traicté de la navigation,* 102.

72. Champlain, *Works* 1:235; 3:302; Hakluyt, *Principal Navigations* 8:63; Ganong, *Crucial Maps,* 68–69. Ganong speculated that Champlain did not differentiate Spanish from Portuguese, as at the time he was writing the two had become one kingdom. The date 1552 for the arrival of the livestock was advocated by George Patterson in "Portuguese on the northeast coast of America," 127–73.

73. Cortesão and Teixeira da Motá, *Portugaliae Monumenta Cartographica* 2: pl. 405.

74. Lanctot, "L'Establissement du Marquis de La Roche," 39.

75. Ganong, *Crucial Maps,* 69. De Laet says that the second Portuguese attempt was on Sable Island (*L'Histoire du Nouveau Monde,* 39).

76. Biggar, *Precursors,* doc. 64a.

77. Sauer, *Sixteenth Century America,* 49–50.

78. Biggar, *Precursors,* 195–97.

79. Wallis, "Historical Background of the Micmac Indians," 42.

80. Cortesão and Teixeira da Motá, *Portugaliae Monumenta Cartographica* 2: pl. 331. The illustration could also be in reference to the name "Labrador," which was derived from the Portuguese "llavrador," meaning small land-holder. However, in that case it could have been expected to have been more widely used; this is the only Portuguese map of Labrador of that period with such an illustration.

81. Alfonce, *Voyages avantureux,* 28.

82. Champlain, *Works* 1:468, 3:418. A repetition of Champlain's version is found in de Laet, *L'Histoire du Nouveau Monde,* 39.

8 The French on the St. Lawrence

1. Brazilwood was a major source of red dye, much in demand for Europe's burgeoning textile industry. Before the discovery of Brazilian stands, India had been Europe's main source of dyewood.

2. Verrazzano (c. 1485–c. 1528), a Florentine by birth, had entered France's maritime service in 1522. His 1524 voyage was financed by Florentine bankers of Lyon. On a subsequent voyage in 1528 to the West Indies and South America, he was reported to have been killed and eaten by Amerindians before the eyes of his crew aboard ship. *See* Wroth, *Verrazzano,* and Mollat, *Premières relations entre la France et le Brésil.*

3. Ramusio, *Navigations et Voyages,* 96.

4. In this connection, it is interesting to note that Juan Ponce de Léon's hostile reception in Florida, 20 April 1513, is the first record of such a reaction upon initial arrival (Sauer, *Sixteenth Century America,* 28). It could well have been that word of their behavior had preceded the Spaniards.

5. Ramusio, *Navigations et Voyages,* 99.

6. Hakluyt, *Principal Navigations* 8:427; Belleforest, *Cosmographie universelle,* 2:2175ff.

7. Ramusio, *Navigations et Voyages,* 107.

8. Hakluyt, *Principal Navigations* 8:437; Wroth, *Verrazzano,* 140.

9. Ramusio, *Navigations et Voyages,* 103.

10. Wroth, *Verrazzano,* 138.

11. Ramusio, *Navigations et Voyages,* 101, 105–6, 108.

12. Wroth, *Verrazzano,* 134, 137.

13. Cartier, *Collection of Documents,* doc. 49.

14. Charlevoix, *Histoire et description* 1:23; Thevet, *Cosmographie* (L'Huillier), 1010.

15. Concerning the name "Canada," *see* Appendix I.

16. D'Avity, *Description générale,* 26; Thwaites, ed., *JR* 3:41; Cartier, *Voyages,* 62, 153, 183.

17. Cartier, *Voyages,* 181. He spoke Portuguese well enough to be used as an interpreter (idem, *Collection of Documents,* 476). For other evidence of a Brazilian connection for Cartier, *see* infra, 210.

18. B.G. Hoffman, "Historical Ethnography," 40. By 1534, French ships were sailing regularly on trading missions to Brazil. Upon arriving offshore they announced their arrival by firing cannon (Mocquet, *Voyages en Afrique,* 88).

19. Thevet, *Singularitez,* 401.

20. Verrazzano had reported a similar reaction in one of his encounters (Ramusio, *Navigations et Voyages,* 104).

21. Thevet, "Grand Insulaire," 156–56v; Belleforest, *Cosmographie universelle,* 2:2184.

22. Cartier, *Voyages,* 66, 100.

23. Thevet, "Grand Insulaire," 143.

24. Ibid., 156v. Later in boundary negotiations with Great Britain, France claimed that Cartier had made an alliance with the Stadaconans and had taken possession of the land (*Mémoires des Commissaires* 1:29).

25. Cartier, *Voyages,* 67.

26. Infra, 224. Thevet, *Cosmographie* (L'Huillier), 1018.

27. Cartier, *Collection of Documents,* doc. 75.

28. La Grange de Chessieux, *La Conduite,* 255.

29. Cartier, *Voyages,* 129. The Stadaconans were not alone in this reaction. In Cayenne, the Amerindians were not pleased when the French appeared fully armed for a ceremonial ratification of a treaty of friendship (Biet, *France Equinioxiale,* 105).

30. Stadacona seems to have been the principal of a cluster of villages. Immediately downstream, in descending order, were Sitadin, Thegnignonde, Tailla, Starnatan, and Ajoasté. Upstream between Achelacy and Stadacona were Tequenonday and Canada (B.G. Hoffman, "Ancient Tribes Revisited," 25). For a somewhat different listing, *see* Trigger and Pendergast in *Handbook of North American Indians* 15:357.

31. Cartier, *Voyages,* 150–61.

32. Verreau, "Jacques Cartier," 129.

33. Supra, 112. However, Bruce Trigger speculates that the willingness to present Cartier with children may have been a forestalling action at least partly inspired by the latter's predilection for kidnapping ("The French Presence in Huronia," 115 n. 37).

34. Cartier, *Voyages,* 140, 188. Biggar has even speculated that Donnacona feared Cartier might arm the upriver Iroquoians (*Early Trading Companies,* 350). Such a fear could have developed if Cartier had refused arms to the Stadaconans. However, we have no hint that the question was even raised; during this period, it was not the European custom to trade firearms with "savages," even those who were considered allies. There is no suggestion in any of the Cartier documentation that Donnacona solicited firearms.

35. Cartier, *Voyages,* 143, 256–59.

36. Ibid., 147. This is illustrated in Gastaldi's drawing of Hochelaga published in Ramusio. It is reproduced in Cartier, *Voyages,* opposite p. 144, and also by Trigger in "Sixteenth Century Ontario," 208–9.

37. Gaffarel, *Histoire de la Floride,* 85.

38. Vespucci, *Letters,* 16.

39. Thevet, "Grand Insulaire," 157.

40. Cartier, *Voyages,* 8. The French in Brazil had a similar experience; Yves reported that the Brazilians raised prices when the French particularly sought certain items (*Voyage dans le Nord du Brésil,* 70).

41. Cartier, *Voyages,* 217.

42. Ibid., 225.

43. La Roncière, "Notre première tentative de colonization au Canada," 284.

44. If one is to credit the Spanish historian Andrés Gonzáles de Barcia Carballido y Zúñiga (1673–1743), this colonization project was originally opposed by Cartier. According to Barcia, Cartier had been profoundly disillusioned upon his return from his second voyage: "Hardly were they in port before they began–Cartier more than anyone else–to spread word of their misfortunes. Cartier maintained the land was not fit for Europeans to live in, for even when there were no contagions such as they had suffered, the cold was intolerable. The few souls he brought back were proof of this fact, he said, and explained they had been forced to leave the place and to lose a ship. If they had re-

mained another fifteen days, none would have returned" (Barcia, *Chronological History,* 20). Charlevoix, however, disputes this, claiming that it agrees neither with Cartier's own reports nor with those of others (*Histoire et description* 1:22).

45. Cartier, *Voyages,* 259.

46. Cartier, *Collection of Documents,* 456–57.

47. Thevet, *Singularitez,* 422–23; *Cosmographie* (L'Huillier), 1012v.

48. Hakluyt, *Principal Navigations* 13:45. Henry Harrisse claimed the story was an invention of Thevet's (*Découverte et évolution cartographique,* 175). But today, historians are not so sure. Hubert Deschamps, for one, blamed Cartier's "brutality" for the hostility of the natives (*Les Méthodes,* 15).

49. Cartier, *Voyages,* 264.

50. Ogilby, *America,* 136.

51. Thevet, *Singularitez,* 423.

52. Cartier, *Collection of Documents,* 463.

53. Cartier, *Voyages,* 267.

54. Thevet, *Cosmographie* (Chaudiere), 1019–20v. A different version of the story appears in Marguerite of Navarre's *L'Heptameron,* which has the husband being cast off on the island and Marguerite voluntarily joining him.

55. Montchrestien, *Traicté,* 214.

56. Cartier, *Voyages,* 268.

57. Montchrestien, *Traicté,* 214.

58. Bergeron, *Traicté de la navigation,* 105.

59. Ganong, *Crucial Maps,* 363.

60. Champlain, *Works* 3:291.

61. Cartier, *Collection of Documents,* doc. 73, September 1538.

62. For a Portuguese estimate of the reliability of Donnacona's statements, *see* Cartier, *Collection of Documents,* doc. 75, January 1539(?).

63. Ribier, *Lettres et mémoires* 1:212–17; Cartier, *Collection of Documents,* doc. 73, September 1538 and doc. 148, April 1541.

64. Bergeron, *Traicté de la navigation,* 105.

65. Cartier, *Bref récit et succincte narration,* 5.

66. Cartier, *Voyages,* 186.

67. Hallowell, in Johnson, ed., *Man in Northeastern North American,* 225. Such an explanation may be more appropriate for more northern hunting tribes than for the Iroquois. In the case of the latter, this kind of behavior could have been part of treaty etiquette, as the Stadaconans considered themselves to be in alliance with the French.

68. Cartier, *Voyages,* 221–22.

69. It went through five printings before 1609, indicating the high level of public interest in that part of the New World (Atkinson, *Nouveaux horizons,* 24).

70. Alfonce, *Voyages avantureux,* 27v; "La Cosmographie," 179.

71. Alfonce, "La Cosmographie," 494. Extracts from the cosmography were reproduced in Cartier, *Voyages,* 278–303. The 1904 edition of "La Cosmographie" was its first publication. Lazare Sainéan, in "La Cosmographie de Jean-Alfonse Saintongeais," described Alfonce's treatise as being largely a literal translation of Enciso's *Suma de geografía.* While Sainéan upholds his point regarding the translation from Enciso, the role of Alfonce is by no means clear. An annotation on the manuscript of "La Cosmographie" says it was the work of Alfonce and Raulin Secalarat, "captains and ship's pilots. . . . Completed by myself, Raulin Secalarat, cosmographer of Honfleur, desiring, by this book, to provide a service for Your Royal Majesty. 1545" (Biggar, *Early Trading Companies,* 224). If Alfonce was the translator, it could well have been that his manuscript was given a direction different from what he had intended after he was killed in action against the Spaniards about 1544. In any event, its concluding section, which contains Cartier-Roberval materials, did not come from Enciso. Sainéan thought it was taken from "Discorso d'uņ Gran Capitano di mare Franceses de Luoco de Dieppa," which Ramusio included in his collection published in 1565. This, however, does not stand up under examination, as the "Discorso" contains no information from the Cartier-Roberval voyages: it is now believed to have been written by Pierre Crignon. The Cartier-Roberval section of "La Cosmographie" is still attributed to Alfonce. *See* B.G. Hoffman, *Cabot to Cartier,* 169–70. Lescarbot had a low opinion of Alfonce's accuracy of geographical description (*History of New France* 2:275–76).

72. Ganong, *Crucial Maps,* 386, 428. "Le Grand Insulaire" seems to have been a partial draft for Thevet's *Singularitez* and *Cosmographie,* in both of which much of its information has been incorporated.

73. Léry, *Histoire d'un voyage* (1578), preface. A similar assessment is found in *Mémoires-Journaux de P. de l'Estoile* bk. 4:381, bk. 5:61–62, in Petitot, *Collection complète des mémoires* XLV–XLIX. Cited by Biggar, *Early Trading Companies*, 241.

74. De Thou, *Histoire universelle* 2:651–52. This passage is cited in part by Winsor, *Narrative and Critical History* 4:31–32; and by Julien, *Voyages de découverte*, 380.

75. Cited by Thorndike, *History of Magic* 6:490–91. André Stegman assesses de Thou in "L'Amerique de Du Bartas et De Thou," 299–309.

76. Trumbull, "Thevet's Specimens of the Indian Language," 239.

77. Thevet, *Cosmographie* (L'Huillier), 913.

78. Supra, 19.

79. Morison, *European Discovery*, 502.

80. Thevet, "Grand Insulaire," 150v. Ganong says that Thevet did not claim to have been in Canada, but only along the coast (*Crucial Maps*, 429). However, as Biggar has pointed out (*Early Trading Companies*, 235), that applies only to what Thevet wrote in *Singularitez;* in his *Cosmographie* (Chaudiere), he claims to have spent twenty days in Canada (1009v).

81. For Ganong's assessment of Thevet, *see Crucial Maps*, 386–87 and 427–29; for B.G. Hoffman's, *Cabot to Cartier*, 171–79; Julien also considered that Thevet's ethnographic descriptions contained much of value (*Voyages de découverte*, 381–94). Also, J.L. Roy, "Un français au Brésil," 363–96.

82. Thevet, *Singularitez*, 417–18.

83. Ibid., 403; "Grand Insulaire," 152. Later Le Jeune, in trying to use snowshoes for the first time, was delighted when he did not end up with his nose in the snow (*Le Dix-Neufiesme tome du Mercure François*, 784).

84. Thevet, *Cosmographie* (Chaudiere), 1014–14v. Earlier, in *Singularitez*, 428, he told of drinking maple sap but with no mention of the reduction process.

85. Thevet, *Singularitez*, 408.

86. Ibid., 421–22; idem, *Cosmographie* (L'Huillier), 1012.

87. Thevet, *Cosmographie* (L'Huillier), 1011v–13; idem, *Singularitez* (Paris, 1558), 155v–58. Thwaites, ed., *JR* 41:83.

88. Thevet, *Singularitez*, 55, 68, 78.

89. Thevet, *Cosmographie* (Chaudiere), 1016. Later, acquaintance with the Huron and Five Nations was to modify this view (Langenes, *Thrésor*, 190; Du Val d'Abbeville, *L'Amerique françoise*, 28.

90. Thevet, *Singularitez*, 418; *Cosmographie* (Chaudiere), 928v.

91. Lescarbot, *History of New France* 2:267–68, and *Nova Francia*, 182. B.G. Hoffman discusses the implications of these references in *Cabot to Cartier*, 203.

92. This is the thesis of Trigger and Pendergast in *Cartier's Hochelaga*, 88–93; and of Trigger in "Trade and Tribal Warfare," 240–56. Other theories concerning the disappearance of the Laurentian Iroquois from the St. Lawrence are discussed by Tooker in *Huron Ethnography*, 3–4 n. 1.

93. Bailey, "Identity and Disappearance of the Laurentian Iroquois," 97–108.

94. B.G. Hoffman, "Souriquois," 79. However, cartography lagged behind the latest information, and cartographers often copied from existing maps.

95. Trigger, "Tribal Warfare," 247.

96. D'Avity, *Description*, 29.

97. B.G. Hoffman, "Souriquois," 79.

98. Thwaites, ed., *JR* 22:215–17; 29:147.

99. Thevet, "Grand Insulaire," 155v and 152v. Thevet was consulted by Hakluyt at the time the latter was preparing his "Discourse on Western Planting" (Taylor, *Two Hakluyts*, 207).

100. Thevet, "Grand Insulaire," 150v. *See also* Appendix I. In connection with mining, one of the rights Cartier's nephews managed to retain when their monopoly was revoked in May 1588 was that of exploiting copper mines. They were to be allowed sixty convicts a year for the task (Biggar, *Early Trading Companies*, 34–35; and La Roncière, *Histoire de la marine française* 4:311).

101. Thevet, "Grand Insulaire," 152v.

102. Thevet, *Singularitez*, 432–36; *Cosmographie* (Chaudiere), 1016; Wytfliet, *Histoire universelle*, pt. 1, 123–24.

103. Montchrestien, *Traicté*, 282.

104. Thevet, "Grand Insulaire," 150v.

105. Girava in Apianus, *Cosmographie*, 166.

106. Whitbourne, *Discourse and Discovery*, preface, 2.

107. Montchrestien, *Traicté*, 269–70.

9 The French in Brazil and Florida

1. Staden, *Histoire d'un pays,* 110; Belleforest, *Cosmographie universelle* 2:2112; Simonsen, *História Econômica,* 55–56.
2. A navigation manual published by Rouennais Jean Cordier in 1547 contained a guide to conversation for Frenchmen in Brazil. The phrases selected recall those of today's tourist manuals (BN, ms.fr. 24269, ff. 53–54v. Cited by Mollat, "Première relations," 72–73).
3. Southey, *History of Brazil* 1:280. *See also* Lescarbot, *History of New France* 1:145–47.
4. *Bref recueil de l'affliction* A(verso). Gaspard de Coligny, Seigneur de Châtillon, *dit l'admiral* (1519–72), had been instrumental in obtaining the ships, as well as a supply vessel and 10,000 francs (at that time francs were the equivalent to the livre) from the king for the enterprise.
5. Ibid.
6. Nowell, "The French in Sixteenth-Century Brazil," 382.
7. The book was displayed in the exhibition "France-Canada" at La Rochelle and Paris in 1955. Listed as item 20 in the exhibition catalogue, it is in the collection of La Bibliothèque de Versailles. Sixteenth-century French writers frequently cited the Tupinambá as examples of natural goodness, despite their cannibalistic ways.
8. The proposition that these Amerindians were Canadians was put forward by Cuoq (1821–98), *Lexique de la langue iroquoise,* 189–90, on the basis of tenuous linguistic evidence. It was discussed by Beaugrand-Champagne in "Les anciens Iroquois du Québec," 195–97. However, an early seventeenth-century writer refers to the visitors as "Toupinambos" (Baudier, *Histoire générale,* 122). *See also* Trigger and Pendergast, *Cartier's Hochelaga,* 90.
9. For this sketch, I have drawn principally upon Métraux, *Handbook of South American Indians* 3:95–133; and Hemming, *Red Gold.*
10. While this was not a top-ranking honor, it did mean that Villegaignon was charged with defending Catholicism (Lewis, *Splendid Century,* 129).
11. Visme, *Précurseurs de l'idée missionnaire,* 2.
12. *Bref recueil de l'affliction,* A(verso); La Popelinière, *Trois Mondes,* bk. 2:17.
13. It was not until about mid-1557, when the project was well on its way, that Coligny became a "more or less conscious Protestant," and by 1559 he was a fully fledged Huguenot (Nowell, "The French in Sixteenth-Century Brazil," 383). However, it is evident that Protestants were more motivated to emigrate than were Catholics, particularly when Henry II moved to extirpate "heresy."
14. Belleforest, *Cosmographie universelle* 2:2066.
15. Hauser, "Les huguenots français," 106.
16. *Histoire des choses memorables,* 7.
17. Haton, *Memoires* 1:37–38.
18. *Histoire des choses memorables,* 13.
19. *Bref recueil de l'affliction,* Biii. This contrasted with the Cartier-Roberval expedition, which had not even attempted to seek volunteers.
20. Gaffarel, *Histoire du Brésil,* 174–75.
21. *Bref recueil de l'affliction,* Avi(verso)–Avii. Nicolas Barré, a pilot who also acted as Villegaignon's secretary and who was later to take part in the Ribault-Laudonnière expedition, wrote that about 600 Amerindians were present. Barré was happy to relegate shipboard water to a bad memory as he noted that the new land was watered by "very beautiful rivers of sweet water, the healthiest I have ever drunk" (*Copie de quelques lettres,* 22).
22. Lescarbot, *History of New France* 1:160; Gaffarel, *Histoire du Brésil,* 384.
23. Thevet, *Singularitez* (Paris, 1558), 49v.
24. Gaffarel, *Histoire du Brésil,* 194–95. According to Thevet, the Tupinambá had originally volunteered in good numbers and had encouraged each other to spare no effort toward the construction of the fort (*Cosmographie* [L'Huillier], 908). *See also* Claude, *Maragnan,* 150v ff. Yves had been impressed with the attitude of Amerindians toward work: he reported they laughed and enjoyed themselves as they labored, encouraging each other (*Voyage dans le Nord de Brésil,* 16–17). Louis de Pezieu also noted an initial Amerindian willingness to work on the French fort (*Bref recueil des particularitez,* 6).
25. *Bref recueil de l'affliction,* Avii. Lescarbot said they were reduced to drinking undiluted water (*History of New France* 1:159).
26. Léry, *Histoire d'un voyage* (1580), 80; Hauser, "Les huguenots français," 104.
27. Barré, *Copie de quelques lettres,* 30.
28. *Histoire des choses memorables,* 25v–26.

29. Oexmelin, *Histoire des Avanturiers* 1:184–94.

30. La Popelinière, *Trois Mondes,* bk. 3:16v; Purchas writes that the Portuguese, after taking the fort, paid the French 30,000 ducats for it (*Hakluytus Posthumus* 17:264).

31. Hauser, "Les huguenots français," 94.

32. Southey, *History of Brazil* 1:293.

33. Léry, *Histoire d'un voyage* (1580), 107.

34. Ibid., 175–78. The acceptance on the part of Amerindians taken prisoner that their fate was to be eaten was noted with surprise by early writers. *See also* Wytfliet, *Histoire universelle,* pt. 1, 85.

35. Hauser, "Les huguenots français," 104.

36. Thevet, *Cosmographie* (L'Huillier), 909.

37. Léry, *Histoire d'un voyage* (1580), 14; Gaffarel, *Histoire du Brésil,* 392–97. Apparently, some effort was made to evangelize the Brazilians, but with little, if any, success (Lescarbot, *History of New France* 1:158).

38. Staden, *Histoire d'un pays,* 177, 211–13.

39. Gaffarel, *Histoire du Brésil,* 208–9; Elliott, *Old World,* 102.

40. Léry, *Histoire d'un voyage* (1580), 36, 229.

41. Maffei, *Histoire des Indes,* 99.

42. *Histoire des chose memorables,* 15.

43. Hauser, "Les huguenots français," 112; Léry, *Histoire d'un voyage* (1580), 182.

44. For the influence of Léry on Jean-Jacques Rousseau, *see* Atkinson, *Nouveaux horizons,* 73–90. Léry has also been credited by Charles Julien with providing Lahontan with the prototype for the Adario type of dialogue. This could well be; however, the dialogue between Amerindian and European is also found in Martire, who in turn could have taken the model from classical literature.

45. Atkinson, *Nouveaux horizons,* 40–41.

46. Léry, *Histoire d'un voyage* (1580), 205–7.

47. Ibid., 226–27.

48. Purchas, *Hakluytus Posthumus* 16:568.

49. Léry, *Histoire d'un voyage* (1580), 185–86, 210–11, 214, 228; Julien, *Voyages de découverte,* 409. Concerning miserliness, Jesuits were to report later from New France that to be called a miser was one of the worst insults in those parts (Thwaites, ed., *JR* 6:237–39).

50. Léry, *Histoire d'un voyage* (1578), 256–58.

51. Léry, *Histoire d'un voyage* (1580), 205.

52. Léry, *Historia navigationis,* 128, 140. Léry records two songs in this edition, one of which refers to birds and the other to fish. *See also* Stevenson, "The Western Hemisphere," in F.W. Sternfeld, ed., *Music from the Middle Ages to the Renaissance* (London, 1973), 430. Stevenson notes that Hector Villa-Lobos incorporated two of these melodies in his *Trois poèmes indiens.*

53. De Thou included accounts of both projects in his *Histoire universelle:* on Villegaignon, 2:647–52; on Ribault-Laudonnière, 5:485–507. The other works are included in the Bibliography. *See also* W.P. Cumming, "The Parreus Map," 27–40.

54. La Popelinière, *Trois Mondes,* bk. 2:26v–27.

55. Cloulas, *Catherine,* 216.

56. Belleforest, *Cosmographie universelle* 2:2037, 2195.

57. Hakluyt, *Principal Navigations* 10:53.

58. Swanton, *Indian Tribes,* 147–52; Muller, "The Southeast," in J.D. Jennings, ed., *Ancient Native Americans,* 281–325; Hodge, *American Indians North of Mexico* 2:470, 752–54, 876–77. According to Métraux, the closest affiliation of the language of the Timucuans was with the Warau of the Orinoco delta in Brazil; the separation may have occurred around 3000–2000 B.C. ("Tupinamba," 554).

59. Trudel, *Vaines tentatives,* 195–201.

60. Le Blanc, *Voyages fameux,* pt. 3:148. Also, Bertrand de la Grassière, *Jean Ribault,* 45.

61. "Copie d'une lettre venant de la Floride," in Gaffarel, *Histoire de la Floride,* 404.

62. Ibid., 89.

63. William Wood described Amerindian self-esteem particularly aptly, when he wrote of a New England sagamore that he "thinks himself little inferior to the great Cham; hee will not stick to say, hee is all one with King Charles. He thinkes he can blow down Castles with his breath, and conquer kingdoms with his conceit. This Pompey can endure no equall" (*New England Prospect,* 74).

64. Laudonnière, *Histoire notable,* 48–49.

65. Gaffarel said that Ribault was not so much asserting French dominance over the Amerindians as he was warning off the Spaniards (*Histoire de la Floride,* 19–20). Le Moyne's painting of one of these occasions was found at Château de

Courance near Paris in 1901. *See* the catalogue, *Canada: An exhibition,* 10.

66. Gaffarel, *Histoire de la Floride,* 29–35. Gaffarel says that the Amerindians taught the French the use of resin and moss for shipbuilding, and provided them with ropes made of twisted vines. *See also* Laudonnière, *Histoire notable,* 56.

67. Hakluyt, *Divers Voyages,* F4(verso).

68. Laudonnière, *Histoire notable,* 44–45. Much later, in Onondaga, a French missionary caused offence during a Feast of the Dead, and was asked to leave (Thwaites, ed., *JR* 53:213–17).

69. Laudonnière, *Histoire notable,* 169–70.

70. Hakluyt, *Principal Navigations* 10:55. Later, the French were to behave similarly in the West Indies and in Cayenne. *See* Du Puis, *Relation,* 27ff.; and Biet, *France Equinoxiale,* 244ff.

71. Lescarbot, *Nova Francia,* 56, 115.

72. Some of this equipment is listed by Gosselin in *Nouvelles Glanes,* 8.

73. Hakluyt, *Principal Navigations* 10:56–58.

74. Laudonnière, *Histoire notable,* 139–40; Le Challeux, *Discours et histoire* 22–23; La Popelinière, *Trois Mondes,* bk. 2:30v.

75. Wytfliet thought the failure was due to lack of subordination, which had led, among other things, to waste of supplies (*Histoire universelle,* pt. 1, 120).

76. Hakluyt, *Principal Navigations* 8:76.

77. Laudonnière, *Histoire notable,* 105–7, 141.

78. Hakluyt, *Principal Navigations* 8:52, 62.

79. *Histoire memorable,* 4. Ribault had the misfortune to return in time to be one of the victims of the slaughter. He was flayed and his skin sent back to Spain, an insult which contributed not a little to the initiative of Gourgues.

80. Maran, *Pionniers de l'Empire,* 330. The Spanish action as well as Gourgues' personal reprisal did not lead to war or threats of war between France and Spain because of the verbal agreement at the Treaty of Cateau-Cambrésis, 1559 (supra, 138–139). However, the French apparently soothed their national pride with a show of force by French galleys off "Ile Floride" during 1565. Galley slaves were given their liberty on condition that they settled there (*Copie d'une lettre.* This letter was reprinted, with a slight change in the title, in 1583. *See also,* Pysière, *Discours de l'Entreprinse).*

81. Laudonnière, *Histoire notable,* 210–11.

82. Trigger, "French Presence," 118.

83. Laudonnière, *Histoire notable,* 217–19.

84. Atkinson, *Nouveaux horizons,* 114–16.

85. Le Challeux, *Discours et histoire,* title page (verso): "Whoever wants to go to Florida, let him go; I have been there."

86. Alexander, *American Colonization,* 203.

87. Sauer, *Sixteenth Century America,* 278.

88. Le Challeux, *Discours et histoire,* 6.

89. Stevenson, *Protestant Church Music in America,* 3–5.

90. Le Challeux, *Brief Discours,* 32–34.

91. Cluvier, *Introduction à la géographie universelle,* 489.

92. Montchrestien, *Traicté,* 218.

93. [Razilly], "Mémoire," 374–83, 453–64. Similar sentiments are also to be found in Biet, *France Equinoxiale,* preface.

94. Hurault, *Français et indiens,* 80.

95. Sauer says the only North American projects that succeeded during the sixteenth century were the cod and whale fisheries. He is forgetting the fur trade, which developed slowly but reasonably steadily along the Atlantic coast and up the St. Lawrence from the time of Cartier's voyages to the first permanent settlements early in the seventeenth century (*Sixteenth Century America,* 280).

96. Hurault, *Français et indiens,* 80. *See* Biet, *France Equinoxiale,* on the disasters experienced by French colonists in Cayenne.

97. Hurault, *Français et indiens,* 80–82.

98. Gomez Canedo, "Différentes attitudes face à l'Indien," 334.

99. It has been held that the rapport between Laudonnière and Satouriona was unique during the sixteenth century (Cummings, et al., *The Discovery of North America,* 17). If this is so, it can only be in a highly qualified sense, because of the eventual falling-out between Laudonnière and Satouriona. The Amerindian leader appears to have got along better with Gourgues.

10 Amerindians in Europe

1. *Troisième tome du Mercure François,* 5. Sir Ferdinando Gorges told of a New England Amerindian who had exhibited in London "for a wonder," apparently one of several who had been so used on that occasion (*Briefe Relation of the Discovery,* 13).
2. Oviedo, *L'Histoire naturelle,* bk. 2:17v.
3. Martire, *De Orbe novo* (Gaffarel), 29.
4. Gaffarel, *Histoire de la découverte* 2:417; Navarrete, *Quatre voyages* 1:469.
5. Hodgen, *Early Anthropology,* 111. There is some doubt about this report as there is no word that the captives arrived at Seville (Sauer, *Early Spanish Main,* 87 n. 25).
6. Navarrete, *Quatre voyages* 1:492.
7. Las Casas, *Oeuvres* 1:256; Herrera, *Histoire générale* 1:188.
8. Gaffarel, *Histoire de la découverte* 2:418.
9. Vespucci, *First Four Voyages,* 22–23. The authenticity of this voyage, supposed to have occurred in 1497–98, has been strongly disputed. Some have assigned this episode to Vespucci's accepted 1499 voyage with Alonso de Ojeda.
10. Schöner (1477–1547), *Reproduction,* 118; Laudonnière, *Histoire notable,* 30; Yves, *Voyage dans le Nord du Brésil,* ix.
11. Newton, *European Nations,* 13.
12. Martire, *De Orbe Novo* (MacNutt) 2:418–20.
13. Herrera, *General History* 6:339.
14. Hanke, in Chiapelli, ed., *First Images* 1:367; Diaz del Castillo, *Historia verdadera de la conquista,* 195ff., 226v–27.
15. Tazbir, "Conquête de l'Amérique," 7.
16. Martire, *De Orbe Novo* (MacNutt) 2:258, 267–68.
17. The account was first published in Fracanzano's *Paesi novamenti retrovati.* Du Redouer's adaptation, *Sensuyt le nouveau monde,* does not include this episode.
18. Alberto Cantino, Lisbon, to Hercules d'Este, Duke of Ferrara, 17 October 1501 (reproduced by Biggar in *Precursors,* 64).
19. Pietro Pasqualigo to the seignory of Venice, 18 October 1501 (reproduced by Biggar, *Precursors,* 66).
20. Harrisse, *Discovery of North America,* 128, 694. These Amerindians, however, were probably Brazilians rather than northerners.
21. Stow, *Annales,* 483–84. The visit of the three Amerindians is also reported by Hakluyt in *Principal Navigations* 12:19.
22. Hale, in Hay, ed., *Age of the Renaissance,* 335. It is likely that Inuit had long since been seen in Denmark and perhaps in Norway. *See* Oleson, *Early Voyages.*
23. Hakluyt, *Third and Last Volume,* 700.
24. Gaffarel, *Découvreurs français,* 86–87; D'Avezac, *Campagne du navire l'Espoir.*
25. De Brosse, *Histoire des Navigations* 1:102–20; Julien, *Voyages de découverte,* 19–20. For a somewhat different version, *see* Hemming, *Red Gold,* 11–12.
26. Paulmier, *Mémoire,* 178.
27. Ibid., introductory letter.
28. One could speculate if Voltaire had this story in mind when he wrote *L'Ingenue,* a play about a "Huron"–really a Frenchman raised by the Huron–who came to Europe.
29. Gaffarel, *Découvreurs français,* 128. This is a translation of a Latin account which appeared in the chronicle of Eusebius as updated by Prosper and Mathieu Paulmier. Hemming says the seven men were from Brazil (*Red Gold,* 12).
30. Ramusio, *Navigations et Voyages,* 113; Harrisse, *Discovery of North America,* 181; Ganong, *Crucial Maps,* 197.
31. Thwaites, ed., *JR* 3:39.
32. *Raccolta di documenti e studi* 2:377. This citation is taken from Bembo's *Historia Veneziana* (1530).
33. La Roncière, *Histoire de la marine française* 3:139.
34. Ramusio, *Navigations et Voyages,* 100.
35. Maran, *Pionniers de l'Empire,* 104, 97.
36. The figure of ten that is usually given refers to Cartier's statement that he sailed back with ten Amerindians (Cartier, *Voyages,* 249). That number would have included the four children who had been presented to him at Stadacona and Hochelay.
37. Ibid., 201, 221.
38. Barcia, *Chronological History,* 20.
39. Cartier, *Collection of Documents,* doc. 76, March 1538/39.
40. Ibid. doc. 72, 22 September 1538.
41. *Edits, Ordonnances royaux* 2:1–4.
42. Cartier, *Jacques Cartier,* doc. 24, 76–77.

43. Cartier, *Voyage de Jacques Cartier*, pt. 2:37.

44. Sagard prepared for his journey to Huronia in 1623 by learning something of the language beforehand, apparently in France (*Long Journey*, xvi).

45. Gaffarel, *Histoire du Brésil*, 137; La Quérière, *Description historique*. *See also* supra, Chapter 1, n. 71.

46. Denis, ed., *Fête brésilienne*, 16; Hemming, *Red Gold*, 78–79, 485.

47. Léry, *Histoire d'un voyage* (1580), 78–79.

48. Cayet, *Chronologie septenaire* 2:415–16.

49. Leymarie, "Le Canada pendant la jeunesse de Louis XIII," 168–69; Vaumas, *L'Eveil missionnaire*, 43.

50. *The London Gazette* no. 348 (1668), news item datelined "Paris March 23" in the Burney Collection of Newspapers, British Museum. For an admiring seventeenth-century view of New World watercraft, in this case a kayak, *see* Rochefort, *Histoire naturelle*, 189.

51. Mocquet, *Voyages en Afrique*, 80–81.

52. *C'est la deduction*. This is a manuscript describing the event, illuminated in color and bound in velour, at the Bibliothèque Municipale de Rouen. Thomas Galiot described the two-day event as being superb and magnificent in his *Inventaire*.

53. *C'est la deduction*, 40v–42.

54. Ibid. *See also* Denis, ed., *Fête brésilienne;* and Gaffarel, *Histoire du Brésil*, 130–36. McGowan, in Schoenbaum, ed., *Renaissance Drama*, 199, said the pageant provided a good example of the range of talent needed when civic authorities decided to combine local traditions with a re-enactment of a Roman triumph. At the time the entry was held, Rouen had been a major center for trade in brazilwood for half a century. To this day Rouen remembers its Brazilian connection. In 1969, La Foire de Rouen featured ballets "Brasiliana" as a major attraction. The event was reported in *Paris-Normandie*, 19 May 1969.

55. Gaffarel, *Histoire du Brésil*, 136.

56. Chinard, *L'Exotisme américain*, 105.

57. Gaffarel, *Histoire du Brésil*, 136.

58. *Cinquième tome du Mercure François*, 111.

59. Tazbir, "Conquête de l'Amérique," 7. It is difficult to determine the exact extent of the influence of America in such costuming, for in spite of the label "à l'amériquaine," this type of masquerade antedated the discovery of the New World. However, that event greatly boosted the popularity of l'homme sauvage for such purposes.

60. An example of such a ceremony is contained in La Vacquerie, *De multiplici haereticorum*, 56ff.

61. Vaumas, *L'Eveil missionnaire*, 155.

62. François's brother, Isaac, was lieutenant-general in New France, 1632–35.

63. A contemporary account of this event can be found in *Troisième tome du Mercure François*, 164ff.

64. Claude, *Maragnan*, 339v–40.

65. Malherbe, *Lettres*, 258.

66. Claude, *Maragnan*, 341v–42.

67. *Troisième tome du Mercure François*, 174.

68. Chinard, *Rêve*, 22–24. Chinard gives the impression that all six were baptized and died afterward. This is not borne out by either Claude's account nor by that in *Le Mercure François*. Neither does Claude mention a plan to marry the Brazilians to suitable *dévots*, as Chinard says.

69. *Troisième tome du Mercure François*, 164–65; Claude, *Maragnan*, 367v–74.

70. Some of these are reproduced in *L'Amerique historique*. Pl. 30 illustrates the Brazilians as they appeared on arrival, and pl. 187 depicts them in their French finery. Their awkwardness in their unaccustomed clothing is only too evident.

71. Thwaites, ed., *JR* 11:99–101. A contemporary report of other such events is found in Le Ber's *Départ pour le Canada en 1639*.

72. Jamet, *Coppie de la lettre*, 7. Recollet Le Clercq told of one such lad who "had been shown what was most important and beautiful at Paris and elsewhere, and the most holy spots"; unfortunately, the boy died at sea on his way back to Canada (*First Establishment* 1:181–83).

73. Thwaites, ed., *JR* 9:107. Such authorities as Bodin had maintained that education would in time alter the customs and ideas of a people, but unless it was consistently maintained primitive traits would reassert themselves (Bodin, *Method*, 145).

74. Thwaites, ed., *JR* 6:85.

75. Ibid. 9:105.

76. Ibid. 11:53. *See also* 5:145; 7:227.

77. Ibid. 7:287.

78. Ibid. 6:85. This was the lad who had been known as Fortuné when he had first been brought to Champlain as an orphan.

79. Ibid. 9:223–25.

80. Ibid. 9:221.

81. Ibid. 27:285–87, 293.

82. Ibid. 2:87.

83. The story of Louis is in *Dictionary of Canadian Biography* 1, s.v. "Amantacha." Louis's baptism in the Cathedral of Rouen had been another of those religious spectaculars that characterized this age of missionary zeal. Le Tac describes the event in *Histoire chronologique,* 136–38.

84. *Dictionary of Canadian Biography* 1, s.v. "Pastedechouan"; Thwaites, ed., *JR* 5:107–9; 6:87; 7:67–71; 9:69–71.

85. Ibid. 6:25.

86. Ibid. 11:95.

87. Ibid. 11:93. That was not an isolated instance; however, it may have been one of the exceptions that proved the rule, for the generality seems to have been that Amerindian children living with the French became unmanageable as soon as their countrymen encamped nearby. They "no longer belonged to us, we dared say nothing," complained Le Jeune (ibid. 6:87–89).

88. Ibid. 15:223–27, 237.

89. Doublet, *Notice sur un reliquaire.*

90. O'Callaghan and Brodhead, eds., *NYCD* 4:206–11, "Mr. Nelson's Memorial about the State of the Northern Colonies in America," 24 September 1696.

91. For Pieskaret's story, *see* Colden, *History of the Five Nations,* 8–15. For Le Berger's, *see* Thwaites, ed., *JR* 36:21–45, and *Dictionary of Canadian Biography* 1, s.v. "Honatteniate."

92. For another example of an Amerindian freeing himself from his bonds, *see* infra, 224.

93. Thirty-six were sent over according to Leclerc, *Marquis de Denonville,* 194–95. This is the figure given by Jesuit Thierry Beschefer (Thwaites, ed., *JR* 63:278). However, a report in *Le Mercure Galant* (novembre 1687) places the figure at between 50 and 60.

94. *Le Mercure Galant* (novembre 1687), 102.

95. Thwaites, ed., *JR* 64:249.

96. Lahontan, *Voyages en Amérique septentrionale* 1:109ff. Eccles has taken the position that Denonville's action had not been planned beforehand ("Denonville," 408–29).

97. PAC, C11A 2:36v–37, Memoire pour la Nouvelle France, de La Rochelle, le 22 janvier 1663.

98. PAC, C11A 2:214v, de Talon à Québec, le 11 novembre 1666.

99. PAC, AC, C11A 6:289v, de Versaills à de La Barre, le 31 juillet 1684.

100. PAC, AC, F1A 4:36, Estat de la depense que le Roy veut, le 1 mars 1688. The item concerns the payment of fifty livres for the subsistence of the Iroquois.

101. Leclerc, *Marquis de Denonville,* 199–200.

102. Leclerc, "Denonville et ses captifs Iroquois," 53–54. He is citing a letter written by Lamberville dated 23 June 1695 (Thwaites, ed., *JR* 64:243). Later, Leclerc took issue with Lamberville, citing official directives that the galley slaves be well treated (*Marquis de Denonville,* 195–96).

103. P.-G. Roy, "Les Iroquois sur les galères," 123–25.

104. PAC, C11A 10:220v, Frontenac au ministre, le 15 novembre 1689.

105. PAC, AC, F3 7:154v, "Explication de trois colliers que deux Iroquois portent aux . . . Indiens catholiques de Canada," le 9 février 1694.

106. PAC, AC, F3 6:401–1v, "Relation de ce qui c'est passé . . . ," le 27 novembre jusqu'au 15 octobre 1691.

107. O'Callaghan and Brodhead, eds., *NYCD* 4:208.

108. PAC, AC, B 57:639, Maurepas à Beauharnois, le 8 avril 1732.

109. Americans later were to have a similar experience when they attempted to impress hostile Amerindians by bringing their chiefs to Washington, where they were wined and dined, met the president, and had carefully arranged opportunities to see American military might. The reports of these delegates were not only often doubted by their fellow tribesmen, they were sometimes openly scoffed at, and the delegates themselves ran the risk of being regarded as traitors because they had associated with the Long Knives on their own ground. *See* Turner, *Red Men Calling.*

110. PAC, AC, B 71:54v, Maurepas à Guillot, le 2 mai 1740.

111. PAC, AC, C11B 23:74–74v, Du Quesnel à Maurepas, le 19 octobre 1741.

112. Laudonnière, *Histoire notable*, 27–31.

113. Mocquet, *Voyages en Afrique*, 94–95, 98.

114. Rochefort, *Histoire naturelle*, 203.

115. Thwaites, ed., *JR* 12:125; 37:77.

116. Ibid. 15:235.

117. Denys, *Description and Natural History*, 441. Sagard had observed: "Since they reckoned that the greatest captains in France were endowed with the greatest mind, and possessing so great a mind they alone could make the most complicated things, such as axes, knives, kettles, etc., they concluded therefore that the King, being the greatest captain and chief of them all, made the largest kettles, and regarding us in the capacity of captains they used sometimes to offer us kettles to mend" (Sagard, *Long Journey*, 183).

118. Thwaites, ed., *JR* 68:215. This reaction was reported of a visit in 1725.

119. Saint-Michel, *Voyages des isles Camercanes*, 143.

120. Ibid. Similarly, Sieur de La Borde reported that love of Amerindians for their own land was so great that individuals brought to France never wanted to stay there ("Relation des Caraïbes," in Justel, *Recueil de diverses Voyages*, 16).

121. Thwaites, ed., *JR* 31:247.

122. For example, their retort to the raillery of certain ladies when they appeared at the French court painted in their own Amerindian fashion. "They have no sense," they remarked of the ladies, "and their reproaches are unjust, because they themselves have their own faces all mottled with black, from which it appears they are always in mourning, judging by their manner of painting themselves" (Le Clercq, *New Relation*, 97–98).

123. A vivid impression of the cruelty and frequency of these events is provided by contemporary journals, such as *Journal d'un bourgeois de Paris; Chroniques du Roy Françoys Ier; Chronique parisienne;* and Galiot, *Inventaire*. *See also* Seward, *Prince of the Renaissance*, 185–86.

124. Mandrou, *Introduction à la France moderne*, 80.

125. Thwaites, ed., *JR* 7:43.

126. Kamen, *Iron Century*, 13.

127. Dent, "Historical Background of the French Renaissance." France counted about thirty-four inhabitants per square kilometer; the densest population in Europe was that of The Netherlands, with fifty-four inhabitants per square kilometer. According to Lewis, when Saint-Simon spoke of "all France," he was referring to between 50,000 and 60,000 people (*Splendid Century*, 77).

128. Mandrou, *Introduction à la France moderne*, 49.

129. Kamen, *Iron Century*, 29–30, 34–35.

130. This is the central thesis of Porchnev, *Soulevements. Also*, Mandrou, *Introduction à la France moderne*, 128; and Hale, *Renaissance Europe*, 27.

131. Kamen, *Iron Century*, 334.

132. Mandrou, *Introduction à la France moderne*, 363.

133. Kamen, *Iron Century*, 42.

134. Ibid., 314; Porchnev, *Soulevements*, 324.

135. Mandrou, *Introduction à la France moderne*, 42.

136. War was traditionally the principal activity of the nobles (Mandrou, *Introduction à la France moderne*, 148).

137. Thwaites, ed., *JR* 6:287–89.

11 Traders Pave the Way

1. *Commissions du Roi*, 4; PAC, AC, C11D 1:32–39, "Lettre par laquelle le roy fait son lieutenant-general le Sr De Monts au pays de l'acadie, 8 janvier 1603." For information on de Monts *see* Morse, ed., *Pierre du Gua* and *Dictionary of Canadian Biography* 1, s.v. "Gua de Monts, Pierre du."

2. Lancre, *Tableau de l'inconstance*, 30; Isasti, *Compendio Historial*, 164.

3. Thevet, "Grand Insulaire," 150, and *Cosmographie* (L'Huillier), 1016; Magini, *Histoire universelle*, 97; Carlysle's discourse in Hakluyt, *Principal Navigations* 8:144–46. Champlain implied in his writings that French trading ships had visited Tadoussac annually from about 1550 (Champlain, *Works* 2:117; 3:307).

4. *Description de l'Amerique et des parties d'icelle*, 2.

5. Wroth, *Verrazzano*, 134.

6. *Commissions du Roi*, 4. However, de Thou, in his *Histoire universelle*, referred to French voyages to Canada, "which had continued until 1611, without much profit" (14:336). Another observer noted that Champlain had returned to St. Malo from one of his New World voyages "in a good enough state, but better furnished with details of savage customes than with merchandize or booty" ([Faye], *Memoires*, 59). Amerindians had already long since incor-

porated European trade goods into their way of life. For instance, Whitbourne reported of Newfoundland Amerindians that they wore hats fashioned like those of Europeans and adorned with beadwork (*Discourse and Discovery*, conclusion).

7. Boyer, *Veritable Relation*, 367–68.

8. De Brosse, *Histoire des Navigations*, 372.

9. Supra, 168–69.

10. Denys, *Description and Natural History*, 446–51.

11. Thwaites, ed., *JR* 13:97; Yves, *Voyage dans le Nord du Brésil*, 70. Yves observed that Brazilians were also capable of capitalizing on situations for their own benefit.

12. Dalton, "Economic Theory and Primitive Society," 21; Heidenreich, *Huronia*, 223–27.

13. Waldseemüller, *Cosmographiae Introductio*, 98; Wood, *New England Prospect*, 69–70.

14. Chatelain, *Atlas historique* 6:85.

15. Biggar, *Early Trading Companies*, 129.

16. Wytfliet, *Histoire universelle*, pt.1, 123–24.

17. *Un festin de guerre*, 18; Jefferys, *Natural and Civil History*, 48, 68.

18. Bailey, *Conflict of European and Eastern Algonkian Cultures*, 9.

19. B.G. Hoffman, "Historical Ethnography," 21, 40.

20. Eckstorm, *Old John Neptune*, 75–76.

21. Thevet, *Cosmographie* (L'Huillier), 1010.

22. B.G. Hoffman, "Historical Ethnography," 31.

23. Thevet, "Grand Insulaire," 150v.

24. Georges Musset, "Manuscript de la second édition de *Les Rochelais à Terre Neuve*," Bibliothèque de La Rochelle, Ms 2566, pt. 2.

25. Bergeron, *Traicté de la navigation*, 122.

26. According to P.G. Adams, Ingram's report, for all its unreliability, was influential in the opening of the north. One who heard it, Sir Francis Walsingham, principal secretary to Queen Elizabeth I, later backed John Davis in his three unsuccessful attempts to find the North-West Passage; another, Richard Hakluyt, within seven years published the first edition of his *Principal Navigations* (in the second edition, 1598, he did not include Ingram's account); and a third, Sir Humphrey Gilbert, within months had sailed twice to North America, losing his life on the second attempt (*Travelers and Travel Liars*, 133–34).

27. Biggar, *Early Trading Companies*, 93. Presumably the pound referred to is English. Although equivalent values are difficult to determine with any degree of precision for the sixteenth and seventeenth centuries, at the beginning of the latter century a French livre approximately equalled an English shilling. As it took twenty shillings to make an English pound, this would have been a valuable cargo indeed.

28. Pring, "A Voyage," 350. A crown was worth five shillings.

29. Carlysle's discourse in Hakluyt, *Principal Navigations* 8:146.

30. Hakluyt, "Discourse on Western Planting," in Taylor, *Two Richard Hakluyts* 2:288.

31. Montchrestien, *Traicté*, 283.

32. Quinn, "Voyage of Bellenger," 328–43.

33. Ganong, *Crucial Maps*, 458–59.

34. Quinn, "Voyage of Bellenger," 332, 341.

35. Taylor, *Two Richard Hakluyts* 2:227, 278; Quinn, "Voyage of Bellenger," 335.

36. Biggar, *Early Trading Companies*, 34.

37. Le Blant, "Les Arrêts du Parlement," 41.

38. *Treizième tome du Mercure François*, 21–22.

39. Bailyn, *New England Merchants;* Moloney, *Fur Trade in New England;* W.I. Roberts, "Fur Trade of New England." As early as 1671, the French foresaw the demise of the fur trade and the rise of agriculture and the timber industry as principal commercial activities in New France (PAC, AC, C11A 3:199v, "Description du Canada," 1671).

40. La Salle, *La Salade*, fol. xxviii(verso).

41. Morse, ed., *Pierre du Gua*, 4.

42. Ibid., 7. Later, in 1627, the charter of the Company of New France also echoed the terms of Roberval's commission.

43. *Le Mercure François* (1611), 294–97. Champlain's subsequent reports also received considerable space. Historian de Thou also accorded these ventures an unusual attention in his prestigious *Histoire universelle* 14:329–36; 15:14–17, 60–67. *Le Mercure François* was the official annual chronicle of events, and was backed by Richelieu. It appeared until the 1630s, when it was superseded by *La Gazette de*

France. See Solomon, "The Gazette and Antistatist Propaganda," 1–17.

44. *Le Mercure François* (1611), 229–29v. The people had made a revelry out of hardship and had held banquets on the ice, which on one occasion cracked, trapping several persons "who in an instant were all carried out to sea by a current . . . they were on the ice as far as Lilo, three leagues below Antwerp, where they were rescued by boat."

45. Ibid., 294v. On another occasion, Marie de l'Incarnation referred to the portable bark houses that Amerindians erected very neatly and in which they preferred to stay during the winter; bark houses were not as cold as those the French erected in stone (Innis, *Select Documents*, 285–86).

46. For instance, when the Ursuline and Hospital Nuns had to wait for a favorable tide to go to Quebec, the party camped on shore in "cabins built in the manner of the savages" (Marie de Saint-Ignace, *Les Annales de l'Hôtel-Dieu*, 17–18). In 1640, a bark chapel erected at Tadoussac was provided with a European board door and padlock.

47. *Le Mercure François* (1611), 294v–95. According to de Laet, scurvy had been unknown in Europe before the discovery of the New World (*L'Histoire du Nouveau Monde*, 62).

48. Lescarbot, *Nova Francia*, 54; Thwaites, ed., *JR* 7:53.

49. Champlain, *Works* 1:206.

50. Ibid. 2:63. He was probably aware that Amerindians generally did not like salt, which they claimed shortened life. *See* Belleforest, *Cosmographie universelle* 2:2191; Du Tertre, *Histoire générale des Antilles* 2:389; Thevet, *New Found worlde*, 46, and *Cosmographie* (L'Huillier), 930. According to one report, Amerindians even regarded salt as poison (Dassié, *Description générale*, preface). Champlain may also have known of Sagard's observation that Amerindians were healthy without salt, which made him wonder if it were as necessary to keep alive, or even in health, as it was believed in Europe (Sagard, *Long Journey*, 80). *See also* Thwaites, ed., *JR* 7:45; 41:256; 44:279.

51. Champlain, *Works* 6:181. In the meantime, Purchas had reported in "Occurents in Newfoundland," 1612, that "turneps" were "as good to recover from the Scurvie as the Aneda tree to Jacques Cartier Company" (*Hakluytus Posthumus* 19:418). The identity of Cartier's "anedda" had been lost.

52. Pierre Boucher, *Histoire veritable*, 2, 4, 142. For other references to the "healthiness" of the New World, see supra, 13, 59. Some Frenchmen apparently did not like the spring break-up; Le Jeune referred to it as a "frightful spectacle" that caused destruction (Thwaites, ed., *JR* 5:185).

53. Montesquieu, *Oeuvres* 2:314.

54. J.E. Murray, "Fur Trade," 49.

55. *Le Dix-huictième tome du Mercure François*, 59. Earlier, explorers such as Verrazzano and Gomez had reported that this new land was certainly occupied because of the fires they had seen along the coast. These were probably also signals; for instance, when Emery de Caën's ships approached Tadoussac in 1632, Amerindians immediately made fires along the shore and sent two of their number in a canoe to greet the French (ibid., 59). It has also been speculated that these fires were the work of Amerindians clearing land for agriculture (Goad, "Relations of the European Invaders," 74).

56. For the effect of the fur trade on the Huron, *see* Trigger, "French Presence," and Heidenreich, *Huronia*, chap. 7.

57. Staden, *Histoire d'un pays*, 151. The Jesuits later accepted the same obligation in order to evangelize, particularly when "those customs are not unreasonable" (Thwaites, ed., *JR* 8:121; 40:167). However, there were limits: French missionaries at first would not willingly use wooden or bark dishes, nor would they wear scarlet porcupine quill work on the grounds that it was not proper (ibid. 32:285).

58. Champlain, *Works* 2:194. Cartier, when he kidnapped Donnacona, received strings of wampum from Stadaconans who came to say farewell to their chief; returning to Stadacona on his third voyage, Cartier again received gifts of wampum, this time from Donnacona's successor, Agona (Cartier, *Voyages*, 232–33, 252).

59. Trigger, "French Presence," 118.

60. B.G. Hoffman, "Historical Ethnography," 231–36.

61. This was a phenomenon that also occurred on the Prairies and on the West Coast. It seems to be characteristic of a contact situation marked first of all by trade, then by domination by the stronger culture.

62. *Juet's Journal*, 14, 28.

63. "Fleet's Journal," in Neill, ed., *Founders of Maryland*, 30–31. The English, for their part, reported that French traders were making incursions into territory the English regarded as theirs (Hamor, *A True Discourse*, 36–37).

64. "Narrative of a Journey into the Mohawk and Oneida Country," in Jameson, ed., *Narratives of New Netherland*,

149; Trelease, "Indian Relations and the Fur Trade in New Netherland," 101–2.

65. Thwaites, ed., *JR* 8:97.

66. Jameson, ed., *Narratives of New Netherland,* 149.

67. *Cinquiesme tome du Mercure François,* 166, reporting the petition of De Queiros to the king.

68. Ibid., 171.

69. Jean de Biencourt de Poutrincourt et de Saint Just, 1557–1615.

70. *La Continuation du Mercure François,* 528v.

71. Delanglez, *Frontenac and the Jesuits,* 49–50; Sigmund Diamond, "Le Canada français du XVII siècle," 327. The French were also motivated by the belief that Christianization would render Amerindians docile and less likely to revolt against European domination. During the seventeenth century, Morgan Godwin cited the loyalty of "praying Indians" to be to the English during the New England Amerindian wars (*The negro's and Indians advocate,* 130).

72. Champlain, *Works* 3:221; Sagard, *Long Journey,* 79.

73. *Le Dix-neufiesme tome du Mercure François,* 781–82. To the city-dwelling Mexica, Spanish ships had appeared at first to be "floating houses."

74. Thwaites, ed., *JR* 2:79.

75. Ibid. 13:127.

76. *Le Treizième tome du Mercure François,* 15.

77. Thwaites, ed., *JR* 4:197. This was later confirmed by Brébeuf (ibid. 8:95) and Chaumonot (ibid. 18:19).

78. Ibid. 5:93.

12 Missionaries Accept the Challenge

1. *Treizième tome du Mercure François,* 14–15.

2. Ibid., 32.

3. Thwaites, ed., *JR* 6:25; Lescarbot, *History of New France* 1:84.

4. Thwaites, ed., *JR* 8:15.

5. Ibid. 23:153.

6. Ibid. 28:53. The English, for their part, reported in detail the searching questions Amerindians asked of the missionaries concerning Christianity, e.g., Thorowgood, *Jewes in America,* 105ff.; Eliot, *Day-Breaking,* 4ff.

7. Thwaites, ed., *JR* 28:55; d'Avity, *Estates, Empires,* 319–21; Du Tertre, *Histoire générale des isles,* 459–62; Saint-Michel, *Voyage des isles Camercanes,* au lecteur; Rochefort, *Histoire naturelle,* 195; Ribier, *Lettres et mémoires,* 1:215.

8. Thwaites, ed., *JR* 9:87–91. The attitude of the French in this regard stood in contrast to that of the English, who in the seventeenth century were not nearly so convinced of the value of evangelizing Amerindians. The English approach is examined by James in "Puritan Missionary Endeavors."

9. Thwaites, ed., *JR* 9:91. Such opinions had long been heard in Spain. One argument in support of this was based on the fact that grapes were not indigenous to the New World, and indeed could be difficult if not impossible to grow. If God himself had not made it possible for Amerindians to make sacramental wine, he obviously was not concerned about them becoming Christian (Commager and Giordanetti, eds., *Was America a Mistake?* 30). *See also* Purchas, *Hakluytus Posthumus* 14:439.

10. Thwaites, ed., *JR* 2:89; 18:91–105.

11. Ibid. 1:165.

12. Ibid. 18:201; 31:241; 15:21. In one case, a Huron woman in good health died so quickly after baptism that her relatives expected gifts from the Jesuits in reparation (ibid. 15:105).

13. Ibid. 10:13–15; 14:13, 23, 65; 17:137; 20:25.

14. Ibid. 12:229.

15. D'Avity, *Estates, Empires,* 320. Biard thought that mutual incomprehension had been a factor in the baptisms performed by Jessé Fléché at Port Royal in 1610 (Campeau, *La Première Mission d'Acadie,* 139–40).

16. Traders had long since accepted the necessity of learning the languages of Amerindians if they wanted to do business with them (supra, Chapter 9, n. 2). When Jacques Savary, for instance, said it was necessary to know the language of the country in order to trade there, he was endorsing accepted practice (*Le Parfait Negociant* [Paris, 1679], 205). However, the point was not easily conceded by French officialdom. In the words of Talon, "it is true that we should have long since made them learn our language, and not forced the King's subjects to learning theirs in order to communicate with them" (PAC, AC, C11A 2:222, Talon à Colbert, le 13 novembre 1666).

17. Thwaites, ed., *JR* 14:125–27. The techniques used by Jesuits for evangelization were studied by Harvey, "Missionary Methods of the French Jesuits."

18. De Vaulx, *History of the Mission,* 70; Burrus, in Nelson, ed., *No Man is Alien,* 98.

19. Thwaites, ed., *JR* 6:243; 16:135. Sometimes Amerindian speeches lasted several hours (Hankins, "Oratory of the American Indians," 19).

20. Thwaites, ed., *JR* 5:63.

21. Ibid. 14:125; 39:49. *See also* Hanzeli, *Missionary Linguistics,* 53–54. Le Jeune did not include the Micmac because at that time it was the Capuchins and not the Jesuits who were working in Acadia.

22. Thwaites, ed., *JR* 9:89; Hennepin, *Louisiane,* 102. The first superior of l'Hôtel-Dieu at Quebec, Marie de Saint-Ignace, wrote that the study of Amerindian languages was "the greatest cross to bear in Canada," adding wistfully that she had never thought it would be necessary "to speak savage" when she had volunteered for service in Canada (Cahingt, ed., "Documents sur le Canada," 94).

23. Biard, for instance, was convinced of the Micmac that their "miserable" level of culture was due to their "perpetually undeveloped language" (Carayon, ed., *Première Mission des Jésuits,* 49; Thwaites, ed., *JR* 2:13). Such a belief had been fostered by misinformed reports from Brazil that the native languages were easy to learn and sterile in their content (Biet, *France Equinoxiale,* 394–95; Malherbe, *Lettres,* 258–59).

24. In Bressani's exact words, "so excellent a System" (Thwaites ed., *JR* 39:119).

25. Ibid. 10:119. The question of language also concerned Amerindians when it came to praying to the Christian God. According to one in New England, "Jesus Christ understood not what Indians spake in prayer, he had been used to heare English men pray and so could well understand them, but Indian language in prayer hee thought hee was not acquainted with it, but was a stranger to it, and therefore could not understand them" (Eliot, *Day-Breaking,* 5).

26. Thwaites, ed., *JR* 39:121.

27. Ibid. 14:11; 16:241; Hanzeli, *Missionary Linguistics,* 50. The importance Brébeuf attached to language studies is illustrated by his concern for the safety of his dictionary and "all that we have of the language" when the mission was threatened (Thwaites, ed., *JR* 15:65).

28. Thwaites, ed., *JR* 10:219; 18:23; 20:71.

29. Ibid. 6:289.

30. Ibid. 9:211; 43:169.

31. Biard's comments illustrate this attitude (ibid. 2:11–13; 3:193–97). Similar sentiments were expressed by Sagard, *Long Journey,* 73.

32. Thwaites, ed., *JR* 7:27.

33. Ibid. 8:133.

34. Ibid. 7:21–33; Hanzeli, *Missionary Linguistics,* 21, 56.

35. Thwaites, ed., *JR* 11:189–91; 28:65. Jesuits Jacques Frémin and Joseph Aubery were among those who adopted speaking mannerisms of Amerindian captains (ibid. 51:205; 66:177–79). On the mannerisms themselves, *see* ibid. 10:257.

36. Ibid. 70:99; 67:163; 10:213. A nineteenth-century missionary observed that an Amerindian in his speech "never uses an inappropriate word, an improper term or a bad construction. This is true even of children and familiar talk; the purity of expression is always preserved. Also, the manner by which they enliven all they say leaves no doubt that they understand the subtlety and beauty of their languages" (*Un festin de guerre,* 19).

37. Thwaites, ed., *JR* 10:213, 259. Amerindians found shocking the French habit of interrupting each other and even speaking two at once (Biet, *France Equinoxiale,* 367).

38. Thwaites, ed., *JR* 10:259; 15:195; 6:213. Earlier, the missionaries had not been so well treated in this regard, as Biard's well-known experiences testify (ibid. 2:11–13; 3:193–95).

39. Ibid. 6:243.

40. Ibid. 12:169.

41. For example, one who knew a certain route (ibid. 7:109).

42. Ibid. 15:157.

43. Some other references to Amerindian intelligence in Thwaites, ed., *JR* are 8:159–61; 15:79. Hennepin wondered how Amerindians could be so clear-sighted about mundane affairs, but so extravagant in their notions about religion (*A New Discovery* 2:65, 59).

44. Thwaites, ed., *JR* 5:33.

45. One was Bonaventure (Fortuné), who had been given to Champlain (supra, 219).

46. Thwaites, ed., *JR* 5:187.

47. Ibid. 10:31; 5:189; 11:221–37.

48. Le Clercq, *First Establishment* 1:172, 176; PAC, Archives National-Paris, ser. E: Arrêts du Conseil d'Etat du roi, vol. 72B, le 11 août 1622, fol. 191.

49. The Capuchins established a school for Amerindian children at Port Royal in 1632, which may have lasted until 1652 or perhaps until the English occupation of 1654 (Candide, *Pages glorieuses,* 141–43, 281ff., and "Une mission capucine en Acadie"). According to a personal communication from Marcel Trudel, these dates are impossible and would more likely be about 1644 (*see also* Trudel's *Initiation à la Nouvelle France,* 54).

50. Thwaites, ed., *JR* 9:219.

51. Ibid. 9:233.

52. Ibid. 9:283.

53. Ibid. 12:53.

54. Ibid. 16:187. In Brazil, Amerindians feared their children would not get enough to eat if they gave them to the French (Yves, *Voyage dans le Nord du Brésil,* 107).

55. Thwaites, ed., *JR* 5:219–21; 6:153–55. Later, however, Christianized Amerindians were reported punishing their children European-style (ibid. 52:249).

56. Ibid. 9:201. Champlain also had acquired three girls whom he had been forced to leave behind when driven out by the English in 1629.

57. Ibid. 9:103; 7:227.

58. Ibid. 9:107.

59. Supra, 217–20.

60. Marie de l'Incarnation, *Correspondance,* 95.

61. Thwaites, ed., *JR* 17:39; 31:269; 68:63; *Le Dix-neufiesme tome du Mercure François,* 849–50. Nearly two centuries later the métis Methodist missionary to the Mississauga, Peter Jones, noted in his diary that the "heathen Indian kneels only when he is resolved to become a Christian" (cited by D.B. Smith, "Mississauga," 209).

62. Thwaites, ed., *JR* 18:41.

63. Marie de l'Incarnation, *Correspondance,* 91.

64. Ibid., 801.

65. Adele de Sainte-Marie and Catherine de Saint-Thomas, *Les Ursulines* 1:409. The longest that an Amerindian girl stayed with the Ursulines at Quebec was ten years. While the Ursulines were making such efforts to encourage intermarriage, the English in Virginia passed laws forbidding it (Horton, "Relations in Virginia," 43).

66. Marie de l'Incarnation, *Correspondance,* 718–20.

67. Ibid., 995.

68. Adele de Sainte-Marie and Catherine de Saint-Thomas, *Les Ursulines* 1:80.

69. Ibid. 1:210.

70. Marie de l'Incarnation, *Correspondance,* 828–29. The Jesuits also found educating Amerindians to be unexpectedly expensive (Thwaites, ed., *JR* 12:113–15).

71. Thwaites, ed., *JR* 11:233. Such conversions were also complicated by the problem of finding suitable wives for the neophytes (ibid. 15:125).

72. Ibid. 10:15; 15:23–25; 17:33.

73. Ibid. 15:109.

74. "Captain" was the term by which the French designated the headman; it roughly corresponded to the Spanish "cacique." Both these designations recognized the fact that Amerindian headmen were not "chiefs" in the European sense.

75. Thwaites, ed., *JR* 15:119. The next year, 1639, the fathers moved their residence from Ihonatiria to Teanaustayé, "the most important of Huron villages" (ibid. 17:11, 59).

76. Ibid. 18:79.

77. Slaves were prisoners of war who were kept in servitude. However, slavery as practised by Amerindians was not synonymous with slavery as practised by Europeans. A major difference was that adoption into the tribe was possible.

78. Marie de Saint-Ignace, *Les Annales de l'Hôtel-Dieu,* 25; Thwaites, ed., *JR* 6:135. Such practices were a necessity of migratory life, and were not followed by sedentary peoples. *See* Virgil J. Vogel, *American Indian Medicine* (Norman, Okla.: University of Oklahoma Press, 1970).

79. Marie de Saint-Ignace, *Les Annales de l'Hôtel-Dieu,* 31. This reflected the general initial reaction among the French to smoked meat. *See* Thwaites, ed., *JR* 5:61; Yves, *Suitte de l'histoire,* 255. Occasionally, necessity caused them to admit that Amerindian food was not so bad, "not even their smoked fish" (Thwaites, ed., *JR* 10:93). *See also* supra, Chapter 4, n. 25.

80. Marie de Saint-Ignace, *Les Annales de l'Hôtel-Dieu,* 31–32. Yves, in describing the improvement in the Tupinambá since their association with the French, noted the transformation of the "stink of smoke," which penetrated and clung to everything, into "good odors" (*Suitte de l'histoire,* 255). Marie de l'Incarnation had a similar reaction (*Ecrits spirituels* 2:370). This odor can still elicit such a reaction

among non-Amerindians today. For most city-dwellers, the only place where they might encounter it would be in shops stocking smoke-tanned Amerindian leather goods.

81. This sentiment was shared by the Jesuits (Thwaites, ed., *JR* 8:129; 19:21).

82. Marie de Saint-Ignace, *Les Annales de l'Hôtel-Dieu,* 95–96; also, Juchereau de la Ferté, *Histoire de l'Hôtel Dieu,* 108–9.

83. Marie de Saint-Ignace, *Les Annales de l'Hôtel-Dieu,* 96. Apparently the Spanish had little better success in attracting native girls into religious orders. Bishop Palafox attributed this to lack of dowries (*L'Indien,* 9). Others held that the difficulties were more profound (Ricard, *Spiritual Conquest of Mexico,* 231).

84. *Dictionary of Canadian Biography,* s.v. "Saint-Etienne de la Tour, Charles de."

85. Ricard, *Spiritual Conquest of Mexico,* 230–31.

86. Hanke, in Chiapelli, ed., *First Images* 1:370. Oddly enough, Protestants, while less eager than Catholics during the sixteenth and seventeenth centuries to undertake missionary work, were more willing to ordain Amerindians, and did so very early. *See* John Eliot, *A brief narrative of the progress of the Gospel among the Indians in New-England* (London, 1671). However, New England Puritans resisted the idea of accepting Amerindians into full membership in their church. *See* James, "Puritan Missionary Endeavors."

87. Gómara, *Voyages et conquestes,* 142v.

88. Ricard, *Spiritual Conquest of Mexico,* 235, 292–95. This was a policy which was to have serious consequences as it caused division in the Mexican church, symbolized by the two Virgins, the Amerindian Virgen de Guadelupe and the Spanish Virgen de los Remedios.

89. Thwaites, ed., *JR* 22:43–45; 52:229–43; 62:125–27. Marie de l'Incarnation felt that in general, converted Amerindians were more devout than the French (Nish, ed., *Le Régime français,* 38).

90. Saint-Vallier, *Estat present de l'Eglise,* 161–62.

91. Thwaites, ed., *JR* 27:67, 311; 62:239–41; 55:277.

92. Ibid. 50:117.

93. Ibid. 27:67–69; 29:275–77; 35:247–49. The Jesuits were particularly pleased with Joseph Chihwatenhwa, whom they described as "a leavening" who raised the mass of the new church in Huronia (ibid. 17:47). *See also Dictionary of Canadian Biography* 1, s.v. "Chihwatenhwa."

94. Reports from Brazil had it that the natives, under the guidance of the Jesuits, were abandoning their vagabond life and organizing themselves into villages and towns, and even adopting laws and forming republics (Wytfliet, *Histoire universelle,* pt. 1:86).

95. "Description du Canada," written by a missionary in 1671 (PAC, AC, C11A 3:210–10v). In Amerindian metaphor, the Algonquin were roving deer, while the French were elk (moose) who did not stray far in their browsing (Thwaites, ed., *JR* 29:221).

96. Letter to François Cardinal de Joyeuse, in Jouve, *Les Franciscains,* 67. It was a vision that was opposed by the fur trading interests, on the grounds that it would be detrimental to their business (Le Clercq, *First Establishment* 1:110–11).

97. Thwaites, ed., *JR* 6:151.

98. Ibid. 8:57.

99. Ibid. 16:75. Also, "Lettre de Père Barthelemy Vimont à Sillery, 1er septembre 1640," reproduced in Cahingt, ed., "Documents sur le Canada," 95–101.

100. Gérin, "La seigneurie de Sillery," 75–115.

101. The Recollets, one of the Franciscan orders, did not endorse segregation of Amerindians from French.

102. Thwaites, ed., *JR* 11:237.

103. Gómara, *Voyages et conquestes,* 356v–57; Yves, *Suitte de l'histoire,* 243–54; Surius, *Histoire ou commentaires,* 320v.

104. Thwaites, ed., *JR* 3:101–3; 2:23, 79. The point was also made by Gaya, *Cérémonies nuptiales,* 182–83.

105. Chaulmer, *Nouveau Monde,* 9.

106. Thwaites, ed., *JR* 56:215–17. When an Iroquois protested to Chaumonot that without polygyny the Amerindian population would not grow, the latter replied by using the example of the French, whom he said were more numerous than Amerindians even though monogamous (Carayon, ed., *Chaumonot,* 55).

107. Thwaites, ed., *JR* 12:165.

108. Ibid. 25:27.

109. Trigger, "Jesuits and the Fur Trade," 44.

110. Thwaites, ed., *JR* 25:269–71; 37:221.

111. Ibid. 37:221. Bailey discusses the dislocations caused to Amerindian life by the missionaries' insistence on monogamy in "Social Revolution," 273–74.

112. Thwaites, ed., *JR* 51:235. In eighteenth-century Europe,

free love was known as "l'amour à la sauvage" (Chinard, *Rêve,* 166).

113. Hennepin, *A New Discovery* 2:70. One very sick woman refused baptism when told she would not be able to separate from her husband afterward (ibid. 13:141).

114. Concerning the coureurs-de-bois, Sagard, *Long Journey,* 134; on envoys in general, Seguin, "La vie libertine en Nouvelle France," 43, 483. Seguin's thesis was published that same year by Leméac in Montreal. *See also* Berquen, *Les merveilles des Indes,* 90.

115. Thwaites, ed., *JR* 60:289.

116. Ibid. 17:93. Later, a missionary reported with satisfaction that he had been able to convoke a council of the Five Nations by ringing a bell (ibid. 47:77).

117. Ibid. 23:211.

118. Ibid. 41:99–101.

119. Ibid. 9:231.

120. Ibid. 12:121.

121. Ibid. Hennepin reported, "the Savages concern themselves very little with French civilities, and mock us when we try to consider theirs." However, he later observed that those who had relations with the French followed the latter's custom of exchanging greetings (*Louisiane,* 51, 56).

122. Thwaites, ed., *JR* 29:127–29. This recalls an episode in Brazil, when several Amerindians went to some lengths to be like the French. They learned to greet each other, kiss hands, say "good day and good bye"; to sit at table, take a napkin, and "take meat with three fingers"; in brief, they had mastered French civilities so well they gave the impression of having lived all their lives in France (Yves, *Voyage dans le Nord du Brésil,* 64). To those who protested that such things were not good enough, Yves replied that in time these people would become fully domesticated and civilized. Razilly, one of the leaders of the colonizing expedition which Yves had accompanied, told Brazilians he was establishing French laws in their country; that he would like the people to continue wearing their hair long, as he approved of that fashion; but would prefer it if they did not pierce their faces. However, he would not force the issue (*Troisième tome du Mercure François,* 175). At other times the missionaries insisted on Christian customs, as at burials. When the family of Membertou prepared to bury the great leader in their traditional manner, Poutrincourt sent an armed guard to demand the body for Christian burial (Carayon, ed., *Première Mission des Jésuites,* 28–29). On a more frivolous side, Lescarbot maintained that Amerindians were the losers for not knowing the joys of kissing (*History of New France* 2:208).

123. Thwaites, ed., *JR* 15:47–49. Objects could also come under suspicion, particularly during a crisis of the proportions of the 1634–40 epidemic. Thus one village rejected trade kettles as being the source of the contagion (ibid. 15:21), while another saw its lack of kettles as the cause (ibid. 13:233).

124. Some of the earliest studies of these effects on eastern Canadian Amerindians are the work of Bailey (*Conflict;* "Social Revolution").

125. Bailey, "Social Revolution," 274; Thwaites, ed., *JR* 18:87.

126. Sagard, *Histoire du Canada* 2:391.

127. Eliade, *Shamanism,* xviii.

128. Hennepin, *A New Discovery* 2:69.

129. Eliot, *Day-Breaking,* 22.

130. Hallowell, *Culture and Experience,* 308.

131. PAC, AC, C11A 2:317v, Talon à Colbert, le 25 août 1667.

132. Marquis Alexandre de Prouville de Tracy was Lieutenant-General in America (1663–67); Daniel Rémy de Courcelle, Governor-General of New France (1665–72). Up until that point the French had marched as allies of Amerindians, with the possible exception of the d'Aulnay-La Tour feud in Acadia, 1635–50. A contemporary report of the departure of the Carignan-Salières regiment for Canada to fight the Iroquois is in *Recueil des Gazettes nouvelles,* 511. In at least one case in the West Indies, the pattern of alliance was the contrary of that of New France, as when the French and the English joined forces against the Caribs (Crouse, *French Pioneers,* 17).

13 Conclusion

1. Du Perier, *Les amours de Pistion,* 6–7. The novel, first published in 1601, was reprinted in 1602 and 1606.

2. White, *The Earliest French Play About America.* In 1973 the University of Ottawa republished *Acoubar* in a critical edition edited by Romeo Arbour.

3. Cõbes, *Coppie d'une lettre,* 10.

4. *Collection de manuscrits* 1:175, "Instructions pour le Sieur de Courcelle au sujet des indiens, 1665."

5. Stanley, "The First Indian 'Reserves' in Canada," 209–10.

6. Vaumas, *L'Eveil missionnaire,* 47. This was the Catholic ideal. During the sixteenth and seventeenth centuries, Protestants were not nearly so certain that such a goal was feasible (Visme, *Précurseurs de l'idée missionnaire*).

7. Thwaites, ed., *JR* 7:257. Because of rivalry with Spain and the fact that the Portuguese did not wish the presence of the French in the Orient, France's missionary aspirations focused on Canada (Vaumas, *L'Eveil missionnaire,* 153).

8. Thwaites, ed., *JR* 13:171; 8:119. Biard reported a similar reaction on the part of the Micmac (ibid. 3:123).

9. Ibid. 6:213; 8:119, 145–47; 10:19; 11:9.

10. Ibid. 21:89.

11. For example, the tenor of Louis XIV's instructions to Courcelle in 1665 was that the governor should strive to make the Amerindians consider it to their advantage to trade with the French (*Collection de manuscrits* 1:175).

12. Dickason, "Louisbourg and the Indians," 155–60. Also, O'Callaghan and Broadhead, eds., *NYCD* 4:206–11, London Document 10, "Mr. Nelson's Memorial about the state of the Northern Colonies in America," 24 September 1696.

13. Hallowell studied the impact of Amerindian culture on the United States in "The Backwash of the Frontier," 229–58.

14. Malouet, *Memoires* 1:151.

15. Ibid. 151–55 passim.

Appendix 1

1. Winsor, *Narrative and Critical History* 4:10; Biggar, *Early Trading Companies,* 175.

2. Langenes, *Thrésor,* 190.

3. Thevet, *Cosmographie* (L'Huillier) 2:1010; idem, "Grand Insulaire," 152v.

4. Charlevoix, *History* 1:113.

5. Belleforest, *Cosmographie universelle* 2:2185.

6. Ibid., 2190. Biggar examines the question of Canada's name and location in Cartier, *Voyages,* 103–5 n. 69.

7. Cartier, *Voyages,* 119.

8. Ballard, "Indian Mode of Applying Names," 447–48.

9. B.G. Hoffman, "Ancient Tribes Revisited," 25.

10. *American Historical Association Report for 1905,* 100.

11. Lescarbot, *History of New France* 2:25–26.

12. Jefferys, *Natural and Civil History,* 1.

13. Patterson, "Portuguese on the Northeast Coast of America," 158–59.

14. Thevet, "Grand Insulaire," 152v.

15. Cartier, *Voyages,* 104–5.

16. Sauer, *Sixteenth Century America,* 15.

Select Bibliography

This bibliography lists a selection of works consulted during the preparation of this book. While most of the titles are cited in the body of the work, some are not, particularly reference works. Conversely, some works referred to only incidentally have not been listed; full bibliographic information about these titles is given in the appropriate note. Classification into primary and secondary sources has been done with reference to the period when the material was written or otherwise prepared. First-hand accounts as well as those reasonably contemporary with topics under consideration are considered primary; all others, secondary. This criterion, of course, has little or no connection with publication dates, and also means that the works of geographers and cartographers are often listed under primary sources, even though they seldom dealt with their subjects at first hand. This is true as well for the works of some chroniclers, such as Pietro Martire d'Anghiera and Francisco López de Gómara, who never visited the New World, but who knew people who did, such as Columbus and Cortés.

As for author's names, national practices have generally been followed, although there are variations in customary usage, both nationally and internationally. In such cases, as well as those of complex names, cross-referencing has been used. Anonymous works are listed alphabetically under titles.

Manuscript Sources

Public Archives of Canada. Ottawa, Canada

MG 1: Archives des Colonies

Série B. Lettres envoyées, vols. 57, and 76
Série C11A. Correspondance générale, Canada, vols. 1, 2, 3, 4, 6, 7, 10, 122
Série C11B. Correspondance générale, Ile Royale, vol. 23
Série C11D. Correspondance générale, Acadie, vol. 1
Série F1A. Fonds des colonies, vol. 4
Série F3. Collection Moreau de Saint-Méry, vols. 6, 7

MG 3: Archives Nationales–Paris

Série E. Arrêts du Conseil d'Etat du roi, vol. 72B

MG 7: Bibliothèques de Paris

Bibliothèque Nationale, Departement de Manuscrits Fonds français:

Ms 15452, "Le Grand Insulaire et Pilotage," par André Thevet;

Ms 24225, "Histoire naturelle, ou la fidelle recherche du tout ce qu'il y a de rare dans les Indes occidentals," par Louis Nicholas

MG 17: Archives de la Province de Paris de la Compagnie de Jésus

Fonds Canada

National Map Collection

V_1/202–1965. Historic Cape Breton, compiled and drawn by George T. Bates

Bibliothèque de La Rochelle. La Rochelle, France
Ms 2556, Manuscrit de la seconde édition de *Les Rochelais à Terre Neuve,* part II, par Georges Musset

Bibliothèque Nationale. Paris, France. Departement de Manuscrits

Ms 1382, "Premier livre de la description de tous les ports de mer de lunivers," par Jehan Mallart. Verses based on Jean Alfonce's *Voyages Avantureux.*

Ms 150, "Les premiers oeuvres," par Jacques Devaulx, Havre de Grace, 1583. Ms sur velin. Cartes marines

II Primary Sources

Abbeville, Claude d'. (*See* Claude (d'Abbeville)).

Acosta, José de. *De natura Novi Orbis libri duo, et de promulgatione Evangelii, apud barbaros... sive De procuranda Indorum salute, libri sex.* Salamanca: Guillelmum Foquel, 1589.

———. *Histoire naturelle et moralle des Indes, tant Orientalles qu'Occidentalles.* Translated by Robert Regnault. Paris: Marc Orry, 1598.

———. *The Naturall and Morall Historie of the East and West Indies.* Translated by Edward Grimstone. London: V. Sims for E. Blount and W. Aspley, 1604.

Agrippa von Nettesheim, Heinrich Cornelius. *Of the vanitie and uncertaintie of artes and sciences.* Englished by James Sandford. London: Henry Wykes, 1569.

Ailly, Pierre, Cardinal d'. *Ymago mundi de Pierre d'Ailly.* 3 vols. Edited by Edmond Joseph Pierre Buron. Paris: Maisonneuve, 1930–31.

Albert le Grand (Albertus Magnus). *Le Livre d'Albert le Grand lequel traite des merveilles du monde.* Lyon: J. Hugudan, 1616.

Alexander, Sir William. *Sir William Alexander and American Colonization.* Boston: Prince Society, 1873.

Aleyrac, Jean-Baptiste d'. *Avantures militaires au XVIIIe siècle, d'après les mémoires de Jean-Baptiste d'Aleyrac (1737–1796).* Edited by Charles Coste. Paris: Editions Berger-Levrault, 1935.

Alfonce, Jean (Jean Fonteneau). "La Cosmographie avec l'espère et régime du soleil et du nord." *Recueil de voyages et de documents pour servir à l'histoire de la géographie depuis le XIIIe jusqu'à la fin du XVIe siècle.* Publiée sous la direction de Ch. Schefer, membre de l'Institut, et Henri Cordier. Paris: Ernest Leroux, 1904.

———. *Les Voyages avantureux du Capitaine Ian Alfonce, Sainctongeois.* Poitiers: Ian de Marnef, 1559.

L'Amérique historique–Recueil des cartes. S.l., 1638.

Anghiera, Pietro Martire d'. *See* Martire d'Anghiera, Pietro.

Apianus (Benewitz), Petrus. *Cosmographie ou description des quatre parties du Monde, contenant la situation, Division, & Estendue de chacune Region & Province d'icelles, Escrite en Latin par Pierre Apian. Corrigée & augmentée par Gemma Frison, excellent Geographe & Mathematicien, avec plusieurs autres Traitez concernans la mesme matiere, composez par le susdit Gemma Frison & autres Autheurs nouvellement traduits en langue Françoise.* Antwerp: Jean Bellere, 1581.

Arber, Edward, ed. *The First Three English Books on America.* Birmingham: Turnbull & Spears (Edinburgh), 1885.

———. *A Transcript of the Registers of the Company of Stationers of London, 1554–1640.* 5 vols. London: Privately printed, 1875–94.

Aristotle. *Nicomachean Ethics.* Translated by H. Rackham. London: Heinemann, 1968.

Arsène (de Paris). *Dernière lettre du Reverend Père Arsène de Paris estant de present en l'Inde Occidentale, en la coste du Brésil, en une isle appelée Maragnan. Qu'il envoye au Reverend Père Provincial des Capucins de la Province de Paris.* Paris: Jean Nigaud, 1613.

Augustine, Aurelius. *The City of God against the Pagans.* 7 vols. Translated by George E. McCracken et al. London: Heinemann, 1957.

Avity, Pierre d', Seigneur de Montmartin. *Description générale de l'Amérique, troisième partie du Monde....* Paris: Claude Sonnius, 1637.

———. *The Estates, Empires & Principallities of the World.* Translated by Edward Grimstone. London: A. Islip for H. Lownes and I. Bill, 1615.

———. *Les Estats, empires et principautez du Monde....* Paris: P. Chevalier, 1619.

Barbier, Edmond-Jean-François. *Journal historique et anecdotique du règne de Louis XV.* 4 vols. Paris: Renouard, 1847–56.

Barcia Carballido y Zúñiga, Andrés González de. *Barcia's Chronological History of the Continent of Florida Containing the Discoveries and Principal Events which came to Pass in this Vast Kingdom.* Translated by Anthony Kerrigan. Gainesville: University of Florida Press, 1951. (Originally published in Madrid, 1723.)

Barré, Nicolas. *Copie de quelques lettres sur la navigation du Chevallier de Villegaignon es terres de l'Amerique oultre l'Aequinoctial, jusques soubz le tropique de Capricorne: côtenant sommairement les fortunes encourues en ce voyage....* Paris: Martin le Jeune, 1557.

Baudier, Michel. *Histoire générale de la religion des Turcs.* Paris: Claude Cramoisy, 1625.

Baugy, Chevalier de. *See* Serrigny, Ernest, Chevalier de Baugy.

Baxter, James Phinney, ed. *Sir Ferdinando Gorges and his Province of Maine.* 3 vols. Boston: Prince Society, 1890.

Belknap, Jeremy. *A discourse intended to commemorate the discovery of America by Christopher Columbus....*Boston: Belknap and Hall, 1792.

Belleforest, François de, and Sebastian Münster. *La Cosmographie universelle de tout le monde.* 2 vols. Paris: M. Sonnius, 1575.

Belon de Mans, Pierre. *Les Observations de plusieurs singularités et choses memorables, trouvées en Grèce, Asie, Judée, Egypte, Arabie, & autre pays estranges....* Paris: Gilles Corrozet, 1553.

Bembo, Pietro [pseud.?] *L'Histoire du Nouveau Monde descouvert par les Portugaloys.* Lyon: Ian d'Ogerolles, 1556.

Benzoni, Girolamo. *Histoire nouvelle du Nouveau Monde... extraite de l'Italien de M. Hierosme Benzoni, Milanois, qui ha voyagé XIIII ans en ces pays-la... enrichie de plusieurs discours & choses digne de memoire, Par M. Urbain Chauveton.* Geneva: Eustace Vignon, 1579. (First published Venice, 1565.)

———. *History of the New World....* Translated and edited by Rear-Admiral W. H. Smyth. London: Hakluyt Society, 1857.

Bergeron, Pierre de. *Traicté de la navigation et des voyages de descouverte & Conqueste modernes, & principalement des François.* Paris: Jean de Heuqueville et M. Soly, 1629.

Berquen, Robert de. *Les Merveilles des Indes Orientales et Occidentales, ou nouveau traitté des Pierres precieuses & des Perles. ...* Paris: C. Lambin, 1669.

Bertius (de Bert), Petrus. *Description d'Amerique, qui est le nouveau monde, tirée des "Tableaux geographiques" de Petrus Bertius.* Amsterdam: Emmanuel Colin, 1622.

Bertrand, Sieur. *Lettre missive touchant la conversion et baptesme du grand Sagamos de la Nouvelle Frãce, qui en estoit auparavant l'arrivée de François le chef & souverain.... Envoyée du Port Royal de la nouvelle France au Sr de la Tronchaie, dattée du 28 juin 1610.* Paris: J. Regnoul, 1610.

Biencourt, Jean de, Sieur de Poutrincourt, Baron de Saint-Just. *Factum du procez entre messire Jean de Biencourt... et Pierre Biard, Evemond Massé et consorts....* *S.l.*, 1613. (Reprint ed. edited by Gabriel Marcel. Paris: 1887.)

Biet, Antoine. *Voyage de la France Equinoxiale en l'isle de Cayenne, entrepris par les François en l'année 1652.* Paris: François Clouzier, 1664.

Blaeu, Willem Janszoon. *Le Theatre du Monde, ou Nouvel Atlas ... mis en lumière par Guillaume et Jean Blaeu.* 5 vols. Amsterdam: G. et J. Blaeu, 1635–54.

Blumenbach, Johann Friedrich. *The Anthropological Treatises of Johann Friedrich Blumenbach.* Translated and edited by Thomas Bendyshe. London: Longman, 1865.

Bodin, Jean. *Method for the Easy Comprehension of History.* Edited and translated by Beatrice Reynolds. New York: Columbia University Press, 1945.

———. *Oeuvres philosophiques de Jean Bodin.* 3 vols. Edited by Pierre Mesnard. Paris: Presses Universitaires de France, 1951.

———. *Les Paradoxes du Seigneur de Malestroict... avec la responce de Jean Bodin....* Paris: Jacques Du Puys, 1578.

———. *Les Six Livres de la Republique.* Paris: Jacques Du Puys, 1577.

———. *Les Six Livres de la Republique.* Lyon: Jacques Du Puys, 1579.

Boem, Johann. *Recueil de diverses histoires touchant les situations de toutes regions & pays contenuz es trois parties du monde, avec les particulieres moeurs, loix, & ceremonies de toutes nations & peuples y habitans. Nouvellement traduict de Latin en Francoys.* Antwerp: Antoine de Goys, 1540.

———. *Recueil de diverses histoires touchant les situations....* Paris, 1542.

———. *Le Recueil des païs selon leur situation, avec les moeurs, loix et cérémonies d'iceux....* Paris: Thibout, 1558.

Boucher, Pierre. *Histoire veritable et naturelle des moeurs et productions du pays de la Nouvelle France, vulgairement dite le Canada.* Paris: Florentin Lambert, 1664. (Facsimile ed., La Société Historique de Boucherville, 1964.)

Bourne, William. *A booke called the Treasure for traveilers....* London: T. Woodcocke, 1578.

Boyer, Paul, Sieur de Petit-Puy. *Veritable Relation de tout ce qui s'est fait et passé au voyage que Monsieur de Brétigny fit à l'Amerique Occidentale.* Paris: Pierre Rocolet, 1654.

Bradford, William. *Of Plymouth Plantation.* New York: Capricorn Books, 1962.

Brant, Sebastian. *La Nef des folz du monde.* Paris: Manstener & de Marnef, 1497.

———. *The shyppe of fooles.* Translated by Henry Watson. London: Wynkyn de Worde, 1509.

Bréard, Charles, ed. *Documents relatifs à la marine nor mande au XVIe et XVIIe siècle....* Rouen: A. Lestringant, 1889.

———. *Journal du corsaire Jean Doublet de Honfleur.* Paris: Charavay Frères, 1883.

———. *Mémoires et documents relatifs aux ports de Normandie (Le Havre, Fécamp, Honfleur).* Rouen: E. Cagniard, 1892.

Bref recueil de l'affliction et dispersion de l'Eglise des fideles au pays du Brésil, partie de l'Amerique Australe. S.l., 1565.

Brosse, Charles de. *Histoire des Navigations aux terres australes. . . .* 2 vols. Paris: Durand, 1756.

Buno, Johann. *Descriptio orbis terrarum veteribus et cogniti et incogniti, In duobus typis exhibita.* Leipzig: J. H. Klosium, 1708.

Burton, Robert [Nathaniel Crouch]. *The Anatomy of Melancholy.* Edited by Floyd Dell and Paul Jordan-Smith. New York: Tudor, 1955.

Burke, Edmund. *An Account of the European Settlements in America.* 2 vols. London: J. Dodsley, 1777. (Reprint ed., New York: Arno Press, 1972.)

Burney Collection of Newspapers. British Museum.

Burrage, Henry Sweetser, ed. *Early English and French Voyages, chiefly from Hakluyt, 1534–1608.* New York: Scribner's, 1906.

Calendar of State Papers, Colonial Series, America and West Indies, 27 October 1697 – 31 December 1698. London: His Majesty's Stationery Office, 1905.

Campeau, Lucien. *La Première Mission d'Acadie (1602–1616) (Momumenta Nova Franciae).* Quebec: Les Presses de l'Université de Laval, 1967

Carayon, Auguste, ed. *Le P. Pierre Chaumonot, de la Compagnie de Jésus, autobiographie et pièces inédites.* Poitiers: Henri Oudin, 1869.

———. *Première Mission des Jésuites au Canada.* Paris: L'Ecureux, 1864. (Vol. 12 of *Documents inédits concernant la Compagnie de Jésus,* 23 vols. [Poitiers and Paris: Henri Oudin, 1863–86].)

Cardano, Girolamo. *De Rerum Varietate. . . . S.l.,* 1556.

Cartes diverses de l'Amérique gravée au XVIIe et au XVIIIe siecles. Paris, *s.d.*

Cartier, Jacques. *Bref récit et succincte narration de la navigation faicte es ysles de Canada, Hochelaga & Saguenay.* Paris: Ponce Roffet *dit* Faucher & Antoine le Clerc frères, 1545.

———. *A Collection of Documents Relating to Jacques Cartier and the Sieur de Roberval.* Edited by Henry Percival Biggar. Ottawa: Public Archives of Canada, 1930.

———. *Discours du voyage fait par le capitaine Jacques Cartier aux Terres-Neufves de Canadas, Norembergue, Hochelage, Labrador, et pays adjacents, dite Nouvelle France; avec particulières moeurs, langage, et ceremonie des habitans d'icelle.* Rouen: R. Du Petit Val, 1598.

———. *Jacques Cartier: documents nouveaux.* Edited by Frédéric Joüon des Longrais. Paris: Alphonse Picard, 1888.

———. *Relation originale du voyage de Jacques Cartier au Canada en 1534. . . .* Edited by H. Michelant and Alfred Ramé. Paris: Librairie Tross, 1867.

———. *The Voyages of Jacques Cartier.* Edited by Henry Percival Biggar. Ottawa: Acland, 1924.

———. *Voyage de Jacques Cartier au Canada en 1534. . . .* Edited by H. H. Michelant and Alfred Ramé. Paris: Librairie Tross, 1865.

Cayet, Pierre-Victor-Palma. *Chronologie septenaire de l'Histoire de la Paix entre les Roys de France et d'Espagne.* 2 vols. Paris: J. Richer, 1605.

C'est la deduction du somptueux ordre plaisantz spectacles et magnifigues theatres dresses et exhibes par les citoyens de Rouen ville Metropolitaine du pays de Normandie, A la sacrée Majesté du Treschristian Roy de France, Henry Second leur soverain Seigneur, Et à Tresillustre dame, ma Dame Katharine de Medicis, La Royne son espouse, lors de leur triumphant joyeulx & nouvelle advenement en icelle ville. . . . Rouen: Robert le Hoy et Jehan dictz du Gord, 1551.

Champlain, Samuel de. *The Works of Samuel de Champlain.* 6 vols. Edited by Henry P. Biggar. Toronto: The Champlain Society, 1922–36. (Reprint ed., Toronto: University of Toronto Press, 1971.)

Chapelain, Jean. *Lettres de Jean Chapelain de l'Academie Française.* 2 vols. Edited by Ph. Tamizey de Larroque *(Documents sur l'histoire de la France,* ser. 2). Paris: Imprimerie Nationale, 1880–83.

Charlevoix, Pierre-François-Xavier. *Histoire et description générale de la Nouvelle France. Avec le Journal historique d'un voyage fait par ordre du roi dans l'Amerique septentrionale.* 6 vols. Paris: Nyon fils, 1744.

———. *History and General Description of New France.* 6 vols. Translated and edited by John Gilmary Shea. New York: J. G. Shea, 1866–72.

Charron, Pierre. *De la Sagesse.* Bordeaux: S. Millanges, 1601. (Reprint ed., Paris: Didot, 1789.)

———. *Les Trois Vérités.* Bordeaux: S. Millanges, 1595.

Chatelain, Henri Abraham. *Atlas historique, ou Nouvelle introduction à l'histoire, à la chronologie & à la géographie ancienne & moderne. . . . Avec des dissertations sur l'histoire de chaque etat par M. [Nicholas] Gueudeville. . . .* 7 vols. Amsterdam: L'Honoré & Chatelain, 1718–32.

Chaulmer, Charles. *Le Nouveau Monde ou l'Amerique chrétienne. . . .* Paris: By the author and S. Piget, 1659.

Chauveton, Urbain. *See* Girolamo Benzoni and Nicolas Le Challeux.

Chevillard, André. *Desseins de son Eminence de cardinal Richelieu pour l'Amerique, ce qui s'y est passé de plus remarquable depuis l'établissement des colonies, et un ample traité du naturel, de la religion et des moeurs des Indiens insulaires de la Terre-Ferme.* Rennes: J. Durand, *s.d.*

Child, Sir Josiah. *A New Discourse of trade, wherein is recommended several weighty points relating to Companies of merchants, the act of navigation, naturalization of strangers and our woolen manufacturers, the ballance of trade....* 2d ed., London: S. Crouch, 1694.

———. *Select tracts relating to colonies....* London: J. Robert, n.d.

Chronique parisienne (1522 à 1535). Edited by Fernand Bournon, in *Mémoires de la Société de l'Histoire de Paris et de l'Isle de France.* Vol. 22 (1895).

Chroniques du Roy Françoys Ier (1515 à 1542). Edited by G. Guiffrey. Paris: Jules Renouard, 1860.

Cicero, Marcus Tullius. *De legibus libri tres.* Translated and edited by W.D. Pearman. Cambridge: J. Hall & Son, 1881.

———. *De Natura Deorum.* Translated by H. Rackham. London: Heinemann, 1956.

Claude (d'Abbeville). *Histoire de la Mission des Pères Capucins en l'Isle de Maragnan et terres circonvoisins.* Paris: François Huby, 1614. (Facsimile ed., Graz: Akademische Druck–u. Verlagsanstalt, 1963.)

Claudin, Anatole, ed. *Diverses pièces curieuses.* 6 vols. Lyon: Perrin et Marinet, 1875–76.

Clodoré, Jean de. *Plaintes et griefs presentés à Monseigneurde Colbert par Monsieur de Clodoré, gouverneur de l'Isle de la Martinique... contre Monsieur de la Barre, Lieutenant-général en l'Amérique. S.l., s.d.*

———. *Relation de ce qui s'est passé dans les Isles et Terre Ferme de l'Amérique, pendant la dernière Guerre avec l'Angleterre....* 2 vols. Paris: G. Clouzier, 1671.

Cluvier, Philippe de (Philipp Clüver). *Introduction à la géographie universelle....* Paris: Henault, 1642.

Cõbes, Sieur de. *See* Combes, Sieur de.

Cobo, Bernabé. *Historia del Nuevo Mundo.* 4 vols. Edited by Marcos Jiménez de la Espada. Seville: E. Rasco, 1890–93.

Colden, Cadwallader. *History of the Five Nations depending on the province of New York in America.* New York: W. Bradford, 1727.

Collection de manuscrits contenant lettres, mémoires et autres documents historiques relatif à la Nouvelle-France. 4 vols. Quebec, 1883–85.

Columbus, Christopher. *La Carta de Colón annunciando el descubrimiento del nuevo mundo 15 febrero–14 marzo 1493. Reproducción del texto original español, impreso en Barcelona (Pedro Posa, 1493).* Annotated by Carlos Sanz. Madrid, 1956.

———. *La Carta de Colón annunciando la llegada a las India y a la Provincia de Catayo....* Facsimile of the 17 known editions, annotated by Carlos Sanz. Madrid: Graficás Yagües, 1958.

———. *The Columbus Letter of 1493; a facsimile of the copy in the William L. Clements Library.* Translated by Frank E. Robbins. Ann Arbor, Mich.: Clements Library Associates, 1952.

———. *Four Voyages to the New World: Letters and Selected Documents.* Translated and edited by R. H. Major. New York: Corinth Books, 1961.

———. *The Journal of Christopher Columbus.* Translated by Cecil Jane. New York: Clarkson N. Potter, 1960.

———. *Oeuvres de Christophe Colombe.* Translated and annotated by Alexander Cioranescu. Paris: Gallimard, 1973.

———. *Select Documents Illustrating the Four Voyages of Columbus.* Edited by Cecil Jane. London: Hakluyt Society, 1930.

———. *The Spanish Letter of Columbus to Luis de Sant'Angel, escribano de racion of the Kingdom of Aragon, dated 15 February 1493.* Reduced facsimile of the original edition printed by Johann Rosenbach at Barcelona, April 1493. London: Bernard Quaritch, 1893.

Combes, Sieur de. *Coppie d'une Lettre Envoyee de la Nouvelle-France ou Canada, par le Sieur de Cõbes, Gentilhomme poictevin à un sien amy.* Lyon: Jean Savine, 1609.

Commission International d'Histoire Maritime. *Rapports.* XIIe Congrès International des Sciences Historiques, Vienna, 1965. Paris: Ecole Pratique des Hautes Etudes, 1965.

Commissions du roi de Monseigneur l'Admiral, au sieur de Monts, pour l'habitation ès terres de Lacadie, Canada, et autres endroits en la nouvelle France. Paris, 1605.

La conversion des sauvages qui ont été baptizés en la Nouvelle France cette année 1610, avec un bref récit du voyage de Poutrincourt. Paris: Millot, *s.d.*

Copie d'une lettre envoyée au gouverneur de la Rochelle par les Capitaines des Galleres de France, faisant mention des assaults & combats qu'ils on soustenus contre les Mores et Sauvages, faisant le voyage de l'Isle Floride. Paris: Pierre de Langre, 1565.

Coppier, Guillaume. *Histoire et voyage des Indes Occidentales....* Lyon: Hugueton, 1645.

Coréal, François. *Voyages de François Coréal aux Indes occidentales, contenant ce qu'il y a vû de plus remarquables pendant son séjour depuis 1666 jusqu'en 1697.* 2 vols. Paris: G. Amaulry, 1722.

Cornut, Jacques. *Canadensium plantarum aliarumque non dum editarum historia.* Paris: S. Le Moyne, 1635.

Cortés, Hernán. *Correspondance de Fernand Cortés avec l'empereur Charles-Quint, sur la conquête de Mexique.* Translated by M. le Vicomte de Flevigny. Paris: Cellot et Jombert fils jeune, *s.d.*

Cortesão, Armando, and Avalina Teixeira da Motá, eds. *Portugaliae Monumenta Cartographica.* 5 vols. Lisbon, 1960.

Couillard, Antoine, Seigneur du Pavillon pres Lorriz. *Les Antiquitez et singularitez du monde.* Paris: Jean Dallier, 1557.

Crouch, Nathaniel [Robert Burton, pseud]. *The English Empire in America.* London: by the Author, 1685. (Reprint ed., California State Library: San Francisco, 1940.)

Crucé, Emeric de. *See* La Croix, Emeric de.

Danckaerts, Jasper. *Journal of Jasper Danckaerts, 1679–1680.* Edited by J. Franklin Jameson and Bartlett Burleigh James. New York: Scribner's, 1913.

Dangeau, Philippe de Courcillon, Marquis de. *Journal de la Cours de Louis XIV (1684–1715).* Paris: Xhrouet, 1807.

Dassié, F. *Description générale des costes de l'Amerique. . . .* Paris: Robert J.-B. de La Caille, 1676.

Davenport, Francis Gardiner. *European Treaties bearing on the History of the United States and its Dependencies.* 4 vols. Washington: Carnegie Institution, 1917.

La Découverte de l'Amérique. Rapport de dixième stage international d'études humanistes. Tours, 1966. Paris: J. Vrin, 1968.

Denys, Nicolas. *Description geographique et historique des Costes de l'Amerique Septentrionale, avec l'histoire naturelle du pais.* 2 vols. Paris: Louis Billaine, 1672.

———. *The Description and Natural History of the Coasts of North America (Acadia).* Edited by William F. Ganong. Toronto: Champlain Society, 1908.

Description de l'Amerique. Paris: Les Marchands de nouveautés, *s.d.*

Description de l'Amerique et des parties d'icelle comme de la Nouvelle France, Floride, des Antilles, Lucaya, Cuba, Jamaica. . . . Amsterdam: Jean Evertsz Cloppenburch, 1619.

Deserpz, François. *Recueil de la diversité des habits qui sont a présent en usaige tant ès pays d'Europe, Asie, Affrique et Illes sauvages; le tout fait après le naturel.* Paris: R. Breton, 1567.

Desjeans, Jean-Bernard, Sieur de Pointis. *Relation de ce qui s'est fait à la prise de Carthagène, située aux Indes-Espagnoles, par l'escadre commandée par M. de Pointis.* Bruxelles: Jean Freix, 1698.

Díaz del Castillo, Bernal. *Historia verdadera de la conquista de la Nueva-España.* Madrid: Imprenta del Reyno, 1632.

Diderot, Denis. *Supplément aux dictionnaires des sciences, des arts et des metiers.* 4 vols. Paris: Stoupe, 1776.

———. *Supplément au Voyage de Bougainville.* In *Oeuvres Complètes,* J. Assézat, ed., vol. 2. Paris: Garnier, 1875.

Diéreville, Sieur de. *Relation of the Voyage to Port Royal in Acadia or New France by the Sieur de Diéreville.* Translated by Mrs. Clarence Webster and edited by John C. Webster. Toronto: Champlain Society, 1933.

Discours et congratulation à la France sur l'arrivée des Pères Capucins en l'Inde Nouvelle de l'Amérique Meridionale. Paris, 1619.

Drake, Sir Francis. *Le Voyage de l'illustre seigneur et chevalier François Drach . . . à l'entour du Monde, augmenté d'une second partie.* Translated by F. de Louvencourt, Sieur de Vauchelles. Paris: Gesselin, 1627.

Du Bartas, Seigneur, Guillaume de Saluste. *See* Saluste, Guillaume de, Seigneur Du Bartas.

Du Choul, Guillaume. *Discours de la religion des anciens Romains. . . .* Lyon: G. Roville, 1567.

Du Périer, Antoine, Sieur de Sarlagues. *Les Amours de Pistion.* Paris: Thomas de la Ruelle, 1601.

Du Puis, Mathias. *Relation de l'établissement d'une colonie françoise dans la Guadeloupe, isle de l'Amérique, et des moeurs des sauvages. . . .* Caen: M. Yvon, 1652.

Du Redouer, Mathurin. *See* under Fracanzano da Montalboddo.

Du Tertre, Jean-Baptiste. *Histoire générale des Antilles habitées par les François. . . .* 4 vols. Paris: Thomas Jolly, 1667–71.

———. *Histoire générale des isles de S. Christophe . . . et autres dans L'Amérique. . . .* Paris: Jacques Langlois, 1654.

Du Val d'Abbeville, Pierre. *L'Amerique françoise ou sont decrites la France Nouvelle, la France Insulaire, la France Equinoctiale, et autres pays.* Paris: Cl. Jollain, *s.d.*

———. *Memoires geographiques de tous les pays du monde; avec plusieurs observations historiques.* Lyon: Jean Certes, 1674.

Duret, Claude. *Thresor de l'histoire des langues de cest univers.* Cologne: Matth. Berjon, 1613.

Edits, Ordonnances royaux, declarations et arrêts du Conseil d'Etat du roi concernant Canada. 3 vols. Quebec: E. R. Fréchette, 1854–56.

Eliot, John. *The Day-Breaking, if not The Sun-Rising of the Gospell with the Indians of New-England.* London: Rich. Cotes, 1647.

Enciso, Martín Fernández de. *See* Fernández de Encisco, Martín.

Engel, Samuel. *Essai sur cette question: Quand et comment l'Amérique a-t-elle été peuplée d'hommes et d'animaux?* 5 vols. Amsterdam: M. M. Roy, 1767.

Estienne, Henri. *Apologie pour Hérodote.* Edited by P. Ristelhuber. 2 vols. Paris: I. Lisieux, 1879. (Based on first French edition of Geneva, 1566.)

———. *L'Introduction au Traité de la conformité des merveilles anciennes avec les modernes, ou Traité preparatif à l'Apologie pour Herodote. ...* Geneva, 1566.

Etablissement de la Compagnie de Canada sous le titre de Nouvelle France par les Articles des vingt-neuf Avril et sept May, mil six cens vingt-sept. Paris: Saugrain & Prault, 1725.

Eusebius Pamphili. *Eusebii Caesariensis Episcopi Chronicon.* Edited by Prosper and Mathieu Paulmier. Paris: Henri Estienne, 1512.

Evreux, Yves d'. *See* Yves (d'Evreux).

[Faye, Charles, Sieur d'Espesses]. *Memoires de plusieurs choses considerables avenuës en France. Avec quelque recit touchant les affaires des pays voisins, depuis le commencement de l'année 1607.* Paris: Thomas Blaise, 1634.

Fénélon, François de Salignac de la Mothe. *Les Avantures de Télémaque* in *Oeuvres choisies.* 6 vols. Paris: Guibert, 1825.

Fernandes de Queiros (de Quir), Pedro. *Copie de la Requeste presentee au Roy d'Espagne par le capitaine Pierre Ferdinand de Quir, sur la descouverte de la cinquiesme partie du monde appelee terre Australle, incogneuë & des grandes richesses & fertilité d'icelle.* Paris, 1617.

Fernández de Enciso, Martín. *Suma de geografía que trata de todas las partidas y provincias del mundo: en especial de las Indias.* Seville: Jacob Kromberg, 1519. (Reprint ed., Madrid, 1948.)

Fernández de Oviedo y Valdes, Gonzalo. *L'Histoire naturelle et generalle des Indes, isles et terre ferme de la grand mer océane. ...* Translated by J. Poleur. Paris: M. De Vascosan, 1555.

———. *Historia General y Natural de las Indias.* 5 vols. Edited by Juan Perez de Tudela Bueso. Madrid: Gráficas Orbe, 1959.

———. *Natural History of the West Indies.* Translated and edited by Sterling A. Stoudemire. Chapel Hill: University of North Carolina Press, 1959.

Un festin de guerre chez les sauvages. Par un missionnaire. Limoges: Barbon Frères, 1861.

Foigny, Gabriel de [pseud. Jacques Sadeur]. *La Terre australe connue, c'est-à-dire la description de ce pays inconnue jusqu'ici, de ses moeurs et de ses coutumes....* Vannes: J. Verneuil, 1676.

Fontaine, Ch. *La Description des terres trouvees de nostre temps, avec le sommaire de plusieurs belles antiquitez, contenant une partie de l'excellence & magnificence des richesses, triomphes & largesses des anciens.* Lyon: Benoit Rigaud, 1559.

———. *Les Nouvelles et antiques merveilles....* Paris: Guillaume le Noir, 1554.

Fontenelle, Bernard Le Bouyer de. *Oeuvres diverses.* 8 vols. Paris: M. Brunet, 1715.

Fournier, Georges. *Hydrographie contenant la théorie et la pratique de toutes les parties de la navigation.* Paris: Michael Soly, 1643.

Fracanzano da Montalboddo. *Le Nouveau monde et navigations faictes par Emeric de Vespucce....* Translated by Mathurin Du Redouer. Paris: G. du Pré, 1516.

———. *Sensuyt le nouveau monde & navigations faictes par Emeric Vespuce Florentin: Des pays & isles nouvellement trouvez auparavant a nous inconnuz tant en l'Ethiope que Arrabie, Calichut et aultres plusieurs regions etranges.* Translated by Mathurin Du Redouer. Paris, 1515. (Facsimile ed., Princeton: Princeton University Press, 1916.)

French, Benjamin Franklin, ed. *Historical Collections of Louisiana and Florida....* New Series. New York: J. Sabin & Sons, 1869.

Frobisher, Martin. *La Navigation du capitaine Frobisher, Anglois, ez régions d'Oest et Nord-West en l'année 1577.* Geneva: Andrée Chuppin, 1578.

Froger, François. *Relation d'un voyage fait en 1695, 1696 & 1697, aux Côtes d'Afrique, Détroit de Magellan, Brézil, Cayenne, et isles Antilles, par une Escadre des Vaisseaux du Roy commandée par M. de Gennes.* Paris: N. de Fer, 1698.

Gage, Thomas. *Nouvelle relation contenant les voyages de Thomas Gage dans la Nouvelle Espagne, ses divers aventures et son retour par la Province de Nicaragua jusqu'à la Havane, etc... Et un traité de la langue Poconchi ou Pacomane....* 2 vols. Translated by Sieur de Beaulieu Huës O'Neil. Paris: G. Clouzier, 1676.

Galard-Terraube. *See* Terraube, Gaillard de.

Galiot, Thomas. *Inventaire de l'histoire journalière.* Paris: Jacques Rezé, 1599.

Garcilasso de La Vega. *Royal Commentaires of the Yncas.* 2 vols. London: Hakluyt Society, 1869–71. (Reprint ed., New York: Burt Franklin, n.d.)

Garimberto, Girolamo. *Les Problemes.* Translated by Jean Louveau d'Orleans. Lyon: Guillaume Rouille, 1559.

Gaya, Louis de. *Cérémonies nuptiales de toutes les nations du monde.* Paris: Estienne Michallet, 1680.

Gellius, Aulus. *Attic Nights.* 3 vols. Translated by John C. Rolfe. London: William Heinemann, 1948–54.

Gerdil, Giacinto Cardinal Sigismondo. *Discours philosophiques sur l'homme considéré Rélativement à l'état de nature & à l'état de Société.* Turin: Reycends, 1769.

Giovio, Paolo. *Histoires de Paolo Jovio, comois, evesque de Nocera, sur les choses faictes et advenues de son temps en toutes les parties du Monde.* 2 vols. Translated by Denis Sauvage, Seigneur du Parc-Champenois. Paris: Jacques Dupuy, 1581.

Godwin, Morgan. *The negro's & Indians advocate, suing for their admission into the church: or, A persuasive to the instructing and baptizing of the negro's and Indians in our plantation....* London: Printed for the Author by J. D., 1680.

———. *A supplement to the negro's & Indians advocate: or, Some further considerations and proposals for the effectual and speedy carrying on of the negro's Christianity in our plantations (notwithstanding the late pretended impossibilities), without any prejudice to their owners.* London: Printed by J. D., 1681.

Goldsmid, Edmund Marsden. *Bibliotheca Curiosa.* Edinburgh: Privately printed, 1884.

Gómara, Francisco López de. *See* López de Gómara, Francisco.

González de Mendoza, Juan. *Histoire du grand royaume de la Chine... avec un itinéraire du Nouveau-Monde et la découverte du Nouveau-Mexique....* Translated by Luc de La Porte. Paris: A. L'Angelier, 1600.

Gordon of Lochinvar, Sir Robert. *Encouragements for such as shall have intention to bee Under-takers in the new plantation of Cape Briton, now New Galloway in America, by Mee Lochinvar.* Edinburgh: John Wriettoun, 1625.

Gorges, Sir Ferdinando. *A Brief Narration of the Originall Undertakings of the Advancement of Plantations into the parts of America....* London: E. E. Brudenell, 1658.

———. *A briefe Relation of the Discovery and Plantation of New England....* London: John Haviland, 1622.

Gosselin, Edouard Hippolyte, ed. *Documents authentiques et inédits pour servir à l'histoire de la marine normande et du commerce Rouennais pendant le XVIe et le XVIIe siècles.* Rouen: Boissel, 1876.

———. *Nouvelles glanes historiques normandes puisées exclusivement dans des documents inédits.* Rouen: Boissel, 1873.

Gottfried, Johann Ludwig. *Newe Welt und Americanische Historien.* Frankfurt am Main: Bey denen Merianischen erben, 1655.

Goulaine de Laudonnière, René de. *Coppie d'une lettre venant de la Floride, envoyée à Rouen, et depuis au seigneur d'Everon, ensemble le plan et portraict du fort que les François y ont faict.* Paris: Normand & Jeanne Bruneau, 1565. (Also reprinted in Paul Gaffarel, *Histoire de la Floride française* [Paris, Firmin Didot, 1875].)

———. *L'Histoire notable de la Floride située es Indes Occidentales, contenant les trois voyages faits en icelle par certains Capitaines et Pilotes François, descrit par le Capitaine Laudonnière, qui y a commandé l'espace d'un an trois moys: à laquelle a esté adiousté un quatriesme voyage fait par le capitaine Gourgues. Mise en lumière par M. Basanier, gentil-homme Mathematicien.* Paris: Guillaume Auvray, 1586. (Reprint ed., Paris: Jannet, 1853.)

Grotius, Hugo (Huigh de Groot). *On the Origin of the Native Races in America. A Dissertation.* Translated and edited by Edmund Goldsmid. Edinburgh: Unwin Bros., 1884.

Guyart, Marie. *See* Marie de l'Incarnation.

Hakluyt, Richard. *Divers Voyages touching the discoveries of America....* London: Thomas Woodcocke, 1582.

———. *The Original Writings & Correspondence of the Two Richard Hakluyts.* 2 vols. Edited by E. G. R. Taylor. London: Hakluyt Society, 1935.

———. *The Principal Navigations, Voyages, Traffiques and Discoveries of the English Nation.* 12 vols. Glasgow: James MacLehose, 1903–5.

———. *The Principall Navigations, Voiages and Discoveries of the English Nation.* 2 vols. Edited by D. B. Quinn and R. A. Skelton. Cambridge: Cambridge University Press, 1965.

———. *The Third and Last Volume of the Voyages, Navigations, Traffiques, and Discoveries of the English Nation, and in some few places, where they have not been, of strangers, performed within and before the time of these hundred yeeres, to all parts of the Newfound world of America, or the West Indies....* London: George Bishop, 1600.

Hamor, Ralph. *A True discourse of the present state of Virginia and the successe of the affaires there till the 18 of June 1614....* London: J. Beale for W. Welby, 1615.

Harangue d'un cacique Indien envoyé aux François, pour se garder de la tyrannie de l'Espagnol. S.l., 1596.

Hariot, Thomas. *Merveilleux et estrange rapport toutesfois fidele, des commoditez qui se trouvent en Virginie... traduit nouvelle-*

ment d'anglois en françois. Frankfurt am Main: Theodor de Bry, 1590.

Haton, Claude. *Mémoires de Claude Haton contenant le récit des événements accomplis de 1553 à 1582, principalement dans la Champagne de la Brie.* 2 vols. Paris: M. Felix Bourquelot, 1857.

Hennepin, Louis. *A New Discovery of a Vast Country in America.* 2 vols. Edited by R. G. Thwaites. Chicago: A. C. McClung, 1903.

———. *Description de la Louisiane nouvellement decouverte au sud-ouest de la Nouvelle-France....* Paris: Sebastien Huré, 1683.

———. *Nouvelle découverte d'un très grand Pays, situé dans l'Amérique entre le Nouveau Mexique et la Mer Glaciale, le tout dédié à sa Majesté Britannique Guillaume III.* Utrecht: Broedelet, 1697.

Henrion, Denis. *Cosmographie, ou traicté general des choses tant celestes qu'elementaires....* Paris: By the Author, 1627.

Herodotus. *The Histories of Herodotus of Halicarnassus.* Translated by Harry Carter. London: Oxford University Press, 1962.

Herrera y Tordesillas, Antonio de. *Description des Indes Occidentales qu'on appelle aujourd'hui le Nouveau Monde....* Amsterdam: E. Colin, 1622.

———. *The General History of the vast continent and islands of America, commonly called the West-Indies, from the first discovery thereof....* 6 vols. Translated by Capt. John Stevens. London: J. Batley, 1725–26.

———. *Histoire générale des voyages et conquestes des Castillans dans les isles et terre ferme des Indes Occidentales.* 3 vols. Translated by N. de La Coste. Paris: N. et J. de la Coste, 1659–71.

Heyns, Pieter. *Le Miroir du Monde....* Antwerp: Christophe Plantin, 1583.

L'Histoire de la Terre-Neuve du Pérou en l'Inde Occidentale, qui est la principale mine d'or du monde, naguere descouverte et conquise et nommé la Nouvelle-Castille. [Translated by Jacques Gohory.] Paris: Vincent Sertenas, 1545.

Histoire des choses memorables advenues en la Terre du Bresil partie de l'Amerique Australe, sous le gouvernement de N. de Villegaignon depuis l'an 1555 jusques à l'an 1558. Geneva, 1561.

Histoire memorable de la reprinse de l'Isle de la Floride, faicte par les François sous la conduite du Capitaine Gourgues Gentilhomme Bourdelois le 24 & 27 de Avril de ceste année, 1568. S.l., 1568.

Histoire véritable de plusieurs voyages avantureux et perilleux faits sur la mer en diverses contrées par I.P.T. capitaine de mer. Rouen: Jean Osmont, 1600.

Hobbes, Thomas. *Leviathan, or The Matter, Forme & Power of a Commonwealth, ecclesiasticall and civill.* London: Andrew Crooke, 1651.

Hondius (Hondt), Jodocus. *See* Langenes, Barent.

Hospital, Michel de l'. *Oeuvres inédites.* 2 vols. Paris: Boulland, 1825.

Horn, Georg. *De Originibus Americanis.* The Hague: A. Vlacq, 1652.

Imhof, Andreas Lazarus von. *Le Grand théâtre historique, ou Nouvelle histoire universelle tant sacrée que profane depuis la création du monde jusqu'au commencement du XVIIIe siècle.* 3 vols. Translated by Nicolas Gueudeville, Leyden: P. Vander Aa, 1703.

l'Incarnation, Marie de. *See* Marie de l'Incarnation.

Innis, Harold Adams, ed. *Select Documents in Canadian Economic History, 1497–1783.* Toronto: University of Toronto Press, 1929.

Isasti, Lope de. *Compendio Historial de la M.N.Y.M.L. Provincia de Guipúzcoa.* San Sebastian: Ignacio Ramon Baroja, 1850.

Jameson, J. Franklin, ed. *Narratives of New Netherland 1609–1664.* New York: Scribner's, 1909.

Jamet, Denys. *Coppie de la lettre Escripte Par le R.P. Denys Jamet, Commissiare des PP. Recollestz de Canada, A Monsieur de Rancé, grand vicaire de Pontoyse, 15 aoust 1620. S.l., s.d.*

Jefferys, Thomas. *Conduite des François par rapport à la nouvelle Ecosse, depuis le premier établissement de cette colonie jusqu'à nos jours.* London: Vaillant, 1755.

———. *The Natural and Civil History of the French Dominions in North and South America.* London: By the Author, 1761.

Jolliet, Louis. *See* under Jacques Marquette.

Le Journal des Jésuits. Edited by Charles Honoré Laverdière and Henri-Raymond Casgrain. Quebec: Léger Brousseau, 1871.

Journal d'un bourgeois de Paris... (1515–1536).... Edited by V. -L. Bourrilly. Paris: Picard, 1910.

Juet's Journal. Edited by Robert M. Lunny. Collections of the New Jersey Historical Society, no. 12. Newark, N.J., 1959.

Justel, Henri, comp. *Recueil de diverses voyages faits en Afrique et en l'Amerique, qui n'ont point esté encore publiez... Le tout enrichi de figures & de cartes geographiques, qui servent à l'intelligence des choses contenuës en ce volume.* Paris: Louis Billaine, 1674.

La Barre, Joseph-Antoine Le Febvre de. *See* Le Febvre de La Barre, Joseph-Antoine.

La Calancha, Antonio de. *Histoire du Perou, partie principale des Antipodes, ou Nouveau Monde. Et du grand progrez de la foy*

Chrestienne, en la conversion de ces Peuples Gentile: par la predication, bons exemples, souffrances, mesme du martyre des PP. FF. de l'Ordre des Hermites du Glorieux Patriarche Sainct Augustin. Comme aussi de plusieurs exemples des choses prodigieuses arrivées en ce Pays-là. Toulouse: François Boude, 1653.

La Croix, A. Phérotée de. *La geographie universelle*.... 4 vols. Paris: La veuve Mabre-Cramoisy, 1693.

La Croix, Emery de (Emeric de Crucé). *Le Nouveau Cynée, ou Discours d'Estat representant les occasions & moyens d'establir une paix generalle, & la liberté du commerce par tout le monde.* Paris: J. Villery, 1623.

La Croix de Chevrières de Saint-Vallier, Jean-Baptiste de. *Estat present de l'Eglise et de la colonie française dans la nouvelle France.* Paris: Pépie, 1688.

La Grange de Chessieux, Gilbert-Armand-François-Simon de. *La Conduite des François justifiée, ou observations sur un écrite anglois*.... Paris: Le Breton, 1756.

La Peyrère, Isaac de. *Men Before Adam.* London, 1656.

La Popelinière. *See* Lancelot-Voisin, Henri, Sieur de La Popelinière.

La Salle, Antoine. *La Salade, nouvellement imprimée, laquelle fait mension de tous les pays du monde*.... Paris: Phillippe Le Noir, 1527.

La Vacquerie, Jean de. *De multiplici haereticorium tentatione, per Io. vacquerium Roïensem, Societatis Sorbonicae Doctorem.* Paris, 1560.

Laet, Johannes de. *L'Histoire du Nouveau Monde, ou Description des Indes occidentales*.... Leyden: B. et A. Elzeviers, 1640.

Lafitau, Joseph-François. *Customs of the American Indians Compared with the Customs of Primitive Times.* 2 vols. Edited and translated by William N. Fenton and Elizabeth L. Moore. Toronto: The Champlain Society, 1974.

———. *Moeurs des sauvages amériquains, comparées aux moeurs des Premier Temps.* 2 vols. Paris: Saugrain l'ainé, 1724.

Lahontan. *See* Lom d'Arce, Louis-Armand de, Baron de Lahontan.

Lancelot-Voisin, Henri, Sieur de La Popelinière. *Les Trois Mondes.* Paris: Pierre L'Huillier, 1582.

Lancre, Pierre de. *Tableau de l'inconstance des mauvais anges et démons, ou il est amplement traicté des sorciers et de la sorcellerie*.... Paris: A. Berjon, 1612.

Langenes, Barent. *Thrésor de chartes, contenant les tableaux de tous les pays du monde*.... Translated by J. de La Haye. The Hague: Albert Henry, pour Corneille Nicolas, [1602].

Laon, Jean de, Sieur d'Aigremont. *Relation du voyages des François fait au Cap de Nord en Amérique par les soings de la Compagnie établie à Paris et sous la conduite de monsieur de Royville leur Général, avec une ample description du Pays, des moeurs et façons de vivre des Sauvages et l'observation des hauteurs.* Paris: E. Pepingué, 1654.

Las Casas, Bartolomé de. *Histoire admirable des horribles insolences, cruautez, & tyrannies exercees par les Espagnols ès Indes occidentales*.... Translated by Jacques de Miggrode. [Paris]: Gabriel Cartier, 1582. (First published in Seville in 1552 as *Brevissima relación de la destruyción de las Indias*....)

———. *Oeuvres.* 2 vols. Edited by J. A. Llorente. Paris: Alexis Eymery, 1822.

———. *Relation des voyages et des découvertes que les Espagnols ont faits dans les Indes occidentales*.... Amsterdam: J. L. de Lorme, 1698.

Laudonnière, René de Goulaine de. *See* Goulaine de Laudonnière, René de.

Le Baillif, Georges. *La Plainte de la Nouvelle France. S.l., s.d.*

Le Beau, C. *Avantures du Sr. C. Le Beau ou Voyage Curieux et nouveau Parmi les Sauvages de l'Amérique Septentrionale.* 2 vols. Amsterdam: Wytwerf, 1738. (Reprint ed., New York: Johnson, 1966.)

Le Ber, Joseph. *Départ pour le Canada en 1639: Lettre inédite d'une Ursuline (Soeur Cécile de Sainte-Croix).* Dieppe: La Vigie de Dieppe, 1939.

Le Blanc, Vincent. *Les Voyages fameux du Sr Vincent Le Blanc ... qu'il a faits, depuis l'âge de douze ans jusques à soixante, aux quatre parties du monde ... le tout recueilly de ses mémoires par le Sr Coulon.* Paris: G. Clousier, 1648.

Le Blant, Robert. "Les Arrets du Parlement de Rouen du 25 juin 1633 et les premières compagnies du Canada." *Revue des Sociétés Savantes de Haute-Normandie—Lettres,* no. 3 (1956).

———. "Nouveau documents additionnels aux 'voyages' de Champlain (1560–1651)." *Bulletin Philologique et Historique (jusqu'à 1610) du Comité des Travaux Historiques et Scientifiques, Année 1959.* Paris: Imprimerie Nationale, 1960.

Le Bouyer de Fontenelle, Bernard. *See* Fontenelle, Bernard Le Bouyer de.

Le Challeux, Nicolas. *Brief discours et histoire d'un voyage de quelques François en la Floride; & du massacre autant iniustement que barbaremēt executé sur eux, par les Hespagnoles ... revue & augmentee de nouveau par M. Urbain de Chauveton.* [Geneva], 1579.

———. *Discours et histoire de ce qui est advenu en la Floride....* *S.l.*, 1566.

Le Clercq, Chrestien. *First Establishment of the Faith in New France.* 2 vols. Translated and edited by John Gilmary Shea. New York: J. G. Shea, 1887. (From the 1691 edition.)

———. *New Relation of Gaspesia by Father Chrestien Le Clercq.* Edited by William F. Ganong. Toronto: Champlain Society, 1910.

———. *Nouvelle relation de la Gaspesie, qui contient les Moeurs & la Religion des Sauvages Gaspesiens.* Paris: A. Auroy, 1691.

Le Febvre de la Barre, Joseph-Antoine. *Description de la France équinoctiale, cy-devant appellée Guyanne... avec... un discours très-utile et nécessaire pour ceuz qui voudront établir des colonies en ces contrées.* Paris: J. Ribou, 1666.

Le Mascrier, Jean-Baptiste. *Memoires historiques sur la Louisiane; contenant ce qui est arrivé de plus memorable depuis l'année 1687, jusqu'à present; avec l'Etablissement de la Colonie Française dans cette partie de l'Amerique Septentrionale....* 2 vols. Paris: Bauche, 1753.

Le Moyne de Morgues, Antoine. *Brevis narratio eorum quae in Florida Americae provĩcia Gallis acciderunt, secunda in illam navigatione, duce Renato de Laudoniere....* Frankfurt am Main: Theodor de Bry, 1591.

Le Moyne, Pierre. *Les Peintures morales....* 2 vols. Paris: S. Cramoisy, 1640–43.

Le Roy, Loys. *Considerations sur l'Histoire Françoise et universelle de ce Temps, dont les merveilles sont succinctement recitées. ...* Paris: Frederic Morel, 1567.

———. *Des differens et troubles advenans entre les hommes par la diversité des opinions en la religion.* Paris: Frederic Morel, 1562.

———. *De l'Excellence du gouvernement royal.* Paris: Frederic Morel, 1575.

———. *De la Vicissitude ou Variété des Choses en l'Univers. Paris:* Pierre l'Huillier, 1579.

Le Sage, Alain-René. *Les Aventures du Monsieur Robert Chevalier dit de Beauchêne, capitaine de Flibustiers dans la Nouvelle France....* 2 vols. Paris: Etienne Garneau, 1733. (Reprint ed., *Oeuvres choisies de Le Sage* 4 [Paris: LeBlanc, 1810].)

Le Tac, Sixte. *Histoire chronologique de la Nouvelle France ou Canada, depuis sa découverte (1504) jusques en l'an 1632.* Paris: G. Fischbacher, 1888.

Le Testu, Guillaume. *Cosmographie universelle–selon les navigateurs tant anciens que modernes. S.l.:* by the Author, 1555.

Lechford, Thomas. *Plain Dealing: or Newes from New-England.* London, 1642. (Reprint ed., Massachusetts Historical Society Collections. Ser. 3, vol. 3, 1833.)

Léry, Jean de. *Histoire d'un voyage fait en la terre du Bresil, autrement dit Amerique.* La Rochelle: Antoine Chuppin, 1578.

———. *Histoire d'un voyage fait en la terre du Brésil.* Lausanne: Bibliothèque Romande, 1972. (Based on the Geneva edition of 1580.)

———. *Historia navigationis in Braziliam, quae et America dicitur.* Geneva: Eustathius Vignon, 1586.

Lescarbot, Marc. *Adieu à la France sur l'embarquement du sieur de Poutrincourt et de son equipage faisant voile en la terre de Canadas, dicte la France occidentale, le 26e de may 1606....* Rouen: J. Petit, jouxte la copie imprimée à La Rochelle, 1606.

———. *La Conversion des Sauvages qui ont esté baptizés en la Nouvelle France, cette année 1610....* Paris: Jean Millot, 1610.

———. *La Defaite des sauvages armouchiquois par le Sagamo Membertou & ses alliez Sauvages, en la Nouvelle France au mois de juillet dernier, 1607....* Paris: Jérémie Perier, *s.d.*

———. *The History of New France by Marc Lescarbot.* 3 vols. Edited by W. L. Grant. Toronto: The Champlain Society, 1907–14. (Based on the third edition, Paris, 1618.)

———. *Nova Francia: or the Description of that part of New France, which is one continent with Virginia.* Translated by Pierre Erondelle. London: George Bishop, 1609.

Lettres edifiantes escrites par quelques missionnaires de la Compagnie de Jesus de l'Amerique septentrionale. Brussels: G. Pauwels, 1771.

Lettres édifiantes et curieuses concernant l'Asie, l'Afrique et l'Amerique.... 4 vols. Edited by L. Aimé-Martin. Paris: Auguste Desrez, 1838–43.

Lisle de La Drevetière, Louis François de. *Arlequin sauvage.* Paris: Hochereau, 1722.

Lom d'Arce, Louis-Armand de, Baron de Lahontan. *Dialogues curieux entre l'auteur et un sauvage de bons sens qui a voyagé et Memoires de l'Amerique Septentrionale.* Edited by Gilbert Chinard. Baltimore: Johns Hopkins Press, 1931.

———. *New Voyages to North America....* Edited by R. G. Thwaites. Chicago: A. C. McClure, 1905.

———. *Voyages... dans l'Amerique septentrionale....* 2 vols. Amsterdam: François l'Honoré, 1705. (Facsimile ed. under series title, *Mémoirs pittoresques de la Nouvelle-France.* [Montreal: Editions Elysées, 1974.])

López de Gómara, Francisco. *Histoire generalle des Indes occidentales & Terres neuves qui jusques à present ont esté descouverte.* Translated by M. Fumée, Sieur de Marly le Chastel. Paris: Michel Sonnius, 1569. (Originally published in Spanish, Saragossa, 1552.)

———. *Voyages et conquestes du Capitaine Ferdinand Courtois, ès Indes Occidentales.* Translated by Guillaume le Breton. Paris: Abel l'Angelier, 1588.

Loskiel, George Henry. *History of the Mission of the United Brethren among the Indians in North America.* Translated by Christian I. LaTrobe. London: Society of the United Brethren for Propagating the Gospel among the Heathens, 1794.

Macer, Joannes. *Les Trois Livres de l'histoire des Indes, acomplie de plusieurs choses memorables, autant fidèlement composez en Latin, & depuis nagueres faictz en François.* Paris: Guillaume Guillard, 1555.

Maffei, Giovanni Pietro. *Histoire des Indes.* Translated by F. A. D. L. B. Lyon: Jean Pillehotte, 1603.

Magini, Giovanni Antonio. *Histoire universelle des Indes et de la conversion des Indiens.* Douay: F. Fabri, 1605.

Magnus, Olaus. *Histoire des Pays Septentrionaux....* Antwerp: C. Plantin, 1561.

[Maillard, Pierre-Antoine-Simon.] *An Account of the Customs and Manners of the Micmakis and Maricheets Savage Nations, Now dependent on the Government of Cape-Breton....* London: S. Hooper and A. Morley, 1758.

Malapart, André de. *La prise d'un seigneur écossois et de ses gens qui pilloient les Navires pescheurs de France, Ensemble le Razement de leur fort el l'establissement d'un autre pour le service du Roy, & l'asseurance des Pescheurs François en la Nouvelle-France. Par M. Daniel de Dieppe, Capitaine pour le Roy en la Marine et Général de la Flotte de la Nouvelle France....* Rouen: Jean le Boullenger, 1630.

Malherbe, François de. *Lettres de Malherbe* [à Peiresc], *dédiées à la ville de Caen.* Paris: J. J. Blaise, 1822.

Malouet, Pierre-Victor. *Memoires de Malouet.* 2 vols. Publiés par son petit-fils le Baron Malouet. Paris: Didier, 1868.

Manesson-Mallet, Allain. *Description de l'univers, contenant les differents systèmes du monde....* 5 vols. Paris: Denys Thierry, 1683.

Mapas Españoles de America. Siglos 15–17. Madrid, 1951.

Marconville, Jean de. *Traicte enseignant d'ou procede la diversite des opinions des hommes.* Paris: Dallier, 1568.

Margry, Pierre, ed. *Découvertes et Etablissements des Français dans l'Ouest et dans le sud de l'Amérique septentrionale (1614–1754).* 6 vols. Mémoires et documents pour servir à l'histoire des origines françaises des pays d'outre-mer. Paris: Maisonneuve, 1879–88.

Marguerite de Navarre. *L'Heptameron....* Paris: J. Caveiller, 1559.

Marie de l'Incarnation. *Marie de l'Incarnation, Ursuline (1599–1672): Correspondance.* Edited by Guy Oury. Solesmes: Abbaye Saint-Pierre, 1971.

———. *Marie de l'Incarnation, Ursulines de Tours; Fondatrice des Ursulines de la Nouvelle France. Ecrits Spirituels et Historiques.* 4 vols. Edited by Albert Jamet. Paris: Desclée-De Brouwer, 1930.

Marie de Saint-Ignace. *Les Annales de l'Hôtel-Dieu de Québec, 1636–1716.* Edited by Albert Jamet. Quebec: L'Hôtel-Dieu de Québec, 1939.

Marquette, Jacques, and Louis Jolliet. *Voyage et découverte de quelques pays et nations de l'Amérique Septentrionale....* Paris: Michallet, 1845.

Martire d'Anghiera, Pietro. *De Orbe Novo.* 2 vols. Translated and edited by Francis Augustus MacNutt. New York: Putnam's, 1912.

———. *De Orbe novo de Pierre Martyr Anghiera.* Translated with comments by Paul Gaffarel. Paris: E. Leroux, 1907.

———. *Extraict ou recueil des Isles nouvellement trouvees en la grand mer Oceane ou temps du roy d'Espaigne Fernand....* Paris: Simon de Colines, 1532.

Martyr, Peter. *See* Martire d'Anghiera, Pietro.

Mastrilli, Niccolò (Nicolas Duran). *Relation des insignes progrez de la religion chrestienne faits au Paraguai, province de l'Amerique-Meridionale, et dans les vastes régions du Guair & d'Uruaig....* Translated by Jacques de Machault. Paris: S. Cramoisy, 1638.

Mather, Cotton. *Magnalia Christi Americana.* 2 vols. Hartford: Silas Andrus, 1820.

Memoire pour servir de breve instruction, tant aux Directeurs & Commissionnaires Provinciaux de la grande Compagnie de l'Amerique qu'à ceux qui d'y voudront interesser, ou passer dans le Pais. Paris: Guillaume de Luyne, 1653.

Memoire pour servir d'instruction à la grande compagnie de l'Amerique, qui s'y voudront interesser, ou passer dans le Pais. Paris: Guillaume de Luyne, 1653.

Mémoires de Commissaires du Roi et de ceux de Sa Majesté Britannique. 4 vols. Paris: Imprimerie Royale, 1755–57.

Mémoires sur le Canada depuis 1749 jusqu'à 1760. Quebec: Cary, 1838.

Mendoza, Juan González de. *See* González de Mendoza, Juan.

Mercator (Kremer), Gerhard. *Atlas Minor....* Translated by Sieur de la Popelinière. Amsterdam: C. Nicolai, 1614.

Le Mercure François ou Suitte de l'histoire de la paix, sous le regne de Henvry IV. Paris: Jean Richer, 1611. *La Continuation du Mercure François ou suite de l'histoire de l'Auguste Regence de la Royne Marie de Medicis.* Paris: Estienne Richer, 1615. *Troisième tome du Mercure François...*, 1617. *Cinquième tome...*, 1619. *L'Onziesmetome...*, 1626. *Treizième tome...*, 1629. *Dix-huictième...*, 1633. *Dix-neufviesme tome...*, 1636.

Le Mercure Galant. Paris: Avril 1681; avril 1683.

Merval, Louis de. *L'Entree de Henri II, roi de France, à Rouen, au mois d'octobre 1550.* Rouen: H. Boissel, 1868.

Mexía, Pedro. *Les Diverses leçons de Pierre Messia gentilhomme de Sevile. Contenans variables & memorables histoires.* Translated by Claude Gruget. Paris: Claude Micard, 1580.

Mocquet, Jean. *Voyages en Afrique, Asie, Indes orientales et occidentales....* Paris: J. Heuqueville, 1617.

Molinet, Jehan. *Les Faictz et dictz de feu de bonne memoire maistre Jehan Molinet.* Paris: Jehan Longis et la veufve feu Jehan Sainct-Denys, 1531.

Monardes, Nicolás. *Histoire des simples medicamens apportés des terres neuves, desquels on se sert en la medecine.* Translated by Anthoine Colin. Lyon: J. Pillehotte, 1602.

Montaigne, Michel de. *The Complete Works of Montaigne.* Translated by Donald M. Frame. Stanford, Calif.: Stanford University Press, 1957.

———. *Les Essais de Michel de Montaigne.* Edited by Pierre-Louis-Joseph Villey. Paris: Presses Universitaires de France, 1965.

Montchrestien, Antoine de. *L'Economie politique patronale, traicté de l'oeconomie politique, dédié en 1615 au Roy et à la Reyne mère du Roy....* Paris: E. Plon, 1889.

———. *Traicté de l'oeconomie politique....* *S.l., s.d.*

Montesquieu. *See* Secondat, Charles-Louis de, Baron de la Brède et de Montesquieu.

More, Sir Thomas. *La Description de l'isle d'Utopie ou est comprins le miroer des republicques du monde....* Translated by Jean Leblond. Paris: C. L'Angelier, 1550.

Morse, William Inglis, ed. *Pierre Du Gua, Sieur de Monts. Records: Colonial and "Saintongeois."* London: Bernard Quaritch, 1939.

Morton, Thomas. *The New English Canaan.* Boston: Prince Society Collection, 1883.

Münster, Sebastian. *La Cosmographie universelle....* Basel, 1556.

———. *La Cosmosgraphie universelle....* Basel, 1568.

Münster, Sebastian, and François de Belleforest. *Cosmographie universelle de tout le monde.* 2 vols. Paris: M. Sonnius, 1575.

Nicolaï, Nicolas de, Seigneur d'Arfeuille. *Les Navigations, peregrinations et voyages faicts en la Turquie.* Antwerp: Guillaume Silvius, 1576.

Nish, Cameron, ed. *Le Régime français 1534–1760.* Histoire du Canada documentaire, vol. 1. Scarborough, Ont.: Prentice-Hall, 1966.

[Nóbrega, Manoel]. *L'Institution des loix, coustumes et autres choses merveilleuses & memorables tant du royaume de la Chines que des Indes....* Paris: Sebastian Nyvelle, 1556.

Nouvelles des choses qui se passent en diverses et lointaines parties du monde. Paris: Fleury Bourriquant, *s.d.*

O'Callaghan, Edmund Bailey, and John Romeyn Brodhead, eds. *Documents Relative to the Colonial History of the State of New York.* 15 vols. Albany: Weed Parsons, 1853–87.

Oexmelin, Alexandre Olivier. *Histoire des Avanturiers qui se sont signalez dans les Indes....* 2 vols. Paris: Jacques Le Febvre, 1686.

Of the newe lãdes and of ye people founde by the messengers of the kynge of portÿgale named Emanuel. Antwerp: Jan van Doesborch, c.1508–11.

Ogilby, John. *America: being the latest and most accurate description of the New World; containing the Original of the Inhabitants and the Remarkable Voyages thither. The Conquest of the Vast Empires of Mexico and Peru, and other large provinces and territories, with the several European plantations in those parts....* London: By the Author, 1671.

Oviedo y Valdés, Gonzalo Fernández de. *See* Fernández de Oviedo y Valdés, Gonzalo.

Palafox y Mendoza, Juan de. *L'Indien ou Portrait au naturel des Indiens....* Paris: A. Cramoisy, 1672.

Pasquier, Estienne. *Les Lettres....* Paris: A. l'Angelier, 1586.

———. *Les Oeuvres d'Estienne Pasquier....* 2 vols. Amsterdam: Compagnie des librairies associez, 1723.

Paulmier de Courtonne, Jean. *Mémoire touchant l'établissement d'une mission chrestienne dans le troisième monde, autrement appellé la Terre australe, méridionale, antarctique et inconnue... par un ecclesiastique originaire de cette mesme terre.* Paris: C. Cramoisy, 1663.

Pausanias. *Pausanias' Description of Greece.* Translated by Arthur Richard Shilleto. London: George Bell, 1886.

Pelleprat, Pierre. *Relation des missions des PP de la Compagnie de Jésus dans les isles et dans la terre ferme de l'Amérique méridionale, devisée en deux parties, avec une introduction à la langue des Galibis sauvages de la terre ferme d'Amérique.* Paris: S. & G. Cramoisy, 1655.

Perrot, Nicolas. *Mémoire sur les Moeurs, Coustumes et Relligion des Sauvages de l'Amérique septentrionale.* Edited by J. Tailhan. Leipzig & Paris: A. Franck, 1864. (Facsimile ed., New York: Johnson, 1968.)

Petit de Montluçon, Pierre. *De ignis et lucis natura exercitationes ad Is. Vossium.* Paris: C. Cramoisy, 1663.

Petitot, Claude Bernard, ed. *Collection complète des mémoires relatif à l'histoire de France.* 52 vols. Paris: Foucault, 1819–26.

Pezieu, Louis de. *Bref recueil des particularitez contenues aux lettres envoyées, par Monsieur de Pezieu, à messieurs ses parents & amis de France. De l'isle de Marignan au Brezil, où il est encores à present, pour le service de Sa Majesté tres-chrestienne Louys XIII, par la grace de Dieu, roy de France & de Navarre.* Lyon: Jean Poyet, 1613. (Reprint ed., Boston, 1930.)

Philostratus, Flavius. *The Life of Apollonius of Tyana.* 2 vols. Translated by F. C. Conybeare. London: Heineman, 1948–50.

Pigafetta, Antonio. *Le voyage et navigation faict par les Espagnolz es Isles des Mollucques....* Translated by Jacques-Antoine Fabre. Paris: Simon de Colines, 1522.

Plinius Secundus, Gaius (Pliny). *Historia Naturalis, The historie of the world. Commonly called The Natural historie of C. Plinius Secundus.* Translated by Philemon Holland. London: A. Islip, 1601.

[Poncelin de la Roche-Tillac, Jean Charles]. *Almanach américain, ou Etat physique, politique, ecclesiastique et militaire de l'Amerique....* Paris: By the Author, 1784.

Postel, Guillaume. *Des Merveilles du Monde, et principalement des admirables choses des Indes, & du nouveau Monde: Histoire extraicte des escriptz tresdignes de foy, tant de ceulx qui encores sont a present audict pays, comme de ceulx qui encores vivantz peu paravant en sont retournez.* Paris: Jean Ruelle, 1553.

Poutrincourt. *See* Biencourt, Jean de, Sieur de Poutrincourt, Baron de Saint-Just.

Privy Council, Judicial Committee. In the Matter of the Boundary between the Dominion of Canada and the Colony of Newfoundland in the Labrador Peninsula. Vol. 7. London: William Clowes, 1927.

Ptolemy, Claude (Claudius, Ptolemaeus). *Geographicae enarrationis libri octo....* Lyon: Trechsel, 1535.

———. *Geography of Claudius Ptolemy.* Translated and edited by Edward Luther Stevenson. New York: New York Public Library, 1932.

———. *Opus geographiae....* Hec bona mente Laurentius Phrisius... in lucem jussit prodire.... Strasbourg: Joannes Grieninger, 1522.

———. *Tetrabiblos.* Translated and edited by F. E. Robbins. Cambridge, Mass.: Harvard University Press, 1940.

Publication du jour de l'entrée du roy treschestien Henry deuxiesme de ce nom, en la ville de Paris.... Paris: J. André et G. Corrozet, 1549.

Purchas, Samuel. *Hakluytus Posthumus or Purchas His Pilgrimes.* 20 vols. Glasgow: MacLehose, 1905–7.

Pyrard de Laval, François. *Discours du voyage des françois aux Indes Orientales, ensembles des divers accidens, adventures & dangers de l'auteur en plusieurs royaumes des Indes & du Seiour qu'il y a fait par dix ans, depuis l'an 1601 iusques en ceste année 1611.* Paris: Louis Billaine, 1679.

Pysière, Giles de. *Discours de l'Entreprinse et saccagement que les Forsaires de l'Isle Floride avoient conclud de faire à leurs Capitaines & Gouverneurs, estans mis en liberté. Avec la description des Bestes sauvages tan marines que terrestres, qui ont estez trouvees dans le circuit de la Floride.* Paris: Pierre de Langre, 1565.

Queiros, Fernandes de, Pedro. *See* Fernandes de Queiros, Pedro.

Raccolta di documenti e studi pubblicati dalla R. Commissione colombiana, pel quarto centenario dalla scoperta dell'America. Vols. 1–3. Rome, 1892.

Ramusio, Giovanni Battista. *Navigations et Voyages (XVIe siècle). A la découverte de l'Amérique du Nord.* Translated by Général Langlois and M. J. Simon. Paris: Centre de Documentation "André Thevet," 1933. (Based on Venice edition of 1556.)

Raudot, Jacques. *See* Silvy, Antoine.

Recueil de divers Voyages faits en Afrique et en l'Amerique qui n'ont point estez encore publiez. Paris: L. Billaine, 1674.

Recueil des Gazettes nouvelles ordinaires et extraordinaires ... pour l'année mil six cent soixante-cinq.... Paris: Bureau d'Adresse, 1666.

Relation de ce qui c'est passé en Amérique, dite la Nouvelle-France, contenant le tremblement de terre épouvantable qui y est arrivé et autres particularités. S.l., s.d.

Relation de l'Etablissement de la Compagnie françoise pour le commerce des Indes Orientales. Paris: Sebastian Cramoisy, 1565.

Ribier, Guillaume. *Lettres et mémoires d'Estat des Roys, Princes, Ambassadeurs, et autres ministres sous les Regnes de François premier, Henry II & François II.* 2 vols. Paris: F. Clousier, 1666.

Rochas, Henry de. *La Physique réformée contenant la réfutation des erreurs populaires et le triomphe des veritez philosophiques.* ... Paris: By the Author, 1648.

Rochefort, César de. *Histoire naturelle et morale des isles Antilles de l'Amérique*.... Rotterdam: A. Leers, 1658.

Sadeur, Jacques. *See* Foigny, Gabriel.

Sagard, Gabriel. *Histoire du Canada depuis l'an 1615.* 4 vols. Paris: Librairie Tross, 1865–66. (Reprint of 1636 edition.)

———. *Histoire du Canada et Voyages que les frères Mineurs Recollects y ont faicts pour la Conversion des Infidelles*.... Paris: Claude Sonnius, 1636.

Saint-Ignace, Marie de. *See* Marie de Saint-Ignace.

———. *The Long Journey to the Country of the Hurons.* Edited by George Wrong. Toronto: Champlain Society, 1939.

Saint-Michel, Maurile de. *Voyages des isles Camercanes, en l'Amerique qui font partie des Indes occidentales*.... Mans: Hierosme Olivier, 1652.

Saint-Vallier, Jean-Baptiste de La Croix de Chevrières de. *See* La Croix de Chevrières de Saint-Vallier, Jean-Baptiste de.

Saluste, Guillaume de, Seigneur Du Bartas. *Les Oeuvres poetiques et chrestiennes de G. de Saluste, seigneur Du Bartas, Prince de Poetes François.* Lyon: Thibaud Ancelin, 1606.

Sanson d'Abbeville, Nicolas. *Atlas nouveau contenant toutes les parties du monde, où sont exactement remarqués les empires, monarchies, royaumes Estats, Republiques & peuples qui s'y trouvent à present.* 2 vols. Paris: H. Jaillot, 1696.

Saulx, Gaspard de, Seigneur de Tavannes. *Memoires.* In Claude Bernard Petitot, ed., *Collection complète des mémoires relatif à l'histoire de France.* Vol. 23. Paris: Foucault, 1822.

Schöner, Johann. *A Reproduction of his globe of 1523, long lost, his dedicatory letters to Reymer von Streytperck and the De Moluccis of Maximilianus Transylvanus*.... Edited by C. H. Coote. London: Stevens, 1888.

Secondat, Charles-Louis de, Baron de la Brède et de Montesquieu. *Oeuvres.* 7 vols. Amsterdam, 1785.

Serrigny, Ernest, Chevalier de Baugy. *Journal d'une expedition contre les Iroquois en 1687, redigé par le chevalier de Baugy, aide-de-camp de M. le marquis de Denonville. Lettres et pièces relatives au fort Saint-Louis des Illinois.* Paris: E. Leroux, 1883.

Signot, Jacques. *La Division du Monde*.... Lyon: B. Rigaud, 1555.

[Silvy, Antoine]. *Relation par lettres de l'Amerique Septentrionale (Années 1709 et 1710).* Edited by Camille de Rochemonteix. Paris: Letouzey et Ané, 1904.

Spenser, Edmund. *The Faerie Queene.* Oxford: Limited Editions Club, 1953.

Staden, Johann von. *The Captivity of Hans Stade of Hesse in A.D. 1547–1555 Among the Wild Tribes of Eastern Brazil.* Edited by Richard F. Burton. London: Hakluyt Society, 1874.

———. *Histoire d'un pays situé dans le nouveau monde, nommé Amérique*.... Marburg, 1557. (Reprinted in Charles-Henri Ternaux-Compans, ed., *Voyages, relations et mémoires originaux pour servire à l'histoire de la découverte d'Amerique.* Vol. 3. [Paris, A. Bertrand, 1837].)

———. *Warhafftiger kurtzer bericht, aller von mir erfarnen händel und sitten des Tuppin Inbas, derer gefangner ich gewesen bin, Wonen in America*.... Frankfurt am Main: Weygandt Han, 1557.

Stow, John. *Annales, or a Generall Chronicle of England. Begun by John Stow: and augmented with matters Foraigne and Domestique, Ancient and Moderne, unto the end of this present yeere, 1631.* Continued by Edmund Howes. London: Richard Meighen, 1631.

Surius, Laurentius. *Histoire ou commentaires de toutes choses mémorables*.... Paris: Guillaume Chaudiere, 1571.

Surlaville, Le Courtois de. *Les Derniers Jours de l'Acadie (1748–1758)*.... Edited by Gaston du Bosq de Beaumont. Paris: Emile Lechevalier, 1899.

Ternaux-Compans, Charles-Henri, ed. *Voyages, relations et mémoires originaux pour servir à l'histoire de la découverte de l'Amérique.* 20 vols. Paris: A. Bertrand, 1837–40.

Terraube, Gaillard de. *Discours des choses plus necessaires & dignes d'estre entendues en la Cosmographie.* Paris: Frederic Morel, 1566.

Thévenot, Melchisédech. *Relations de divers voyages curieux qui n'ont point esté publiés*.... 4 vols. Paris: A. Cramoisy (T. Moette), 1672–96.

Thevet, André. *La Cosmographie Universelle.* 2 vols. Paris: Guillaume Chaudiere, 1575.

———. *La Cosmographie Universelle.* 2 vols. Paris: Pierre L'Huillier, 1575.

———. *La Cosmologie Universelle*. Paris: Presses Universitaires de France, 1953.

———. "Le Grand Insulaire et Pilotege." *See* Manuscript Sources, Bibliothèque de Paris.

———. *The New Found worlde, or Antarctike*. . . . Translated by T. Hacket. London: Henrie Bynneman for Thomas Hacket, 1568.

———. *Les Singularitez de la France Antarctique*. . . . Edited by Paul Gaffarel. Paris: Maisonneuve, 1878. (Reprint of Paris edition, 1558.)

———. *Les Singularitez de la France Antarctique*. . . . Paris: Chez les heritiers de Maurice de la Porte, 1558.

Thorowgood, Thomas. *Jewes in America; or, Probabilities that the Americans are of that race*. . . . London: Slater, 1650.

Thou, Jacques-Auguste de. *Histoire universelle*. 16 vols. London, 1734. (First published in Latin, Paris, 1604–20.)

Thwaites, Reuben Gold, ed. *Jesuit Relations and Allied Documents*. 73 vols. Cleveland: Burrows Bros., 1896–1901.

Tonty, Henri de. *Dernières decouvertes dans l'Amerique septentrionale de M. de La Sale*. . . . Paris: Jean Guignard, 1697.

Topsell, Edward. *The History of Foure-footed Beastes*. London: Iaggard, 1607.

Trudel, Marcel, ed. *Atlas de Nouvelle-France*. Quebec: Les Presses de l'Université Laval, 1968.

Tyson, Edward. *Orang-Outang, Sive Homo Sylvestris: or the Anatomy of a Pygmy Compared with that of a Monkey, an Ape, and a Man*. London: 1699. (Facsimile ed., London: Dawsons of Pall Mall, 1966.)

Vadianus, Joachim, (Joachim von Watt). *Epitome trium terrae partium*. . . . Zürich: C. Froschauer, 1534.

Vairasse d'Alais, Denis. *Histoire des Sévérambes, peuples qui habitent une partie du troisième continent, communément appelée Terre Australe*. . . . 5 vols. Paris: C. Barbin, 1677–79.

Les Veritables Motifs de Messieurs et Dames de la Société de Notre Dame de Montreal, pour la conversion des sauvages. Paris: 1643.

Vespucci, Amerigo. *The First Four Voyages of Amerigo Vespucci*. London: Bernard Quaritch, 1893. (Facsimile of Florence edition, 1505–6.)

———. *The Letters of Amerigo Vespucci*. Edited by Sir Clements Robert Markham. London: Hakluyt Society, 1894.

Villiers, Baron Marc de. *Les Raretés des Indes* ("Codex Canadiensis"). Montreal: Les Editions de Bouton d'Or, 1974.

Virgilio, Polydoro. *An abridgemēt of the notable works of Polidore Vergile conteygning the devisers and first finders out as well. . .as of Rites, Ceremonies commonly used in the churche, and the originall beginnyng of the same*. London: R. Grafton, 1546.

Vitoria, Francisco de. *De Indis et de Jure Belli Relectiones*. Edited by Ernest Nys. In James Brown Scott, ed., *The Classics of International Law*. Washington: Carnegie Institution, 1917.

Voltaire (François Marie Arouet). *Oeuvres complètes de Voltaire*. 52 vols. Paris: Garnier Frères, 1878.

Von Nettesheim, Heinrich Cornelius Agrippa. *See* Agrippa von Nettesheim, Heinrich Cornelius.

Waldseemüller, Martin. *Cosmographiae Introductio*. Translated by Joseph Fischer and Franz von Wieser. March of America Facsimile Series, no. 2. Ann Arbor: University Microfilms, 1966. (Facsimile of 1507 edition.)

Whitbourne, Sir Richard. *A Discourse and Discovery of New-found-land, with many reasons to prove how worthy and beneficiall a Plantation may there be made, after a far better manner than now is*. London: Felix Kyngston, 1620.

White, Margaret Adams. *The Earliest French Play About America. Acoubar, ou La Loyauté Trahie*. New York: Publishers of the Institute of French Studies, 1931.

Wood, William. *Wood's New England Prospect*. Boston: Prince Society, 1865. (Reprint of London edition, 1634.)

Wytfliet, Cornelius. *Histoire universelle des Indes Orientales et Occidentales*. . . . Douay: F. Fabri, 1605.

Yves (d'Evreux). *Suitte de l'histoire des choses plus memorables advenues en Maragnan, ès annees 1613 & 1614. Second traite. Des fruits de l'evangile qui tost parurent par le baptesme de plusieurs enfans*. Paris: François Huby, 1615.

———. *Voyage dans le Nord du Brésil fait durant les années 1613 et 1614*. Edited by Ferdinand-Jean Denis. Leipzig and Paris, 1864. (Original title: *Suitte de l'histoire des choses plus memorable advenues en Maragnan ès annees 1613 & 1614*.)

III Secondary Sources

Abler, Thomas S., and Sally M. Weaver. *A Canadian Indian Bibliography 1960–1970*. Toronto: University of Toronto Press, 1974.

Adams, Percy G. *Travelers and Travel Liars, 1660–1800*. Berkeley and Los Angeles: University of California Press, 1962.

Adele de Saint-Marie and Catherine de Saint-Thomas. *Les Ursulines de Québec depuis leur établissement jusqu'à nos jours*. 4 vols. Quebec: C. Darveau, 1863–66.

Adkinson, Henry Magee. "Conceptions of Property Among North American Indians." M.A. thesis, University of Chicago, 1897.

Alden, Dauril. "Black Robes Versus White Settlers: The Struggle for 'Freedom for the Indians' in Colonial Brazil." In Harold Peckham et al., *Attitudes of Colonial Powers Toward the American Indian.* (Salt Lake City: University of Utah Press, 1969.)

Allen, Don Cameron. *The Legend of Noah.* Studies in Language and Literature, vol. 33, nos. 3–4. Urbana, Ill., 1949.

Anderson, Andrew Runni. *Alexander's Gate, Gog and Magog and the Inclosed Nations.* Cambridge, Mass.: Medieval Academy of America, 1932.

Anick, Norman. "A History of the Fur Trade in Eastern Canada." Report prepared for national Historic Sites, Parks Canada, 1973.

Archenholtz, Johann Wilhelm von. *Histoire des Flibustiers.* [Translated by J. F. Bourgoing.] Paris: Henrichs, 1804.

Ashley, Maurice. *England in the Seventeenth Century (1603–1714).* Harmondsworth: Penguin, 1963.

Atkinson, Geoffroy. *The Extraordinary Voyage in French Literature Before 1700.* New York: Columbia University Press, 1920. (Reprint ed., New York: AMS Press, 1966.)

———. *Les Nouveaux horizons de la Renaissance française.* Paris: Droz, 1935.

———. *Les Relations des voyages du XVIIe siècle et l'évolution des idées. Contribution à l'étude de la formation de l'esprit du XVIIIe siècle.* Paris: E. Champion, 1924. (Reprint ed., New York: Burt Franklin, 1971.)

Avenel, Georges, Vicomte d'. *Histoire économique de la propriété, des salaires, des denrées et de tous les prix en général depuis l'an 1200 jusqu'en l'an 1800.* 6 vols. Paris: Ernest Leroux, 1913–24.

———. *La fortune privée à travers sept siècles.* Paris: A. Colin, 1895.

Avezac, Armand d'. *Campagne du navire l'Espoir, de Honfleur, 1503–1505. Relation authentique du voyage du Capitaine de Gonneville....* Paris: Challamel Aîné, 1869.

Bailey, Alfred Goldsworthy. *The Conflict of European and Eastern Algonkian Cultures, 1504–1700; a study in Canadian civilization.* Toronto: University of Toronto Press, 1969. (First edition, Saint John: New Brunswick Museum, 1937.)

———. "The Indian Problem in Early Canada." *América Indígena* 2 (1942): 35–39.

———. "The Significance of the Identity and Disappearance of the Laurentian Iroquois." Transactions of the Royal Society of Canada, 27 (1933): ser. 3, sec. 2, 97–108.

———. "Social Revolution in Early Eastern Canada." Canadian Historical Review 19 (1938): 264–76.

Bailyn, Bernard. *The New England Merchants of the Seventeenth Century.* Cambridge, Mass.: Harvard University Press, 1955.

Baker, Donald G. "Color, Culture and Power: Indian–White Relations in Canada and America." *The Canadian Review of American Studies* 3, no. 1 (Spring 1972): 3–20.

Ballanche, Pierre-Simon. *Essai sur les institutions sociales.* Paris: Bureau de l'Encyclopédie des Connaissances Utiles, 1833. (Facsimile ed., Geneva: Slatkine, 1967.)

Ballard, Edward. "Indian Mode of Applying Names." Collections of the New Hampshire Historical Society, vol. 8., pp. 446–50. Concord, 1866.

Barber, Richard, and Anne Riches. *A Dictionary of Fabulous Beasts.* London: Macmillan, 1971.

Barkham, Selma de L. "A note on the Strait of Belle-Isle during the period of Basque contact with Indians and Inuit." *Etudes Inuit Studies* 4, nos. 1–2 (1980): 51–58.

Barros e Sousa de Mesquita de Macedo Leïtão e Carvalhosa, Manuel Francisco de, Vicomte de Santarem. *Essai sur l'histoire de la Cosmographie et de la Cartographie pendant le Moyen-Age....* 3 vols. Paris: Maulde et Renou, 1849–52.

Bataillon, Marcel. "La Découverte spirituelle du Nouveau Monde." Annuaire du Collège de France, (1952), 276–86.

Bauman, Robert F. "Ottawa Fleets and Iroquois Frustration." *Northwest Ohio Quarterly* 33 (1960–61): 7–40.

———. "The Ottawa Trading System." *Northwest Ohio Quarterly* 36, no. 2 (1964): 60–78; and no. 3 (1964): 146–67.

Beaugrand-Champagne, Aristide. "Les anciens Iroquois du Québec." *Cahiers des Dix* 1 (1936): 171–99.

Beawes, Wyndham. *Lex Mercatoria Rediviva: or, A Complete code of commercial law.* 5th ed. Revised by Thomas Mortimer. London: R. Baldwin, 1792.

Bendyshe, Thomas. "The History of Anthropology." *Memoirs read before the Anthropological Society of London* 1 (1863–64): 353–54.

Bernheimer, Richard. *Wild Men in the Middle Ages: a Study in Art, Sentiment, and Demonology.* Cambridge, Mass.: Harvard University Press, 1952.

Bertrand de la Grassière, Paul. *Jean Ribault.* Paris: La Pensée Universelle, 1971.

Biggar, Henry Percival. *Early Trading Companies.* Toronto: University of Toronto Library, 1901.

———. *The Precursors of Jacques Cartier 1497–1534.* Ottawa: Government Printing Bureau, 1911.

Bissell, Benjamin H. *The American Indian in English Literature of the Eighteenth Century.* New Haven: Yale University Press, 1925.

Boas, George. *Essays on Primitivism and Related Ideas in the Middle Ages.* Baltimore: Johns Hopkins University Press, 1948.

Boas, George, Arthur O. Lovejoy, and Gilbert Chinard, eds. *A documentary history of primitivism and related ideas.* Baltimore: Johns Hopkins University Press, 1935.

Bollème, Geneviève. *Les Almanachs populaires aux XVIIe et XVIIIe siècles; essai d'histoire sociale.* Paris: Mouton, 1969.

———. *La Bibliothèque bleue; littérature populaire en France du XVIIe au XIXe siècle.* Paris: Julliard, 1971.

Boucher, Philip Poulin. "France 'Discovers' America: The Image of Tropical America in Sixteenth- and Seventeenth-Century France and its Impact on Early French Colonialism." Ph.D. thesis, University of Connecticut, 1974.

Bourque, Bruce J. "Aboriginal Settlement and Subsistence on the Maine Coast." *Man in the Northeast* 6 (1973): 3–11.

Bowen, Noel H. "The Social Condition of the Coast of Labrador." Transactions of the Literary and Historical Society of Quebec, 1st ser., vol. 4 (1854), pt. 4: 329–41.

Braudel, Fernand. *La Méditerranée et le monde méditerranéen à l'époque de Philippe II.* Paris: Armand Colin, 1949.

Brinton, Daniel G. *The Myths of the New World: A Treatise on the Symbolism and Mythology of the Red Race of America.* New York: Leopold & Holt, 1876.

Bruzen de La Martinière, Antoine-Augustin. *Le Grand Dictionnaire géographique, historique et critique.* 6 vols. Paris: P. G. Le Mercier, 1739–41.

Burke, Edmund. *An Account of the European Settlements in America.* 2 vols. London: J. Dodsley, 1777. (Reprint ed., New York: Anno Press, 1972.)

"The Cabot Legends." Proceedings and Transactions, Royal Society of Canada, 2d ser., vol. 3 (1897), sec. 3: app. to sec. 2, 429–50.

Cahingt, Henri, ed. "Documents sur le Canada (1639–1660)." Bulletin de la Commission Départementale des Antiquités de la Seine-Inférieure, vol. 16, pp. 84–110. Rouen, 1912.

Campbell, Joseph. *The Mythic Image.* Princeton, N.J.: Princeton University Press, 1974.

Canada: An Exhibition Commemorating the Four Hundredth Anniversary of the Discovery of the Saint Laurence by Jacques Cartier, 1534–1535. New York: New York Public Library, 1935.

Candide (de Nant). "Une Mission capucine en Acadie (1635–1655)." *Etudes franciscaines* 37 (1925): 45–70, 229–58, 446–85, 638–57; 38 (1926): 337–73; 39 (1927): 113–59.

———. *Pages glorieuses de l'epopée canadienne.* Montréal: Le Devoir, 1927.

Carrington, Richard. "The Natural History of the Mermaid." *Horizon* 2, no. 3 (1960): 129–30.

Cawley, Robert Ralston. "Shakespeare's Use of the Voyagers." *Publications of the Modern Language Association of America* 41 (1926): 688–726.

Chaunu, Pierre. *L'Amérique et les Amériques.* Paris: A. Colin, 1964.

———. *L'Expansion européenne du XIIIe au XVe siècle.* Paris: Presses Universitaires de France, 1969.

———. "La Légende noire antihispanique." *Revue de Psychologie des Peuples* (1964): 188–223.

Chevalier, Jean. *Dictionnaire des Symboles.* Paris: Robert Laffont, 1969.

Chiapelli, Fredi, ed. *First Images of America.* 2 vols. Los Angeles and Berkeley: University of California Press, 1976.

Chinard, Gilbert. *L'Amérique et le rève exotique.* Paris: Droz, 1934.

———. *L'Exotisme américain dans la litterature française au XVIe siècle.* Paris: Hachette, 1911.

———. *L'Homme contre la nature. Essais d'histoire de l'Amérique.* Paris: Hermann, 1949.

Church, E. D. *Church Catalogue of Books.* 5 vols. Compiled by George Watson Cole. New York: Peter Smith, 1951.

Cioranescu, Alexandre. *Bibliographie de la litterature française du seizième siècle.* Paris: Klincksieck, 1959.

———. *Bibliographie de la litterature française du dix–septième siècle.* 3 vols. Paris: Centre National de la Recherche Scientifique, 1965.

Clarke, George Frederick. *Someone Before Us: Our Maritime Indians.* Fredericton: Brunswick Press, 1968.

Clignet, Remy. "Sociologie de la colonisation américaine en territoire indien." *Cahiers Internationaux de Sociologie* (janvier–juin 1956). Paris: Les Presses Universitaires de France, 1956.

Cloulas, Ivan. *Catherine de Medici.* Paris: Fayard, 1979.

Cohn, Norman. *The Pursuit of the Millennium.* London: Secker & Warburg, 1957.

Commager, Henry Steele, and Elmo Giordanetti, eds. *Was America a Mistake? An Eighteenth Century Controversy.* Columbia, S.C.: University of South Carolina, 1968.

Concessa, Sister M. "Père Gabriel Druillettes, Missionary Extraordinary." M.A. thesis, University of Duquesne, 1950.

Cook, Sherburne F., and Woodrow Borah. *Essays in Population History: Mexico and the Caribbean.* 2 vols. Berkeley and Los Angeles: University of California Press, 1974.

Cope, Robert Samuel. "Slavery and Servitude in the Colony of Virginia in the Seventeenth Century." Ph.D. thesis, Ohio State University, 1950.

Corneille, Thomas. *Dictionnaire universel, géographique et historique....* 3 vols. Paris: Jean-Baptiste Coignard, 1708.

Couillard-Després, Azarie. *Charles de Saint-Etienne de la Tour, gouverneur, lieutenant-général en Acadie, et son temps, 1539–1666.* Arthabaska, P.Q.: Imprimerie d'Arthabaska, 1930.

Creeny, William Frederick. *A Book of Fac-similes of Monumental Brasses of the Continent of Europe, with brief descriptive notes.* Norwich: A. H. Goose, 1884.

Crone, Gerald Roe. *The Discovery of America.* London: Hamilton, 1969.

Crosby, Alfred W., Jr. *The Columbian Exchange: Biological and Cultural Consequences of 1492.* Westport, Conn.: Greenwood, 1972.

Crouse, Nellis M. *Contributions of the Canadian Jesuits to the geographical knowledge of New France, 1632–1675.* [Ithaca, N.Y.], 1924.

———. *French pioneers in the West Indies, 1624–1664.* New York: Columbia University Press, 1940.

Cumming, William Patterson. "The Parreus Map (1562) of French Florida." *Imago Mundi* 17 (1963): 27–40.

Cumming, William Patterson, Raleigh Ashlin Skelton, and David Beers Quinn. *The Discovery of North America.* Toronto: McClelland and Stewart, 1971.

Cuoq, Jean-André. *Lexique de la langue iroquoise.* Montreal: J. Chapleau, 1882.

Dacos, Nicole. "Présents américains à la Renaissance: L'Assimilation de l'exotisme." *Gazette des Beaux Arts,* VIe période, 73 (1969): 57–64.

Dalton, George. "Economic Theory and Primitive Society." *American Anthropologist* 63 (1961): 1–25.

Davidson, Marshall B., ed. *The Horizon Book of Lost Worlds.* New York: American Heritage Publishing, 1962.

Day, Gordon. *The Mots loups of Father Mathevet.* Ottawa: National Museum of Man, 1975.

Découverte de l'Amérique. Dixième Stage International d'Etudes Humanistes, Tours, 1966. Paris: J. Vrin, 1968.

Delanglez, Jean. *Frontenac and the Jesuits.* Chicago: Institute of Jesuit History, 1939.

Denis, Ferdinand-Jean, ed. *Une Fête brésilienne célébrée à Rouen en 1550....* Paris: J. Techener, 1850.

Dent, Julian. "The Historical Background of the French Renaissance." Paper presented at the National Gallery of Canada, 3 April 1973, in connection with the exhibition, "Fontainebleau."

Deschamps, Hubert. *Les Méthodes et les doctrines coloniales de la France.* Paris: Librairie Armand Colin, 1953.

Desroches, Henri. "Micromillénairisme et communautarisme utopique en Amérique du Nord du XVIIe au XIXe siècle." *Archives de Sociologie des Religions* 4 (1957): 57–92.

Diamond, Sigmund. "Le Canada français du XVII siècle: Une société préfabriquée." *Annales* 16, no. 2 (1961): 317–54.

Diamond, Stanley. *Primitive Views of the World.* New York: Columbia University Press, 1969.

Dickason, Olive Patricia. "The Concept of *l'homme sauvage* and early French colonialism in the Americas." *Revue française d'histoire d'outre-mer* 64, no. 234 (1977): 5–32.

———. "European and Amerindian: Some Comparative Aspects of Early Contact." Canadian Historical Association, *Historical Papers,* (1979): 182–202.

———. "Louisbourg and the Indians: A Study in Imperial Race Relations." *History and Archaeology* 6 (1976): 1–206.

———. "Renaissance Europe's View of Amerindian Sovereignty and Territoriality." *Plural Societies* 8, nos. 3–4 (Autumn–Winter 1977), 97–107.

Dickinson, John A. "La guerre iroquoise et la mortalité en Nouvelle-France, 1608–1666." *Revue d'histoire de l'Amérique française* 35, no. 1 (1892): 31–34.

Dictionary of Canadian Biography. Toronto: University of Toronto Press, 1966–.

Dictionnaire de l'Academie française. 2 vols. Paris: Jean-Baptiste Coignard, 1694.

Dictionnaire Encyclopédique Quillet. 8 vols. Paris: Librarie Aristide Quillet, 1968.

Dictionnaire universel françois et latin, vulgairement appellé Dictionnaire de Trevoux. 6 vols. Trevoux, 1742.

———. "Sociopsychological Aspects of Acculturation." In Ralph Linton, ed., *The Science of Man in the World Crisis* 171–200. New York: Columbia University Press, 1945.

Halpin, Marjorie, and Michael Ames, eds. *Manlike Monsters on Trial.* Vancouver: University of British Columbia Press, 1980.

Hamilton, Earl Jefferson. *American Treasure and the Price Revolution in Spain.* Cambridge, Mass.: Harvard University Press, 1934. (Reprint ed., New York: Octagon, 1970.)

———. "American Treasure and the Rise of Capitalism." *Economica* 9 (1929): 338–57.

Handbook of North American Indians. Washington: Smithsonian Institution, 1978–.

Handbook of South American Indians. Vol. 3. Julian H. Steward, ed. Washington: Government Printing Office, 1946–63.

Hanke, Lewis. *Aristotle and the American Indians: a study in race prejudice in the modern world.* Bloomington: Indiana University Press, 1970.

———. *Colonisation et conscience chrétienne au 16e siècle.* Translated by François Durif. Paris: Plon, 1957.

———. "The Cultural Contribution of Bishop Juan de Zumárraga to Mexican Culture." *The Americas* 5 (1948): 276–77.

———. "Pope Paul III and the American Indians." *The Harvard Theological Review* 30 (1937): 65–102.

———. *The Spanish Struggle for Justice in the Conquest of America.* Philadelphia: University of Pennsylvania Press, 1949.

Hankins, John Erskine. "Oratory of the American Indians." M.A. thesis, University of California, 1925.

Hanotaux, Gabriel-Albert-Auguste. *Etudes historiques surle XVIe et le XVIIe siècles en France.* Paris: Hachette, 1886.

———. *Pour l'Empire coloniale français.* Paris: Kapp, 1933.

Hanotaux, G.-A.-A., and Alfred Martineau. *Histoire des colonies françaises et de l'expansion de la France dans le monde.* 6 vols. Paris: Plon, 1929–33.

Hanzeli, Victor Egon. *Missionary Linguistics in New France; a study of seventeenth- and eighteenth-century descriptions of American Indian languages.* The Hague: Mouton, 1969.

Harrisse, Henry. *Bibliotheca Americana Vetustissima: A Description of Works Relating to America Published Between the Years 1492 and 1551.* New York: Philes, 1866.

———. *Bibliotheca Americana Vetustissima, Additions.* Paris: Tross, 1872.

———. *Jean et Sébastien Cabot, leur origine et leurs voyages....* Paris: E. Leroux, 1882.

———. *John Cabot, The Discoverer of North America and Sebastion his Son.* London: B. F. Stevens, 1896. (Reprint ed., New York: Argosy-Antiquarian, 1968.)

———. *Découverte et évolution cartographique de Terre-Neuve et des pays circonvoisins, 1497–1501–1769.* Paris: H. Welter, 1900. (Reprint ed., Ridgewood, N.J.: Gregg Press, 1968.)

———. *The Discovery of North America.* London: H. Stevens, 1892. (Reprint ed., Amsterdam: N. Israel, 1961.)

———. *Notes pour Servir à l'histoire, à la bibliographie et à la cartographie de la Nouvelle-France et des Pays adjacente, 1545–1700.* Paris: Tross, 1872.

Harvey, Theodore Vespasian Lee. "Missionary Methods of the French Jesuits Among the Hurons." B.D. thesis, University of Chicago, 1934.

Harwood, Thomas Franklin. "The Indian Problem on the First Frontier: Virginia, 1584–1622." M.A. thesis, University of Texas, 1954.

Hauser, Henri. "Les Huguenots français au Brésil (1560–1584) d'après des documents portugais." *Bulletin de la Société de l'Histoire du Protestantisme français* (1937): 93–115.

Hay, Denys, ed. *The Age of the Renaissance.* London: Thames & Hudson, 1967.

Heagerty, John J. *Four Centuries of Medical History in Canada and a Sketch of the Medical History of Newfoundland.* Toronto: Macmillan, 1928.

Heard, Joseph Norman. *White into red; a study of the assimilation of white persons captured by Indians.* Metruchen, N.J.: Scarecrow Press, 1973.

Heidenreich, Conrad E. *Huronia: A History and Geography of the Indians 1600–1650.* Toronto: McClelland and Stewart, 1971.

———. "Maps relating to the first half of the 17th century and their use in determining the location of Jesuit Missions in Huronia." *The Cartographer* 3, no. 2 (1966): 103–126.

Hemming, John. *Red Gold.* London: Macmillan, 1978.

Heraldry in Miniature, containing all the arms, crests, supporters and mottos of the peers, peeresses and bishops of England, Scotland and Ireland.... London: T. C. Hansard, 1808.

The Heraldry of Nature.... London: M. Smith, 1785.

Herman, Mary Woody. "Indian Fur Trade of New France in the Seventeenth Century." Ph.D. thesis, University of California, 1953.

Hérouville, Pierre d'. *Les Missions des Jésuites au Canada, XVIIe et XVIIIe siècles. Analyses des documents exposés. Exposition rétrospective des colonies française de l'Amerique du Nord.* Paris: Gabriel Enault, 1929.

Herrmann, Paul. *Conquest by Man.* Translated by Michael Bullock. London: H. Hamilton, 1954.

———. *The World Unveiled; the Story of Exploration from Columbus to Livingstone.* Translated by Arnold Pomerans. London: H. Hamilton, 1958.

Hodge, Frederick W. *Handbook of American Indians North of Mexico.* 2 vols. Bureau of Ethnology, no. 30. Washington, 1912.

Hodgen, Margaret T. *Early Anthropology in the Sixteenth and Seventeenth Centuries.* Philadelphia: University of Pennsylvania Press, 1964.

Hoffman, Bernard Gilbert. "Ancient Tribes Revisited: A Summary of Indian Distribution and Movement in the Northeastern United States from 1534 to 1779." *Ethnohistory* 14 (1967): 1–46.

———. *Cabot to Cartier: Sources for a Historical Ethnography of Eastern North America.* Toronto: University of Toronto Press, 1961.

———. "Historical Ethnography of the Micmac of the Sixteenth and Seventeenth Centuries." Ph.D. thesis, University of California, 1955.

———. "Souriquois, Etchemin, and Kwedech – A Lost Chapter in American Ethnography." *Ethnohistory* 2 (1955): 65–87.

Hoffman, Paul E. "Diplomacy and the Papal Donation." *The Americas* 30 (1973–74): 151–83.

Honigman, John J. "War and Social Structure." M.A. thesis, Yale University, 1943.

Honour, Hugh. *The European Vision of America.* Exhibition catalogue. Cleveland: The Cleveland Museum of Art, 1975.

Horton, Ralph. "The Relations Between the Indians and the Whites in Colonial Virginia." M.A. thesis, University of Chicago, 1921.

Howley, James P. *The Beothucks or Red Indians.* Cambridge, Mass.: Harvard University Press, 1915. (Facsimile ed., Toronto: Cole Publishing, 1974.)

Huddleston, Lee Eldridge. *Origins of the American Indians.* Austin: University of Texas Press, 1967.

Hughes, Thomas Aloysius. *History of the Society of Jesus in America, colonial and federal.* 3 vols. London: Longmans Green, 1907–17.

Huguet, Adrian. *Jean de Poutrincourt.* Paris: A. Picard, 1932.

Huizinga, Johann. *The Waning of the Middle Ages.* London: Edward Arnold, 1924.

Hulton, Paul, and David Beers Quinn. *The American Drawings of John White, 1577–1590, with Drawings of European and Oriental Subjects.* 2 vols. London: British Museum and University of North Carolina Press, 1964.

Hunt, George T. *The Wars of the Iroquois.* Madison: University of Wisconsin Press, 1967.

Hurault, Jean-Marcel. *Français et indiens en Guyenne: 1604–1972.* Paris: Union générale d'éditions, 1972.

Husband, Timothy. *The Wild Man, Medieval Myth and Symbolism.* New York: The Metropolitan Museum of Art, 1980.

Jaccard, Pierre. *Le Sens de la direction et l'orientation lointaine chez l'homme.* Paris: Payot, 1932.

James, Francis Godwin. "Puritan Missionary Endeavors in Early New England." M.A. thesis, Yale University, 1938.

Jamieson, John. *An Etymological Dictionary of the Scottish Language....* 4 vols. Paisley: A. Gardner, 1879–82.

Janson, Horst Waldemar. *Apes and ape lore in the Middle Ages and Renaissance.* London: Warburg Institute, 1952.

———. "A 'Memento Mori' Among Early Italian Prints." *Journal of the Warburg and Courtauld Institutes* 3 (1939–40): 248.

Jenness, Diamond. *Indians of Canada.* National Museum of Canada Bulletin no. 65. Ottawa, 1958.

Jennings, Francis. *The Invasion of America.* Chapel Hill: University of North Carolina Press, 1975.

———. "Virgin Land and Savage People." *American Quarterly* 23, no. 4 (1971): 519–41.

Jennings, Jesse D., ed. *Ancient Native Americans.* San Francisco: W. H. Freeman, 1979.

Jensen, Adolf E. *Myth and Cult Among Primitive Peoples.* Chicago and London: University of Chicago Press, 1973.

Jilek-Aall, Louise M. "What is a Sasquatch – or, the Problematics of Reality Testing." *Canadian Psychiatry Association Journal* 17 (1972): 243–47.

Johnson, Frederick, ed. *Man in Northeastern North America.* Andover, Mass.: Phillips Academy, Robert S. Peabody Foundation for Archaeology, 1946.

Jones, W. R. "The Image of the Barbarian in Medieval Europe." *Comparative Studies in Society and History* 13 (1971): 376–407.

Jordan, Winthrop. *White over Black: American Attitudes toward the Negro, 1550–1812.* Chapel Hill: University of North Carolina Press, 1968.

Joseph, Mary Anna. *See* Mary Anna Joseph.

Josephy, Alvin M., ed. *The American Heritage Book of Indians.* New York: American Heritage Publishing, 1961.

Juchereau de La Ferté, Soeur Jeanne-Françoise. *Histoire de l'Hotel-Dieu de Québec.* Montauban: Legier, *s.d.*

Julien, Charles-André. *Les Débuts de l'expansion et de la colonisation Française (XVe–XVIe siècles).* Paris: Presses Universitaires de France, 1947.

———. *Les François en Amérique pendant la première moitié du XVIe siècle.* Edited by Ch. -A. Julien, R. Herval, and Th. Beauchesne. Paris: Presses Universitaires de France, 1946.

———. *Les Voyages de découverte et les premiers établissements (XVe–XVIe siècles).* Paris: Presses Universitaires de France, 1948.

Kamen, Henry. *The Iron Century: Social Change in Europe, 1550–1660.* New York: Praeger, 1971.

Kavalyk, Nicholas John. "The Dutch Fur Trade in New Netherland, 1609–1664." M.A. thesis, Columbia University, 1948.

Keller, Arthur S., Oliver J. Lissitzyn, and Frederick J. Mann. *Creation of Rights of Sovereignty through Symbolic Acts, 1400–1800.* New York: Columbia University Press, 1938. (Reprint ed., New York: AMS Press, 1967.)

Kennedy, John Hopkins. *Jesuit and Savage in New France.* New Haven: Yale University Press, 1950. (Reprint ed., Hamden, Conn.: Archon, 1971.)

Kermode, Frank, ed. Shakespeare's *The Tempest.* London: Methuen, 1976.

Kimmey, Fred M. "Christianity and Indian Lands." *Ethnohistory* 7 (1960): 44–60.

Kroeber, Alfred Louis. *An Anthropologist Looks at History.* Edited by Theodora Kroeber. Berkeley and Los Angeles: University of California Press, 1963.

———. *Cultural and natural areas of native North America.* University of California Publications in American Archaeology and Ethnology, 38 (1939).

La Berge, Lionel. *Rouen et le commerce du Canada de 1650 à 1670.* Quebec: Editions Bois-Lotinville, 1972.

La Curne de Sainte-Palaye, J. B. *Dictionnaire historique de l'ancien langage françois ou glossaire de la langue françoise depuis son origine jusqu'au siècle de Louis XIV.* 10 vols. Niort: Le Favre, 1875–82.

La Quérière, Eustache de. *Description historique des maisons de Rouen, les plus remarquables par leur decoration extérieure et par leur ancienneté....* 2 vols. Paris: F. Didot, 1821–41.

La Roncière, Charles Germain Marie Bourel de. *La Floride française: Scène de la vie indienne, peinte en 1564 (par Jacques Le Moyne De Morgues).* Paris: Les Editions Nationales, 1928.

———. *Histoire de la marine française.* 6 vols. Paris: Plon-Nourrit, 1909–23.

———. "Notre première tentative de colonisation au Canada." *Bibliothèque de l'Ecole de Chartres* 73 (1912): 228–300.

Ladurie, Emmanuel Le Roy. *Montaillou, The Promised Land of Error.* Translated by Barbara Bray. New York: Vintage, 1979.

Lanctot, Gustave. "L'Establissement du Marquis De La Roche à l'Isle de Sable." *Canadian Historical Association Report* (1933): 33–42.

———. *Histoire du Canada.* 3 vols. Montreal: Beauchemin, 1959.

Landucci, Sergio. *I filosofi e i selvaggi 1580–1780.* Bari: Laterza, 1972.

Lanning, Edward P. *Peru Before the Incas.* Englewood Cliffs, N.J.: Prentice-Hall, 1967.

Larousse, Pierre. *Grand Dictionnaire Universel.* 17 vols. Paris, 1905.

Lauvrière, Emile. "Les Jésuites en Acadie." *Revue de l'histoire des colonies françaises* 13 (1925).

Lavisse, Ernest. *Histoire de France, depuis les origines jusqu'à la Revolution.* 9 vols. Paris: Hachette, 1903–11.

Le Moine, Roger. *L'Amérique et les poètes français de la Renaissance.* Ottawa: Université d'Ottawa, 1972.

Leakey, Richard E., and Roger Lewin. *Origins.* New York: Dutton, 1977.

Leclerc, Jean. "Denonville et ses captifs Iroquois: Jean de Lamville et les quarante delégués Iroquois." *Revue d'histoire de l'Amérique française* 14, no. 4 (1961): 545–58; 15, no. 1 (1961): 41–58.

———. *Le Marquis de Denonville, gouverneur de la Nouvelle-France 1685–1689.* Montreal: Fides, 1976.

Lehner, Ernst and Johanna. *How They Saw the New World.* New York: Tudor, 1966.

Leithauser, Joachim. *Mappaemundi. Die geistige Eroberung der Welt.* Berlin: Gestaltung Fritz Kolling, 1958.

Levi-Strauss, Claude. "L'Anthropologie sociale devant l'histoire." *Annales* 15, no. 4 (August 1960): 625–37.

———. *La Pensée sauvage.* Paris: Plon, 1962.

———. *Race et histoire.* Paris: Editions Gonthier, 1961.

———. *Structural Anthropology.* London: Allen Lane, Penguin Press, 1968.

———. *Les Structures elementaires de la Parenté.* Paris: Les

Presses Universitaires de France, 1949.

———. "La Théorie du pouvoir dans une société primitive." In *Les Doctrines Politiques Modernes*, pp. 41–63. New York: Brentano's, 1947.

———. *Tristes Tropiques*. Paris: Plon, 1955.

Lewis, Warren Hamilton. *The Splendid Century*. London: Eyre & Spottiswoode, 1953.

Leymarie, A. -Léo. "Le Canada pendant la jeunesse de Louis XIII." *Nova Francia* 1, no. 4 (1926): 168–69.

Linden, H. Vander. "Alexander VI and the Demarcation of the Maritime and Colonial Domains of Spain and Portugal, 1493–1494." *American Historical Review* 22 (1916–17): 1–20.

Linton, Ralph, ed. *The Science of Man in the World Crisis*. New York: Columbia University Press, 1945.

———. *The Cultural Background of Personality*. New York: Appleton-Century, 1945.

Littré, Emile. *Dictionnaire de la langue française....* 7 vols. Paris: Gallimard/Hachette, 1956.

Loeb, Edwin Meyer. "Cannibalism." M.A. thesis, Yale University, 1921.

———. "The Origin and Evolution of Human Sacrifice." Ph.D. thesis, Yale University, 1922.

Lorant, Stefan, ed. *The New World: The First Pictures of America*. New York: Duell, Sloan and Pearce, 1965.

Lovejoy, Arthur Oncken. *The Great Chain of Being; a study of the history of an idea*. Cambridge, Mass.: Harvard University Press, 1936.

MacLeod, Murdo J. *Spanish Central America: a socioeconomic history, 1520–1720*. Berkeley and Los Angeles: University of California Press, 1973.

Mandrou, Robert. *De la Culture populaire aux XVIIe et XVIIIe siècles: la Bibliothèque Bleue de Troyes*. Paris: Stock, c.1964.

———. "Les Français hors de France aux XVIe et XVIIe siècles." *Annales* 14, no. 4 (octobre–décembre 1959): 662–75.

———. *Introduction à la France moderne (1500–1640)*. Paris: Albin Michel, 1961.

Manso, J. A. "The Quest of El Dorado." *Bulletin of the Pan American Union* 34 (1912): 55–56, 165–76.

Maran, René. *Les pionniers de l'Empire....* Paris: Albin Michel, 1943.

Marcel, Gabriel. *Cartographie de la Nouvelle-France, supplement à l'ouvrage de M. Harrisse....* Paris: Maisonneuve frères et C. Leclerc, 1885.

———. *Les Corsaires français au XVIe siècle dans les Antilles*. Paris: E. Leroux, 1902.

———. *Reproductions de cartes et de globes relatifs à la découverte de l'Amérique du XVIe au XVIIIe siècle, avec texte explicatif*. Paris: E. Leroux, 1893.

———. *Sur quelques documents peu connus relatifs à la découverte de l'Amérique*. Paris: May et Metteroz, 1893.

———. *Un texte ethnographique inédit du XVIII siècle*. Mâcon: Protat frères, 1904.

Marion, Marcel. *Dictionnaire des institutions de la France aux XVIIe et XVIIIe siècles*. Paris: A. Picard, 1923.

Markham, Sir Clements Robert, ed. *The Letters of Amerigo Vespucci*. London: Hakluyt Society, 1894.

Marshak, Alexander. "The Message of the Markings." *Horizon* 18, no. 4 (1976): 62–73.

Martin, Calvin. "The European Impact on the Culture of a Northeastern Algonquian Tribe: An Ecological Interpretation." *William and Mary Quarterly* 21 (1974): 3–54.

Martin, François-Xavier. *History of Louisiana from the earliest period*. 2 vols. New Orleans: Lyman & Beardslee, 1827.

Martineau, LaVan. *The Rocks Begin to Speak*. Las Vegas: KC Publications, 1973.

Mary Anna Joseph (Mary Genevieve Hennesey). "French and English Pressures on the Indians of Acadia and Eastern New England (1667–1727)." M.A. thesis, University of New Brunswick, 1962.

Masselman, George. *The Cradle of Colonialism*. New Haven: Yale University Press, 1963.

Mateos, Francisco. "Ecos de América en Trento." *Revista de Indias* 6, no. 22 (1945): 359–605.

Maurault, Joseph-Pierre-Anselme. *Histoire des Abénakis depuis 1605 jusqu'à nos jours*. Montréal: Gazette de Sorel, 1866.

Mauss, Marcel. *Sociologie et anthropologie*. Paris: Les Presses Universitaires de France, 1960.

Mayer, Hans Eberhard. *The Crusades*. Translated by John Gillingham. London: Oxford University Press, 1972.

McIntyre, Loren. "The Lost Empire of the Incas." *National Geographic* 144, no. 6 (1973): 729–87.

McKee, David R. "Isaac de la Peyrère, a Precursor of Eighteenth Century Critical Deists." *Publications of the Modern Language Association* 59 (1944): 456–85.

McKeon, Jesse C. "A comparative Study of the Indian Policy of Spain, France and England in Colonial America." M.A. thesis, Pennsylvania State College, 1934.

McManus, John C. "An Economic Analysis of Indian Behavior in the North American Fur Trade." *Journal of Economic History* 32, no. 1 (1972): 36–53.

Ménage, Gilles. *Dictionnaire étymologique de la langue françoise.* ... 2 vols. Edited by A. F. Jault. Paris: Briasson, 1750.

Menzi, Hermine. "The Relation of the Indians to the Economic Life of Colonial New England." M.A. thesis, University of Chicago, 1926.

Mesnard, Pierre. *L'Essor de la philosophie politique au XVIe siècle.* Paris: Vrin, 1969.

Mollat, Michel. *Le Commerce maritime normand à la fin du Moyen Age.* Paris: Plon, 1952.

———. *Premières relations entre la France et le Brésil, du Verrazano à Villegaignon.* Cahiers de l'Institut des Hautes Etudes de l'Amérique Latine. Paris, 1964.

Mollat, Michel, and Paul Adam, eds. *Les Aspects internationaux de la découverte océanique aux XVe et XVIe siècles. Actes du cinquième colloque international d'histoire maritime, Lisbonne, 1960.* Paris: S.E.V.P.E.N., 1966.

Molnár, Erik. "Les Fondements économiques et sociaux de l'absolutisme." In *Nouvelles Etudes Historiques,* pp. 285–97. Vienna, 1965. (XIIe Congrès International des Sciences Historiques, *Rapports.*)

Moloney, Francis X. *The Fur Trade in New England 1620–1676.* Cambridge, Mass.: Harvard University Press, 1931. (Reprint ed., Hamden, Conn.: Archon, 1967.)

Morgan, Dale et al. *Aspects of the Fur Trade.* St. Paul: University Historical Society, 1967.

Morgan, Lewis Henry. *League of the Ho-dé-no-sau-nee or Iroquois.* Edited by Herbert M. Lloyd. New York: Dodd-Mead, 1901.

———. *League of the Iroquois.* New York: Corinth, 1969.

Morison, Samuel Eliot. *Admiral of the Ocean Sea.* Boston: Little, Brown, 1942.

———. *The European Discovery of America.* New York: Oxford University Press, 1971.

———. *Portuguese Voyages to America in the Fifteenth Century.* New York: Octagon Books, 1965.

Morley, Sylvanus Griswold. *The Ancient Maya.* Stanford: Stanford University Press, 1947.

Morrison, Alvin H., and Thomas H. Goetz. "Membertou's Raid on the Chouacoet 'Almouchiquois'–the Micmac Sack of Saco, 1607." Papers of the Sixth Algonquian Conference, 1974, pp. 141–79. Ottawa: National Museum of Man, 1975.

Morrison, Alvin Hamblen. "Dawnland Decisions: Seventeenth-Century Wabanaki Leaders and Their Responses to the Differential Contact Stimuli in the Overlap Area of New France and New England." Ph.D. thesis, State University of New York at Buffalo, 1974.

Muntz, Earl Edward. "Race Contact, A Study of the Social and Economic Consequences of Contact Between Civilized and Uncivilized Races." Ph.D. thesis, Yale University, 1925.

Murray, David. *Museums, their history and their use.* 3 vols. Glasgow: MacLehose, 1904.

Murray, Jean Elizabeth. "The Fur Trade in New France and New Netherland prior to 1645." Ph.D. thesis, University of Chicago, 1936.

Musset, Georges. *Les Rochelais à Terre-Neuve 1500–1789.* La Rochelle: By the Author, 1899.

Myres, Sir John Linton. *The Influence of Anthropology on the Course of Political Science.* University of California Publications in History, vol. 4, no. 1. Berkeley and Los Angeles: University of California Press, 1916.

Nant, Candide de. *See* Candide (de Nant).

Nash, Gary B. *Red, white and black: the peoples of early America.* Englewood Cliffs, N.J.: Prentice-Hall, 1974.

Navarrete, Martin Fernández de. *See* Fernández de Navarrete, Martin.

Navières, J. "Un Voyage inédit à la Nouvelle-France (Canada) sous Louis XV (1734), relation inédite de J. Navières." Edited by L. Drapeyron. *Revue de géographie* 1 (1882): 81–105.

Neill, Edward D. *The Founders of Maryland....* Albany: Munsell, 1876.

———. *The History of Minnesota from the earliest French Explorations to the Present Time.* Philadelphia: Lippincott, 1858.

Nelson, Robert J., ed. *No Man is Alien.* Leyden: Brill, 1971.

Newton, Arthur Percival. *The European Nations in the West Indies 1493–1688.* London: A. & C. Black, 1933.

Nordenskiöld, Nils Adolf Erik. *Periplus: An Essay on the Early History of Charts and Sailing Directions.* Translated by Francis A. Bather. Stockholm: Norstedt, 1897. (Accompanying facsimile Atlas published in 1889.)

Nowell, Charles E. "The French in Sixteenth-Century Brazil." *The Americas* 5, no. 4 (1949): 381–93.

Oakeshott, Walter Fraser, ed. *Some woodcuts by Hans Burgkmair.* Oxford: Roxburghe Club, 1960.

O'Gorman, Edmundo. *The Invention of America.* Bloomington: Indiana University Press, 1961.

Oleson, Tryggvi J. *Early Voyages and Northern Approaches, 1000–1632.* Toronto: McClelland and Stewart, 1963.

Owen, Roger C., James J. F. Deetz, and Anthony Fisher, eds. *The North American Indians: A Sourcebook.* Toronto: Macmillan, 1972.

Pannier, Jacques. "Quand et comment l'influence des Jésuites s'est substituée à l'influence des protestants dans les entreprises français au Canada (1610–1611)." *Bulletin de la Société de l'Histoire du Protestantisme français* (1912): 508-12.

Paredes, J. Anthony. "A Case Study of 'Normal Windigo'." *Anthropologica* 14, no. 2 (1972): 97–116.

Parker, Robert J. "The Iroquois and the Albany Fur Trade, 1609–1701." Ph.D. thesis, University of California, 1932.

Parry, John Horace. *The Age of Reconnaissance.* New York: New American Library, 1964.

———. *The Spanish Theory of Empire in the Sixteenth Century.* Cambridge: Cambridge University Press, 1940.

Pastor, Ludwig. *The History of the Popes,* 40 vols. London: Kegan Paul, 1923–53.

Patterson, George. "Beothick Vocabularies, with a few Notes on Paper on the Beothiks in 'Transactions of Royal Society of Canada' for 1891." Proceedings and Transactions, Royal Society of Canada, 1st ser., vol. 10 (1892), sec. 2: 19–30.

———. "The Beothicks or Red Indians of Newfoundland." Proceedings and Transactions, Royal Society of Canada, 1st ser., vol. 9 (1891), sec. 2: 123–71.

———. "Portuguese on the northeast coast of America and the first European Attempt at Colonization there: A Lost chapter in American history." Proceedings and Transactions, Royal Society of Canada, 1st ser., vol. 8 (1890), sec. 2: 127–73.

———. "Sable Island: Its History and Phenomena." Proceedings and Transactions, Royal Society of Canada, 1st ser., vol. 12 (1894), sec. 2: 3–49.

———. "Sir William Alexander and the Scottish Attempt to Colonize Acadia." Proceedings and Transactions, Royal Society of Canada, 1st ser., vol. 10 (1892), sec. 2: 79–107.

Pearce, Roy Harvey. "The Significance of the Captivity Narratives." *American Literature* 19, no. 1 (March 1947): 1–20.

Peckham, Howard, and Charles Gibson, eds. *Attitudes of Colonial Powers Toward the American Indian.* Salt Lake City: University of Utah Press, 1969.

Peddie, Robert Alexander. *Fifteenth Century Books.* London: Grafton, 1913. (Reprint ed., New York: Burt Franklin, 1969.)

Penrose, Boies. *Travel and Discovery in the Renaissance, 1420–1620.* Cambridge, Mass.: Harvard University Press, 1955.

Phelan, John Leddy. *The Millennial Kingdom of the Franciscans in the New World.* Berkeley and Los Angeles: University of California Press, 1956.

Porchnev, Boris. *Les Soulèvements populaires en France au XVIIe siècle.* Paris: Flammarion, 1972.

Porter, Harry Culverwell. *The Inconstant Savage.* London: Duckworth, 1979.

Post, J. B., comp. *An Atlas of Fantasy.* Baltimore: Mirage Press, 1973.

Pouliot, Léon. "Etats mystiques chez les Convertis Indiens dans la Nouvelle France." Société Canadienne d'Histoire de l'Eglise Catholique, Rapport 1939-1940 (1940): 99–106.

———. *Etude sur les Relations de Jésuites de la Nouvelle-France (1632–1672).* Montreal: Compagnie de Jésus, 1940.

Priestly, Herbert Ingram. *The Coming of the White Man, 1492–1848.* New York: Quadrangle, 1971.

Pring, Martin. "A Voyage Set out from the Cities of Bristoll, 1603." In H. S. Burrage, ed., *Early English and French Voyages. . . .* New York: Scribner's 1906.

Quinn, David Beers. "The Voyage of Etienne Bellenger to the Maritimes in 1583: A New Document." *Canadian Historical Review* 43 (1962): 328–43.

Quinn, D. B. and N. M. Cheshire. *The New Found Land of Stephen Parmenius.* Toronto: University of Toronto Press, 1972.

Quirk, Robert E. "Some Notes on a Controversial Controversy: Juan Ginés de Sepúlveda and Natural Servitude." *Hispanic American Historical Review* 34 (1954): 357–64.

Ramsey, Peter H., ed. *The Price Revolution in Sixteenth Century England.* London: Methuen, 1971.

[Razilly, Claude]. "Mémoire du Chevalier de Razilly." *Revue de Géographie* 19, (1886): 374–83, 453–64.

Renfrew, Colin. *Before Civilization.* London: Pelican Books, 1976.

Ricard, Robert. *La Conquête spirituelle du Mexique*. Paris: Institut d'Ethnologie, 1933.

———. *The Spiritual Conquest of Mexico; an essay on the apostolate, and the evangelizing methods of the mendicant orders in New Spain, 1523–1572*. Translated by Lesley Byrd Simpson. Berkeley and Los Angeles: University of California Press, 1966.

Rich, Edwin Ernest. "Trade Habits and Economic Motivation Among the Indians of North America." *Canadian Journal of Economic and Political Science* 26, no. 1 (1960): 35–53.

Richelet, Pierre. *Dictionnaire françois contenant les mots et les choses, plusieurs nouvelles remarques sur la langue françoise....* Geneva: Jean Herman Widerhold, 1680.

Robbins, Russel Hope. *The Encyclopedia of Witchcraft and Demonology*. New York: Crown Publishers, 1966.

Roberts, Lewes. *The Merchants Map of Commerce; Wherein the Universal Manner and Matter of Trade Is Compendiously Handled*. London: Printed for R. Horn, 1671.

———. *The Treasure of Trafficke or A Discourse of Forraigne Trade*. London: Printed for Nicholas Bourne, 1641.

Roberts, William I., III. "The Fur Trade of New England in the Seventeenth Century." Ph.D. thesis, University of Pennsylvania, 1958.

Robertson, Samuel. "Notes on the Coast of Labrador." Transactions of The Literary and Historical Society of Quebec. 1st ser., vol. 4 (1841), pt. 1: 27–53.

Rochemonteix, Camille de. *Les Jésuites et la Nouvelle-France au XVIIe siècle, d'après beaucoup de documents inédits*. 3 vols. Paris: Letouzey et ainé, 1895–96.

Rose, John Holland, et al. *Cambridge History of the British empire*. 8 vols. Cambridge: Cambridge University Press, 1929–59.

Rothkrug, Lionel. *Opposition to Louis XIV*. Princeton: Princeton University Press, 1965.

Rousseau, François. *L'Idée missionnaire au XVIe et XVIIe siècles*. Paris: Editions Spes, 1930.

Rowe, John Howland. "Ethnography and Ethnology in the Sixteenth Century." The Kroeber Anthropological Society Papers, no. 30, pp. 1–19. Berkeley and Los Angeles: University of California Press, 1964.

Roy, Jean-L. "Un Français au Brésil au XVIe siècle: André Thevet, Cosmographe." *Revue d'histoire de l'Amérique française* 21, no. 3 (décembre 1967): 363–96.

Roy, Pierre-Georges. "Les Iroquois sur les galères." *Bulletin des recherches historiques* 4, no. 4 (1898): 123–25.

Ruyer, Raymond. *L'Utopie et les Utopies*. Paris: Les Presses Universitaires de France, 1950.

Sabin, Joseph, Wilberforce Eames, and R. W. G. Vail. *A Dictionary of Books Relating to America*. 29 vols. New York, 1868–1936. (Reprint ed., Amsterdam: N. Israel, 1961.)

Sainéan, Lazare (Saineanu, Lazar). "La Cosmographie de Jean-Alfonse Saintongeais." *Revue des études rabelaisiennes* 10 (1912): 19–67.

Saint-Martin, Antoine-Jean. *Mémoires historiques et géographiques sur l'Armenie suivis du texte arménien de l'Histoire des princes Orpilians*. 2 vols. Paris: Imprimerie Royale, 1818–19.

Sainte-Marie, Adele de. *See* Adele de Sainte-Marie.

Sainte-Palaye, J. B. La Curne. *See* La Curne de Sainte-Palaye, J. B.

Salone, Emile. "Les Sauvages du Canada et les maladies importées de France au XVIIe et au XVIIIe siècles: la picote et l'alcoolisme." *Journal de la Sociéte des Américanistes* 4 (1907): 7–20.

Sandars, Nancy K. *The Epic of Gilgamesh*. London: Penguin, 1964.

Sandford, Charles L. *The Quest for Paradise*. Urbana: University of Illinois Press, 1961.

Santarem, Manuel Francisco de Barros. *See* Barros e Sousa de Mesquita de Macedo Leitão e Carvalhosa, Manuel Francisco de, Vicomte de Santarem.

Sauer, Carl Ortwin. *The Early Spanish Main*. Berkeley and Los Angeles: University of California Press, 1969.

———. *Northern Mists*. Berkeley and Los Angeles: University of California Press, 1968.

———. *Sixteenth Century North America*. Berkeley and Los Angeles: University of California Press, 1971.

Savary, Jacques. *Le Parfait Negociant Ou Instruction Generale Pour Ce Qui Regarde Le Commerce des Marchandises de France, & des Pays Estrangers....* Paris: Louis Billaine, 1679.

Savelle, Max. *The Diplomatic History of the Canadian Boundary 1749–1763*. New Haven: Yale University Press, 1940.

Schafer, Edward H. *The Vermilion Bird*. Berkeley and Los Angeles: University of California Press, 1967.

———. *The Golden Peaches of Samarkand*. Berkeley and Los Angeles: University of California Press, 1963.

Scheele, Raymond. "Warfare of the Iroquois and Their Northern Neighbors." Ph.D. thesis, Columbia University, 1950.

Schlesier, Karl H. "Epidemics and Indian Middlemen: Rethinking the Wars of the Iroquois, 1609–53." *Ethnohistory*

23, no. 2 (1976): 129–45.

Schoenbaum, Samuel, ed. *Renaissance Drama*. Evanston, Ill.: Northwestern University Press, 1968.

Sealey, Donald Bruce, and Verna J. Kirkness, eds. *Indians Without Tipis: A Resource Book*. Vancouver: W. Clare, 1973.

Seguin, Jean Pierre. *L'Information en France avant la periodique: 517 canards imprimés entre 1529 et 1631*. Paris: Maisonneuve et Larose, 1964.

———. *L'Information en France, de Louis XII à Henri II*. Geneva: Droz, 1961.

Seguin, Robert-Lionel. "La Vie libertine en Nouvelle-France au XVIIe siècle." Thèses de D. ès Lettres d'État, Sorbonne, 1972. (Published in 2 vols., Montreal: Lemeac, 1972.)

Séjourné, Laurette. *Burning Water: Thought and Religion in Ancient Mexico*. Translated by Irene Nicholson. London: Thames and Hudson, c.1956.

Seward, Desmond. *Prince of the Renaissance*. London: Cardinal, 1974.

Shorter Oxford Dictionary on Historical Principles. 2 vols. Revised and edited by C. T. Onions. Oxford: The Clarendon Press, 1973.

Simonsen, Roberto C. *História Econômica do Brasil (1500/1820)*. São Paulo: Companhia Editora Nacional, 1962.

Smith, Donald B. "The Mississauga, Peter Jones, and the White Man: the Algonkian's Adjustment to the Europeans on the North Shore of Lake Ontario to 1860." Ph.D. thesis, University of Toronto, 1975.

———. *Le Sauvage*. Ottawa: National Museums of Canada, 1974.

Smith, James Morton, ed. *Seventeenth Century America: Essays on Colonial History*. Chapel Hill: University of North Carolina Press, 1959. (Reprint ed., New York: Norton, 1972.)

Snow, Dean. *The American Indians: their archaeology and prehistory*. London: Thames and Hudson, 1976.

Solomon, Howard M. "The Gazette and Antistatist Propaganda: The Medium of the Print in the first half of the Seventeenth Century." *Canadian Journal of History* 9, no. 1 (1974): 1–17.

Southey, Robert. *History of Brazil*. 3 vols. London: Longmans, 1822. (Reprint ed., New York: Greenwood Press, 1969.)

Spiro, Milford E., ed. *Context and Meaning in Cultural Anthropology*. New York: Free Press, 1965.

Stanley, George F. G. "The First Indian 'Reserves' in Canada." *Revue de l'histoire de l'Amerique française* 4 (1950): 178–209.

Starna, William A. "Mohawk Iroquois Population: A Revision." *Ethnohistory* 27, no. 4 (1980): 371–82.

Stegman, André. "L'Amérique de Du Bartas et De Thou." In *La Découverte d'Amérique*. Xe Stage International d'Études Humanistes, Tours, 1966. Paris: J. Vrin, 1968.

Stephenson, Mill. *A List of Monumental Brasses in the British Isles*. London: Headley Bros., 1926. (Based upon *A Manual of Monumental Brasses* by Herbert Haines.)

Stevenson, Robert. *Protestant Church Music in America*. New York: Norton, 1966.

Stilwell, Margaret Bingham. *Incunabula and Americana*. New York: Cooper Square.

Stocking, George W. "French Anthropology in 1800." *Isis* 55 (June 1964): 134–50.

Streit, Robert. *Bibliotheca Missionum*. 29 vols. Rome: Herder, 1916–.

Such, Peter. *Riverrun*. Toronto: Clarke Irwin, 1973.

Sulte, Benjamin. "The Valley of the Grand River, 1600– 1650." Proceedings and Transactions, Royal Society of Canada, vol. 4, sec. 2 (1898): 107–135.

Suttles, Wayne. "Subhuman and Human Fighting." *Anthropologica*, n.s. 3 (1961): 148–63.

Swan, Conrad M. J. F. "American Indians in Heraldry." *Coat of Arms* 12, no. 87 (July 1971): 96–106; and no. 88 (October 1971): 148–59.

Swanton, John R. *The Indian Tribes of North America*. Washington: Smithsonian Institution Press, 1968.

Tazbir, Janusz. "La Conquête de l'Amérique à la lumière de l'opinion polonaise." *Acta Poloniae Historica* 17 (1968): 5–22.

Ternaux-Compans, Charles-Henri (Charles Navarin). *Bibliothèque américaine des ouvrages relatifs à l'Amérique qui ont paru depuis sa découverte jusqu'à l'an 1700*. Paris: A. Bertrand, 1837.

Thompson, H. Paul. "A Technique Using Anthropological and Biological Data." *Current Anthropology* 7, no. 4 (1966): 417–49.

Thompson, Stith. *Motif Index of Folk Literature*. 6 vols. Bloomington: Indiana University Press, 1956.

Thorndike, Lynn. *A History of Magic and Experimental Science*. 8 vols. New York: Columbia University Press, c.1923–58.

———. "The Survival of Medieval Intellectual Interests into Modern Times." *Speculum* 2 (1927): 147–59.

Thwaites, Reuben Gold. *France in America, 1497–1663*. New York: Cooper Square, 1968.

Tilley, Arthur A. *Studies in the French Renaissance*. New York:

Barnes and Noble, 1968.

Tooker, Elizabeth. *An Ethnography of the Huron Indians 1615–1649.* Midland, Ont.: Huronia Historical Development Council, 1967.

———. "The Iroquois Defeat of the Huron: A Review of the Causes." *Pennsylvania Archaeologist* 33 (1963): 115–23.

———. "Northern Iroquoian Sociopolitical Organization." *American Anthropologist* 72 (1970): 90–97.

Trelease, Allen William. "Indian Relations and the Fur Trade in New Netherland, 1609–1664." Ph.D. thesis, Harvard University, 1955.

Trigger, Bruce G. "Champlain Judged by His Indian Policy: A Different View of Early Canadian History." *Anthropologica* 13 (1971): 85–114.

———. *The Children of Aataentsic.* 2 vols. Montreal: McGill-Queen's University Press, 1976.

———. "The Destruction of Huronia: A Study in Economic and Cultural Change, 1609–1650." Transactions of the Royal Canadian Institute, vol. 33, pt. 1, no. 68 (1960): 14–45.

———. "The French Presence in Huronia: The Structure of Franco-Huron Relations in the First Half of the Seventeenth Century." *The Canadian Historical Review* 49, no. 2 (1968): 107–41.

———. *The Huron Farmers of the North.* Case Studies in Cultural Anthropology, Stanford University. New York: Holt Rinehart and Winston, 1969.

———. "The Jesuits and the Fur Trade." *Ethnohistory* 12, no. 1 (1965): 30–53.

———. "Order and Freedom in Huron Society." *Anthropologica* 5 (1963): 151–68.

———. "Sixteenth Century Ontario: History, Ethnohistory and Archaeology." *Ontario History* 71, no. 4 (1979): 205–23.

———. "Trade and Tribal Warfare on the St. Lawrence in the Sixteenth Century." *Ethnohistory* 9, no. 3 (1962): 240–56.

Trigger, Bruce G., and James F. Pendergast. *Cartier's Hochelaga and the Dawson Site.* Montreal: McGill-Queen's University Press, 1972.

Trudel, Marcel. *Initiation à la Nouvelle-France.* Montreal: Holt, Rinehart & Winston, 1971.

———. *Histoire de la Nouvelle-France: Les vaines tentatives 1524–1603.* Montreal: Fides, 1963.

———. *Histoire de la Nouvelle-France: Le comptoir 1604–1627.* Montreal: Fides, 1966.

Trumbull, J. Hammond. "Thevet's Specimens of the Indian Language of Norumbega." *Historical Magazine,* ser. 2 (1870): 239.

Tuck, James A. "A Current Summary of Newfoundland Prehistory." *The Newfoundland Quarterly* 68 (1971).

———. "The Iroquois Confederacy." *Scientific American* 224, no. 2 (1971): 32–42.

———. *Onondaga Iroquois Prehistory.* Syracuse: Syracuse University Press, 1971.

Turner, Katherine C. *Red Men Calling on the Great White Father.* Norman: University of Oklahoma Press, 1951.

Turney-High, Harry Holbert. *Primitive Warfare: Its Practices and Concepts.* Columbia, S.C.: University of South Carolina Press, 1949.

Tylor, E. Burnet. "Wild Men and Beast Children." *Anthropological Review* 1 (1863): 21–32.

Umstead, Kenneth. "The French in the Americas during the Sixteenth Century." Ph.D. thesis, University of California, 1939.

Vander Linden, H. *See* Linden, H. Vander.

Van Gennep, Arnold. *Manuel de folklore français contemporain.* 4 vols. Paris: A. Picard, 1937–58.

Vaucheret, Etienne. "Jean Nicot et l'entreprise de Villegaignon." In *La Découverte d'Amérique,* pp. 89–104. Xe State International d'Etudes Humanistes, Tours, 1966. Paris: J. Vrin, 1968.

Vaulx, Bernard de. *History of the Missions: From the beginning to Benedict XV–1914.* Translated by Reginald F. Trevett. London: Burns & Oates, 1961. (Faith and Fact Books, no. 98.)

Vaumas, Guillaume de. *L'Eveil missionnaire de la France (d'Henri IV à la fondation du seminaire des Missions étrangères).* Lyon: Imprimerie Express, 1942.

Vellard, Jehan. "La Conception de l'âme et de la maladie chez les Indiens d'Amérique." *Revue de psychologie des peuples* (1960).

Verlinden, Charles. "Les Influences médiévales dans la colonisation de l'Amérique." *Revista de Historia de America,* no. 30 (décembre 1950): 440–50.

Verreau, Hospice. "Jacques Cartier: Questions de droit public, de législation et d'usages maritimes." Mémoires, Société Royale du Canada, vol. 9 (1891): sec. 1, pp. 77–83.

Vetromile, Eugene. *The Abnakis and their history.* New York: J. B. Kerker, 1866.

Villey, Pierre-Louis-Joseph. *Les Sources et l'évolution des "Essais" de Montaigne*. 2 vols. Paris: Hachette, 1908.

Visme, Jean-Daniel de. *Les Précurseurs de l'idée missionnaire en France au XVIe et XVIIe siècles*. Paris: Société des missions évangéliques, 1923.

Vitet, Louis. *Histoire des anciennes villes de France*. 2 vols. Paris: Mesnier, 1833.

Wagner, Sir Anthony. *Heralds and Ancestors*. London: British Museum, 1978.

Wagner, Henry R. "Creation of Rights of Sovereignty through Symbolic Acts." *Pacific Historical Review* 7, no. 4 (1938): 297–326.

Walker, James W. St. G. "The Indian in Canadian Historical Writing." Canadian Historical Association, *Historical Papers* (1971): 21–47.

Walker, Joseph B. "The Valley of the Merrimack." Collections of the New Hampshire Historical Society, vol. 7. Edited by Nathaniel Bouton. Concord, 1863.

Wallace, Anthony, F. C. *The Death and Rebirth of the Seneca*. New York: Alfred A. Knopf, 1970.

———. "The Institutionalization of cathartic and control strategies in Iroquois religious psychotherapy." In Marvin K. Opler, ed., *Culture and Mental Health: Cross-Cultural Studies*. New York: Macmillan, 1959.

Wallis, Wilson Dallam. "Historical Background of the Micmac Indians of Canada." National Museums of Canada Bulletin, no. 173. Ottawa, 1961.

Warwick, Jack. *The Long Journey: Literary Themes of French Canada*. Toronto: University of Toronto Press, 1968.

Washburn, Wilcomb E. "History, Anthropology and the American Indian." *American Studies* 11, no. 1 (1972): 25–36.

———. "The Writing of American Indian History: A Status Report." *Pacific Historical Review* 40 (1971): 261–81.

Wasserman, Maurice Marc. *The American Indian as seen by seventeenth century chronicles*. Philadephia: University of Pennsylvania Press, 1954.

Wauchope, Robert. *Lost Tribes and Sunken Continents: Myth and Method in the Study of American Indians*. Chicago: University of Chicago Press, 1962.

Weckmann-Muñoz, Luis. *Las Bulas Alejandrinas de 1493 y la teoría politica del papado medieval*. . . . Mexico: Universidad Nacional Autónoma de Mexico, 1949.

Weissmann, Elizabeth Wilder. *Mexico in Sculpture 1521–1821*. Cambridge: Harvard University Press, 1950. (Reprint ed., Westport, Conn.: Greenwood Press, 1971.)

White, Helen Constance. *Social criticism in popular religious literature of the sixteenth century*. New York: Macmillan, 1944.

Wieser, Franz von and Jos. Fischer. *The Oldest Map with the Name America of the year 1507, and the Carta Marina of the year 1516, By M. Waldseemüller (Ilacomilus)*. Innsbrück: Wagner'sche Universitäts-Buchhandlung, 1903.

Winsor, Justin. *Narrative and Critical History of America*. 8 vols. Boston: Houghton Mifflin, 1884–89.

Wissler, Clark. *The relation of nature to man in aboriginal America*. London: Oxford University Press, 1926. (Reprint ed., New York: AMS Press, 1971.)

Wright, James Valliere. *The Ontario Iroquois Tradition*. National Museum of Canada Bulletin, no. 120. Ottawa, 1966.

Wright, Joseph. *The English Dialect Dictionary*. . . . 6 vols. London: H. Frowde, 1898–1905.

Wroth, Lawrence C. *The Voyages of Giovanni da Verrazzano, 1524*–1528. New Haven: Yale University Press, 1970.

Wroth, Lawrence C., and Gertrude L. Annan. *Acts of French royal administration concerning Canada, The West Indies, and Louisiana prior to 1791*. New York: New York Public Library, 1930.

Wyman, Walker D. and Clifton B. Kroeber. *The Frontier in Perspective*. Madison: University of Wisconsin Press, 1957.

Yerkes, Robert M. and Ada W. *The Great Apes*. New Haven: Yale University Press, 1929.

Index

C

D

E

Q

R

S

T